MUST FAITH ENDURE

FOR SALVATION TO BE SURE?

MUST FAITH ENDURE

FOR SALVATION TO BE SURE?

A Biblical Study of the
Perseverance Versus
Preservation of the Saints

Thomas L. Stegall

Grace Gospel Press
Duluth, Minnesota

ISBN 978-1-939110-11-4

GGP◄
Grace Gospel Press
201 W. Saint Andrews St.
Duluth, MN 55803
U.S.A.
(218) 724-5914
www.gracegospelpress.com

Printed in the United States of America

To Dennis and Nancy Rokser, with deep appreciation for your faithful, loving, and sacrificial ministry to the Lord and His saints over the years. Your lives have been a testimony to me and many others of what it means to be looking unto Jesus in the race, strengthened and kept by His grace.

CONTENTS

Chapter 1

Introduction

The book you are reading addresses a crucial question that every professing Christian must answer: Does your eternal salvation from hell to heaven depend on your perseverance as a Christian? Put another way, we could ask, must your faith endure to the end of your life for your salvation to be sure or guaranteed? What if your faith falters along the way or fails to be fruitful or fails to endure to the end of your earthly life? Will you be lost for eternity? To begin answering these questions and to clarify the issue of perseverance even further, consider the story of two professing Christians named Jack and Jill.

Meet Jack Van Due

Jack Van Due was born and raised in Grand Rapids, Michigan, the son of devout Dutch Reformed parents. While still an infant, Jack's parents had him baptized as a sign that he was a member of God's covenant community of grace. Jack's family regularly attended services at the neighborhood Christian Reformed church each Lord's Day, not wanting to break the Christian Sabbath. While a teen, he struggled to memorize the entire Westminster Shorter Catechism, but he persisted, and his persistence paid off. By his eighteenth birthday, he achieved his goal and knew the entire Catechism by heart—something many Reformed adults never even accomplish.

As a freshman in college, Jack determined to finish reading Calvin's Institutes by the end of the school year. Despite a heavy course load and a part-time job, he managed through self-discipline to carve out just enough extracurricular time to finish the last chapter of Calvin's classic right before spring semester ended. Though it was close, his commitment paid off once again as he accomplished another major goal in his Christian life.

Now being well-grounded in the classical Calvinist point of view, Jack sought to fortify his soul with the teachings of leading contemporary Calvinists such as John Piper and John MacArthur. He downloaded dozens of their sermons on his iPod, devoured the majority of their books, and even attended annual Passion conferences with thousands of other young Reformed evangelicals. Jack Van Due was officially young, restless, and Reformed.

From Piper, he learned that "Election is unconditional, but glorification is not," and that "those who do not hold fast to Christ can be lost in the end."[1] While Jack always believed the fifth point of Calvinism about the perseverance of the saints, this belief was reinforced through Piper's solemn warning to all ministers: "One final word on eternal security. It is a community project. And that is why the pastoral ministry is so utterly serious, and why our preaching must not be playful but earnest. We preach so that saints might persevere in faith to glory. We preach not only for their growth, but because if they don't grow, they perish."[2] The more Jack learned from Piper, the more he determined to grow, lest he ultimately perish.

He also learned from MacArthur to spurn the notions of "cheap grace" and "easy believism"[3] and to "count the cost" of his salvation.[4] He learned that though Christ paid for all sin on the cross, "there is a cost in terms of salvation's impact on the sinner's life. This paradox may be difficult but it is nevertheless true: salvation is both free and costly."[5] Jack took to heart MacArthur's challenge about the nature of true, saving faith.

> Thus in a sense we pay the ultimate price for salvation when our sinful self is nailed to a cross. It is a total abandonment of self-will, like the grain of wheat that falls to the ground and dies so that it can bear much fruit (cf. John 12:24). It is an exchange of all that we are for all that Christ is. And it

---

1. John Piper, *Five Points: Towards a Deeper Experience of God's Grace* (Ross-Shire, Scotland: Christian Focus, 2013), 63.

2. John Piper, *Brothers, We Are Not Professionals: A Plea to Pastors for Radical Ministry* (Nashville: Broadman & Holman, 2002), 110-11.

3. John F. MacArthur, Jr., *The Gospel According to Jesus* (Grand Rapids: Zondervan, 1988), 183.

4. Ibid., 140-41.

5. Ibid., 140.

denotes implicit obedience, full surrender to the lordship of Christ. Nothing less can qualify as saving faith.[6]

If this was the kind of dedication and commitment necessary to reach final justification and heavenly glorification and to prove the genuineness of his faith, then Jack was determined to fulfill the covenant of his salvation by upholding his pledge of obedience to God—enabled by God's grace, of course. After all, he learned from MacArthur that the covenant of his salvation was "a covenant of obedience" that required him to fulfill his responsibility.

> Self-discipline comes when you look back to the covenant of your salvation. That is to say, when you remember that at the point of your salvation you made a promise to submit to the Lord. You made a pledge at that time to be obedient to Christ. You confessed Him as Lord, and Lord means that He is above all. . . . It's essential then as believers to remember that we made a covenant of obedience when we confessed Jesus as Lord. . . . That pledge was inherent in salvation. God at the time you came to Him for salvation promised you forgiveness and eternal life and all the grace necessary to fulfill His will, and the Holy Spirit, and you pledged obedience. And you need to go back and remember that and have the integrity to be faithful to your original promise.[7]

While Jack Van Due believes he must live out this covenant of obedience with God, he knows enough Scripture and theology to admit that Jesus Christ paid the price for sin. But he is quick to add that there is still a cost he must incur. To prove the genuineness of his faith and go to heaven, he believes there are many things he must still do, such as pray, heed the warnings and exhortations of Scripture, keep the commandments, live a holy life, use the "means of grace," and endure in his own personal faith. He confesses that he is confident he himself is saved but also admits that he does not know this with absolute certainty since no one can be 100-percent sure of salvation without first persevering in faith and good works to the end of life.

Though Jack is still relatively young in life and in his faith, he appears to be doing quite well. He is determined to live in obedience

---

6. Ibid.

7, "Fundamental Christian Attitudes: Self-Discipline, Part 2," transcription. See www.gty.org/MediaPlayer/ sermons/90-131 (accessed March 16, 2012).

to God's will for the rest of his life because he is convinced that perseverance in faith and holiness are necessary for final salvation. By all accounts, he is succeeding. He is widely regarded to be a moral and upstanding member of society; and his church peers consider him to be an earnest, committed, productive Christian with a positive testimony for the Lord. But is it possible that someone as zealous and seemingly faithful as Jack has never truly trusted in Jesus Christ and His work alone for salvation but may in fact have been trusting all along in his own perseverance and devotion to gain final salvation? Is it possible that Jack has never really been born again?

Meet Jill Van Dunn

Jill Van Dunn was also born and raised in Grand Rapids, Michigan, to parents of Dutch descent, and her family lived in the same neighborhood as Jack Van Due. In fact, Jack and Jill were childhood friends. But Jill's family decided to attend a Bible Church across town that emphasized expository teaching from the Bible. Though she memorized no Protestant catechisms or confessions, her church did have an AWANA (Approved Workmen Are Not Ashamed) program where she memorized dozens of Bible verses, especially salvation verses. She was taught in AWANA that the condition for receiving eternal life had nothing to do with giving or surrendering her life to Christ, forsaking all, promising to serve Him, praying the sinner's prayer, asking Jesus into her heart, dedicating her life to Christ, or making a commitment of obedience to Him as Lord.[8] She learned from the founder of AWANA, Lance "Doc" Latham, that these were all meritorious works and that salvation was free to her because all of the cost was fully paid by her Savior. Latham taught:

> You have lied, stolen, been immoral and covetous; you cannot be justified (i.e., accepted as righteous) by rectifying your conduct. To stop your lying, stealing, and other deeds will in no way make you acceptable to God. Believing on Christ is distinctly not "turning the direction of your life over to Him." It is looking in faith to our Saviour crucified for our sins on Calvary! It is not of works, devotion or full surrender. It is His work and His death that avails.[9]

---

8. "Scriptural Evaluation of Salvation Invitations," www.faithprofiles.org/Portals/0/AWANA-answers.pdf

9. Lance B. Latham, *The Two Gospels* (Streamwood, IL: Awana Clubs Interna-

One who discovers the gospel will instantly realize that the sole basis of his salvation is the work of Christ on Calvary's cross. Saving faith depends alone on the value of Calvary. All other possible sources for the assurance of salvation are counterfeit. . . . The GOSPEL is the 'GOOD NEWS.' It is not a new set of obligations or duties to be performed—new strivings—more agonizings—but rather an announcement of WHAT HAS BEEN DONE for us. . . . We present a wonderful FREE OFFER by God Himself to the sinner who BELIEVES.[10]

Jill believed and accepted this message that was taught to her as a child, which was reinforced on a weekly basis by her pastor's preaching from the Bible and the church's emphasis on the gospel and evangelism. In her teenage years, she began systematically reading through the entire Bible, checking all the footnotes in her study Bible, which was the same study Bible that her pastor used and recommended—the Scofield Reference Bible. She rejoiced in the simplicity of God's plan of individual salvation as she read notes such as the following: "For salvation, faith is personal trust, apart from meritorious works, in the Lord Jesus Christ, as delivered for our offences and raised again for our justification (Rom. 4:5, 23-25)."[11]

After graduating from high school, Jill continued studying her Bible and taking her faith seriously. Since she cherished her Scofield Reference Bible and was already quite familiar with C. I. Scofield's dispensational interpretations, she decided to purchase and read some of his other books. From these she continued learning about the freeness of God's saving grace.

That is the simplicity that is in Christ; that is the blessed gospel of God's free grace. But it is all a gift; it is not for sale. God is not trading in this matter of salvation; He is not giving a little salvation for a little goodness, and a little more salvation for a little more goodness. There is no trading; it is a free gift.[12]

As a result of such teaching, Jill had been sure of her salvation since she was a girl going through her church's AWANA program.

tional, 1984), 54.

10. Ibid., 43.

11. C. I. Scofield, ed., *The Scofield Reference Bible*, rev. ed. (New York: Oxford University Press, 1917), 1302.

12. C. I. Scofield, "By Grace through Faith," in *In Many Pulpits* (Greenville, SC: Gospel Hour, n.d.), 92.

She knew she was a citizen of heaven who belonged to Jesus Christ, and she rejoiced in the fact that she was eternally secure in Him.

Then one day, she ran into Jack in the parking lot of a grocery store in Grand Rapids, and after spending several minutes catching up on their lives, Jill shared with Jack about the joy of her salvation. She had heard that Jack had grown up to become a very devout, committed Christian. He affirmed this to her as they talked, explaining that Jesus was his passion too. In fact, right there in the parking lot he invited her to attend an upcoming Passion conference in Atlanta where she could meet thousands of other young adults who were just as passionate about Jesus. Intrigued and excited, Jill decided to go. Her life would never be the same.

Once there, she was introduced to the "doctrines of grace" as they were called. Though she thought she was already quite familiar with the term and concept of grace, she was challenged to delve deeper into grace by studying Calvinist Reformed theology. Growing up in a heavily Dutch community, she already knew about Calvinism in a general sense, but she had never studied it for herself. Now, surrounded by so many people her own age who seemed so excited about the "true" grace they found in Calvinism, she wondered if she had missed something very important growing up. As she began listening to sermons by popular Reformed teachers online and reading their books, she developed a growing sense of unrest. She was upset, concluding that she had been deceived by her Bible Church upbringing, saying, "Why didn't anyone ever tell me about the necessity of perseverance in faith and good works as the evidence of true, saving faith?" After attending the Christian Reformed church with the Van Due family for a year, Jill became a full five-point Calvinist.

As she strove to live a life of nothing less than total abandonment of self-will, full exchange of self for the Savior, with implicit obedience and full surrender to the lordship of Christ, Jill became weary. The joy of her salvation had been tempered with a somberness that she initially mistook for godliness. The more Jill strove, she could not shake the sense of restlessness she had about not living up to the standards of "true, saving faith." For the first time that she could remember, doubts began creeping into her mind that she may not really be saved after all. When she confided such thoughts to a few other ladies at her Reformed church, she was told that such thoughts were common among Christians and actually healthy since they reflected reverence for the Lord. Upon hearing this, she did not think it was wise to reveal to others just how discouraged and defeated she really felt inside. So she kept her doubts and discouragement to herself and speculated that this was just her cross to bear—the cross of the normal Christian life.

At this low point, a new employee at Jill's company showed up. Steve Smith was handsome, charming, and humorous. He had a zest for life that she was lacking. Soon, she started looking forward to seeing him each day, especially when he began showing special interest in her. But there was one problem: Steve was not a believer in the Lord Jesus Christ and didn't even claim to be. Despite this "minor" detail, a romantic interest developed between Jill and Steve as he pursued her and wooed her to himself and she gave her heart to him. During this time, Jill's church attendance waned, as Steve candidly expressed he had no interest in attending church. At times, he even poked fun at Christianity and the Bible. But despite such comments and a gnawing internal conviction that the whole relationship was wrong, Jill chose to follow her feelings and was determined to have a happy life with Steve. Her relationship with the Lord was fading away. Jill was now "in love" with Steve and after several months, they were openly living an immoral lifestyle together. A year later, she was pregnant.

By now, Jill had not attended church in over a year, and her former friends at the Reformed church shunned her. She became bitter. Partly out of spite, she decided to become unequally yoked together in marriage with Steve, who was still as much of an unbeliever as ever. Word was now out at the Reformed church that Jill was married to an unbeliever, and questions about the status of Jill's salvation became an occasional topic of conversation. When Jill caught wind of it, she spiritually shut down even further. But at least she had the birth of her baby to look forward to.

When her baby girl entered the world, Jill found a new joy and satisfaction in life. In the following weeks, she and Steve affectionately fawned over their precious little one. But such joy was short lived, as their baby lay motionless one morning. Lifeless. Dead. SIDS had claimed its latest victim. After many days of sobbing and deep, gut-wrenching anguish, Jill went numb. She was empty. As each minute of each day ticked and tocked, Jill slipped away, becoming increasingly reclusive and withdrawn, unable to function. She was shutting down emotionally, psychologically, and spiritually. As the endless minutes faded into days, and days passed into weeks, Jill became completely disillusioned and hardened. Her husband's response turned her already-cold heart to stone. His daily antagonism toward her and her God was too much to bear as he scorned and mocked the idea of a supposed "God" who could let such a thing like this happen. Jill's faith was now shattered. Tragically, if you were to ask her today what she believes, she will tell you that she is no longer a Christian and does not profess to believe the gospel anymore.

Meanwhile, Jack and his peers at the Reformed church still talk about Jill. They speculate whether she was ever truly saved. Some hold out hope that maybe her faith hasn't totally disappeared and that maybe, after she repents, she will still persevere to the end of her life and prove to be one of God's elect. Others conclude that since she appears to have gone apostate by denying the faith, she must have never really believed in Christ to begin with. In their eyes, she is eternally lost. But they are confident of their own salvation as they persevere in their faith and good works.

The Purpose of This Book

It may relieve you to know that the previous saga is entirely fictional—made up. On the other hand, it may not be so relieving to realize that the previous story portrays characters and events that are far too common in evangelical Christianity. But this story and the current state of affairs in evangelicalism raise several vital questions that have eternal ramifications.

- If a person has genuine faith in Jesus Christ for salvation, will that faith necessarily persevere to the end of his or her life?

- Must faith be constant and continuous, without any gaps or lapses, in order to be genuine and saving?

- Can faith temporarily lapse during one's Christian life as long as it is still present at the time of death?

- When does belief become unbelief?

- Can a person have doubts about the gospel and truly believe it at the same time?

- Does the presence of doubt in one's Christian life mean the absence of faith?

- What constitutes apostasy or turning away from the faith in unbelief?

- Are good works the proof of initial faith in Christ for salvation or the proof of a walk of faith in the Christian life?

- Can a person have genuine faith in Christ for salvation and not manifest it by a life of good works?

- If a person is trusting in his or her own works to be accepted by God while professing to also believe in Christ, will that person be saved?

- If faith is the condition to get saved in the first place, and it is not meritorious, then how can it be meritorious as an ongoing condition for final salvation?

How should we answer these questions? Since the Bible is the only authoritative and infallible source of spiritual truth available, the book you are reading will focus on the interpretation of numerous biblical passages that deal with the relationship between faith and salvation, eternal security, and perseverance. Unfortunately, it is all too common for people to follow the path of tradition, or a mixture of biblical truth with tradition, in seeking to answer the preceding questions.

One traditional approach to the issue of faith and perseverance is that of Arminianism. Although this view teaches correctly from the Bible that genuine faith in Christ may not necessarily endure to the end of one's life, it errs by teaching that eternal salvation can be lost if one's faith does not persevere. According to Arminianism, the believer must persevere and stay faithful to God in order to be eternally secure and reach final salvation.

In contrast to Arminianism is the theological system of Calvinism, which says that although salvation can never be lost, you will and must necessarily persevere in faith and good works to the very end of your Christian life in order to receive final salvation. If you do not persevere to the end, this simply proves you were never truly born again. If you do not have persevering faith and personal holiness, then according to Calvinism, you are not a genuine *possessor* of salvation but only a *professor* of salvation. According to Calvinism, genuine believers are incapable of apostasy or losing their faith completely and finally. This doctrine is known as the "perseverance of the saints," which will be explained more thoroughly in chapter three.

This book presents a third view that is more consistent with Scripture than either Calvinism or Arminianism. This view sees in Scripture the preservation of the saints or the eternal security of all who have believed in Jesus Christ alone for their eternal salvation. This view understands the Bible to teach that once a person has been regenerated by God's grace alone through faith alone in Christ alone, he will never be in danger of God's condemnation or loss of salvation, but he is kept eternally secure solely by God's grace and power based on the finished work of Christ, not because of any fruitfulness, faithfulness, holiness, or perseverance on his part. Thus, the preservation of the saints (eternal security) is distinct from the traditional Calvinist doctrine of the "perseverance of the saints."

While the focus of this book is not on eternal security per se,[13] it will examine the key biblical passages on salvation that contain the words "faith" and "believe," showing that genuine faith in Christ for eternal salvation may not necessarily endure to the end of one's earthly life; and when that is the case, God in His grace, based on the enduring sufficiency of Christ's work, will still safely preserve His own unto His heavenly kingdom (1 Thess. 5:23-24; 2 Tim. 4:18; Jude 1). Thus, the Bible teaches the preservation of the saints by Christ rather than the perseverance of the saints.

This reassuring truth was illustrated well by the famous Bible expositor of the nineteenth century, James H. Brookes, who recounted the testimony of a dying Scottish woman.

> A young minister was in the habit of visiting an aged Scotch woman in his congregation who was familiarly called "Old Nanny." She was bedridden and rapidly approaching the end of her "long and weary pilgrimage," but she rested with undisturbed composure and full assurance of faith upon the finished work of Christ. One day he said to her, "Now, Nanny, what if, after all your confidence in the Saviour, and your watching and waiting, God should suffer your soul to be lost?" Raising herself on her elbow, and turning to him with a look of grief and pain, she laid her hand on the open Bible before her, and quietly replied, "Ah, dearie me, is that a' the length you have got yet, man? God," she continued ear-

---

13. For an excellent book focusing on the believer's eternal security in Christ, see Dennis M. Rokser, *Shall Never Perish Forever: Is Salvation Forever or Can It Be Lost?* (Duluth, MN: Grace Gospel Press, 2012).

nestly, "would have the greatest loss. Poor Nanny would but lose her soul, and that would be a great loss indeed, but God would lose His honor and His character. Haven't I hung my soul upon His 'exceeding great and precious promises'? and if He brak' His word, He would make Himself a liar, AND A' THE UNIVERSE WOULD RUSH INTO CONFUSION.[14]

Brookes goes on to comment insightfully on this story.

This anecdote reveals the true ground of the believer's safety. It is as high as the honor of God; it is as trustworthy as His character; it is as immutable as His promises; it is as broad as the infinite merits of His Son's atoning blood. There has long been a sharp controversy between theological writers concerning the doctrine of "the perseverance of the saints," as it is called, but, like most controversies among true Christians, it is owing largely to a misapprehension or misapplication of the terms employed in the dispute. The question, properly presented, is not about the perseverance of the saints, but the perseverance of the Lord. If the saints were left to themselves, it is not only probable, but certain, that they would not persevere, but if the Lord perseveres in His purpose of grace, it is not only probable, but certain, that they will be saved. Inasmuch, then, as the phrase, "perseverance of the saints," is not found in the Bible, and as it may possibly turn our attention from the Saviour to ourselves, which is always fraught with evil, I prefer to think of the perseverance of the Lord in speaking of the believer's safety.[15]

With this critical distinction in mind between the perseverance of the saints and the perseverance of the Savior, we can now return to the main question of this book: Must faith endure for salvation to be sure? As this book will go on to explain, the biblical answer to this question is "no" since the perseverance of the saints in faith, holiness, and good works is neither the necessary result of genuine, "saving faith" in Jesus Christ for eternal life nor is it an ongoing condition for final salvation. Rather, eternal life is predicated only upon the perseverance of the Savior and the preservation of the saints by Jesus Christ from the moment of their initial faith in Him alone. This

14. James H. Brookes, *The Way Made Plain* (Grand Rapids: Baker, 1967), 194.
15. Ibid., 194-95.

results in a salvation that is "sure" both in the sense of being eternally secure and personally assured.

What a joy and encouragement it is to know the truth of one's eternal security and preservation by God's grace and power based solely on the finished work of Christ and the unfailing promises of God! But as amazing as this sounds, you may be wondering, Is this really true? If it is, then how can it be possible? This is explained clearly in the saving message of the gospel of Christ, which is the subject of the next chapter. So read on!

Part I

Answering Key Questions about Perseverance

Chapter 2

The Gospel of the Grace of God

The biblical truth of the preservation and eternal security of the saints by Christ is based upon an accurate understanding of the biblical gospel of God's grace. Without a proper and correct understanding of the gospel, the marvelous and reassuring truth of the eternal security and preservation of the saints by Christ cannot be grasped. But in order to appreciate and understand the good news of the gospel, you must first understand the bad news and accept the fact of your own sinful, lost spiritual condition before God. If you do not acknowledge this, you will never see your need for Jesus Christ and believe in Him for your own salvation.

The Bad News

According to the Bible, all mankind (except Jesus Christ) is born spiritually dead in trespasses and sins (Eph. 2:1). No one is a child of God at birth. All people are born physically alive yet spiritually dead and in need of regeneration or new birth (John 3:3-7; 6:53; Eph. 4:18). Just like the symptoms of physical sickness stem from the root cause of the disease itself, the many individual acts of sin that people commit are symptomatic of their real root problem—being born spiritually dead toward God, with a sinful nature and disposition bent toward self-will and disobedience (Gen. 8:21; Ps. 51:5, 58:3; Isa. 48:8; Eph. 2:2). By nature, every person is a congenital rebel and guilty before God (Rom. 3:19; Gal. 3:22), and is the object of His wrath (John 3:36; Eph. 2:3; 5:6). In this sinful condition, man is essentially and unchangeably bad apart from God's grace (Jer. 17:9; Mark 7:20-23; Rom. 7:18) and completely incapable of either regenerating himself

(John 1:13; Eph. 2:4-5; Col. 2:13; James 1:18) or successfully justifying himself in God's sight (Job 25:4; Ps. 130:3; Rom. 3:19-20; 8:33).

Since the standard of righteousness is God's own perfect holiness, all people fall far short of being worthy of salvation (Rom. 3:23). This is why no one can get to heaven on the basis of his or her own goodness or righteousness. We would have to be as good and righteous as God to be admitted to heaven on that basis. And God has already given His estimation of man's righteousness and worthiness for salvation, and it is not good! According to His Word, there are "none righteous" before Him, "no, not one" (Rom. 3:10). There is "none who does good, no, not one" (Rom. 3:12; see also Eccl. 7:20). In fact, Isaiah 64:6 says that all of our supposedly righteous deeds are like filthy rags in God's sight, and the apostle Paul even calls them "dung" (Phil. 3:8). Thus, no man in this sinful condition is capable of doing truly "good" works that are acceptable to God (Rom. 8:6-7; Eph. 2:8-9; Titus 3:5-7).

The Good News

This bad news about man's complete inability to merit salvation or save himself means that salvation must come from a source outside of himself. Thankfully, God has graciously provided such deliverance through His Son, the Lord Jesus Christ. He alone is the unique God-man, God's only begotten Son, the Savior and Redeemer of mankind, and the one Mediator between God and man. Scripture declares that there is only *one* Savior of mankind from sin (Isa. 43:11; 45:21-22) and Jesus Christ is that Savior (John 14:6; Acts 4:12). This deliverance for man provided by another, Jesus Christ, is in keeping with the scriptural principle that "salvation is of the Lord" (Jonah 2:9). Since salvation is "of the Lord" and not of us, it cannot be a joint effort of collaboration between God and sinful man, even between those whom God has already regenerated as His own dear children, because even children of God are still sinners while on the earth. God has no co-saviors, co-mediators, or co-redeemers (1 Tim. 2:4-5), even among His own children. This means that we cannot keep and preserve our own salvation. It is all God's work.

The bad news of man's unworthiness of salvation is also met by good news from God. Since man is not worthy or deserving of salvation, the only way salvation can be possible is if it is all by God's grace. Grace is God's unmerited, undeserved kindness and favor toward those who deserve the very opposite, namely, His just condemnation. Therefore, salvation cannot be partly earned and partly by grace. If it is by grace, then it cannot be mixed with our works (Eph. 2:8-9), "otherwise, grace is no longer grace" (Rom. 11:6). Believers are not initially elected, regenerated, and justified by grace but then sanctified and preserved unto final salvation by a collaborative effort between God and man, as if God's grace "helps" us fulfill a supposedly ongoing "condition" of perseverance in faith and holiness to the end. Salvation is unearned (and thus solely by God's grace), but it is not this way only *initially* and then *afterward* partly earned by a mixture of God's grace and our ongoing obedience. No, it is all by His grace![1]

The reality of the bad news about man's lost, sinful, spiritually dead status before God also means that man has a spiritual debt of sin that must be paid, as Romans 6:23 says, "the wages of sin is death." This means that what we naturally deserve because of our sin is death. In the Bible, death never means that something no longer exists, as we tend to think; rather, it always speaks of some kind of separation—like the soul and spirit from the body (James 2:26). If this separation persists throughout one's lifetime and one is never reconciled to God through Christ, that person will die separated from God and remain separated from Him forever in hell (John 8:24; 2 Thess. 1:9; Rev. 21:8). But God is not only a just and holy God, He is also a loving and gracious God. He knew we had a debt we could not pay and that our own moral and religious efforts were insufficient to save us. Therefore, in love and grace, He gave His own Son to pay the debt of sin that we could not pay, as Christ bore our debt by dying as our substitute to satisfy the just and righteous penalty we deserved because of our sin, as 1 Peter 3:18 says,

> For Christ also died for sins once for all, the just for the unjust, so that He might bring us to God, having been put to death in the flesh, but made alive in the spirit. (NASB)

Thus, the good news of the gospel is that salvation has already been paid in full by another, Jesus Christ, when He died on the cross for us all (John 3:14-16; 12:32). As He died, He cried out, "It is finished" (John 19:30), meaning that the price for all sin, for all time, had been paid in full. No more work was necessary to satisfy the

---

1. The relationship of God's grace to all three phases of salvation—justification before God, the process of practical sanctification, and glorification—is addressed in chapters 7 and 8.

infinite justice of a holy and righteous God, as Isaiah 53:11 explains how God the Father views the propitiatory death of His Son, "He shall see the labor of His soul, and be satisfied." Because the price for sin has been fully paid, salvation is free to all people who will receive it by faith, though it cost God His very own Son. Like all gifts, salvation was paid for by another—in this case, the Redeemer Himself. And since Christ is risen from the dead and has overcome the wages and effects of sin, He is able to grant eternal life as a free gift to undeserving sinners who place their faith in Him rather than relying upon their own good works. Salvation is free to us because the cost was already borne by Jesus Christ. When a person recognizes this, only then can he appreciate the gospel for what it truly is—"good news" from God to man.[2]

The sacrificial death of Christ on Calvary's cross was the only work that has ever effectively resolved man's debt of sin, making it the heart of God's saving message—the "good news" of the gospel. This was certainly the case in the ministry of the apostle Paul, as he wrote to the Corinthians, "For I determined not to know anything among you except Jesus Christ and Him crucified" (1 Cor. 2:2). That is why the Corinthians (and all Christians) were later commissioned with the same message of Christ's substitutionary death on the cross for man's sin (2 Cor. 5:19-21). No human works can ever be added to Christ's work on the cross as the basis of eternal salvation without nullifying God's grace and Christ's work in the process, as Paul wrote to the Galatians, "I do not nullify the grace of God, for if righteousness *comes* through the Law, then Christ died needlessly" (Gal. 2:21, NASB).

When the true "evangel" or gospel is proclaimed, there will be no room left for boasting in human works. All boasting will be in Jesus Christ alone because of His perfect and sufficient work of redemption. Every Christian who holds to the true "evangel" should therefore be able to affirm, for time and all eternity, "God forbid that I should boast except in the cross of our Lord Jesus Christ" (Gal. 6:14).

According to the Bible, salvation is all the work of God for man, never the work of man for God, as the Scriptures proclaim, "For by grace you have been saved through faith, and that not of yourselves;

---

2. The word "gospel" is the English translation of the Greek word *euangelion*, which is a compound word made up of the prefix *eu* (meaning "good") and the root *angel-* (meaning "message"). Literally, the *euangelion* is the good message or good news. Our English term "evangelical" comes directly from the Greek word *euangelion*. Thus, whoever holds to the good news of the gospel may be considered a true "evangelical."

it is the gift of God, not of works, lest anyone should boast" (Eph. 2:8-9). Notice that salvation is *not* of us; it is *not* of works. Salvation is *not* given to the one who believes *and* works for salvation, but to the one who does *not work* but simply believes in Christ. As Romans 4:4-6 declares, "Now to him who works, the wages are not counted as grace but as debt. But to him who does *not work but believes* on Him who justifies the ungodly, his faith is accounted for righteousness, just as David also describes the blessedness of the man to whom God imputes righteousness *apart from works*." So, for a lost sinner to be justified in God's sight, he must actually *stop* relying on his works and believe only in Jesus Christ.

But if no one is justified before God by good works, then why should anyone do them? The teaching of salvation by grace alone through faith alone in Christ alone does not mean that believers *should not* persevere in faith and good works, only that they will not always do so, and in fact they do *not need to* do so in order for God in grace to keep them eternally saved. However, the Bible is emphatic that every believer should persevere in faith and good works. Ephesians 2:8-9 clearly says that believers are not saved by good works since salvation is God's gracious gift. But Ephesians 2:10 goes on to say that we *should* do good works because they are part of His plan and will for every believer's life: "For we are His workmanship, created in Christ Jesus for good works, which God prepared beforehand that we should walk in them."

Even though we are not saved by perseverance in faith and good works, we still should walk by faith in fellowship with God as His child (1 John 1:3-4) so as to:

(a) become more like God in His character (Rom. 8:29; 12:2; Phil. 3:10);
(b) serve Him through good works (Rom. 7:6; Col. 3:24);
(c) benefit others (Gal. 5:13; Titus 3:8);
(d) receive an eternal reward one day (1 Cor. 3:10-15; 2 Cor. 5:9-10); and
(e) ultimately please and glorify God (1 Cor. 10:31).

Thus, there is a definite need to persevere in the Christian life,[3] but not in order to reach heaven or final salvation. This explains why there are no passages in the Bible, including Ephesians 2:10, that say

---

3. For the role, place, and value of perseverance in faith and good works in the Christian life, see chapters 6–8 and 15.

true believers in Christ *will* necessarily persevere to the end, but only that they *should*.

Adding to the Gospel

It is imperative that every lost, unsaved person comes to realize and accept that the gospel is not a message of obligation announcing what man must do for God, but rather that it is the good news of what God has already done for man through His Son in providing salvation as a free gift of His grace to undeserving sinners. The gospel is not a message of "DO!" but of "DONE!" When Christ cried out on the cross as He died for our sins, "It is finished" (John 19:30), this did not mean that there was still some work left for us to do to become acceptable to God. No, it was truly done!

However, when the gospel is turned into a message of human obligation, it ceases to have the character of good news and is no longer a message that God can use to save people. It becomes "another gospel," which cannot save (Gal. 1:6-9). In addition, it actually becomes "bad news" to those who humbly recognize that they are helpless "sinners" and "without strength" to save themselves (Rom. 5:6, 8). According to the Bible, lost, weak, and sinful man simply cannot save himself. That is why we are saved solely by God, not by ourselves, once we place our faith in Christ (Eph. 1:13-14). Though we must respond to the gospel with faith in Christ out of our own volition, which we would not even be able to do apart from the gracious, pre-salvation drawing of God (John 6:44; Acts 18:27), God then does all the work of eternally saving and securing us in Christ. We are preserved in Christ and by Christ (1 John 5:18, NASB; Jude 1), as He alone faithfully perseveres to the end in keeping saved all those who have trusted solely in Him for eternal life.

Unfortunately, confusion about the gospel abounds today even in so-called evangelical church circles. Today, the emphasis is placed on many unscriptural *human requirements* to be saved, such as:

- praying the sinner's prayer,
- giving your life to Christ,
- making a commitment to Christ,
- dedicating one's life to serve Christ,
- making a public confession of Christ,

- trying to keep Christ's commands,
- making Christ Lord of your life, or
- asking Jesus into your heart.[4]

Aside from the fact that none of these statements or conditions are found in the Bible, none of these emphasize the work of Jesus Christ nor are they even synonymous with faith in Christ. In fact, they are all works that man must do for God, rather than faith in what God has already accomplished for us through His Son. Unfortunately, most contemporary "gospel" presentations give little emphasis to *Christ* and what *He* has done to secure the salvation of sinners through His all-sufficient work.

Of course, many in Christendom readily affirm that sinners are justified by faith in Christ. But then they practically deny that affirmation by adding qualifications to faith that still require works to be saved in the end, saying such things as, "Faith alone saves, but saving faith is never alone; it must also be fruitful and have good works attached to it, or else it is not genuine faith." Or, they often say, "Yes, faith alone saves, but you still must faithfully endure to the end." When such qualifying statements are made, the gospel is no longer the "good news" of what God has done in giving His Son to die for all sin, thereby providing salvation freely to undeserving, helpless sinners who receive it by personal faith in Christ and His work. When such qualifications are placed upon faith, the whole character of the gospel is changed from the "good news" of what God has done for you to the "bad news" of what you must strive to do for God in order to get saved, stay saved, or prove that you were originally saved.

The biblical gospel assures us that when a sinner believes that Jesus Christ died to completely pay for all his sins, so that no other means of satisfying the holy justice of God is necessary, and he believes that God raised His Son from the dead to freely give eternal life on the sole condition of faith in Him, the Bible promises that such an individual presently has eternal life and will be saved forever from that point on. Our entire salvation, whether past, present, or future, is based entirely upon the lasting, satisfactory work of Christ and the enduring faithfulness of God in keeping His gracious

---

4. For an excellent resource clarifying the sole condition of faith in Christ for salvation and why one is not saved by asking Jesus into his or her heart, see Dennis M. Rokser, *Don't Ask Jesus into Your Heart: A Biblical Answer to the Question: "What Must I Do to be Saved?"* (Duluth, MN: Grace Gospel Press, 2007).

promises. We are not saved by our persevering faithfulness as saints but by the persevering faithfulness of our Savior!

The Sole Condition of Faith in Christ

If our eternal salvation were dependent, even in the smallest measure, upon our faithfulness or ability to persevere in holding on to Christ, then surely we would all perish! That is why the Bible never states that "faithfulness" is required for eternal salvation, only "faith" in Jesus Christ. Faith is the only human condition that is exempt from the category of meritorious works in God's eyes. According to Scripture, salvation is "of faith that it might be according to grace, so that the promise might be sure to all" (Rom. 4:16). Salvation is through faith because faith is non-meritorious and thus consistent with grace.

Faith in Jesus Christ for salvation cannot be meritorious since it does not rely upon one's own works but the work of another—Christ. That is why Romans 4:5 states, "But to him who does not work but believes on Him who justifies the ungodly, his faith is accounted for righteousness." Did you catch that? "To him who does *not work but believes.*" This indicates that believing is not a work! Working and believing are antithetical, just like works and grace (Rom. 11:6). So, technically, we are not saved *by* our faith but *through* faith since biblical "saving faith" relies upon the work and merits of Christ. That is why if a man has one foot resting upon solid ground (i.e., Christ) and another foot on quicksand (i.e., his works), he will sink just as surely and quickly as if he had both feet resting upon the quicksand (i.e., trusting solely in his works). Do you see the analogy? The man who says he believes in Christ yet claims that good works are also necessary to be saved does not really believe in Christ at all. While he may know and accept certain basic facts about Jesus Christ that are true, he certainly has not understood nor believed in Christ's substitutionary, satisfactory, sufficient death for his sins, otherwise he would not still be relying upon his own works to save him. Hence, that man's faith is not really in the right object, namely, Jesus Christ and His finished work. That is why Romans 4:5 says that one must "believe on Him who justifies the ungodly" in order to be counted righteous in God's estimation. True "saving faith" is faith in the right *object*.

The expression "saving faith" is often used by many perseverance advocates to refer to a special *quality* of faith, such as working faith, obedient faith, persevering faith, heart faith versus head faith, and so forth. Though many perseverance proponents speak of "saving faith" in these terms, nowhere in Scripture does God require a special *quality* or *kind* of faith to be eternally saved.[5] Salvation in the Bible is a matter of who or what someone is relying upon to be saved. It is a matter of having the right *content* and *object* of one's faith. Therefore, to believe certain facts about Christ while still trusting in one's own works does not result in justification or eternal salvation. But to have faith in Christ and His work alone is to have a faith that will save, hence a "saving faith." So, the real question with salvation is never, "What *kind* of faith do I have?" but *"Whom or what am I trusting to be saved?"*

We may summarize these points about grace, faith, and Christ alone as the object of faith by concluding that the basis of salvation is God's *grace alone*; the instrumental means of salvation is *faith alone*; and the object of faith for eternal salvation is *Christ alone*. So, to be theologically precise, we must conclude from Scripture that we are saved by grace alone, through faith alone, in Christ alone.

All of this leads to another very important question. If faith is inherently non-meritorious because it relies upon the work of another, Jesus Christ, then how can continual faith be considered meritorious just because it extends over a longer period of time? The answer is that in such a case, faith itself is not really the ongoing condition, but rather faithfulness becomes the condition. Perseverance in faith as a condition for final salvation is indeed meritorious because it changes the object of faith from Christ to self. It results in a person having faith in his faith! When a lost person is told that Jesus Christ can and will save him but he must persevere in holding on to Christ, faith is no longer a matter of relying upon Jesus Christ to do the work of saving, but the person holding on is actually doing the necessary work of salvation. This point is vividly illustrated by comparing two ships in the Bible.

The Two Ships of Preservation and Perseverance

The single act of believing in Christ for eternal life is clarified by the contrast between two ships—Noah's ark and Paul's ship bound for

---

5. For a highly recommended critique of the Reformed concept of saving faith, see J. B. Hixson's chapter, "Establishing the Standard: What Is Saving Faith?" in his book, *Getting the Gospel Wrong: The Evangelical Crisis No One Is Talking About*, rev. ed. (Duluth, MN: Grace Gospel Press, 2013), 85-136.

Rome. Noah's ark was entered once and resulted in the preservation of its occupants whereas Paul's ship sailing for Rome broke to pieces and secured none of its occupants. This contrast clearly portrays the biblical truth of eternal security and preservation in Christ versus attempted salvation by perseverance in faith and good works.

Noah's Ark: Preservation

The ark of Genesis 6–8 is a clear picture of God's salvation through Christ. Just as the ark had one door to enter (Gen. 6:16), so God has one door of salvation for sinners to enter, namely, Jesus Christ (John 10:9). Just as God miraculously drew all the animals to the ark (Gen. 6:20), so God must supernaturally draw all men to Christ before they can believe in Him and enter the door of salvation (John 6:44; 12:32; 16:8). And just as it was God Himself who shut the door of the ark and secured its occupants (Gen. 7:16), so God seals the believer in Christ and eternally secures his or her salvation (Eph. 1:13-14; 4:30).

Once aboard the ark, its occupants may have lost their faith in the ark's ability to save them from the storm of God's judgment, yet the ark would have continued to keep them secure despite their loss of faith. It was not the passengers' ability to continually hold on to the ark that guaranteed their salvation. What secured them was the integrity of the ark and its ability to withstand the waves of God's wrath.

In just the same way, it is not a person's faith that secures his or her salvation; it is the reliability of the Object of faith that saves a believer and then keeps that soul secure. Salvation should never be likened to someone outside the ark who realized it was seaworthy and then determined to faithfully clutch its sides in an effort to be rescued from the rising floodwaters. That picture of faith for salvation amounts to a *Christ-plus-works* approach to salvation that will surely end in eternal perdition. In contrast, biblical faith and salvation are likened to a person who enters the door of the ark one time by faith, trusting in the ark's ability to save, even before that person sees the impending judgment. Once inside, that person can rest, secure from the threat of destruction. This is a *Christ-plus-nothing* approach to salvation, which is the only approach consistent with God's saving grace. The Word of God declares the wonderfully gracious truth that once a sinner believes in the Lord Jesus Christ alone for eternal salvation, God keeps that person secure in

Christ forever, even if that person falters due to doubt, denial, or unfaithfulness.

However, many today misunderstand or reject this marvelous truth, claiming that while Christ must save a person, that person must also continually hold on to Christ to reach heaven. According to this approach, Christ does not really do the work of saving a person, but that person saves himself. With this approach, a person is not really saved by faith *in Christ* but ultimately by faith *in his faith*, as he thinks it is his "faithfulness" to Christ that will ultimately bring him eternal life. Harry Ironside, a dispensational Bible teacher of the past, addressed this very problem as he answered the objection: "But must I not hold on to the end if I would be saved at last?" Using the illustration of Noah's ark, he replied as follows:

> May I, without irreverence, venture to recast a Bible story? If the account of Noah and the flood went something like this, what would you think of it? Suppose that after the ark was completed God said to Noah, "Now, get eight great spikes of iron and drive them into the side of the ark." And Noah procured the spikes and did as he was bidden. Then the word came unto him, "Come thou and all thy house and hang on to these spikes." And Noah and his wife, and the three sons and their wives, each held onto a spike. And the rains descended and the flood came, and as the ark was borne up on the waters their muscles were strained to the utmost as they clung to the spikes. Imagine God saying to them, "If you hang on till the deluge is over you will be saved!" Can you even think of such a thing as anyone of them going safely through?
>
> But oh, how different the simple Bible story. "And the Lord said unto Noah, Come thou and all thy house into the ark." Ah, that is a very different thing than holding on! Inside the ark they were safe as long as the ark endured the storm. And every believer is in Christ and is as safe as God can make him. Look away then from all self-effort and trust Him alone. Rest in the ark and rejoice in God's great salvation.
>
> And be sure to remember that it is Christ who holds you, not you who hold Him. He has said, "I will never leave thee, nor forsake thee." "For if, when we were enemies, we were reconciled to God by the death of his Son, much more, being reconciled, we shall be saved by his life" (Rom. 5:10). He who

died for you, now lives at God's right hand to keep you, and
the Father sees you in Him. "He hath made us accepted in
the beloved." Could anything be more sure?[6]

Paul's Shipwreck: Perseverance

In contrast to Noah's ark and that picture of salvation by grace
stands the example of Paul's ship bound for Rome, which broke apart
and saved none of its occupants. However, many who hold to the
doctrine of the perseverance of the saints for final salvation use the
example of Paul's ship in Acts 27 to support their view.[7] They teach
that, although God promised that no one aboard the ship would perish (vv. 22-25, 34), the passengers still needed to heed Paul's warning to stay aboard if they would ultimately survive: "Paul said to
the centurion and soldiers, 'Unless these men stay in the ship, you
cannot be saved'" (v. 31). Though this chapter deals with physical
salvation or deliverance, it is theologically applied (i.e., misapplied)
to eternal salvation by teaching that once a person is saved by God,
that person must heed God's "warnings," which are the "means"
of perseverance in the Christian life to stay aboard the ship of faith
and not perish eternally outside of Christ.[8] As most commentators
recognize, Acts 27 is a passage dealing with the relationship between
divine sovereignty and human responsibility. However, in contrast
to Noah's ark in Genesis 6–8, neither the immediate context of Acts
27 nor any other passages of Scripture indicate that eternal deliverance from God's wrath is the divinely intended picture of this chapter. Therefore, it is illegitimate to use Acts 27 to establish the doctrine
of perseverance for salvation.

In addition, the details of the passage do not even correspond
with salvation by grace through faith, as taught elsewhere in Scrip-

---

6. H. A. Ironside, *Full Assurance*, rev. ed. (Chicago: Moody Press, 1968), 102-103.

7. Louis Berkhof, *Systematic Theology*, 4th ed. (Grand Rapids: Eerdmans, 1991), 548;
John H. Fish, "God's Sovereignty and Human Responsibility: An Important Lesson
from Acts 27," *Emmaus Journal* 10 (Winter 2001): 237-49; Anthony A. Hoekema, *Saved
By Grace* (Grand Rapids: Eerdmans, 1989), 246; Thomas R. Schreiner and Ardel B.
Caneday, *The Race Set Before Us: A Biblical Theology of Perseverance & Assurance* (Down-
ers Grove, IL: InterVarsity Press, 2001), 209-12.

8. The Canons of the Synod of Dort state that believers must use the "means" of
perseverance, which include God's "exhortations, threatenings, and promises" (Article XIV on the Perseverance of the Saints). Calvinist theologian Charles Hodge
writes: "This perseverance in holiness is secured partly by the inward secret influence of the Spirit, and partly by all the means adapted to secure that end—instructions, admonitions, exhortations, warnings, the means of grace" (*Systematic Theology*
[Grand Rapids: Eerdmans, reprinted 1989], 3:112-13).

ture. First of all, unlike the passengers on Noah's ark, those onboard Paul's ship do not represent believers, who have been regenerated, who must supposedly thereafter persevere in faith to remain saved and onboard the ship of faith. Apart from Paul, Luke, and Aristarchus (v. 2), the other 273 passengers (v. 37) were likely all unregenerate men who had never come to faith in Christ or even to a profession of faith. However, the eight souls inside Noah's ark pictured only those who had "found grace in the eyes of the Lord" (Gen. 6:8; 7:1), in sharp contrast to all the spiritually and physically lost who were outside the ark (Gen. 6:5; 7:21-23; 1 Peter 3:20; 2 Peter 2:5). Second, the means of preservation for the passengers in Acts 27 was actually not the ship, since it broke apart (27:41, 44), which would be a very poor picture of Christ. Instead, the means of preservation for those who suffered shipwreck was the island of Melita (vv. 26, 44; 28:1). Finally, the passengers actually swam to their physical salvation after the ship broke apart (Acts 27:42-44), picturing salvation by works rather than salvation by grace through faith in Christ's finished work.

The contrast between these two ships demonstrates that when continual faith is made the requirement for final salvation, Jesus Christ is really no longer the sole object of faith or trust. If perseverance in faith were the requirement for final salvation, one would invariably end up relying upon his or her own ability to hold on to the object of faith. This really amounts to faith in one's faith, rather than faith in Christ. Consequently, the condition for eternal life is transformed from *faith in Christ* to *faithfulness toward Christ*.

Faith vs. Faithfulness

A comparison of the Greek words for "believe," "faith," and "faithfulness" helps clarify further that the condition for salvation is simply a single act of faith in Christ alone rather than ongoing faithfulness to Christ. The Greek word translated "faithful" in the New Testament is *pistos*. Of the 67 occurrences of this adjective in the New Testament, not once is it used as a requirement for salvation or any synonymous salvation-related concept, such as eternal life, justification, forgiveness, redemption, or regeneration. According to God's Word, faithfulness is not considered to be a condition for eternal salvation, but it is stated to be a condition for receiving a future crown or reward (Rev. 2:10), which is distinct from the free gift of salvation. Though *pistos* is never used as a *condition* for eternal salvation, it is sometimes used as a *description* of believers, or those who are already saved (Acts 10:45, 16:1; Rev. 17:14); though even the saved can be unfaithful or unbelieving (*apistos*), as the example of Thomas reveals in John 20:27.

Pistos should be properly distinguished from the noun *pistis* (faith) and the verb *pisteuō* (believe), which are used repeatedly in the New Testament as the sole condition for salvation. It must be emphatically noted that when *pistis* or *pisteuō* are used in Scripture, they always have as their object either Jesus Christ or necessary propositional truth related to Christ, such as the promises of Christ or the gospel. (See, for example, Mark 1:15; John 3:15-16, 18, 36; 6:40; 8:30; 11:27; 20:31; Acts 10:43; 11:17; 16:31; Rom. 3:22, 26; Gal. 2:16; 3:22, 26; Phil. 3:9; 1 John 5:1, 5.) Not once does the faith or belief required for eternal salvation have as its object anything related to human works or self. This simply means that a person's trust must be in Christ alone. It is not sufficient, therefore, to say that we are saved simply through "faith alone," but through "faith alone in Christ alone."

The saving value of one's faith, therefore, does not lie in the quality, amount, or duration of faith itself, but solely in the quality, character, worthiness, or "faithfulness" of its object. It is technically not our faith that saves us since faith is simply the instrument by which God saves us. Instead, the object of our faith is what (or who) saves us—the Lord Jesus Christ. Our faith in Christ is simply the non-meritorious (Rom. 3:27; 4:5, 16) response to the gospel that God requires before He will do all the work of eternally saving and securing us in Christ.

Who Does the Saving, Keeping, and Persevering?

So who does all of the work of saving and keeping? Believers? God? Believers with the help of God? Must believers continually collaborate with the sanctifying grace of God in their lives in order to maintain their faith and achieve final salvation? That is what many professing Christians believe. But notice that in numerous passages of Scripture it is *God alone* who does the work of saving, keeping, securing, and persevering:

> In John 6:39, Christ specifically says that *He* will not lose any saint: "This is the will of the Father who sent Me, that of all He has given Me I should lose nothing, but should raise it up at the last day."

In John 10:28-29, it is *Christ* and *the Father* who hold on to believers and never let go, not believers who faithfully hold on to God: "And I give them eternal life, and they shall never perish; neither shall anyone snatch them out of My hand. My Father, who has given them to Me, is greater than all; and no one is able to snatch *them* out of My Father's hand." It bears pointing out here that sheep have no hands or fingers with which to hold on to Christ; instead they only have hooves. Thus, Christ must hold on to His sheep.

In John 17:11-12, it is *Christ* and *the Father* who do the keeping: "Now I am no longer in the world, but these are in the world, and I come to You. Holy Father, keep through Your name those whom You have given Me, that they may be one as We are. While I was with them in the world, I kept them in Your name. Those whom You gave Me I have kept; and none of them is lost except the son of perdition, that the Scripture might be fulfilled."

In Romans 5:9-10, it is strictly the *Person* and *work of Christ* that secures our future, final salvation: "Much more then, having now been justified by His blood, we shall be saved from wrath through Him. For if when we were enemies we were reconciled to God through the death of His Son, much more, having been reconciled, we shall be saved by His life." When it comes to the question of whether the redeemed child of God will ever face the wrath of God in the future, the inspired Word emphatically denies such a possibility based upon "His blood" and "the death of His Son." Christ's blood and death are the only answer for our sin problem. Thanks be to God that the Holy Spirit does not say our future deliverance is by *our* Christian life but "by *His* life!"

In Romans 8:29-30, it is *God* alone who accomplishes the work of our salvation from start to finish: "For whom He foreknew, He also predestined to be conformed to the image of His Son, that He might be the firstborn among many brethren. Moreover whom He predestined, these He also called; whom He called, these He also justified; and whom He justified, these He also glorified." In these verses, there is absolutely no mention of man and God partnering together in the earthly process of progressive sanctification, which many so-called evangelicals claim is necessary for one to receive final glorification.

In Romans 8:34, it is strictly the *death, resurrection,* and *intercession of Christ* that answer to all possible condemnation of God's children. Again, no appeal is made to the earthly life or on-going faith of the saint: "Who is he who condemns? It is Christ who died, and furthermore is also risen, who is even at the right hand of God, who also makes intercession for us."

In 2 Timothy 1:12, Paul was confident that it was *God who was able to keep* what he had entrusted to Him: "For this reason I also suffer these things; nevertheless I am not ashamed, for I know whom I have believed and am persuaded that He is able to keep what I have committed to Him until that Day."[9] Our salvation and security is *not* based on *our* ability to endure, nor on any ability which God might give to *us* to endure, but on *God's* ability to keep what lies within His power.

In 2 Timothy 4:18, it is simply *the Lord who preserves us* unto final salvation: "And the Lord will deliver me from every evil work and preserve me for His heavenly kingdom. To Him be glory forever and ever. Amen!"

In Hebrews 7:25, it is *Christ's continual intercession* that is stated to be the basis for our complete salvation: "Therefore He is also able to save to the uttermost those who come to God through Him, since He always lives to make intercession for them."

---

9. Some interpret this verse to mean that God is able to keep or protect that which was "entrusted to me until that day" (RSV, NET Bible). The Greek literally states that "He is able to protect 'my deposit' or 'my entrustment' (*tēn parathēkēn mou*) until that day." Those who interpret this deposit to be the Gospel ministry that God had entrusted to Paul base this on the contextual references to the gospel in verses 11 and 14. Those who interpret this to mean Paul's entrustment of his eternal destiny, or the deposit of the welfare of his soul into the safekeeping of God, base their interpretation on the contextual reference to salvation in verses 9-10 and on the normal sense of verse 12, namely, that God was able to protect what resided with Him rather than with Paul. This has been the traditional translation and interpretation of this verse (KJV, NKJV, NASB, NIV, NRSV) and even the basis for the hymn "I Know Whom I Have Believed," by Daniel W. Whittle.

The Word of God abundantly and repeatedly testifies that it is God who keeps His children secure through His own power and grace. When a sinner fulfills the simple gospel command to "believe" in Christ for his salvation, from *that moment* forward God accomplishes several irreversible, mighty, eternal works on his behalf. From the moment a sinner first believes, the Holy Spirit permanently regenerates him (Titus 3:5), indwells him (John 14:16), baptizes him into Christ's own body (1 Cor. 12:12-13), and seals him in Christ (Eph. 1:13). God also adopts him (Eph. 1:5), forgives him (Col. 2:13), justifies him (Rom. 5:1), reconciles him (2 Cor. 5:19), redeems him (Eph. 1:7), gives him everlasting life in Christ (Rom. 6:23), and guarantees his future bodily glorification (Rom. 8:18-23).

Which one of these blessings are ever said in Scripture to be lost or forfeited through disobedience, doubt, or even outright denial of Christ after one has believed? None! They all remain true of us who have believed in Christ because we are kept in Christ by God's undeserved favor. These salvation-blessings are all promised to believers strictly on the basis of God's grace (Eph. 2:8-9) and the work of Christ (Rom. 5:9-10). Thus, we are kept secure by God, not because we are so faithful to Him, but because He is so faithful to us, and because He always keeps His promises: "If we are faithless, He remains faithful; He cannot deny Himself" (2 Tim. 2:13).

Chapter 3

The Roman Catholicism of Calvinism

If you are devoted to Reformed, Calvinist theology, then be advised: you may find the contents of this chapter very disturbing. This chapter admittedly makes some very strong and unsettling claims. It seeks to demonstrate through extensive quotations by Calvinists themselves that Calvinism's doctrine of the perseverance of the saints effectively denies the biblical truth that salvation is solely by God's grace and not by works, and in this respect, Calvinism bears a striking resemblance to Roman Catholicism's doctrine of salvation. Both views practically destroy personal assurance of salvation; both make perseverance in faith and good works an actual "condition" for final salvation; and both teach that God's saving grace comes through works, such as prayer and the sacraments. While the goal of this chapter is not to disturb you, it should lead you to pause and seriously reconsider whether the doctrine of the perseverance of the saints is truly biblical. If Calvinism's doctrine of perseverance is found to be based largely on religious tradition rather than the Bible, then it needs to be "reformed" further until it agrees with the only infallible rule of faith and practice—the Bible.

The Bible repeatedly declares that God has only one requirement for lost, sinful mankind to be saved, namely, to believe in the Lord Jesus Christ alone for one's salvation (John 3:16; Acts 16:31). But is receiving God's gift of salvation really as simple as believing in Christ? Or must you do more than believe? While many evangelical Christians today adamantly affirm that salvation is through "faith alone," in the same breath they practically deny that biblical truth by redefining "genuine" faith to include some necessary component of good works for final salvation.

But how is this appreciably different from Roman Catholicism? According to Catholic teaching, faith in Jesus Christ is necessary for salvation, but so is perseverance to the end in a supposedly grace-enabled life of good works, including participation in the sacraments as the means of God's sanctifying and saving grace. According to Catholicism (as with Calvinism), man does not initiate the process of salvation, but once it is initiated by God, man must thereafter utilize the grace and strength provided by God to avoid mortal sins and persevere to the end of life in faithful obedience to God; otherwise, he will end up in hell for eternity.

Calvinism vs. Arminianism

While the Protestant doctrines of Arminianism and Calvinism teach that initial salvation is by God's grace, they also teach that faith must endure to the end of one's life and be fruitful for salvation to be sure and truly secure. Though these two doctrinal positions claim to be in opposition to each other and to Roman Catholicism, all three agree that you must continue holding on to Christ by faith until the time of death and have a life of faithfulness, holiness, obedience, and good works to reach heaven's glory one day.

Whether it is the Protestant doctrine of Arminianism stemming from Jacob Arminius and his followers in the early seventeenth century, or the doctrine of Calvinism derived from John Calvin and his followers in the sixteenth century, both of these Protestant traditions teach that if your faith in Christ ceases or completely fails at any point along your earthly path, then God considers you to be lost and in need of His salvation. Arminianism teaches that salvation will be *lost* if you lose your faith. In such a case, your salvation is not eternally secure, and it is dependent upon your faithfulness. On the other hand, Calvinism has traditionally taught that if your faith fails to endure to the end of your life, then it simply proves you were *never truly* saved in the first place because you had mere temporary, spurious faith and not genuine, saving faith. In either case, whether you lose your salvation (Arminianism) or prove that you were never really saved to begin with (Calvinism), your salvation still ultimately requires your faithfulness and endurance. Thus, there really is no practical difference between Arminianism and Calvinism when it comes to the ultimate requirement of perseverance in faith, holiness, and good works for eternal salvation.

Undoubtedly, many Calvinists will balk at such an assessment, for they often claim that their system of salvation is uniquely a grace-method of salvation, while Arminianism or any belief system contrary to Calvinism is a works-based approach to salvation. Here is a small sampling of such claims:

> Calvinism is the Gospel and to teach Calvinism is in fact to preach the Gospel. It is questionable whether a dogmatic theology which is not Calvinistic is truly Christian.[1]

> The doctrines of grace distilled in the five points of Calvinism have been shown to be the consistent testimony of Scripture. Ultimately Arminianism finds its support not in Scripture but in the pride of sinful men by teaching that a person plays the decisive part in his own salvation.[2]

> Arminianism denies this doctrine of Perseverance, because it is a system, not of pure grace, but of grace and works; and in any such system the person must prove himself at least partially worthy.[3]

> The doctrine that men are saved only through the unmerited love and grace of God finds its full and honest expression only in the doctrines of Calvinism.[4]

> Arminianism is a "works religion" at least to the extent that man must accomplish the good works of repentance and faith. . . . Calvinism is strictly a "not of works, lest any man should boast" religion (Ephesians 2:8-9) because it insists on giving God all the glory for all that is good.[5]

This is the one point of Calvinistic soteriology which the "five points" are concerned to establish and Arminianism in all its

---

1. Arthur C. Custance, *The Sovereignty of Grace* (Phillipsburg, NJ: Presbyterian & Reformed, 1979), 302.

2. Keith Mathison, *Dispensationalism: Rightly Dividing the People of God?* (Phillipsburg, NJ: Presbyterian & Reformed, 1995), 78.

3. Lorraine Boettner, *The Reformed Doctrine of Predestination* (Phillipsburg, NJ: Presbyterian & Reformed, 1932), 187.

4. Ibid., 95.

5. Duane E. Spencer, *TULIP: The Five Points of Calvinism in the Light of Scripture* (Grand Rapids: Baker, 1979), 84.

forms to deny: namely, that sinners do not save themselves in any sense at all, but that salvation, first and last, whole and entire, past, present and future, is of the Lord.[6]

If you do not know the Five Points of Calvinism, you do not know the Gospel but some perversion of it.[7]

Roman Calminianism

With the preceding claims of the Calvinists in mind, the following list of quotations provides a helpful exercise to illustrate the fact that there is practically no difference between the two theologies of Arminianism and Calvinism when it comes to their requirements for eternal salvation. Listed below are over thirty quotations on perseverance and salvation from Arminian, Calvinist, and Roman Catholic sources. As you read these quotes, try guessing which of the three theological persuasions is held by the writer of each quote. You may be shocked by some of the answers in the footnotes. And don't be surprised if you find yourself saying after a while, "I give up. They all sound the same!" Though some may wonder why so many quotations are given below, the point of this exercise is to show that the similarity of Calvinism's teaching on salvation to that of Arminianism and Catholicism is far more pervasive than most Calvinists care to admit.

There is no valid assurance of election and final salvation for any man, apart from deliberate perseverance in faith.[8]

The only evidence of election is . . . the production of holiness. And the only evidence of the genuineness of this call and the certainty of our perseverance, is a patient continuance in well-doing.[9]

There is no cleansing from sin, and no salvation, without a continual walking in God's light.[10]

---

6. J. I. Packer, as quoted in Daniel N. Steele and Curtis C. Thomas, *The Five Points of Calvinism* (Phillipsburg, NJ: Presbyterian & Reformed, 1963), 22.

7. Fred Phelps, "The Five Points of Calvinism," *The Berea Baptist Banner*, February 5, 1990, p. 21.

8. Robert Shank (Arminian), *Life in the Son* (Springfield, MO: Westcott, 1960), 293.

9. Charles Hodge (Calvinist), *Commentary on Romans* (Grand Rapids: Eerdmans, 1994), 292.

10. Guy Duty (Arminian), *If Ye Continue* (Minneapolis: Bethany House, 1966), 141.

Let us not then take refuge in our sloth or encouragement in our lust from the abused doctrine of the security of the believer. But let us . . . recognize that we may entertain the faith of our security in Christ only as we persevere in faith and holiness to the end.[11]

The Scriptures repeatedly exhort us to persevere, to "hang in there." It is only the one who endures to the end who will be saved.[12]

Endurance in faith is a condition for future salvation. Only those who endure in faith will be saved for eternity.[13]

Believing in Jesus Christ and in the One who sent him for our salvation is necessary for obtaining that salvation. . . . therefore without faith no one has ever attained justification, nor will anyone obtain eternal life "but he who endures to the end."[14]

Let us hear the conclusion of the whole matter: Objectively, the elect will persevere, and they who persevere are elect. Subjectively, the individual is elect only as he perseveres.[15]

We can never know that we are elected of God to eternal life except by manifesting in our lives the fruits of election—faith and virtue, knowledge and temperance, patience and godliness, love of brethren. . . . It is idle to seek assurance of election outside of holiness of life.[16]

And since, without faith, it is impossible to please God, and to attain to the fellowship of his children, therefore without

---

11. John Murray (Calvinist), *Redemption—Accomplished and Applied* (Grand Rapids: Eerdmans, 1955), 155.

12. Joseph Kindel (Roman Catholic), *What Must I Do to be Saved?* (Milford, OH: Riehle Foundation, 1995), 79.

13. R. C. Sproul (Calvinist), *Grace Unknown: The Heart of Reformed Theology* (Grand Rapids: Baker, 1997), 198.

14. (Roman Catholic) *Catechism of the Catholic Church* (Bloomingdale, OH: Apostolate for Family Consecration, 1994), 44, §161.

15. Robert Shank (Arminian), *Life in the Son*, 301.

16. Benjamin B. Warfield (Calvinist) as favorably quoted by Lorraine Boettner in *The Reformed Doctrine of Predestination* (Phillipsburg, NJ: Presbyterian & Reformed, 1932), 309 (ellipsis original to Boettner).

faith no one has ever attained justification, nor will any one obtain eternal life unless he shall have persevered in faith unto the end.[17]

Holiness in this life is such a part of our "salvation" that it is a necessary means to make us meet to be partakers of the inheritance of the saints in heavenly light and glory.[18]

In like manner [God] could cause His people to grow in grace, make them fruitful unto every good work, and preserve them from everything injurious to their welfare, without requiring any industry and diligence on their part; but it has not so pleased Him to dispense with their concurrence. Accordingly we find Him bidding them *"Work out your own salvation with fear and trembling"* (Phil. 2:12), *"Labour therefore to enter into that rest, lest any man fall after the same example of unbelief"* (Heb. 4:11).[19]

As the believer's salvation is received, not by an act of righteousness but by an act of faith, so the believer's salvation is maintained, not by acts of righteousness but by a life of faith. . . . his security is never in doubt as long as his faith in Christ is steadfast, for he is kept by faith.[20]

Furthermore, we are protected through faith. Our continued faith in Christ is the instrument of God's sustaining work. God didn't save us apart from faith, and He doesn't keep us apart from faith. . . . It is our faith. We believe. We remain steadfast. We are not passive in the process. The means by which God maintains our faith involves our full participation.[21]

---

17. (Roman Catholic) Vatican I, Dogmatic Constitution on the Catholic Faith, Chapter III, "On Faith," in *The Creeds of Christendom: With a History and Critical Notes*, ed. Philip Schaff, rev. by David S. Schaff, 6th rev. ed. (New York: Harper and Row, 1931; reprint, Grand Rapids: Baker, 1993), 2:245.

18. Walter Marshall (Calvinist), as favorably quoted by A. W. Pink (Calvinist) in *The Doctrine of Sanctification* (Great Britain: Christian Focus, 1998), 25.

19. A. W. Pink (Calvinist), *The Saint's Perseverance* (Lafayette, IN: Sovereign Grace, 2001), 81.

20. Assemblies of God (Arminian) Position Paper, *The Security of the Believer* (Springfield, MO: General Council of the Assemblies of God, 1978), 3.

21. John MacArthur (Calvinist), *Faith Works* (Dallas: Word, 1993), 185.

Having stressed the sovereignty and grace of God, it is also imperative to bring the free will and responsibility of the believer into focus. God does not withdraw the power of choice from the person who believes. By the exercise of free will the believer becomes a child of God, and by the continued exercise of free will he remains a child of God. To keep on believing is the believer's responsibility.[22]

The saints are *"kept by the power of God through faith"* (1 Pet. 1:5). He does not deal with them as unaccountable automatons, but as moral agents, just as their natural life is maintained through their use of means and by their avoidance of that which is inimical to their wellbeing, so it is with the maintenance and preservation of their spiritual lives. God preserves His people in this world through their perseverance—their use of means and avoidance of what is destructive.[23]

[A]lthough the Bible tells us that we are kept by the grace of God, it does not encourage the idea that God keeps us without constant watchfulness, diligence, and prayer on our part.[24]

Just as the Bible teaches God's protection and preservation of His people, it is equally emphatic that only those will be saved who endure to the end, abide in Christ and his Word, and continue in the faith (please read Matt 24:13; John 8:31; John 15:6; 1 Cor 15:1, 2; Col 1:22, 23).[25]

Saving faith is no simple thing. It has many dimensions. "Believe on the Lord Jesus" is a massive command. It contains a hundred other things. Unless we see this, the array of conditions for salvation in the New Testament will be utterly perplexing.[26]

---

22. Assemblies of God (Arminian) Position Paper, *The Security of the Believer*, 5.

23. A. W. Pink (Calvinist), *The Saint's Perseverance*, 11.

24. Louis Berkhof (Calvinist), *Systematic Theology* (Grand Rapids: Eerdmans, 1991), 548.

25. (Roman Catholic), www.justforcatholics.org/d17.htm (accessed September 9, 2015).

26. John Piper (Calvinist), *Desiring God* (Sisters, OR: Multnomah, 1986), 65. This quote also appeared verbatim in the 1996 reprinting of *Desiring God*, but it was

The New Testament clearly teaches that bare faith cannot save and that works are necessary for final justification or final salvation.[27]

Jesus taught salvation to be conditional upon a man denying himself, and taking up his cross, and following Him continuously. . . . True faith reveals itself in continual obedience to Christ's conditions for salvation.[28]

It means we obey his commands. It means we are always prayerful, embedded in Christian community, worshiping Jesus in all of life, and living on mission with him every day. In the absence of all this, no one can be assured of salvation.[29]

These are just some of the conditions that the New Testament says we must meet in order to inherit final salvation. We must believe on Jesus and receive him and turn from our sin and obey him and humble ourselves like little children and love him more than we love our family, our possessions or our own life. This is what it means to be converted to Christ. This alone is the way of life everlasting.[30]

There is a marked theme in [Jesus'] teachings regarding people who say they believe, or who believe only for a little while, but whose works are false, missing, or incomplete. It is these who are lost. These teachings warn us that people are damned not merely for lack of faith, per se, but for not following through with their faith, i.e., for not doing works of obedience. But most importantly, not once does Jesus say or teach that someone can be eternally saved by a one-time act of faith.[31]

Salvation for sinners cost God His own Son; it cost God's Son His life, and it'll cost you the same thing. Salvation isn't the result of an intellectual exercise. It comes from a life lived in

---

rephrased in the 2003 and 2011 editions.

27. Thomas R. Schreiner (Calvinist), *Faith Alone—The Doctrine of Justification* (Grand Rapids: Zondervan, 2015), 191.

28. Guy Duty (Arminian), *If Ye Continue*, 65.

29. Sam Storms (Calvinist), *Kept for Jesus* (Wheaton, IL: Crossway, 2015), 57.

30. John Piper (Calvinist), *Desiring God*, 65-66.

31. Robert A. Sungenis (Roman Catholic), *How Can I Get to Heaven? The Bible's Teaching on Salvation Made Easy to Understand* (Santa Barbara, CA: Queenship, 1998), 139.

obedience and service to Christ as revealed in the Scripture; it's the fruit of actions, not intentions.[32]

Divine preservation always presupposes human persever-ance. Perseverance proves faith's genuine character, and is therefore indispensable to salvation. To be sure, no one can continue in the faith in his own strength (John 15:5). The enabling grace of God is needed from start to finish (Phil. 2:12, 13). This, however, does not cancel human responsibil-ity and activity. Yes, *activity*, continuous, sustained, strenu-ous effort (Heb. 12:14).[33]

We have seen that God's salvation covenant is a Continuing Covenant. And it is a monstrous deception to teach that the continual sinner will be saved by a continuing covenant that demands his continual obedience.[34]

Holiness, which is defined by love of God and neighbor, is usually something that is seen by others rather than by us. Nevertheless, it is the indispensable condition of our glori-fication: no one will be seated at the heavenly banquet who has not begun, however imperfectly, in new obedience.[35]

We cannot "earn" our salvation through good works, but our faith in Christ puts us in a special grace-filled relationship with God so that our obedience and love, combined with our faith, will be rewarded with eternal life.[36]

[Christians] are to refrain from speaking evil and from guile so that they will obtain the eschatological reward, eternal life itself. We must insist again that such a theology is not works righteousness, nor does it compromise the theme that salva-

32. John MacArthur (Calvinist), *Hard to Believe: The High Cost and Infinite Value of Following Jesus* (Nashville: Thomas Nelson, 2003), 93. While this quote has been revised and softened in subsequent printings of *Hard to Believe,* MacArthur's revised paragraph still teaches the necessity of faith plus works for final salvation.

33. William Hendricksen (Calvinist), *Exposition of Colossians and Philemon,* New Testament Commentary (Grand Rapids: Baker, 1964), 85.

34. Guy Duty (Arminian), *If Ye Continue,* 169.

35. Michael Horton (Calvinist), *Introducing Covenant Theology* (Grand Rapids: Baker, 2006), 183.

36. (Roman Catholic) *Pillar of Fire, Pillar of Truth* (San Diego: Catholic Answers, 1993), 23.

tion is by grace. Peter believed that those who have received new life from God will live transformed lives and that such lives provide evidence (necessary evidence!) that they have been converted.[37]

There is a deadly and damnable heresy being widely propagated today to the effect that, if a sinner truly accepts Christ as his personal Saviour, no matter how he lives afterwards, he cannot perish. That is a satanic lie, for it is at direct variance with the teaching of the Word of truth. Something more than believing in Christ is necessary to ensure the soul's reaching heaven.[38]

If you have taken the time to carefully read each of the preceding quotations, then it should be evident by now that there is no practical difference between Calvinism, Arminianism, and Roman Catholicism in their requirement of faithful perseverance and good works to make it to heaven. While many Calvinists readily acknowledge that Roman Catholicism and Arminianism promote a works-gospel, they remain spiritually blind to the fact that the same error is endemic to their own system of salvation and its unscriptural doctrine of the perseverance of the saints. At this point, you may be wondering how Calvinists, who purport so strongly at times to believe in salvation by grace alone, can simultaneously and just as vehemently require works for eternal salvation. The answer is apparent in understanding the relationship of Calvinism's first four points to its fifth point—the perseverance of the saints.

The Five Points of Calvinism

Since the time of the Calvinist Synod of Dordrect (Dort) in 1618–1619, the basic doctrines of orthodox, confessional Calvinism have traditionally been summarized and set in contrast to Arminianism by five points that are commonly known by the acrostic TULIP.

---

37. Thomas R. Schreiner (Calvinist), 1, 2 Peter, Jude, New American Commentary (Nashville: Broadman & Holman, 2003), 167 (parenthesis and exclamation point original).

38. A. W. Pink (Calvinist), as quoted in Iain H. Murray, The Life of Arthur W. Pink (Edinburgh: Banner of Truth, 1981), 248-49.

T	-	Total Depravity
U	-	Unconditional Election
L	-	Limited Atonement
I	-	Irresistible Grace
P	-	Perseverance of the Saints

To properly understand Calvinism's doctrine of perseverance, one must understand its four points leading up to this fifth point since all five points are logically interrelated.

In its first point, Calvinism teaches that every man is "totally depraved" in sin, spiritually dead before God, and therefore incapable of saving himself, which is all true to Scripture. However, Calvinism also interprets mankind's total depravity to mean "total inability." This view teaches that a lost person is utterly incapable of positively exercising his will, so he is spiritually incapable of believing in Christ unless the Holy Spirit first regenerates him to give him the gift of faith and make him willing to believe in Christ.

Based on the false conclusion that man is totally incapable of believing in Christ of his own volition before he is born again, the second point of Calvinism then concludes that God must have "unconditionally elected" only certain people to be saved. This unconditional election is made strictly on the basis of God's sovereign choice, completely apart from any foresight or recognition of man's volition or choice to believe in Christ.

Traditional Calvinism also teaches that since God determined only a select number of people to be elect and destined for salvation, it would be superfluous for Christ to purchase the salvation of the nonelect when He died for sin on Calvary's cross. Calvinism believes that Christ died on the cross not only to make salvation available but also to make it effectual so that all whom Christ died for must (and will) be saved. Therefore, Calvinism has traditionally taught that Christ provided a "limited atonement" by dying for the sins of only the elect rather than the whole world of the elect and non-elect.

The fourth point of traditional Calvinism is the teaching of "irresistible grace." This point teaches that since God unconditionally chose certain people to be saved and Christ paid for the sins of only these elect, God will work in their lives in such a way that they will be irresistibly drawn to Christ. God then supposedly draws the elect completely apart from their own volition, regenerates them, and gives them the gift of faith so that thereafter they always believe in Jesus Christ.

Finally, the "perseverance of the saints" teaches that all whom God irresistibly draws to Himself and regenerates apart from their own volition will prove their election by living a predominantly faithful, productive life of holiness and good works. Calvinism teaches that a failure to continue in the faith does not mean a person has lost his salvation; it simply means he never had genuine faith and salvation in the first place. Calvinism concludes that the saint's perseverance in faith is guaranteed because God not only sovereignly bestows the gift of saving faith on His elect but He also causes it to endure and be productive.

Calvinism's Guaranteed Perseverance

Because this book will regularly make reference to the Calvinist doctrine of the perseverance of the saints and compare it with Scripture, it is essential to understand precisely what this doctrine claims. For centuries, Calvinists have followed the Synod of Dort's position on the perseverance of the saints. Under Dort's fifth point on the perseverance of the saints, article four acknowledges that the elect are capable of "great and heinous sins by the flesh." Article five goes on to say that "such enormous sins" may even temporarily "interrupt the exercise of faith." Yet, article seven declares that when the elect sin in such a manner, they will certainly and effectually be renewed to repentance before their deaths. In addition, article eight concludes that genuinely elect believers can "neither totally fall from faith and grace nor continue and perish finally in their backslidings." Therefore, the teaching of traditional Calvinism states that true believers will never completely nor finally stop believing in Christ since a failure to persevere to the end with at least some degree of faith is an impossibility for those who are truly elect.[39]

Anthony Hoekema, a late professor of systematic theology at Calvin Theological Seminary, summarizes this critical point of Calvinist teaching.

What the doctrine of the perseverance of true believers does mean is this: those who have true faith can lose that faith neither totally nor finally. The real question at issue, there-

---

39. Berkhof, *Systematic Theology*, 548-49; Boettner, *Reformed Doctrine of Predestination*, 187; Curt Daniel, *Biblical Calvinism* (Springfield, IL: Reformed Bible Church, n.d.), 10; Gerstner, *Wrongly Dividing the Word of Truth*, 221; A. W. Pink, *The Saint's Perseverance* (Lafayette, IN: Sovereign Grace, 2001), 77.

fore, is this: Can a person who has true faith ever lose that faith? To this question the person of Reformed persuasion says: No. It should immediately be added, however, that the Calvinist gives this answer not on the basis of the superior spiritual strength of the believer, but on the ground of God's faithfulness to his promise. The Calvinist believes that God will never permit those to whom he has given true faith to fall away from that faith.[40]

In Calvinism, there is a very close connection between the sovereign, unconditional bestowal of faith and one's perseverance in that faith, as Edwin Palmer writes, "But when we realize that faith is not man's gift to God, but is rather God's gift to man, then we realize that man will never lose his faith."[41] Similarly, John MacArthur claims, "As a divine gift, faith is neither transient nor impotent. It has an abiding quality that guarantees its endurance to the end."[42] Contemporary Reformed scholar Keith Mathison concurs, explaining, "True living faith is a gift from God that begins at a person's new birth and never ends. . . . At some stages in the Christian's life, faith may be very weak, but if it is true faith it will never die. The true believer must and will, by the grace of God, persevere until the end."[43]

Calvinism's doctrine of the unfailing nature of true, saving faith leads some of its proponents at times to claim near invincibility for their faith. According to one leading Calvinist, if your faith is genuine, then it must always persist through life's many trials and temptations, and it must respond positively to church discipline, and you can never apostatize. John MacArthur expresses these stark, practical implications of Calvinism's doctrine of perseverance.

> Temptations . . . and tests don't weaken or shatter real faith — just the opposite. They strengthen it. People who lose their faith in a trial only show that they never had real faith to begin with.[44]

The church discipline process our Lord outlined in Matthew 18 is predicated on the doctrine of perseverance. Those

---

40. Anthony A. Hoekema, *Saved by Grace* (Grand Rapids: Eerdmans, 1989), 234-35.
41. Edwin H. Palmer, *The Five Points of Calvinism* (Grand Rapids: Baker, 1980), 70.
42. MacArthur, *Gospel According to Jesus*, 173.
43. Mathison, *Dispensationalism: Rightly Dividing the People of God?* 77.
44. MacArthur, *Faith Works*, 186.

who remain hardened in sin only demonstrate their lack of true faith. Those who respond to the rebuke and return to the Lord give the best possible evidence that their salvation is genuine. They can be sure that if their faith is real it will endure to the end—because God Himself guarantees it.[45]

True believers will persevere. If a person turns against Christ, it is proof that person was never saved. . . . No matter how convincing a person's testimony might seem, once he becomes apostate he has demonstrated irrefutably that he was never saved.[46]

According to MacArthur and other Calvinists, your preservation by God and eternal security in Christ are inseparably connected to your perseverance. If you truly believe, your faith will never fail to persevere. If your faith does fail, it proves your faith was never genuine and you were never really born again. Calvinism teaches that true faith, just like salvation, can never be lost. In this sense, Calvinism weds eternal security to the believer's perseverance in faithfulness.

Perseverance versus Eternal Security

While Calvinism affirms that believers are eternally secure in one sense, this security is still directly connected to an unfailing, productive, and enduring faith. MacArthur explains: "Security in Christ is tied to perseverance. . . .When somebody abandons Christ, abandons gospel truth, abandons virtue and holiness—walks away—that is not a failure of eternal life; that is evidence of superficial faith. They never did believe or they would remain."[47] According to Calvinism's doctrine of the perseverance of the saints, a believer's salvation is never in question from God's point of view; it is eternally secure. But from the believer's human standpoint, salvation still requires faithful perseverance to the end of one's earthly life.

Calvinists themselves routinely distinguish between the *eternal security of the saints* and the *perseverance of the saints*. For instance, MacArthur states:

---

45. Ibid, 192.
46. MacArthur, *Gospel According to Jesus*, 98.
47. John MacArthur, "The Faith That Doesn't Fail," audio recording, GTY155, 2015.

I am committed to the biblical truth that salvation is forever. Contemporary Christians have come to refer to this as the doctrine of eternal security. Perhaps the Puritans' terminology is more appropriate; they spoke of the perseverance of the saints. The point is not that God guarantees security to everyone who will say he accepts Christ, but rather that those whose faith is genuine will prove their salvation is secure by persevering to the end in the way of righteousness.[48]

[The Westminster divines] understood "perseverance of the saints" to be a better expression of the truth than "eternal security." Eternal security has come to be a more popular designation, but it's not nearly as accurate. Eternal security doesn't describe the necessary means by which our eternal life is secured. Even though believers may sin, may sin seriously, may sin repeatedly, there are some things they will never abandon. They will not come under the full dominion of sin. They will not lose trust and confidence in the Lord and the gospel. They will not shun holiness and fully embrace iniquity.[49]

Keith Mathison is critical of the doctrine of eternal security held by many dispensationalists. In the following statement, he distinguishes between the supposedly false view of eternal security held by many dispensationalists versus his Reformed doctrine of perseverance:

According to the dispensational doctrine of eternal security, once a person "believes," nothing he does—even persistent unconfessed sin—can affect his eternal salvation. This, however, differs from the doctrine of the perseverance of the saints. The Reformed doctrine of perseverance says that all who were chosen, redeemed, and regenerated by God are eternally saved and are kept in faith by the power of God. They must and will, therefore, persevere in holiness to the end.[50]

---

48. Ibid.

49. MacArthur, "The Faith That Doesn't Fail." When speaking of "the necessary means by which our eternal life is secured," MacArthur is simply using centuries-old, standard Reformed terminology for the human responsibility in reaching glorification or final salvation, which provides the opening for works to be added to the gospel. This crucial concept of "necessary means" for final salvation is explained later in this chapter.

50. Mathison, *Dispensationalism: Rightly Dividing the People of God?* 76.

Popular author and ardent Calvinist John Piper also underscores the necessity for saints to persevere in order to be considered eternally secure.

> It follows from what was just said that the people of God WILL persevere to the end and not be lost. The foreknown are predestined, the predestined are called, the called are justified, and the justified are glorified. To belong to this people is to be eternally secure. But we mean more than this by the doctrine of the perseverance of the saints. We mean that the saints will and must persevere in the obedience which comes from faith. Election is unconditional, but glorification is not. There are many warnings in Scripture that those who do not hold fast to Christ can be lost in the end.[51]

As the previous quotations show, Calvinism's view of eternal security still requires faithfulness and good works throughout one's Christian life, which is really no different from Arminianism. This explains why Calvinist theologian Anthony Hoekema openly admits his agreement with Robert Shank on the conditions for final salvation even though Shank was a leading Arminian of the twentieth century who wrote an entire book opposing the "notion" of eternal security. Hoekema states:

> As we have noted, the Bible teaches that God does not preserve us apart from our watchfulness, prayer, and persevering faith. The expression "once saved, always saved" is therefore not an accurate way of stating the doctrine of the perseverance of true believers. Such an expression could easily be understood to mean "once saved, always saved" regardless of how we live, and such a notion is clearly contrary to Scripture. On this point I quite agree with Robert Shank.[52]

According to the previous statements by leading Calvinists, salvation still depends on "how we live" and whether you as a believer do the following:

---

51. John Piper and Pastoral Staff, *What We Believe About the Five Points of Calvinism* (Minneapolis: Bethlehem Baptist Church document, 1998), capitalization original.
52. Hoekema, *Saved by Grace*, 245.

- endure to the end in "the way of righteousness,"
- do not have "persistent unconfessed sin,"
- "persevere in the obedience which comes from faith,"
- "hold fast to Christ," and
- have "watchfulness" and "prayer."

Though Calvinists vociferously deny that this is salvation by works, how can it be otherwise when good works are still viewed ultimately as a requirement for eternal life? Thus, there is little practical difference between the plan of salvation taught by Calvinism, Arminianism, and Roman Catholicism since each maintains that faith must be coupled with divinely enabled good works to obtain eternal salvation.

For too long, many Bible-believing Christians have wrongly assumed that the Calvinist doctrine of the "perseverance of the saints" is synonymous with the biblical doctrine of eternal security. But the two are clearly *not* the same. According to Scripture, a person's eternal security rests solely upon the gracious perseverance of the *Savior* as He perseveres in keeping saved all who have trusted in Him alone for their eternal salvation but who are still sinners (1 Tim. 1:15-16). When the perseverance of the *saints* is required for final salvation rather than the perseverance of the *Savior*, it has several tragic consequences, starting with the loss of the believer's assurance.

Perseverance & Assurance

If you must persevere in your faith to the end of your life to be saved eternally, but you have not yet reached the end of your life, how can you really know with certainty whether you will escape God's condemnation in hell? According to Calvinism's doctrine of the perseverance of the saints, you cannot even take solace in the fact that you presently believe in Christ, for this is no guarantee that you will still believe upon your deathbed. If you think you are a believer now but you end up dying in unbelief, that will simply show that you had false, spurious faith all along. And if that is the case, then you were merely a *professor* of salvation but not an actual *possessor*. So much for the "blessed assurance" of your salvation! Though Calvinists profess that some degree of assurance can be attained in this life, according to the logic of Calvinism's perseverance of the saints, no one can really be sure of their salvation until they cross the finish line of their earthly lives and die in a state of faith and grace. For this reason, the doctrine of perseverance practically destroys personal assurance of salvation even though New Testament saints possessed it (Phil. 4:2-3; Col. 3:1-4; 1 Peter 1:3-5; 1 John 3:1-2) and God promises it to every believer (1 John 5:9-13).

It is no wonder that so many Calvinists down through the centuries have lacked complete assurance of salvation, especially upon their deathbeds. One author states regarding the most prominent Puritan theologian of the late-sixteenth century, William Perkins, "Believing in Christ to Perkins means sooner or later to descend inside ourselves; the eventual result is not merely introspection, but a doctrine of faith that could easily breed legalism."[53] It is no wonder that he goes on to say, "Perkins reportedly died 'in the conflict of a troubled conscience.'"[54]

Tragically, many other Puritans cried out to God for mercy upon their deathbeds, being afflicted with the uncertainty that they were numbered among God's elect. For this reason, John MacArthur admits,

> Most of the Puritans taught that believers could not expect assurance until long after conversion, and only after a life of extended faithfulness. They tended to make assurance dependent on the believer's ability to live at an almost unattainable level of personal holiness. . . . As we might expect, the Puritans' demanding preaching led to a widespread lack of assurance among their flocks. Christians became obsessed with whether they were truly elect, and many lapsed into morbid introspection and despair.[55]

Writing on the subject of assurance, one Reformed author candidly admits the real problem plagueing so many Puritans: "The

---

53. R. T. Kendall, *Calvin and English Calvinism to 1649* (Great Britain: Paternoster, 1997), 53, 75.

54. Ibid.

55. MacArthur, *Faith Works*, 161. It is astonishing that MacArthur speaks of the "unattainable level of personal holiness" required by the Puritans for personal assurance of salvation when he himself proclaims, "Thus in a sense we pay the ultimate price for salvation when our sinful self is nailed to a cross. It is a total abandonment of self-will, like the grain of wheat that falls to the ground and dies so that it can bear much fruit (cf. John 12:24). It is an exchange of all that we are for all that Christ is. And it denotes implicit obedience, full surrender to the lordship of Christ. Nothing less can qualify as saving faith" (MacArthur, *Gospel According to Jesus*, 140). Can anyone honestly say that in this earthly life they have met this demand for complete ("total," "all," "full") obedience to Christ?

Puritan doctrine of assurance is a form of salvation by works. A doctrine of works is necessarily also a doctrine of doubt."[56] But personal assurance of salvation was not only lacking among many of the Puritans, for even the original Calvinist himself apparently did not possess complete assurance of salvation.

John Calvin indicated in his will before his death in 1564 that he still did not know with absolute certainty whether he was one of the "elect," evidently because he had not yet persevered to the very end of his life in faith and holiness. Thus, he could only *wish* for final salvation, declaring in his will, "I testify also and profess that I humbly seek from God, that He may so will me to be washed and purified by the great Redeemer's blood, shed for the sins of the human race, that it may be permitted me to stand before His tribunal under the covert of the Redeemer Himself."[57] How unfortunate that this esteemed reformer toward the end of his life apparently still did not know with certainty whether "it may be permitted" him to be saved and whether God "may so will" his salvation, when in fact the Word of God plainly declares that God "is not willing that any should perish" (2 Peter 3:9) and that He "desires all men to be saved" (1 Tim. 2:4).

Not coincidentally, even some prominent modern-day proponents of Calvinism's doctrine of perseverance admit that they lack assurance because of sin patterns in their lives. Piper plainly confesses,

> I know people, and I would say this about myself, for whom the greatest threat to my perseverance and my ultimate salvation is the slowness of my sanctification. It's not theoretical questions like "Did He rise from the dead?" or the problem of evil. I've got answers. But why I sin against my wife the same at age 62 that I did at age 42 causes me sometimes to doubt my salvation or the power of the Holy Spirit.[58]

While there is definitely a place to ask ourselves whether we truly possess eternal life or are self-deceived in thinking we are saved, the answer to such a question must be based solely upon the *object* of our

---

56. David J. Engelsma, *The Gift of Assurance* (South Holland, IL: Evangelism Committee of the Protestant Reformed Church, 2009), 12.

57. As quoted in Norman F. Douty, *The Death of Christ,* Revised Edition (Irving, TX: Williams & Watrous, 1978), 176.

58. John Piper, "Why God Is Not a Megalomaniac in Demanding to be Worshiped," 60th Annual Meeting of the Evangelical Theological Society, Providence, RI, November 20, 2008. www.desiringgod.org/messages/why-god-is-not-a-megalo-maniac-in-demanding-to-be-worshiped

faith—whether it is Jesus Christ and His work alone or whether it includes our own practical righteousness in the form of our efforts, commitment, obedience, faithfulness, prayers, sacramental rituals, good deeds, and perseverance. C. I. Scofield, a dispensational Bible teacher of the past, understood this truth well.

> Assurance is the believer's absolute conviction that he is in the present possession of a salvation in which he will be eternally kept. This assurance is based on his perfect righteousness in Christ Jesus. Note: It follows, therefore, that the believer's assurance does not rest upon sanctification, but justification—not upon works, but upon faith in Christ alone.[59]

The assurance of salvation does not come from analyzing the *nature* of our faith or the *productivity* of our faith, as if we need a certain *kind* of faith, *amount* of faith, *duration* of faith, or *output* of faith. Instead, assurance comes by looking to the right *object* of faith—the Lord Jesus Christ and His finished work alone. While it is certainly possible for people to have false assurance and think they are saved when they are not, the reason people are self-deceived is invariably because they are trusting in the wrong object of faith, namely, themselves and their own works rather than Christ alone (Matt. 7:22; 19:16-26; 21:31-32; Luke 18:9-14).

The "Condition" of Ongoing Faith & Works

Besides the loss of personal assurance of salvation, Calvinism's doctrine of perseverance also leads to faithfulness and good works becoming actual "conditions" for eternal salvation and not just the "results" of regeneration. Calvinists often qualify their doctrine of perseverance by teaching that although God regenerates and justifies by His grace alone through faith alone in Christ alone, regeneration and "saving faith" will never be alone. They will always be accompanied by perseverance and good works. Thus, MacArthur insists, "But make no mistake—real faith will always produce righteous works."[60]

But if perseverance in faith and good works must always accompany regeneration and faith so that good works are considered to be the necessary result of "saving faith," then doesn't Calvinism still

---

59. C. I. Scofield, *Twenty-Six Great Words of Scripture*, Scofield Bible Correspondence Course, 6 vols. (Chicago: Moody Bible Institute, 1960), 5:1076.

60. MacArthur, *Faith Works*, 50.

ultimately require works to be saved from hell? Calvinists often deny the logical implications of their own position by adamantly professing that they are *not* making good works a "condition" for eternal salvation. Thus, MacArthur avers, "To say that works are a necessary *result* of faith is *not* the same as making works a *condition* for justification."[61] Really? If this is the case, then why do so many leading Reformed theologians liberally employ the word "condition" or "conditions" to describe the necessity of perseverance in faith and good works for eternal salvation? This can be observed in the following statements, where the words "condition," "conditions," and "contingent" are italicized for emphasis:

> Faith may appropriately be regarded as a unique *condition* of justification in the manner explained above, but there are other *conditions* (that without which justification will not be) as well, and these *conditions* are indeed subsumed under the notion of evangelical obedience.[62]

> Evangelical obedience is an absolute necessity, a *"condition"* in man's justification.[63]

> Endurance in faith is a *condition* for future salvation. Only those who endure in faith will be saved for eternity.[64]

> Jesus' words indicate that perseverance to the end is the necessary *condition*. Perseverance is the means that God has appointed by which one can be saved.[65]

> This passage teaches that perseverance is a *condition* of final salvation. . . . Continuing to believe the Gospel is indispensable to final salvation.[66]

> The New Testament lays before us a vast array of *conditions* for final salvation. Not only initial repentance and faith, but

---

61. Ibid., 53.

62. Samuel T. Logan, Jr., "The Doctrine of Justification in the Theology of Jonathan Edwards," *Westminster Theological Journal* 46 (Spring 1984): 38.

63. Ibid., 43.

64. Sproul, *Grace Unknown*, 198.

65. Thomas R. Schreiner and Ardel B. Canaday, *The Race Set Before Us: A Biblical Theology of Perseverance & Assurance* (Downers Grove, IL: InterVarsity, 2001), 151-52.

66. Robert A. Peterson, "The Perseverance of the Saints: A Theological Exegesis of Four Key New Testament Passages," *Presbyterion* Vol. 17, No. 2 (1991): 98.

perseverance in both, demonstrated in love toward God and neighbor, are part of that holiness without which no one shall see the Lord (Heb. 12:14).[67]

Holiness, which is defined by love of God and neighbor, is usually something that is seen by others rather than by us. Nevertheless, it is the indispensable *condition* of our glorification: no one will be seated at the heavenly banquet who has not begun, however imperfectly, in new obedience.[68]

Saving faith is no simple thing. It has many dimensions. "Believe on the Lord Jesus" is a massive command. It contains a hundred other things. Unless we see this, the array of *conditions* for salvation in the New Testament will be utterly perplexing.[69]

These are just some of the *conditions* that the New Testament says we must meet in order to inherit final salvation. We must believe on Jesus and receive him and turn from our sin and obey him and humble ourselves like little children and love him more than we love our family, our possessions or our own life. This is what it means to be converted to Christ. This alone is the way of life everlasting.[70]

Nevertheless, we must also own up to the fact that our final salvation is made *contingent* upon the subsequent obedience which comes from faith. . . . This is why those who do not lead a life of faith with its inevitable obedience simply bear witness to the fact that their first act of faith was not genuine.[71]

As Tom Schreiner says, the book "tackles one of the fundamental questions of our human condition: how can a person be right with God?" The stunning Christian answer is: *sola fide*—faith alone. But be sure you hear this carefully and precisely: He says *right with God* by faith alone, not *attain heaven* by faith alone. There are other *conditions* for attaining heaven,

---

67. Horton, *Introducing Covenant Theology*, 182.
68. Ibid., 183.
69. Piper, *Desiring God*, 65.
70. Ibid., 65-66.
71. John Piper and Pastoral Staff, *What We Believe About the Five Points of Calvinism*.

but no others for entering a right relationship to God. In fact, one must already be in a right relationship with God by faith alone in order to meet the other *conditions*.[72]

Thus, good works may be said to be a *condition* for obtaining salvation in that they inevitably accompany genuine faith. . . . The question is not whether good works are necessary for salvation, but in what way are they necessary. As the inevitable outworking of saving faith, they are necessary for salvation.[73]

These quotes reveal the meritorious perspective behind many Calvinists' quests for everlasting life. From the human standpoint, they think they must still work to obtain salvation in the end even though their theology also affirms that it is really God's work in and through them and He will cause them to faithfully persevere to the end. Despite repeated denials that they adhere to a works-gospel, the Calvinist requirement of perseverance in faith and good works is clearly not just the inevitable *result* of regeneration but the ongoing *condition* that all saints must fulfill for final salvation. While Calvinists correctly affirm that works are not necessary for initial salvation (i.e., regeneration and justification before God), they undermine the truth of salvation by grace alone when they also insist that good works must always accompany "saving faith," so that without such works no one will obtain glorification, final salvation, or "final justification."[74] But doesn't this still undermine salvation by grace alone? If works cannot be a "condition" for initial salvation lest they nullify grace (Rom. 11:6; Gal. 2:21), then doesn't making works a "condition" for final salvation also nullify grace and the biblical truth that salvation is solely by God's grace from start to finish?

In addition, though Calvinists rightly affirm that the meritorious ground of any sinner's acceptance before God is solely the finished work of Christ, they then go beyond this biblical truth to ultimately make a sinner's acceptance before God conditioned on faith plus works. For example, John Gerstner declares:

---

72. John Piper, Foreword to Thomas R. Schreiner, *Faith Alone—The Doctrine of Justification* (Grand Rapids: Zondervan, 2015), 11.

73. Gerstner, *Wrongly Dividing the Word of Truth: A Critique of Dispensationalism*, 210.

74. See chapters 7 and 8 for the distinction between the three tenses of salvation and the concept of "final justification" in vogue among many contemporary Calvinists.

Good works, while a necessary complement of true faith, are never the meritorious grounds of justification, of acceptance before God. From the essential truth that no sinner in himself can merit salvation, the antinomian draws the erroneous conclusion that good works need not even accompany faith in the saint. The question is not whether good works are necessary for salvation, but in what way are they necessary. As the inevitable outworking of saving faith, they are necessary for salvation.[75]

In response to Gerstner's claim we must ask, If a sinner has trusted solely in Christ's finished work for his eternal salvation, but at the final judgment he is found not to have sufficient good works of his own accompanying his faith to finally justify him, will he not be rejected by God according to Calvinism? If faith plus good works are necessary to be accepted by God for eternity at the "final judgment," then how is a sinner's acceptance by God *not* meritoriously based on his own works in addition to Christ's finished work? Ultimately, Calvinism's distorted doctrine of perseverance leads to a system of salvation by faith plus works, just like Roman Catholicism.

Works and Sacraments as Means of Saving Grace

The use of the supposed "means of grace" is further evidence that Calvinism's doctrine of the perseverance of the saints really does make salvation rest upon the meritorious grounds of human works and not solely upon the Savior's work. Reformed, Calvinist theology has historically maintained that the use of certain means by believers enables them to persevere in their faith and be saved. What are these God-ordained "means" that believers are instructed to appropriate in order to obtain final salvation? According to Calvinism, these "means of grace" include heeding the Word of God (including the "threatenings" of the Law),[76] "the practice of devout prayer,"[77] renewing our "covenant oath" to keep God's "commandments,"[78] and partaking of the "sacraments."

---

75. Gerstner, *Wrongly Dividing the Word of Truth,* 210.

76. Herman Witsius, *The Economy of the Covenants Between God and Man* (Grand Rapids: Reformation Heritage, 2010), 2:39.

77. Hoekema, *Saved by Grace,* 245-47. See also, Witsius, *Economy of the Covenants,* 2:42.

78. Witsius, *Economy of the Covenants,* 2:43. Here Witsius writes, "It is also expedient, that we renew our covenant with God, and those promises by which we formerly bound ourselves to the sincere observance of his commandments."

Regarding the sacrament of baptism as a means of salvation in addition to faith, John Calvin wrote, "In baptism, the Lord promises forgiveness of sins: receive it, and be secure. I have no intention however, to detract from the power of baptism. I would only add to the sign the substance and reality, inasmuch as God works by external means. But from this sacrament, as from all others, we gain nothing, unless in so far as we receive in faith."[79] This statement, among other similar comments by Calvin, reflects the inroads of Roman Catholicism upon Reformed theology that continue to this day. While Roman Catholicism does not require faith on the part of the one baptized for sacramental graces to be received, nevertheless, faith plus the sacraments supposedly assist believers in their Christian lives to obtain final salvation just as they do in Calvinism.

Historically, Calvinism has always taught that salvation comes through the "means of grace." This explains why in the century after Calvin, the Synod of Dort formulated its response to Arminianism and stated in article 14 on the perseverance of the saints, "As it has pleased God, by the preaching of the gospel, to begin this work of grace in us, so He preserves, continues, and perfects it by the hearing of His Word, by meditation thereon, and by the exhortations, threatenings, and promises thereof, and by the use of the sacraments."[80] A few decades later, the Westminster Shorter Catechism also explicitly affirmed that salvation comes through the sacraments as the means of God's grace.

Q. 85. What doth God require of us that we may escape his wrath and curse due to us for sin?
A. To escape the wrath and curse of God due to us for sin, God requireth of us faith in Jesus Christ, repentance unto life, with the diligent use of all the outward means whereby Christ communicateth to us the benefits of redemption.

Q. 88. What are the outward means whereby Christ communicateth to us the benefits of redemption?
A. The outward and ordinary means whereby Christ communicateth to us the benefits of redemption, are his ordinances, especially the word, sacraments, and prayer; all which are made effectual to the elect for salvation.

---

79. John Calvin, *Institutes of the Christian Religion*, Vol. IV, XV, 15.
80. *The Articles of the Synod of Dort*, trans. Thomas Scott (Harrisonburg, VA: Sprinkle, 1993), 321.

Q. 91. How do the sacraments become effectual means of salvation?

A. The sacraments become effectual means of salvation, not from any virtue in them, or in him that doth administer them; but only by the blessing of Christ, and the working of his Spirit in them that by faith receive them.[81]

According to Calvinists, the use of such means are effective for a believer's eternal salvation. This is why such traditional Calvinist stalwarts as Charles Hodge, Louis Berkhof, John Murray, Anthony Hoekema, and Herman Ridderbos continued to attest to the use of the supposed means of grace for salvation centuries after Calvin, Dort, and Westminster. Consider the following quotes:

> Faith sanctifies because it is the necessary condition of the efficacy of the means of grace. It is through the Word, sacraments, and prayer, that God communicates constant supplies of grace. They are the means of calling the activities of spiritual life into exercise. But these means of grace are inoperative unless they are received and used by faith. Faith does not, indeed, give them their power, but it is the condition on which the Spirit of God renders them efficacious.[82]

> It must be remembered that what the Apostle argues to prove is not merely the certainty of the salvation of those that believe; but their certain perseverance in holiness. Salvation in sin, according to Paul's system, is a contradiction in terms. This perseverance in holiness is secured partly by the inward secret influence of the Spirit, and partly by all the means adapted to secure that end—instructions, admonitions, exhortations, warnings, the means of grace, and the dispensations of his providence. Having, through love, determined on the end, He has determined on the means for its accomplishment.[83]

The first point clearly taught on this subject in the Symbols of the Reformed Church is that the sacraments are real means of

---

81. Westminster Shorter Catechism in *The Creeds of Christendom*, 3:695-96.
82. Charles Hodge, *Systematic Theology*, 3 vols. (reprint, Grand Rapids: Eerdmans, 1968), 3:109-10.
83. Ibid., 3:112-13.

grace, that is, means appointed and employed by Christ for conveying the benefits of his redemption to his people. They are not, as Romanists teach, the exclusive channels; but they are channels. A promise is made to those who rightly receive the sacraments that they shall thereby and therein be made partakers of the blessings of which the sacraments are the divinely appointed signs and seals. The word grace, when we speak of the means of grace, includes three things. 1st. An unmerited gift, such as the remission of sin. 2d. The supernatural influence of the Holy Spirit. 3d. The subjective effects of that influence on the soul.[84]

The third point included in the Reformed doctrine is, that the sacraments are effectual as means of grace only, so far as adults are concerned, to those who by faith receive them. They may have a natural power on other than believers by presenting truth and exciting feeling, but their saving or sanctifying influence is experienced only by believers.[85]

It is confidently asserted that the doctrine of perseverance leads to indolence, license, and even immorality. A false security is said to result from it. This is a mistaken notion, however, for, although the Bible tells us that we are kept by the grace of God, it does not encourage the idea that God keeps us without constant watchfulness, diligence, and prayer on our part. . . . But these warnings regard the whole matter from the side of man and are seriously meant. They prompt self-examination, and are instrumental in keeping believers in the way of perseverance. They do not prove that any of those addressed will apostatize, but simply that the use of means is necessary to prevent them from committing this sin.[86]

While the Spirit can and does in some respects operate immediately on the soul of the sinner, He has seen fit to bind Himself largely to the use of certain means in the communi-

---

84. Ibid., 3:499.

85. Ibid., 3:500.

86. Berkhof, *Systematic Theology*, 548. Berkhof considers the Word and sacraments to be the ordinary means of grace but not prayer. In this, he disagrees with his predecessor Charles Hodge (ibid., 604).

cation of divine grace. . . . The Church may be represented as the great means of grace which Christ, working through the Holy Spirit, uses for the gathering of the elect, the edification of the saints, and the building up of His spiritual body. He qualifies her for this great task by endowing her with all kinds of spiritual gifts, and by the institution of the offices for the administration of the Word and the sacraments, which are all means to lead the elect to their eternal destiny.[87]

The perseverance of the saints reminds us very forcefully that only those who persevere to the end are truly saints. We do not attain to the prize of the high calling of God in Christ Jesus automatically. Perseverance means the engagement of our persons in the most intense and concentrated devotion to those means which God has ordained for the achievement of his saving purpose.[88]

Do passages of this sort, and others like them, overthrow the doctrine of perseverance? No, they do not. But they warn us against a misunderstanding of this teaching. They underscore our responsibility in our perseverance. They tell us that it is only as we prayerfully endure to the end, hold fast to what we have, continue in Christ's word, and remain in Christ that we can enjoy the blessing of perseverance. And they also remind us that God, in preserving us, uses means.[89]

[W]e find baptism, in harmony with the whole of the early Christian proclamation, characterized as the symbol of and means of salvation for the washing away of and cleansing from sin.[90]

Baptism is . . . the place where this union is effected (*en tō baptismatō*; Col. 2:12), the means by which Christ cleanses his church (*katharisas tō loutrō*; Eph. 5:26), and God has saved it (*esōsen hēmas dia loutrou*; Titus 3:5), so that baptism itself can be called the washing of regeneration and of the renewing

---

87. Ibid., 604.
88. Murray, *Redemption: Accomplished and Applied*, 155.
89. Hoekema, *Saved by Grace*, 246.
90. Herman Ridderbos, *Paul: An Outline of His Theology*, trans. John R. de Witt (Grand Rapids: Eerdmans, 1975), 397.

by the Holy Spirit (Titus 3:5). All these formulations speak clearly of the significance of baptism in mediating redemption; they speak of what happens in and by baptism and not merely of what happened before baptism and of which baptism would only be the confirmation.[91]

The teaching of traditional Calvinism on the use of the supposed "means of grace" has not died out. Today's leading Calvinists maintain the same doctrine. For example, popular contemporary preacher and author John Piper admits, "I probably pray the prayer, 'Keep me and preserve me' as often as I pray any prayer. I mean, 'Keep me saved,' because I think God uses means to cause us to persevere."[92] But does the Bible really teach that the prayers of the saints keep them saved? On the contrary, the Word of God says that the *Savior's* intercession for His own keeps saints saved (Rom. 8:34; Heb. 7:25). To teach that *our* prayers keep us saved is salvation by works, not salvation solely by grace through faith in Christ alone.

Prayer and the use of the sacraments for salvation are also taught by other contemporary Calvinists, such as Keith Mathison and Michael Horton, who are quoted below.

[W]e understand that there are several means of grace: the Word, sacraments, and prayer. These means of grace are . . . the channels through which Christ communicates to his people the benefits of redemption.[93]

The Westminster Shorter Catechism adds that the sacraments become effectual means of salvation only "in them that by faith receive them" (A. 91). . . . Because of the sacramental union established by God, the sacraments effectually confer grace to those who receive them in faith. As several Reformed confessions indicate, for those with faith God performs spiritually what the sacraments signify physically.[94]

Baptism functions as a means of grace both as a sign and as a seal. It visibly signifies the believer's union with Christ, the

---

91. Ibid., 409.

92. John Piper, *Stand: A Call for the Endurance of the Saints,* p. 142.

93. Keith A. Mathison, "God's Means of Assurance," in *Assured by God: Living in the Fullness of God's Grace,* 2nd ed., ed. Burk Parsons (Phillipsburg, NJ: Presbyterian and Reformed, 2007), 140.

94. Ibid., 144.

believer's regeneration, and the remission of the believer's sin. It is a visible word testifying to the truth of those realities. It is also a seal, confirming God's covenantal promises. To those with faith, the spiritual realities promised in the sacraments are "not only offered, but really exhibited and conferred by the Holy Ghost" (Westminster Confession of Faith 28.6).[95]

Worthy partakers, namely, those who partake of the Lord's Supper with true faith, "receive and apply unto themselves Christ crucified, and all the benefits of his death" (Westminster Larger Catechism, A. 170).[96]

The sacraments are not mere badges of profession or "bare signs"; far less are they made sacraments by the piety of the individual or the community. It is neither the action of the signs themselves nor of the people but the action of God that makes the sacraments, in the words of the Westminster Larger Catechism, "effectual means of salvation" (Question 161). The benefits offered by the sacraments are the same as those offered by the gospel itself: Christ and all his treasures. The sacraments signify and seal to the individual believer the promise that is heard in the preaching of the gospel.[97]

Surely the Sacraments can remind us of grace, help us to appreciate grace, and exhort us to walk in grace, but do they actually give us the grace promised in the Gospel? The Reformed and Presbyterian confessions answer "yes" without hesitation: A Sacrament not only consists of the signs (water, bread and wine), but of the things signified (new birth, forgiveness, life everlasting).[98]

Furthermore, a sacrament not only reveals; it confers. Through the Word and sacrament, God actually gives that which he promises in his gospel—forgiveness of sins, freedom from the tyranny of sin and eternal life. The sacraments

---

95. Ibid., 146.
96. Ibid., 151.
97. Horton, *Introducing Covenant Theology*, 167.
98. Michael Horton, "Mysteries of God and Means of Grace," Alliance of Confessing Evangelicals, 1997.

not only testify to or signify divine activity in salvation, but are part of that divine redemptive activity.[99]

It is one thing for an evangelical to believe that the Word is a means of grace. It is quite another to add that the sacraments are a further means of grace. Even the word "sacrament" sounds "Catholic" to many evangelical ears. In fact, it is a biblical concept.[100]

Could Calvinist theologians, scholars, authors, and preachers be more clear? Their method of salvation is strikingly similar to Catholicism's in that both believe God's grace is funneled to the believer by means of good works—sacraments—which supposedly become effective for ensuring the believer's eternal salvation.

Yet some may reasonably wonder how Calvinists can claim on the one hand that salvation is all by grace while on the other hand simultaneously prescribe works for salvation such as prayer and the sacraments. The answer according to traditional Reformed theology is that God supplies the faith for the elect to believe and the means of grace that believers use for their salvation as sovereignly moved by the Holy Spirit, so in a very distorted way God is credited with doing all the work necessary for salvation. He supposedly determines the will of the elect to such an extent that He effectively makes the believer pray and use the sacraments of baptism and the Lord's Supper as means of saving grace. This is why Witsius claims that "man can and will savingly use those means."[101]

But this system of salvation is completely out of sync with the Bible's teaching that salvation is solely by God's grace and "not of works" (Eph. 2:8-9). Salvation cannot be by works such as prayer and the sacraments and "not of works" at the same time! If, according to the Bible, salvation is to him who does "not work, but believes" (Rom. 4:5) and it is "not by works of righteousness" (Titus 3:5), then how can salvation simultaneously be by good works such as prayer, sacraments, and keeping the commandments? Furthermore, what difference does it make if God is the one determining the will of man so as to cause man to use the "means of grace" for salvation, or as in Catholicism man simply chooses to use such means out of his own

---

99. Michael Horton, *In the Face of God: The Dangers and Delights of Spiritual Intimacy* (Nashville: Thomas Nelson, 1997), 219.

100. Ibid., 139.

101. Witsius, *Economy of the Covenants*, 2:39.

volition? In either case, the supposed "means of grace" are still used by man supposedly to obtain sanctification and final salvation. In both cases, grace comes through a work and faith is no longer the only requirement for salvation. If works are truly a means of God's grace, then grace is no longer grace (Rom. 11:6)!

The Word of God: The Only Way Forward

It must seem strange for many evangelical, Bible-believing Christians who are not familiar with traditional Calvinism to hear so many esteemed Calvinist leaders touting faith plus works as the means of salvation. Yet, it should not be too surprising since the doctrine of the perseverance of the saints has always been based more on rational or philosophical deduction and historical theology than on biblical exegesis. Thus, we should also not be too surprised to find Calvinists in expressed agreement with Roman Catholics on the ultimate conditions for eternal salvation.

However, our faith must not stand on the shifting opinions of men, nor on historical theology or religious tradition (even Protestant tradition), but only upon the sure footing of the inspired Word of God. For this reason, this book will now shift its focus and attention to explaining biblical passages related to faith, perseverance, and salvation. These passages clearly show that faith alone in Christ alone is the sole human condition to receive eternal life, and that perseverance in faith and good works is not required by God to possess everlasting life. Christ alone perseveres in keeping His own eternally saved by His grace.

Chapter 4

Does Eternal Salvation Require Momentary or Continual Belief?

Centuries ago, the slave trader turned preacher, John Newton, penned the now famous words to the classic hymn "Amazing Grace": "How precious did that grace appear the hour I first believed." The hour Newton first believed was a moment that changed his eternal destiny. This is true of all who believe in Christ and are born again into the family of God forever. While many professing Christians happily sing these lyrics to "Amazing Grace," few stop to consider their theological implications and even whether they agree with Scripture. Does the Bible teach that eternal salvation is conditioned on the moment of initial faith in Christ or on continual belief throughout one's lifetime? In Acts 16:30, an unsaved Gentile poses the ultimate question to Paul and Silas, saying, "Sirs, what must I do to be saved?" Their authoritative reply was simple: "Believe on the Lord Jesus Christ, and you will be saved, you and your household" (v. 31). Paul and Silas did not answer by commanding him to "Believe, and continue to believe" or "believe and persevere in your faith to the end, and you shall be saved." But this is exactly what we would expect Paul and Silas to say if they held to the teaching of the perseverance of the saints. In contrast, the Bible repeatedly teaches that belief in Christ for everlasting life occurs at a moment in time; it is not an ongoing condition that must be fulfilled, such as perseverance in faith and good works to the end of one's life.

The Bible uses several pictures or metaphors to demonstrate the momentary nature of belief in Christ for eternal life. These include the single acts of a look, a drink, and eating bread. While many claim that the Greek present tense of the verb "believe" proves that perseverance in faith is necessary for final salvation, this chapter goes on to show that this is not supported by either Greek syntax or the biblical pictures of belief in Christ for eternal life.

Actions Illustrating the Single Act of Belief

There is perhaps no better book in the entire Bible for illustrating the meaning of the word "believe" than the Gospel of John. Believing in Christ for eternal life was in fact the very reason this Gospel was written according to its purpose statement in John 20:30-31. The various forms of the Greek verb and participle for "believe" (*pisteuō*) occur 241 times in the New Testament with 98 of these occurring in the Gospel of John. This means that over 40 percent of all New Testament occurrences of *pisteuō* as a verb or verbal part of speech are found in John's Gospel alone. No wonder John is often referred to as the "Gospel of Belief." John's Gospel uses three metaphors for believing that demonstrate the momentary nature of belief in Christ for eternal life.

Belief Illustrated by Looking

In John 3, Christ uses a basic Old Testament object lesson from Numbers 21:5-9 to explain to the religious Pharisee Nicodemus how to be born again. In John 3:14, Christ refers to Numbers 21, where many Israelites complained about Moses's leadership and God's provision for them as they wandered in the desert. Consequently, the Lord judged the Israelites with serpents so that many died. In Numbers 21, the Lord gives to Moses the remedy for this snake problem.

> 8 Then the Lord said to Moses, "Make a fiery serpent, and set it on a pole; and it shall be that everyone who is bitten, when he looks at it, shall live." 9 So Moses made a bronze serpent, and put it on a pole; and so it was, if a serpent had bitten anyone, when he looked at the bronze serpent, he lived. (Num. 21:8-9)

From this episode in Israel's history, the Lord Jesus illustrates for Nicodemus what it means to believe in Him for everlasting life. He says to Nicodemus,

> 14 And as Moses lifted up the serpent in the wilderness, even so must the Son of Man be lifted up, 15 that whoever believes

[*ho pisteuōn*] in Him should not perish but have eternal life.
(John 3:14-15)

Just as the Israelites had to acknowledge their sinful, snake-bitten condition and look in faith to the bronze serpent, which was God's symbol of judgment upon their sin, even so lost people today must look in faith to Christ-crucified as God's provision for their own snake-bitten, sinful condition. All that was required of the Israelites was a look of faith, and they were instantaneously and permanently healed. They were not required to keep on looking at the brass serpent for the rest of their lives in order to stay healed (Arminianism) or to prove that they were truly healed initially (Calvinism). When a lost sinner places his faith in Christ for salvation, at that instant, he receives God's gift of eternal life by grace and is instantaneously born again (John 5:24). Robert Gromacki explains well that ongoing faith is *not* required to complete the heavenly transaction: "How many times did the people have to look at the serpent to be healed? Just once. One look prompted by faith was enough. So it is with Calvary. How many times must one look at Christ in faith to be saved? Just once. The faith that heals or saves is an act, a completed event, not an attitude."[1]

However, some perseverance advocates cannot let the simplicity of Christ's statement in John 3:14-15 stand as it is written. Amazingly, one famous Calvinist author and Bible teacher morphs the simple look of faith described by Christ into a meritorious human work:

A more careful study of Numbers 21 reveals that Jesus was not painting a picture of easy faith. . . . In order to look at the bronze snake on the pole, they had to drag themselves to where they could see it. They were in no position to glance flippantly at the pole and then proceed with lives of rebellion.[2]

This caricature completely distorts the biblical account of Numbers 21 and Jesus' use of it in John 3 as an illustration of faith in Him for eternal life. Nowhere does Numbers 21 say that the Israelites "had to drag themselves" to where they could see the bronze serpent. In fact, the reason for setting the serpent on a pole (vv. 8-9)

---

1. Robert Gromacki, *Salvation Is Forever* (Schaumburg, IL: Regular Baptist Press, 1989), 88.
2. John F. MacArthur, Jr., *The Gospel According to Jesus* (Grand Rapids: Zondervan, 1988), 46.

was to elevate it so that all could see it, thereby picturing Christ's own lifting up on the cross to make salvation available to all, just as it says in John 12:32-33: "'And I, if I am lifted up from the earth, will draw all peoples to Myself.' This He said, signifying by what death He would die."

Second, the Israelites' look at the raised bronze serpent in Numbers 21 was deliberate in response to God's prescription spoken through Moses. There was nothing "flippant" or superficial about it. Facing one's sin and its judgment in the symbol of the serpent and then accepting God's prescribed remedy and substitute required at that moment personal accountability, humility, and trust—not strenuous activity.

Third, the Israelites actually did "proceed with lives of rebellion" against the Lord after their look of faith at the bronze serpent in Numbers 21. In fact, the wilderness generation of Israelites was notorious for its ongoing unbelief, idolatry, and rebellion against the Lord, despite having initially believed in Him and His Word. Read the Bible's own description of that generation in Exodus 14:31: "Thus Israel saw the great work which the Lord had done in Egypt; so the people feared the Lord, and believed the Lord and His servant Moses" (Ex. 14:31). This is consistent with the testimony of Psalm 106, which says that the wilderness generation initially believed God's Word but afterward departed from Him: "Then they believed His words; they sang His praise. They soon forgot His works; they did not wait for His counsel, but lusted exceedingly in the wilderness, and tested God in the desert" (Ps. 106:12-14). Consequently, a few chapters after the incident of the brass serpent in Numbers 21, the book of Numbers goes on to say that the Israelites "began to commit harlotry with the women of Moab . . . and bowed down to their gods," so that "Israel was joined to Baal of Peor, and the anger of the Lord was aroused against Israel" (Num. 25:1-3). Those who died in that plague were 24,000 Israelites (v. 9). This sad account demonstrates that genuine believers do not necessarily persevere to the end of their lives in faith and holiness (1 Cor. 11:28-32). However, this account also illustrates that God in His sovereignty and grace is still willing to save (Ex. 4:31; 14:31) and heal (Num. 21:5-9), simply on the basis of a one-time look of faith, knowing full well in His omniscience that rebellion and sin leading to death may transpire afterward.

The incident in Numbers 21 is used by the Lord in John 3 to illustrate the true requirement for eternal life—a simple look of faith in Jesus Christ and His work on the cross in dying a substitutionary death for one's sins, rather than relying upon one's own human goodness or works. This solitary act of trust in Christ and His finished work would have been humbling for a moral and religious man such as Nicodemus, but it was necessary. Whether a person is moral (like Nicodemus in John 3) or immoral (like the Israelites in Numbers 25 and the Samaritan woman in John 4), the sole condition for eternal life today is the same — a single act of belief in Jesus Christ.

Belief Illustrated by Drinking

When the Lord Jesus encountered the sinful Samaritan woman at the well of Sychar, He used the analogy of drinking physical water to picture believing in Him for eternal life.

> 13 Jesus answered and said to her, "Whoever drinks [*ho pinōn*] of this water will thirst again, 14 but whoever drinks [*hos piē*] of the water that I shall give him will never thirst. But the water that I shall give him will become in him a fountain of water springing up into everlasting life." 15 The woman said to Him, "Sir, give me this water, that I may not thirst, nor come here to draw." (John 4:13-15)

In this passage Christ equates believing in Him with drinking from the well. According to John 6:35, drinking is used as a metaphor for appropriating eternal life by faith. People had to *keep drinking* from the well of Sychar to satisfy their physical thirst, and thus they would "thirst again" (4:13). But Jesus offered this woman *a drink* that would leave her spiritual thirst quenched for eternity. Gromacki captures again the essence of Christ's teaching in John 4, stating that a person "just has to have one spiritual drink of Christ and he will have spiritual life. There is a contrast in thirsts. Men are always thirsty for natural water, but Jesus said that *one* spiritual drink will forever quench man's spiritual thirst."[3] Jesus Christ is not teaching in John 4 that we must keep on drinking, and drinking, and drinking in order to either maintain the gift of eternal life (Arminianism) or prove that we possess it (Calvinism).

In John 4, Jesus is also not requiring the woman at the well to make some sort of costly commitment to serve Christ before He would grant her eternal life, as some Lordship Salvation teachers suppose.

---

3. Gromacki, *Salvation Is Forever*, 89.

Some people hold the view that saving faith involves no idea of obedience or commitment. . . . Can we concede that the verb "drink" conveys the idea of appropriation apart from commitment? Certainly not. Matthew 20:22 ("Are you able to drink the cup that I am about to drink?") and John 18:11 ("the cup which the Father has given Me, shall I not drink it?") both use *drink* in a way that clearly implies full compliance and surrender. Furthermore, to attempt to define faith with a metaphor is unwarranted selectivity.[4]

There is nothing unwarranted about using the very metaphors of looking, drinking, and eating that the Lord Jesus Himself instituted to picture the act of believing in Him for eternal life. However, it is completely unwarranted to use Christ's own drink from the cup of God's wrath as a comparison with freely drinking the water of eternal life. In Christ's case, the cup He drank amounted to His sacrificial, substitutionary death in the place of sinners. In the case of the woman at the well of Sychar, the cup Jesus was offering her to drink was not the cup of God's wrath that required her own work of dying to pay for sin but was in fact the water of life that was without cost to her because it would be purchased in full by the Offeror Himself (John 19:30). To equate drinking the water of life that Jesus offers sinners to Christ's drinking the cup of wrath merely proves that perseverance advocates are adding the believer's works to Christ's work as a condition for salvation. In contrast, the Lord Jesus' offer of eternal life in John 4:10 is described as the "gift of God"; and it was conditioned only upon a single drink—a single act of belief in Him. This is perfectly consistent with the gracious invitation to salvation found at the end of Revelation (which John also wrote): "And whosoever will, let him *take* of the water of life *freely*" (Rev. 22:17, KJV, italics added).

Belief Illustrated by Eating

In John 6, the Lord Jesus contrasted the Israelites' continual eating of manna in the desert to receiving Him by faith as the Bread of eternal life.

31 Our fathers ate the manna in the desert; as it is written, "He gave them bread from heaven to eat." 32 Then Jesus said

---

4. MacArthur, *Gospel According to Jesus*, 52-53.

to them, "Most assuredly, I say to you, Moses did not give you the bread from heaven, but My Father gives you the true bread from heaven. 33 For the bread of God is He who comes down from heaven and gives life to the world." 34 Then they said to Him, "Lord, give us this bread always [*pantote*]." 35 And Jesus said to them, "I am the bread of life. He who comes to Me shall never hunger, and he who believes [*ho pisteuōn*] in Me shall never thirst." (John 6:31-35)

The contrast could not be more evident. The Jews first failed to realize that Christ was the Bread from heaven. Furthermore, they mistakenly thought that repeated consumption of this Bread was necessary to sustain life as with the Israelites' collection of manna in the desert for forty years (Ex. 16; Josh. 5:12). Their confusion is seen in John 6:34 where they ask Christ to "always" give them this Bread. The Greek adverb *pantote* in verse 34 modifies the verb "give." This Greek word means "always" (NKJV), "evermore" (KJV), or "at all times."[5] The Jews who followed Jesus presumed that this Bread must be constantly, repetitiously given and constantly, repetitiously received in order to meet their need. They were still thinking of their ancestors who had to consume manna daily because of their unsatisfied physical hunger. Yet, in verse 35, Christ promises that if they would believe in Him, they would "never hunger." The Jews missed Jesus' point that the receiving of eternal life and satisfaction of spiritual hunger were not received by repeated consumption of some spectacular "Wonder Bread" but instead by a solitary act of eating, or believing in the right object, the Lord Jesus Christ—the Bread of eternal life.

Regarding the metaphor of eating as a picture of believing in Christ for eternal life, there is an ironic contrast between the first Adam and "the last Adam" (1 Cor. 15:45). Once again, Gromacki insightfully states, "How many times did Adam have to eat to bring condemnation upon himself and the human race? Only once! One eating brought death. So it is with salvation; one eating brings eternal life."[6] But many perseverance advocates reject this conclusion and claim that Jesus teaches in the Bread of Life Discourse that eter-

---

5. One lexicon defines *pantote* as "duration of time, with reference to a series of occasions—'always, at all times, on every occasion'" (Johannes P. Louw and Eugene Nida, eds. *Greek-English Lexicon of the New Testament Based on Semantic Domains* [New York: United Bible Societies, 1988], 1:641, §67.88).

6. Gromacki, *Salvation Is Forever*, 90.

nal life is guaranteed only through perpetual eating (i.e., believing). Calvinist James White claims:

> Throughout this passage [John 6:35-45] an important truth is presented that again might be missed in many English translations. When Jesus describes the one who comes to Him and who believes in Him, He uses the present tense to describe this coming, believing, or, in other passages, hearing or seeing. The present tense refers to a continuous, ongoing action. . . . The wonderful promises that are provided by Christ are not for those who do not truly and continually believe. The faith that saves is a living faith, a faith that always looks to Christ as Lord and Savior. . . . The true Christian is the one continually coming, always believing in Christ. Real Christian faith is an ongoing faith, not a one-time act. If one wishes to be eternally satiated, one meal is not enough. If we wish to feast on the bread of heaven, we must do so all our lives. We will never hunger or thirst if we are always coming and always believing in Christ.[7]

Do the biblical metaphors in John's Gospel for believing in Christ really require ongoing belief? The present tense certainly does not indicate this, as will be explained later in this chapter; nor do the contexts of the metaphors themselves. According to the original context of Numbers 21 referred to in John 3:14, continual looking at the brass serpent was not required either to get healed or stay healed. In John 4, Jesus promised the woman at the well that she would "never thirst" (4:14a) again if she believed in Him. This quenching of her thirst was not because of the continuance of the act of drinking but because of the permanence of the water within the one who believes: "But the water that I shall give him will become in him a fountain of water springing up into everlasting life" (v. 14b). The perpetual wellspring of eternal life does not continue to flow within a person because it is continually being fed from outside by the believer's perpetual acts of drinking or ingestion. According to Jesus Christ Himself, one drink initiates eternal hydration and satiation from within.

Likewise in John 6:35, when Jesus promises that "he who comes to Me shall never hunger, and he who believes in Me shall never thirst," the satisfaction of hunger and thirst is because of the perpetual nature

---

7. James White, *Drawn by the Father* (Lindenhurst, NY: Great Christian Books, 2000), 19-20.

of what is consumed (the eternal food and drink—Jesus Christ), not because of the perpetual faithfulness of the believer in eating and drinking. To conclude otherwise is to destroy the intended contrast in each passage between the insufficient physical-temporal metaphor and the spiritual-eternal meaning of the metaphor. In other words, the Lord Jesus uses an intentional contrast between the repeated consumption of bread and water to keep satisfying one's physical hunger and thirst versus the one act of appropriating Him by faith to eternally and permanently satisfy one's spiritual need. In the physical realm, a person must eat and drink continually because physical food and water is only temporal in duration and satisfaction. By contrast, the Bread of Life and the Living Water that Christ gives never ceases, and therefore it needs to be received only once. But to say that this Bread and Water must be continually and repeatedly consumed by the believer in order to either maintain or guarantee salvation ends up contradicting Christ's statements about "never" hungering or thirsting again. After all, why would a person need to eat and drink again if that person was "never" hungry and thirsty anymore?

Moreover, to interpret John's metaphors of believing in Christ for eternal life as requiring ongoing appropriation of Christ actually reflects the very same works-oriented thinking as the unregenerate Jews whom Jesus is correcting in John 6. This reveals what is ultimately behind the doctrine of the perseverance of the saints—a doctrine of salvation that is not solely by God's grace but leaves room for human merit. Notice how A. W. Pink uses John 6 to teach the necessity of laboring in one's continual appropriation of Christ for final salvation.

> God has purposed the eternal felicity of His people and that purpose is certain of full fruition, nevertheless it is not effected without the use of means on their part, any more than a harvest is obtained and secured apart from human industry and persevering diligence. God has made promise to His saints that "bread shall be given" them and their "water shall be sure" (Isa. 33:16), but that does not exempt them from the discharge of their duty or provide them with an indulgence to take their ease. The Lord gave a plentiful supply of manna from heaven, but the Israelites had to get up early and gather it each morning, for it melted when the sun shone on it. So His people are now required to "labour for the meat which endureth unto everlasting life" (John 6:27).[8]

8. A. W. Pink, *The Saint's Perseverance* (Lafayette, IN: Sovereign Grace, 2001), 65-66.

This interpretation misses the whole point of Christ's metaphor of eating the Bread of Life by simply believing in Him rather than working for it. Jesus is not teaching in John 6:27 that the Jews should work for eternal life or that faith in Him inherently includes good works or "the use of means." The Lord Jesus uses the term "labor" (v. 27) because the Jewish crowd had been traveling around the Sea of Galilee to diligently "seek" Him out (v. 26) because of the sign-miracle He performed of multiplying the loaves and fishes (vv. 1-15). Yet, in seeking out a mere miracle worker, they sought or labored for the wrong thing. They misunderstood Christ's reference to "labor" (v. 27) and thought in terms of works, saying, "What shall we do that we may work the works of God?" (v. 28). Mankind naturally thinks in terms of meriting the favor and salvation of God. Consequently, Christ corrects them in verse 29, replying, "This is the work of God, that you believe in Him whom He sent." Christ clarifies that God is not requiring them to "work" but to "believe" in Him. We do not "labor" or "work" to receive the "gift of God" (John 4:10), otherwise we turn His gift into an earned reward, thereby nullifying grace (Rom. 11:6).

According to the Gospel of John—the Gospel of Belief—believing in Christ is described as a non-meritorious look, drink, or act of eating. In these three metaphorical illustrations of belief, the Lord Jesus Christ consistently portrays belief in Him for eternal salvation as a simple, momentary act rather than an ongoing activity. Many deny this truth by arguing that while faith in Christ is necessary for salvation, a person must also continually hold on to Christ in order to reach final salvation in heaven.

"Believe" in New Testament Greek

The previous pictures of biblical belief in Christ for eternal life require little to no technical explanation. They are rather straightforward in teaching that such belief does not require a lifelong commitment or habitual action. While the previous passages should be sufficient in themselves to establish the premise that "saving" faith is momentary or instantaneous, this conclusion is further clarified and confirmed by an accurate understanding of verbs and participles in New Testament Greek.

Present-Tense Verb Form

One major claim often made to support perseverance in faith as a requirement for eternal life is the frequent use of the present-tense form of the verb "believe" (*pisteuō*) in New Testament salvation passages. The mere fact of the present tense supposedly denotes a continual act or state of believing. The following quotes reveal that whether a person holds to Calvinism, Arminianism, or neither, the misconception is prevalent that the present-tense form of *pisteuō* makes continual belief necessary for eternal life:

> But it is not a biblical view of faith to say that one may have it at the moment of salvation and never need to have it again. The continuing nature of saving faith is underscored by the use of the present tense of the Greek verb *pisteuō* ("believe") throughout the gospel of John (cf. 3:15-18, 36; 5:24; 6:35, 40; 7:38; 11:25-26; 12:44, 46; 20:31; also Acts 10:43; 13:39; Romans 1:16; 3:22; 4:5; 9:33; 10:4, 10-11). If believing were a one-time act, the Greek tense in those verses would be aorist.[9]

> Do I Have a Present Trust in Christ for Salvation? Paul tells the Colossians that they will be saved on the last day, "pro-vided that you *continue in the faith,* stable and steadfast, not shifting from the hope of the gospel which you heard" (Col. 1:23). . . . In fact, the most famous verse in the entire Bible uses a present tense verb that may be translated, "whoever contin-ues believing in him" may have eternal life (see John 3:16).[10]

> In the New Testament, when belief is said to lead to eter-nal life, as is the case here, the tense expressing continuous action is always used while the tense expressing a single action is never used. The stress is thus placed on continuous faith rather than on an isolated moment of faith.[11]

It misses the mark to say that one only needs faith for salva-tion and then never needs it again. The very word "faith" in the Greek New Testament indicates ongoing belief in Christ. The Greek verb for faith, *pisteuo*, is usually found in the con-tinuous present tense in the New Testament. *Pisteuo* is in only a very few cases found in the aorist, indicating one-time

---

9. MacArthur (Calvinist), *Gospel According to Jesus,* 172.

10. Wayne Grudem (Calvinist), *Systematic Theology* (Grand Rapids: Zondervan, 1994), 803.

11. George Allen Turner (Arminian) and Julius R. Mantey, *The Gospel According to John,* Evangelical Commentary (Grand Rapids: Eerdmans, n.d.), 99. (Though coau-thored with Mantey, Turner wrote the portion of the commentary quoted above.)

action. Therefore, the overall pattern of the use of *pisteuo* in the New Testament indicates that faith in a believer's life will be continuous and vital.[12]

John is not concerned so much with the momentary, individual acts of sin as with the overall characteristic tendencies and inclinations of someone's life. John is not taking a snapshot, but a moving picture. His repeated use of the Greek present tense appears to bear this out. He focuses on the habitual character of the activity in view.[13]

[I]n the overwhelming majority of passages like these, the "believing" is consistently presented as a progressive action (present tense in Greek). Thus, for example . . . *John 3:16*—". . . that everyone who *is believing* (present participle) may *be having* (present subjunctive) eternal life."[14]

The result, to be sure, is security ("never die") but in this passage [John 11:26] "living" and "believing" (progressive presents denoting a continuous state) are necessary prerogatives. In other words, perseverance in the present life from God is necessary to maintain the future certainty of life in the next age.[15]

Similar statements and claims could be multiplied ad infinitum. The view that the present tense in New Testament Greek inherently indicates a continuous, habitual, linear action or state is a deeply ingrained misconception. Despite the popularity of this view, it is a well-known fallacy among current Greek language scholars. The use of the present tense does not automatically refer to an ongoing action or state;[16] and similarly the use of the aorist-tense form does not auto-

---

12. David Dunlap (neither), *Written Aforetime: Selected Articles from Bible & Life Newsletter from 1993–2009* (Land O' Lakes, FL: Bible & Life Ministries, 2009), 171. Dunlap is a Plymouth Brethren writer who strongly advocates the necessity of the perseverance of the saints for final salvation while also rejecting several major tenets of Calvinism. See David Dunlap, *Limiting Omnipotence: The Consequences of Calvinism—A Study of Critical Issues in Reformed and Dispensational Theology* (Port Colborne, Ontario: Gospel Folio Press, 2004).

13. Sam Storms (Calvinist), *Kept for Jesus: What the New Testament Really Teaches about Assurance of Salvation and Eternal Security* (Wheaton, IL: Crossway, 2015), 167.

14. Robert E. Picirilli (Arminian), *Grace, Faith, Free Will: Contrasting Views of Salvation: Calvinism & Arminianism* (Nashville: Randall House, 2002), 201.

15. Grant R. Osborne (Arminian), "Soteriology in the Gospel of John," in *The Grace of God and the Will of Man*, ed. Clark H. Pinnock (Minneapolis: Bethany House, 1989), 251.

16. David L. Mathewson, "The Abused Present," *Bulletin for Biblical Research* 23.3

matically mean a once-for-all action or state.[17] Greek tense forms do not inherently determine a verb's function or actual, objective kind of action (*Aktionsart*), whether linear or punctiliar. Instead, tense forms indicate the subjective portrayal of that action or state by the writer (aspect).[18] A biblical writer may choose to portray a momentary, instantaneous action using the present-tense form in order to bring the reader more vividly into a scene or he may choose to zoom out and use the aorist-tense form to more broadly and remotely portray an action that is continuous and repeated but presented in a summary statement. This difference in subjective portrayal between the present and aorist tenses is often illustrated by two different vantage points for viewing a parade. The present-tense form effectively places the reader on the street curb to see the parade passing right in front of him, and the aorist-tense form would be used to view the parade from a helicopter with a bird's-eye view.

This explains why Gospel writers oftentimes portray the same objective action in Christ's earthly ministry using two different verb tenses. For example, Matthew 4:1 says, "Then Jesus was led up by the Spirit into the wilderness to be tempted [*peirasthēnai*] by the devil." Here the infinitive form of "to be tempted/tested" (*peirazō*) is in the aorist tense. But in Luke's parallel account, the participle form of *peirazō* is present tense: "Then Jesus, being filled with the Holy Spirit, returned from the Jordan and was led by the Spirit into the wilderness, being tempted [*peirazomenos*] for forty days by the devil" (Luke 4:1-2). In cases where one passage has one tense form and a parallel Gospel passage uses another tense form, the Gospel writers are not making different, conflicting claims about the nature of the Lord's actions or speech; rather they are simply choosing to portray His actions or speech from a vantage point that is either more proximate or remote.

Recognizing this difference between verbal *aspect* (subjective portrayal of an action or state) and *Aktionsart* (the objective nature

---

(2013): 343-63.

    17. Frank Stagg, "The Abused Aorist," *Journal of Biblical Literature* 91 (1972): 222-31.

    18. Constantine R. Campbell, *Advances in the Study of Greek* (Grand Rapids: Zondervan, 2015), 105-33; idem, *Basics of Verbal Aspect in Biblical Greek* (Grand Rapids: Zondervan, 2008), 19-25; Rodney J. Decker, *Temporal Deixis of the Greek Verb in the Gospel of Mark with Reference to Verbal Aspect* (New York: Peter Lang, 2000), 26-27; Buist M. Fanning, *Verbal Aspect in New Testament Greek* (New York: Oxford University Press, 1990), 84-85; Stanley E. Porter, *Verbal Aspect in the Greek New Testament, with Reference to Tense and Mood* (New York: Peter Lang, 1989), 75-109; Richard A. Young, *Intermediate Greek: A Linguistic and Exegetical Approach* (Nashville: Broadman & Holman, 1994), 105-7.

or kind of action) helps to understand how Greek present and aorist tenses function. Contrary to popular opinion among many Bible
teachers, the present tense can be used for momentary, instantaneous, punctiliar action; but when it does so, it is portraying an action
or state with greater proximity. Conversely, the aorist tense can be
used for continuous action that is perceived and portrayed remotely.
An example of the latter occurs in Revelation 20:4. There, the aorist
tense is used to summarize an action that will occur continually and
repeatedly for a thousand years after Christ's Second Coming:

> And I saw thrones, and they sat on them, and judgment was
> committed to them. Then I saw the souls of those who had
> been beheaded for their witness to Jesus and for the word of
> God, who had not worshiped the beast or his image, and had
> not received his mark on their foreheads or on their hands.
> And they lived and reigned with Christ for a thousand years.

The Greek verbs for "lived" and "reigned" are both in the aorist
tense, but the context is explicit that the living and reigning transpire
over a period of one thousand years. Here, the aorist tense is used to
remotely summarize the living and reigning that will occur during
the millennial kingdom. This use of the aorist tense is not uncommon
in the New Testament, nor is the use of the present tense for punctiliar action. An example of the latter occurs in Matthew 3:13: "Then
Jesus came from Galilee to John at the Jordan to be baptized by him."
The word "came" (*paraginetai*) is in the present tense, which certainly
does not mean that Jesus "was continually or habitually arriving"[19]
at the Jordan River to meet John the Baptist.

The examples of Matthew 3:13 and Revelation 20:4 demonstrate
a very important point with respect to verbs in the Greek New Testament—the verb's *Aktionsart* or kind of action (whether habitual or
momentary) is not determined by the verb's tense but by the context
in which it occurs and by the lexical meaning or nature of the verb
itself. In the context, there may be adverbs or prepositional phrases
that modify the verb and provide clues to its duration or kind of
action (e.g., "immediately," "at once," "in that hour," "continually").[20]
Some verbs by their very nature tend to express either more momentary or continual action. For example, the verb for "crucify" (*stauroō*)

---

19. Mathewson, "The Abused Present," 346.
20. Daniel B. Wallace, *Greek Grammar Beyond the Basics: An Exegetical Syntax of the New Testament* (Grand Rapids: Zondervan, 1996), 499-504.

inherently means a one-time act based on the nature of crucifixion leading to imminent death. The same is often true with verbs such as "born" (Matt. 2:4) or "die" (John 11:51), unless an unusual meaning is indicated by other modifying words in the context, such as Paul exclaiming, "I die *daily*" (1 Cor. 15:31). Though the verb for "crucify" (*stauroō*) normally occurs in the aorist-tense form, it occasionally occurs in the present-tense form (Matt. 27:38; Mark 15:27; Luke 23:21), showing that the present tense can certainly be used to portray a one-time event.

In the Gospel of John—the "Gospel of Belief"—the present tense is used to portray several events that are one-time occurrences by their very nature. The Second Coming of Christ is spoken of using the present-tense form (14:2-3, 18, 28), along with His ascension (20:17), as are the disciples going fishing one night (21:3). Not only can the present-tense form be used to describe one-time, non-repeatable events occurring in the *present*, such as the Crucifixion, or *future* events from the disciples' standpoint, such as the Ascension and Second Coming, but the present tense even portrays *past*, completed, instantaneous events, such as Christ's coming to earth at the Incarnation (John 6:33, 50). In each of these examples, the inherent meaning of the verb's action and other contextual factors, not the verb's tense form, determine whether the action of the verb is momentary or continual.

Present Tense, Articular, Substantival Participle

The present tense, articular participle construction for "believe" is quite common in John's Gospel and deserves special attention. This is the construction that occurs in the most popular evangelistic verse in the Bible, John 3:16, which says, "whoever believes [*ho pisteuōn*] in Him should not perish but have everlasting life." When a definite article such as *ho* is used with the present-tense participle form of a verb such as *pisteuōn*, the combination is known as a present-tense, articular, substantival participle construction. In Greek, the articular, present-tense form of a participle commonly functions as a substantival noun or descriptive title, so that a phrase like "he who believes" (*ho pisteuōn*) simply means "the believer," without denoting anything specific about the nature of believing, its duration, or even the time when it occurred. The belief may occur at a point in time or repeatedly over a period of time, but the Greek tense does not inherently indicate this information. Though substantival participles in Greek are normally articular (have an article), they do not need to be articular in order to still function substantivally as nouns. But the addition of the article definitely nominalizes the participle (i.e., turns it into a noun in function). Since tense is a function of verbs and the articular participle construction is substantival as a virtual noun phrase, it practically and functionally has a zero-tense value, just like nouns or articles themselves. For this reason, a substantival participle construction such as *ho pisteuōn* is best understood as simply a generic title or description, meaning "he who believes," "the believing one," "whoever believes," or even just "the believer."

Even if an action occurs once, that solitary act can identify the entire person and serve as a descriptive title for that person. For example, Adam's one act of sin was enough to identify him thereafter as "a sinner" and all of his descendants as "sinners," just as Romans 5:17-19 declares:

> 17 For if by the one man's offense death reigned through the one, much more those who receive abundance of grace and of the gift of righteousness will reign in life through the One, Jesus Christ. 18 Therefore, as through one man's offense judgment came to all men, resulting in condemnation, even so through one Man's righteous act the free gift came to all men, resulting in justification of life. 19 For as by one man's disobedience many were made sinners, so also by one Man's obedience many will be made righteous.

A similar point is made in James 2:10-11, which states that a person who breaks God's law only once is "guilty of all." The person who violates God's law is known as a "transgressor," regardless of whether he broke God's law once or a thousand times.

> 10 For whoever shall keep the whole law, and yet stumble in one point, he is guilty of all. 11 For He who said, "Do not commit adultery," also said, "Do not murder." Now if you do not commit adultery, but you do murder, you have become a transgressor of the law.

According to these passages, all it takes is one sin for a person to be justly counted as a "sinner" or "transgressor" in God's sight. Virtually all perseverance advocates agree with this point as it pertains to original sin, and they readily agree that in our society a person's one-time donation is enough to identify him thereafter as a "benefactor." But if perseverance advocates are willing to acknowledge these examples to be true, why do they deny that one act of belief is enough to constitute a person a "believer" in God's sight? If all it takes is one act of sin to become a "sinner" or one donation to become a "benefactor," then all it takes is one act of belief to become a "believer" (*ho pisteuōn*).

This view of *ho pisteuōn* is consistent with the conclusions of leading Greek grammarians. Nigel Turner explains this use of the present-tense, articular, substantival participle, saying that in these grammatical constructions the "action (time or variety) is irrelevant and the participle has become a proper name; it may be under Hebraic influence, insofar as the Hebrew participle is also timeless and is equally applicable to past, present and future."[21] The present-tense construction *ho pisteuōn* found throughout John's Gospel is best understood, therefore, as having a gnomic function. According to Wallace, this use of the present tense involves generic subjects and most often occurs with "*generic* statements to describe something that is true *any* time."[22] Other generic, gnomic-type statements using the same grammatical construction that are commonly used by John include "he who hears" (*ho akouōn*), "he who loves" (*ho agapōn*), and "he who does" (*ho poiōn*). The Johannine expression "he who believes" (*ho pisteuōn*) definitely qualifies as a generic subject or statement.[23] Regarding the generic nature of the gnomic present tense, Fanning says the "sense of a generic statement is usually an *absolute* statement of what each one does once, and not a state-

---

21. Nigel Turner, "Syntax," Vol. III, *A Grammar of New Testament Greek*, ed. James Hope Moulton (Edinburgh: T & T Clark, 1963), 150-51.

22. Wallace, *Greek Grammar Beyond the Basics*, 523.

23. In his standard and popular grammar book, Wallace considers the use of *ho pisteuōn* in passages like John 3:16 to be a customary or habitual present tense usage based on his *theological* conclusion that John's Gospel stresses continual belief, while admitting that grammatically "this could also be taken as a gnomic present" (*Greek Grammar Beyond the Basics*, 522). Wallace states that "when a participle is *substantival*, its aspectual force is more susceptible to reduction in force" and that "many substantival participles in the NT are used in generic utterances. The *pas ho akouōn* (or *agapōn, poiōn*, etc.) formula is always or almost always generic. As such it is expected to involve a *gnomic* idea. Most of these instances involve the present participle" (ibid., 615). Yet Wallace, who holds to the doctrine of the perseverance of the saints, interprets the same present, articular participle construction of *ho pisteuōn* exceptionally, as meaning "he who [continually] believes." His reason for treating *ho pisteuōn* differently is that allegedly in John's Gospel "there seems to be a qualitative distinction between the ongoing act of believing and the simple fact of believing" (ibid, 522. See also, 523 n. 26; 616 n. 9; 621 n. 22). By claiming this, Wallace is essentially admitting that his interpretation of *ho pisteuōn* is theologically driven rather than a purely grammatical conclusion.

ment of the individual's customary or habitual activity."[24] Thus, for a group of people who fit the description of *ho pisteuōn*, such as in John 3:36, Fanning says this describes "a group doing an act a single time, rather than repeatedly."[25]

This function of the present-tense, substantival participle is quite common in the New Testament. The following examples are theologically unrelated to the issue of perseverance but are grammatically identical to the *ho pisteuōn* ("he who believes") construction. Each scriptural example demonstrates that the articular, substantival participle in the present-tense form does not inherently refer to continual, habitual perseverance in faith. Because this is so commonly misunderstood, ten biblical examples are given below to thoroughly demonstrate this point.

- When morning came, all the chief priests and elders of the people plotted against Jesus to put Him to death. And when they had bound Him, they led Him away and delivered Him to Pontius Pilate the governor. Then Judas, His betrayer [*ho paradidous*], seeing that He had been condemned, was remorseful and brought back the thirty pieces of silver to the chief priests and elders. (Matt. 27:1-3)

  Here in Matthew 27:3, the present tense, articular participle *ho paradidous* functionally becomes a noun or title for Judas—"the betrayer" or "he who betrays." The construction here should not be translated, "he who is betraying" or "he who is continuing to betray," since Judas's act of betrayal was a one-time, past event by this point in Matthew 27; and he was even remorseful afterward for this sinful act, though he was still not repentant in the sense of changing his mind by believing in Jesus as the Messiah and Savior. Judas's single act of betrayal earned him the infamous title in Scripture of "the betrayer" or "he who betrays," even after his deed was accomplished.

- Then two robbers were crucified with Him, one on the right and another on the left. And those who passed by blasphemed Him, wagging their heads and saying, "You who destroy the temple and build it in three days [*ho*

---

24. Fanning, *Verbal Aspect in New Testament Greek*, 217.
25. Ibid., 216-17.

kataluōn . . . kai . . . oikodomōn], save Yourself! If You are the Son of God, come down from the cross." (Matt. 27:38-40)

Here in Matthew 27:40, the crowd gathered around Jesus at His crucifixion mocks Him by recounting His prophetic prediction from the beginning of His public ministry when He said, "Destroy this temple, and in three days I will raise it up" (John 2:19). As John 2:20-22 goes on to explain, this statement refers to His crucifixion and bodily resurrection. Ironically, Jesus proved Himself to be the true Christ and Son of God by not coming down off the cross but staying there to die and pay for mankind's sin. But in Matthew 27:40 (and in Mark 15:29), the unbelieving crowd jeeringly calls Jesus "the one who destroys . . . and . . . builds" (*ho kataluōn . . . kai . . . oikodomōn*). This use of the present-tense form of the participle with the article clearly shows that Jesus was not habitually or continually destroying and building (i.e., dying and rising) since His death and resurrection were singular events that each took place within the stated span of "three days."

- Now as they sat and ate, Jesus said, "Assuredly, I say to you, one of you who eats with Me will betray Me." And they began to be sorrowful, and to say to Him one by one, "Is it I?" And another said, "Is it I?" He answered and said to them, "It is one of the twelve, who dips [*ho embaptomenos*] with Me in the dish." (Mark 14:18-20)

Mark 14:20 uses the present-tense, articular participle construction "he who dips" (*ho embaptomenos*) to identify Judas Iscariot as the betrayer. There are two reasons why the Lord could not possibly have meant "he who continually or habitually dips." First, the context establishes that the dipping took place during one meal in one particular evening. Second, the parallel passage in John's Gospel clarifies even further that Jesus was referring to only one particular dipping gesture that evening. John 13:26 says, "'It is he to whom I shall give a piece of bread when I have dipped it.' And having dipped the bread, He gave it to Judas Iscariot, the son of Simon."

- Then He took the cup, and when He had given thanks He gave it to them, and they all drank from it. And He said to them, "This is My blood of the new covenant, which is shed [to ekchynnomenon] for many." (Mark 14:23-24)

In Mark 14:24, the Lord Jesus institutes the Lord's Supper and refers to His sacrificial blood that will be "shed" the next day on the cross. The present-tense, articular participle construction to ekchynnomenon cannot possibly refer to a continual, habitual action since Christ's "shedding" of His blood occurred once and for all as a finished event the following day when He died on the cross.

- Then Mary said to the angel, "How can this be, since I do not know a man?" And the angel answered and said to her, "The Holy Spirit will come upon you, and the power of the Highest will overshadow you; therefore, also, that Holy One who is to be born [to gennōmenon] will be called the Son of God." (Luke 1:34-35)

In Luke 1:35, the Lord Jesus is described as that Holy One "who is to be born" (to gennōmenon). The present-tense form of the substantival, articular participle obviously cannot mean that Jesus is being "continually or habitually born" since birth by its very nature is a one-time, momentary event.

- Whoever divorces his wife and marries [ho apoluōn . . . kai gamōn] another commits adultery; and whoever marries her who is divorced from her husband commits adultery. (Luke 16:18)

In Luke 16:18, the substantival expression "whoever divorces . . . and marries" contains two participles (apoluōn and gamōn) in their present-tense form preceded by the same article (ho). These present-tense, articular participles function substantivally and cannot possibly be denoting continuous, habitual action for two reasons. First, the very nature of the act of divorce is momentary or punctiliar as a legal, judicial decision. Second, the acts of divorce and marriage are opposite of one another and cannot occur both concurrently and continuously. It is not possible to be continuously and habitually divorcing one's wife while continuously and habitually marrying one's wife. Divorce and marriage are separate momentary, instantaneous acts.

- The next day John saw Jesus coming toward him, and said, "Behold! The Lamb of God who takes away [*ho airōn*] the sin of the world!" (John 1:29)

John 1:29 records Jesus' introduction to Israel and the beginning of His public ministry. The forerunner and herald of the Messiah, John the Baptist, correctly identified Jesus, using the title, "The Lamb of God." The additional phrase, "who takes away [*ho airōn*] the sin of the world," modifies and explains "Lamb of God." Thus, the entire construction "the Lamb of God who takes away the sin of the world" becomes a proleptic statement indicating Jesus' future accomplishment before it happened. Jesus was not at that moment taking away the sin of the world, but since it was certain that He would do so in the sovereign plan of God three years later, John used the nominal phrase *ho airōn* ("he who takes away")—a present-tense, articular participle—to describe Jesus before the actual moment when our sins were laid on Him as the sacrificial Lamb and taken away by His work at Calvary (John 19:30; Col. 2:14).

- Jesus said to her, "I am the resurrection and the life. He who believes [*ho pisteuōn*] in Me, though he may die, he shall live. And whoever lives and believes in Me shall never die. Do you believe this?" She said to Him, "Yes, Lord, I believe that You are the Christ, the Son of God, who is to come [*ho erchomenos*] into the world." (John 11:25-27)

This passage contains two present-tense, articular participles functioning substantivally. In the second instance, Martha described Jesus as "He who is to come [*ho erchomenos*] into the world." Since Jesus had already come into the world at this point in John's narrative, interpreting the present tense here with linear *Aktionsart* ("He who is continually coming into the world") results in a historical anachronism and ignores the fact that this phrase is being

used as a messianic title for the One who fulfilled centuries of prophetic anticipation. (See also Matthew 11:3).[26]

- Christ has redeemed us from the curse of the law, having
  become a curse for us (for it is written, "Cursed is everyone who hangs [*ho kremamenos*] on a tree"). (Gal. 3:13)

Galatians 3:13 contains another use of a present-tense,
articular participle functioning as a substantival noun
phrase where Christ is described as the One "who hangs"
(*ho kremamenos*) upon the cross. Once again, the reference
to Christ's crucifixion indicates that this event was not
a continual, habitual action but a one-time, momentary
event. The Old Testament passage quoted in Galatians
3:13 also confirms this conclusion, for it states that those
who were cursed and hanged on a tree were not to remain
there overnight: "his body shall not remain overnight on
the tree, but you shall surely bury him that day, so that
you do not defile the land which the Lord your God is
giving you as an inheritance; for he who is hanged is ac-
cursed of God" (Deut. 21:23).

- By faith he kept the Passover and the sprinkling of blood,
  lest he who destroyed [*ho olothreuōn*] the firstborn should
  touch them. (Heb. 11:28)

In this description of Moses and the Israelites keeping
the Passover by faith, the present-tense participle form of
the verb *olothreuō* ("destroy") is used with the article to
form a substantival, articular participle construction (*ho
olothreuōn*). Though it contains the present-tense form,
the phrase "he who destroyed" is clearly not indicating an action occurring in the present, which is why it is
translated into English with the past tense—"destroyed."
Nor is the statement "he who destroyed the firstborn" indicating an act of destruction that is continual or habitual
since this is an unmistakable reference to a single, unparalleled event of destruction by God in Israel's ancient
past, namely, the tenth plague against the Egyptians, recorded in Exodus 11–12.

---

26. Michael F. Bird, *Are You the One Who Is to Come? The Historical Jesus and the
Messianic Question* (Grand Rapids: Baker, 2009).

Many similar examples from the New Testament could be given, but these have been selected specifically for two reasons. First, each example is framed by contextual clues or markers that give information about the time of action and/or kind of action completely apart from the grammatical form of the present-tense, articular participle itself. Second, these examples were chosen because they do not include the word *pisteuōn* and are therefore theologically neutral with respect to the issue of perseverance in the faith.[27] Although these ten examples are non-theological with respect to faith, they provide ample proof that the grammatical construction in the phrase "he who believes" (*ho pisteuōn*) does not inherently indicate continuous, habitual, persevering belief. Instead, grammatical constructions in the New Testament that are identical to *ho pisteuōn* function as substantival nouns without reference to time or even kind of action. Therefore, the nominal phrase *ho pisteuōn* describes one who either has believed at some point in the past, believes at some point in the present, or will believe at some point in the future, without denoting anything in itself about ongoing belief.

Aorist-tense Verb Form

Those who teach erroneously that the present tense must indicate continual or habitual belief often make a similar unfounded claim regarding the use of the aorist tense of "believe" (*pisteuō*). They sometimes say that there are no examples of *pisteuō* in the aorist-tense form in eternal salvation contexts[28] or that such instances occur so infrequently compared to the present tense that we must conclude that the New Testament writers used the present tense predominantly to make a theological point about the ongoing nature of true, "saving" faith.[29] Both of these claims are patently false.

In terms of frequency of usage, of the 98 uses of *pisteuō* in John's Gospel, 32 are in the aorist-tense form.[30] Though the occurrences of the present-tense form of "believe" (*pisteuō*) outnumber the aorist in

---

27. For New Testament passages containing the present tense, articular participle form of the verb *pisteuō* used as a substantival participle, see Matthew 18:6; Mark 9:23, 42; John 3:15, 16, 18, 36; 5:24; 6:35, 40, 47; 7:38; 11:25, 26; 12:44, 46; 14:12; 17:20; Acts 2:44; 10:43; 13:39; 22:19; Romans 1:16; 3:22; 4:11, 24; 9:33; 10:4, 11; 1 Corinthians 1:21; 14:22; Galatians 3:22; Ephesians 1:19; 1 Thessalonians 1:7; 2:10, 13; 1 John 5:1, 5, 10, 13; 1 Peter 2:6, 7.

28. Turner, *Gospel According to John*, 99.

29. Wallace, *Greek Grammar Beyond the Basics*, 621 n. 22.

30. See John 1:7; 2:11, 22, 23; 4:39, 41, 48, 50, 53; 6:30; 7:31, 39, 48; 8:24, 30; 9:18, 36; 10:42; 11:15, 40, 42, 45; 12:38, 42; 13:19; 14:29; 17:8; 19:35; 20:8, 25, 29, 31.

John, it is only by a ratio of two to one, which is hardly significant enough to justify a major theological distinction based on differing tense-form usage. Furthermore, the aorist-tense form of *pisteuō* is used several times in key evangelistic, salvation passages in John's Gospel.

- John 1:7: "This man came for a witness, to bear witness of the Light, that all through him might believe [*pisteusōsin*]." This verse declares that the main purpose of John the Baptist's ministry was to bear witness to the Savior so "that all through him might believe."

- John 2:11: "This beginning of signs Jesus did in Cana of Galilee, and manifested His glory; and His disciples believed [*episteusan*] in Him." This verse refers to Jesus' first sign miracle in the Gospel of John, where He turns water into wine. In response to this sign, John 2:11 says, "His disciples believed in Him." According to the purpose statement for the entire book, the miraculous signs done by the Lord were recorded in John's Gospel to lead people evangelistically to "believe" in Jesus as the Christ, the Son of God and have eternal life. Concerning Jesus' signs, which began in John 2, the evangelistic purpose statement of John 20:30-31 says, "And truly Jesus did many other signs in the presence of His disciples, which are not written in this book; but these are written that you may believe that Jesus is the Christ, the Son of God, and that believing you may have life in His name."

- John 8:24: "Therefore I said to you that you will die in your sins; for if you do not believe [*pisteusēte*] that I am, you will die in your sins." Here the Lord Jesus warns His audience that a failure to identify Him as the "I am" (the God of Israel) would result in dying in one's sins—unsaved.

- John 12:42: "Nevertheless even among the rulers many believed [*episteusan*] in Him, but because of the Pharisees they did not confess Him, lest they should be put out of the synagogue." This verse uses the aorist tense ("believed") to describe genuine believers, who in the immediate context (12:37-40) are contrasted with unbelievers.

- John 19:35: "And he who has seen has testified, and his testimony is true; and he knows that he is telling the truth, so that you may believe [*pisteusēte*]." John 20:31: "but these are written that you may believe [*pisteusēte*] that Jesus is the Christ, the Son of God, and that believing you may have life in His name." All but two surviving Greek manuscripts (Codices Vaticanus and Sinaiticus) have the aorist-tense form of "believe" in John 19:35 and 20:31. These two verses are the only places in the entire book where John the narrator breaks through the story to directly address the readers, using the second-person pronoun "you." In so doing, he gives an evangelistic invitation to the readers to "believe."

Besides these significant uses of *pisteuō* in the aorist tense in eternal salvation contexts in John's Gospel, several other verses use the aorist-tense verbs "received" (1:12), "drinks" (4:14), and "eat" (6:53) as synonyms for believing in Christ. John 1:12 is particularly significant since it uses both the aorist- and present-tense forms: "But as many as received [*elabon*] Him, to them He gave the right to become children of God, to those who believe [*tois pisteuousin*] in His name." The phrase "those who believe" (*tois pisteuousin*) is another instance of the substantival participle function of the present-tense, articular participle form of *pisteuō*; but it occurs in apposition to those who "received" (*elabon*), which is an aorist-tense verb. This effectively equates the aorist-tense verb "received" with the present-tense participle "believe." The claim that the present tense portrays ongoing belief in contrast to the aorist tense is disproven by this verse since the action of receiving (aorist tense) Christ is used interchangeably with believing (present tense) in His name.

Michael Bird provides a more accurate and up-to-date perspective on the significance of tenses as they relate to John's depiction of the act or state of believing.

> The tense of the verb alone will not tell you whether the type of belief is initial or continual. The tense-form, either aorist or present, does not give us any grounds for supposing that John is talking about belief caused by evangelism (i.e. conversion) or belief reinforced through teaching (i.e. discipleship). The evangelist can use either tense-form of *pisteuō* to signify coming to faith or continuing in the faith. . . . The

present-tense form highlights the general state of believing, not the persistence of belief.[31]

In addition to the Gospel of John, the book of Acts contains one of the clearest passages in the New Testament on belief in Christ as the sole condition for salvation, and it uses the aorist tense for "believe." In Acts 16:30-31, the Philippian jailer asks Paul and Silas the ultimate question: "Sirs, what must I do to be saved?" They reply, "Believe [*pisteuson*] on the Lord Jesus Christ, and you shall be saved, you and your household." In verse 31, Paul and Silas state the condition for salvation using the aorist-tense, imperative-mood form of *pisteuō*. Since the Greek imperative mood occurs only in the present- and aorist-tense forms, there were only two tense forms for Paul and Silas to choose from to command the jailer to believe. If, for the sake of argument, we assume that the present-tense form necessarily indicates habitual, continual action, then why did Paul and Silas opt for the aorist tense of "believe" if they meant to say that the condition for eternal life is continual belief? Furthermore, why didn't Paul and Silas just remove all ambiguity regarding tenses by adding certain modifying words that clearly mean continuous, enduring belief, such as "Believe on the Lord Jesus Christ *until the end*, and you shall be saved" or "Believe on the Lord Jesus Christ *and continue to believe, and you shall be saved*"?

Besides these significant passages in John's Gospel and Acts 16:31 using the aorist-tense form of "believe," there are at least two other significant aorist-tense uses of "believe" in Paul's epistles. In Romans 13:11, Paul exclaims, "Now is our salvation nearer than when *we believed* [*episteusamen*]" (KJV). Significantly, he does not use the present tense of *pisteuō* as if to say, "Our salvation is nearer now that *we believe*." Again, this distinction raises the fundamental question: if present, ongoing faith in the Christian's life is necessary to reach final salvation, then why does Paul connect future, final salvation to *past, initial belief* as expressed here by his choice of the aorist, indicative form for "we believed"? Why not connect it to present, ongoing belief, which is purportedly the real proof of the genuineness of initial, saving faith?

A similar question arises when realizing that Paul writes to the Thessalonians and tells them they will be saved from eternal judgment at Christ's return "because [*hoti*] our testimony among you was believed [*episteuthē*]" (2 Thess. 1:10). The aorist-tense, indicative-mood

---

31. Michael F. Bird, *Jesus Is the Christ* (Downers Grove, IL: InterVarsity, 2012), 136.

verb *episteuthē* ("was believed") is stated as the reason (*hoti*) that the Thessalonians would not experience everlasting destruction. But if the present tense necessarily indicates ongoing action and the aorist tense indicates momentary action, as is commonly claimed, and if continual belief is necessary for final salvation, then why didn't Paul use the present-tense, indicative-mood form of *pisteuō* to say "because our testimony among you *is believed*"? Instead, Paul uses the aorist tense of *pisteuō* in 2 Thessalonians 1:10 to describe the moment of their *initial belief* (Acts 17:1-5) as the reason why they will not face eternal judgment. If perseverance in faith were truly a requirement for final salvation, as perseverance proponents teach, then why didn't Paul refer to the Thessalonians' *present* faith that persevered from the point of their initial faith up to the time of Paul writing 2 Thessalonians? In that case, Paul should have said, "because our testimony among you *has been believed*" (perfect tense, indicative mood) or "because our testimony among you *is being believed*" or *"is still believed."* So why did Paul point to their past, initial belief as the reason for their final salvation, which was yet future when he wrote to them, if indeed final salvation requires perseverance in faith to the end?

The answer to these questions is clear. Eternal salvation is not predicated upon perseverance in faith, holiness, and good works to the end of one's life, but upon a single, non-meritorious act of belief in Christ. This conclusion is supported by Jesus' metaphors of belief in Him for eternal life found in John's Gospel and by the grammar and syntax of New Testament Greek for the verb *pisteuō*. The only view that is true to Scripture and consistent with eternal salvation by grace is the one that teaches eternal life is conditioned solely upon initial faith, not faithful perseverance. Only this view allows the Christian to joyfully sing:

> Amazing grace! How sweet the sound
> That saved a wretch like me!
> I once was lost, but now am found;
> Was blind, but now I see.

> 'Twas grace that taught my heart to fear,
> And grace my fears relieved;
> How precious did that grace appear
> The hour I first believed.

Chapter 5

When Does Belief Become Unbelief?

Many questions about the nature of faith accompany the popular, but erroneous, doctrine that God requires perseverance in faith to the end of one's life to get to heaven one day. If this doctrine were true, then what would happen if your faith falters, slips, and falls along the way? What would happen if doubts arise or your faith fails amidst a trial? Can your faith gradually decrease over time or must it continue growing for you to be saved? If it can decrease, how little could it become before salvation would be nullified? What happens if your faith lapses for a period of time? How long could these lapses be before your initial faith would no longer be regarded as genuine? How much biblical truth is required to be believed for eternal salvation—all of the Bible or just the gospel? Does the presence of doubt in your life mean the absence of faith? What constitutes the threshold of unbelief that would disqualify you from everlasting life and glorification? All of these questions can essentially be boiled down to one: According to the Bible, when does belief become unbelief?

According to the traditional doctrine of the perseverance of the saints, a believer may fall in his or her walk of faith with the Lord, but not "totally" or "finally." The Synod of Dort, where the five points of Calvinism were first formulated in 1619, states in Article 8 on the perseverance of the saints: "Thus, it is not in consequence of their own merits or strength, but of God's free mercy, that they do not totally fall from faith and grace, nor continue and perish finally in their backslidings."[1] Based on this statement, Calvinists generally

---

1. *The Canons of the Synod of Dort*, in Philip Schaff, *The Creeds of Christendom: With a History and Critical Notes*, rev. David S. Schaff (New York: Harper & Brothers, 1877;

adhere to the operative terms "totally" and "finally" when teaching the doctrine of the perseverance of the saints. Anthony Hoekema, a late professor of systematic theology at Calvin Theological Seminary, provides an example.

> What the doctrine of the perseverance of true believers does mean is this: those who have true faith can lose that faith neither totally nor finally. The real question at issue, therefore, is this: Can a person who has true faith ever lose that faith? To this question the person of Reformed persuasion says: No. It should immediately be added, however, that the Calvinist gives this answer not on the basis of the superior spiritual strength of the believer, but on the ground of God's faithfulness to his promise. The Calvinist believes that God will never permit those to whom he has given true faith to fall away from that faith.[2]

Popular Bible teacher and author John MacArthur also holds to the notion that genuine faith may falter but not "totally" or "finally."[3] In seeking to clarify this concept of total and final unbelief, he states, "Those who turn away completely (not *almost* completely, 90 percent, or 50 percent) demonstrate that they never had true faith."[4]

However, such attempts to clarify the doctrine of perseverance lead only to more confusion and contradiction. For if God were to sovereignly cause His unconditionally elect to persevere in faith and good works, as Reformed theology claims, so that He would not permit a true believer to reach the fatal level of 0-percent faith, then why would He sovereignly allow a believer's faith to fall to only 50-percent faith or even to 1-percent faith or for that matter to anything less than 100-percent faith? If a genuine believer's faith were based entirely on God's sovereign choice rather than man's, then logically all responsibility for perseverance in faith must rest with God. Consequently, if God would never permit those to whom He has given true faith to fall away from that faith completely, why would He sovereignly permit them to fall away from it to any degree?

reprint, Grand Rapids: Baker, 1977), 3:594.
    2. Anthony A. Hoekema, *Saved by Grace* (Grand Rapids: Eerdmans, 1989), 234-35.
    3. John F. MacArthur, Jr., *Faith Works: The Gospel According to the Apostles* (Dallas: Word, 1993), 177.
    4. Ibid., 191.

Though the explanations of MacArthur and most Calvinists are offered to help provide parameters for believers to gauge the genuineness of their faith, such quantifications turn out to be not very helpful. After all, what does 50-percent faith mean practically? How could I really know whether I had lost half of my faith or when I entered the "danger zone," below 10-percent faith, or that I had reached the critical, threshold level of 1-percent faith? The overarching assumption that faith is genuine and saving as long as it is not "total" or "final" unbelief is fraught with problems and contradictions of Scripture.

In order to base our beliefs on a consistently biblical foundation, several basic subjects related to faith must be clarified, such as faith's content and object, the nature of faith (involving both trust and persuasion), the relationship between faith and doubt, and the question of whether all faith is the same or if there are degrees of faith.

The Content & Object of Faith

Faith in Christ for eternal salvation involves believing the gospel message about Christ and believing in the person of Christ. There is no dichotomy between believing a message versus a person. When an unsaved person hears, understands, and believes the gospel of Christ (also called in the Bible the gospel of the grace of God, gospel of peace, and the gospel of our salvation), that person has simultaneously trusted in the person of Christ. This conclusion about the object and content of faith is integral to understanding the nature of faith and discerning when belief becomes unbelief in God's sight.

It is a false dichotomy to pit the person of Christ against the facts of the gospel,[5] as though someone believing the message of the gospel believes only in a set of revealed, propositional facts, or certain doctrines, versus having a deeper, genuine faith in the person of Christ. Though it may sound pious for someone to claim he believes only in the person of Christ and not a set of propositions or doctrines, this distinction is patently unbiblical. J. Gresham Machen explains:

> The truth is that the whole opposition between faith in a person and acceptance of a message about the person must be given up. It is based, as we have already seen, upon a false psychology; a person cannot be trusted without acceptance

5. Gordon H. Clark, *Faith and Saving Faith* (Jefferson, MD: Trinity Foundation, 1990), 56-57, 82-83.

of the facts about the person. But in the case of Jesus the notion is particularly false; for it is just the message about Jesus, the message that sets forth his Cross and resurrection, that brings us into contact with Him. Without that message He would be forever remote—a great Person, but one with whom we could have no communion—but through that message He comes to be our Savior.[6]

All faith requires assent to certain propositions and therefore has informational content.[7] If faith comes by hearing the Word of Christ (Rom. 10:17) and God desires everyone to be saved and to come to the knowledge of the truth (1 Tim. 2:4), then faith requires specific divine information. Though this need for requisite knowledge from God is downplayed in our postmodern culture, we should not pit faith against divine revelation, as Machen states, "Far from being contrasted with knowledge, faith is founded upon knowledge."[8]

What determines whether a person's faith is saving or not is a matter of what knowledge, information, or propositions are believed—whether divinely revealed truth (the gospel) or messages of human or satanic origin (false gospels). Both Jesus Christ, who is the incarnate Word (John 1:14, 18), and the message about Jesus Christ, which is the word of the gospel (Gal. 1:11-12), are divine revelations that must be believed. Therefore, when a person believes the gospel of Christ, he also believes in the person of Christ for eternal life.

Though there is a semantic distinction between the person of Christ and gospel content pertaining to Christ, in Scripture we see that the object of faith (Jesus Christ) and the content of that faith (the gospel message about Jesus Christ) are spoken of interchangeably. There are dozens of passages in the New Testament that condition eternal salvation solely upon belief. Several of these use the verb "believe" intransitively. For example, observe the use of "believes," "believed," and "believe" in the following salvation verses:

> Therefore let it be known to you, brethren, that through this Man is preached to you the forgiveness of sins; 39 and by Him everyone who *believes* is justified from all things from which you could not be justified by the law of Moses. (Acts 13:38-39)

---

6. J. Gresham Machen, *What Is Faith?* (New York: Macmillan, 1925; reprint, Grand Rapids: Eerdmans, 1946), 151.

7. Clark, *Faith and Saving Faith*, 118.

8. Machen, *What Is Faith?* 46.

Now when the Gentiles heard this, they were glad and glorified the word of the Lord. And as many as had been appointed to eternal life *believed*. (Acts 13:48)

But the Scripture has confined all under sin, that the promise by faith in Jesus Christ might be given to those who *believe*. (Gal. 3:22)

In these verses, there is no stated object to receive the action of believing. In such instances, the object of faith is not specifically mentioned and the verb "believe" appears by itself. Nothing is stated to the effect that "they believed *in Him*" or "they believed *the gospel*," though the object or content of what is believed may be inferred from the context.

However, many other salvation passages use "believe" transitively. In these, the object of belief is variously stated to be the *person* of Jesus, whether it is "the Lord Jesus Christ," or "Christ," or even just "Him." In the following verses, note the person of Christ as the object of belief:

And he brought them out and said, "Sirs, what must I do to be saved?" 31 So they said, *"Believe on the Lord Jesus Christ*, and you will be saved, you and your household." (Acts 16:30-31)

[K]nowing that a man is not justified by the works of the law but by *faith in Jesus Christ*, even we have *believed in Christ Jesus*, that we might be justified by *faith in Christ* and not by the works of the law; for by the works of the law no flesh shall be justified. (Gal. 2:16)

However, for this reason I obtained mercy, that in me first Jesus Christ might show all longsuffering, as a pattern to those who are going to *believe on Him* for everlasting life. (1 Tim. 1:15)

Finally, there are passages where the verb "believe" is used transitively (i.e., taking an explicit object) and that require belief in some specific form of propositional truth or divine revelation in order to be saved. Sometimes the content of belief is implied by the immediate context, such as in 1 Corinthians 1 when it speaks of believing "the word of the cross" (v. 18) or "the message preached" (1 Cor. 1:21). In other passages, it is the "testimony" or "truth" that must be believed.

These shall be punished with everlasting destruction from the presence of the Lord and from the glory of His power, 10 when He comes, in that Day, to be glorified in His saints and to be admired among all those who believe, because *our testimony* among you was *believed*. (2 Thess. 1:9-10)

And for this reason God will send them strong delusion, that they should believe the lie, 12 that they all may be condemned who did not *believe the truth* but had pleasure in unrighteousness. (2 Thess. 2:11-12)

He who believes in the Son of God has the witness in himself; he who does not believe God has made Him a liar, because he has not *believed the testimony* that God has given of His Son. (1 John 5:10)

The Gospel of John also demonstrates that believing *in* and believing *that* occur simultaneously and should not be viewed as separate sequential steps in the act of believing. Gordon Clark explains that to "believe in Christ Jesus simply means to believe that Jesus died and rose again. In John especially *to believe in* and *to believe that* are constantly used interchangeably."[9] For example, in John's Gospel to "believe that" (*pisteuō* + *hoti*) Jesus is the I Am of the Old Testament (i.e., the Lord God) is necessary not to perish in one's sins, for Jesus says in John 8:24, "Therefore I said to you that you will die in your sins; for if you do not believe that I am, you will die in your sins." Likewise, according to John 20:30-31, it is necessary to "believe that" (*pisteuō* + *hoti*) Jesus is the Christ, the Son of God, to have eternal life: "And truly Jesus did many other signs in the presence of His disciples, which are not written in this book; but these are written that you may *believe that Jesus is the Christ, the Son of God*, and that believing you may have life in His name." But John's Gospel also says that one must believe "in" (*pisteuō* + *eis/en*) Jesus Christ for eternal life: "that whoever *believes in Him* (*ho pisteuōn en autō*) should not perish but have eternal life. For God so loved the world that He gave His only begotten Son, that whoever *believes in Him* (*ho pisteuōn eis auton*) should not perish but have everlasting life" (3:15-16).[10] This

---

9. Clark, *Faith and Saving Faith*, 101.

10. Leon Morris, *Jesus Is the Christ: Studies in the Theology of John* (Grand Rapids: Eerdmans, 1989), 188-89; Robert L. Reymond, *Faith's Reasons for Believing* (Ross-Shire, Scotland: Christian Focus, 2008), 13.

shows that belief in some divinely revealed *proposition* about Jesus (i.e., that He is God, the Christ, the Son of God) is inherent to belief in His *person*.

Practically, all of this means that when someone believes the gospel message, he or she also believes in the person of Jesus Christ and vice versa. Ephesians 1:13 demonstrates this principle when it says in reference to Christ: *"In Him* you also trusted, after you heard *the word of truth, the gospel* of your salvation; in whom also, having believed, you were sealed with the Holy Spirit of promise." Though the gospel sets forth propositional truth to be believed, it also sets forth a person to be believed. If belief in the gospel is required for eternal salvation (Rom. 1:16; 1 Cor. 4:15; 15:1-4; Eph. 1:13; 2 Thess. 1:8-10), and belief in the person and work of Christ is also required (John 3:15, 16, 18; 6:47; 20:30-31; Acts 13:38-41), and there is only one condition to be saved, then believing the gospel and believing in Christ must be inseparable and simultaneous rather than being two separate, chronological steps to receiving eternal life.[11] This foundational principle has major ramifications for the teaching that faith must endure for salvation to be sure.

Unbelief Among the Galatians

The Epistle to the Galatians sheds significant light on the question of when belief becomes unbelief. The apostle Paul personally preached the gospel of God's grace to the Galatians (Acts 13–14), but within only a year or two Jewish legalizers introduced into the Galatian church another gospel—a gospel of works for salvation. Not surprisingly, Paul expresses dismay in his introduction to the Galatians: "I marvel that you are turning away so soon from Him who called you in the grace of Christ, to a different gospel, which is not another; but there are some who trouble you and want to pervert the gospel of Christ" (1:6-7). Paul's opening salvo must have shocked the Galatians. In their religious legalism and self-deception, they probably thought they were measuring up quite well in their Christian lives. It probably never occurred to them that some of them had departed from the true gospel and the person of the Savior since they were still professing faith in Christ and the gospel while they added works to grace.

---

11. For more information on the content of saving faith, see Thomas L. Stegall, *The Gospel of the Christ: A Biblical Response to the Crossless Gospel Regarding the Contents of Saving Faith* (Milwaukee: Grace Gospel Press, 2009). A free pdf copy of this book is available online at www.gracegospelpress.org.

Those who advocate the doctrine of the perseverance of the saints might suppose that the unbelief of the Galatians was not "total" since they were "just" adding works to grace while still fully affirming other gospel truths, such as the deity of Christ and His resurrection. But is a person really persevering in his faith in the person and work of Christ when he is also denying the sufficiency of God's grace in salvation? Is it possible to maintain genuine belief in Christ and the gospel while simultaneously trusting in good works to be saved?

Calvinist Teaching on Believing the Gospel

According to Calvinism, saints must persevere in believing the gospel lest they fail to obtain final salvation. Robert Peterson writes regarding one gospel passage, "This passage teaches that perseverance is a condition of final salvation. . . . Continuing to believe the Gospel is indispensable to final salvation."[12] But this raises a legitimate question, does Scripture teach that the Galatians continued to believe the gospel? The Westminster Shorter Catechism also links saving faith to believing the gospel. Question 86 asks: "What is faith in Jesus Christ?" Answer: "Faith in Jesus Christ is a saving grace, whereby we receive and rest upon him alone for salvation, as he is offered to us in the gospel."[13] According to Westminster, the very definition of saving faith requires believing in Christ as He is presented in the gospel. Again we must ask, did the Galatians continue to believe the gospel of Christ that was originally presented to them by Paul? John Piper is another perseverance proponent who states that it is the gospel itself that must be believed for new birth and thereafter for preservation: "Our faith must endure to the end if we are to be saved. This means that the gospel is God's instrument in the preservation of faith as well as the begetting of faith."[14]

Once again, we must ask the crucial question, did the Galatians persevere in believing the same gospel that was instrumental in their new birth? The answer to these questions should be obvious. In abandoning the truth of justification by faith alone, the Galatians

---

12. Robert A. Peterson, "The Perseverance of the Saints: A Theological Exegesis of Four Key New Testament Passages," *Presbyterion* Vol. 17, No. 2 (1991): 98.

13. *Westminster Shorter Catechism*, in Philip Schaff, *The Creeds of Christendom: With a History and Critical Notes*, rev. David S. Schaff (New York: Harper & Brothers, 1877; reprint, Grand Rapids: Baker, 1977), 3:695.

14. John Piper, *Five Points: Towards a Deeper Experience of God's Grace* (Ross-Shire, Scotland: Christian Focus, 2013), 63.

no longer believed *the* gospel though they did continue believing in *a* gospel—another gospel (1:7).

In addition to requiring perseverance in believing the gospel message, Calvinists also teach that true believers will never depart from the person of Christ Himself. Lorraine Boettner says that "the elect are secured on both sides. Not only will God not depart from them, but He will so put His fear into their hearts that they shall not depart from Him."[15] Likewise, Edwin Palmer declares, "The term perseverance of the saints emphasizes that Christians—saints, as Paul calls them in his letters—will persevere in trusting Christ as their Savior. They will not turn on and then turn off, but they will continue believing forever. Thus they will always be saved."[16]

However, the example of the Galatian Christians clearly contradicts these claims since Galatians 1:6 and 5:4 declare that the Galatians not only embraced another gospel but in doing so departed from the Lord Himself.

> I marvel that you are turning away so soon from Him who called you in the grace of Christ, to a different gospel, 7 which is not another; but there are some who trouble you and want to pervert the gospel of Christ. (Gal. 1:6-7)

> You have become estranged from Christ, you who attempt to be justified by law; you have fallen from grace. (Gal. 5:4)

Unbelief in the Gospel of Grace Is Not Perseverance

Earlier it was demonstrated that there is no dichotomy between believing the gospel and believing in the person of Christ. Galatians 1:6 reveals that the Galatians' departure from the true gospel of grace coincided with their departure from the person of Christ. Note these two aspects of the Galatians' defection in verse 6: "you are turning away so soon from *Him* who called you in the grace of Christ, to a different *gospel*." Apostasy is never a matter strictly of doctrinal defection; it is primarily a breakdown in one's vertical relationship with the Lord. Legalism always has this effect of fostering pride and self-reliance while diminishing one's perceived need for Christ; whereas, grace reminds us that we are not sufficient in

---

15. Lorraine Boettner, *The Reformed Doctrine of Predestination* (Phillipsburg, NJ: Presbyterian & Reformed, 1932), 201.

16. Edwin H. Palmer, *The Five Points of Calvinism* (Grand Rapids: Baker, 1980), 68.

ourselves but need Christ for everything and that He is all-sufficient (2 Cor. 3:5-6; 12:9-10).

By embracing a gospel of works, the finished work of Christ was treated by the Galatians as being no longer sufficient for salvation. For this reason, Paul emphasizes the Cross in every chapter of the epistle (1:3-4; 2:20-21; 3:1, 13-14; 4:4-5; 5:11, 24; 6:12-14). When a false gospel of good works for salvation was accepted by some Galatians, Christ was no longer viewed as the sole object of trust, reliance, or dependence. In this respect, some of the Galatians not only stopped believing the true gospel, but they departed from the person of Christ in the process though they probably did so unwittingly in their religious self-deception and spiritual blindness.

The Galatians most likely thought they were being even more faithful to the Lord by adding law and works to grace. They may have contested Paul's claim that they were turning to another gospel and had departed from the Lord. But Galatians 5:4 gives God's perspective about the true spiritual state of those within the Galatian church who embraced a false gospel: "You have become estranged (*katērgēthēte*) from Christ, you who attempt to be justified by law; you have fallen (*exepesate*) from grace."

The word for "estranged" (*katērgēthēte*) is a strong term and is translated in other English versions as "severed" (NASB, ESV) and "alienated" (NIV). Though the Lord in His grace did not turn away from those Galatians who sought justification through law-keeping, they turned away from Him. They were still justified in His sight and eternally secure, but their fellowship with Christ was ruptured so that they became "estranged" from their Savior! They were not merely on the verge of this breach; it actually happened according to Galatians 5:4. We know this from the fact that the words "estranged" (*katērgēthēte*) and "fallen" (*exepesate*) are both aorist-tense, indicative-mood verbs, which normally indicate a past, completed event. Their estrangement from Christ and fall from grace had already occurred. This does not mean that those Galatians described in verse 4 fell out of Christ and the Father's hands and were no longer saved since John 10:28-30 promises that this will never happen and every child of God is eternally secure.

Nor does falling from grace in this context mean what religion today often assumes it means, namely, that these fallen, estranged Galatians must have lived so immorally and licentiously that they no longer deserved to go to heaven. "Grace" means they never deserved heaven in the first place! Instead, those within the Galatian church described in Galatians 5:4 had fallen from grace only in the sense that they no longer viewed grace as solely sufficient for their justification and sanctification. They fell from grace by rejecting it and replacing it with something else—works of human merit.

This leads us to the sobering realization that while many legalistic Christians today profess to believe the gospel and follow the person of Christ, in reality, from God's point of view they no longer truly believe the gospel and have departed from their Savior! From the Lord's perspective the Galatians' continuing, religious, legalistic belief in another gospel amounted to unbelief in His sight.

Not much has changed since the first century. While many legalistic Christians today also maintain belief in certain elements or parts of the gospel's content, such as Christ's deity, humanity, and resurrection, the gospel's content pertaining to God's grace and the substitutionary, sufficient death of Christ for our sins are not truly believed. Perseverance proponents may see this as merely "partial" unbelief in the gospel and "partial" departure from Christ that stops short of "total" unbelief and failure to persevere. But according to the example of the Galatians, unbelief in part of the gospel's content (Christ's finished, satisfactory work and salvation solely by God's grace) means unbelief of the very gospel itself.

Bible-believing Protestants have rightly concluded for centuries that a person is still unregenerate and considered an unbeliever until that person believes Christ's death was a sufficient payment for one's sins, so one's faith must rest upon Christ and His finished work alone rather than one's own good works for eternal salvation. Since the Reformation, Protestants have agreed with the biblical truth that to be born again one must believe the gospel truth of justification by grace alone through faith alone in Christ alone rather than trusting in one's own good works (Acts 13:38-39; Rom. 4:4-5). We accept the fact that a person is still unregenerate if he or she has not believed the gospel, not accepting the truth of Christ's finished work and justification by grace alone through faith alone. And if we readily accept this truth, then it is utterly inconsistent to deny that genuine saints such as the Galatians have stopped believing the gospel when they trust in their own works to be justified before God. The example of the Galatians proves that even genuine children of God, who have believed the gospel, can later reject the gospel and return to a state of unbelief and apostasy.

The example of the Galatians is inconsistent with Calvinism's claim that a genuine believer can never experience total unbelief.

But total unbelief is not the same as final unbelief. A person may stop believing the gospel at any point in time (total unbelief) and then later repent and believe the gospel. To die in a state of unbelief would be final unbelief. Classical Calvinist formulations of the doctrine of perseverance state that a true believer will have neither total unbelief at any point after regeneration nor final unbelief at the very end of life. While the Galatians ceased believing the gospel of grace for a time (total unbelief), they did not necessarily continue in unbelief until the end of their lives (final unbelief). In Galatians 5:10, Paul sounds a note of optimism about their repentance after receiving his letter, saying, "I have confidence in you, in the Lord, that you will have no other mind." Though the unbelief of some Galatians in the gospel was total, it was not necessarily a permanent or irreversible condition.

Trust & Persuasion

Just as belief in the gospel message and the person of Christ are inseparably connected, even so belief in Christ for eternal salvation is a matter both of trusting in the person of Christ and of being persuaded that the gospel message is true. In other words, *trust* and *persuasion* ("mental assent") are necessary, simultaneous, and inseparable elements of faith in Christ for eternal life. This means that when someone trusts in the person of Christ as his Savior, that belief or trust is inseparable from his persuasion that the gospel message is true. When someone understands and is persuaded about the person of Christ (being both Lord God[17] and man) and His work (His substitutionary, sufficient death for sin and resurrection from the dead),

---

17. To believe in Jesus as *Lord* as a requirement for salvation (Acts 10:42; 16:30-31; 17:31; Rom. 10:9-10) means to believe in His *deity* as One possessing the divine attribute and position of absolute sovereignty—the One with the authority to render eternal judgment and grant either eternal life or eternal condemnation. See Charles C. Bing, *Lordship Salvation: A Biblical Evaluation and Response*, GraceLife Edition (Burleson, TX: GraceLife Ministries, 1992), 104; Thomas R. Edgar, "What Is the Gospel?" in *Basic Theology: Applied*, ed. Wesley and Elaine Willis & John and Janet Master (Wheaton, IL: Victor, 1995), 158; J. B. Hixson, *Getting the Gospel Wrong: The Evangelical Crisis No One Is Talking About*, Revised Edition (Duluth, MN: Grace Gospel Press, 2013), 63; Robert P. Lightner, *Sin, the Savior, and Salvation: The Theology of Everlasting Life* (Nashville: Thomas Nelson, 1991), 204; Lou Martuneac, *In Defense of the Gospel: Biblical Answers to Lordship Salvation*, Revised Edition (n.p.: Xulon, 2010), 195-200; Charles C. Ryrie, *So Great Salvation: What It Means to Believe In Jesus Christ* (Wheaton, IL: Victor, 1989), 69-70. Adherents of Lordship Salvation and the perseverance of the saints practically nullify salvation solely by grace when they combine active submission to Christ's lordship in one's daily Christian life with belief in Christ as Lord.

that person has thereby become convinced that Jesus is the Christ, the Son of God and possesses everlasting life (John 20:31). Trust and persuasion occur simultaneously because they are inherent to faith.

This conclusion is significant for at least three reasons. First, if saving faith is a matter of being persuaded about the gospel, then what happens when doubts arise later about the gospel? Since doubt is the opposite of faith, saints who have doubts are not actually persevering in faith. This important subject will be discussed in more detail in the following section.

Second, if faith is a matter of being convinced or persuaded about the gospel of Christ, then how likely is it that someone may become unconvinced or unpersuaded only moments later? Perseverance-of-the-saints proponent John MacArthur attempts to discredit the position of eternal security by painting a scenario in which a lost person hears and believes the gospel one moment and then is immediately persuaded not to believe the next moment, so he goes from being a believer to an atheist in a matter of moments.[18] But if belief in Christ is a matter of becoming convinced or persuaded about the gospel as the Lord supernaturally draws, illuminates, and convinces (Matt. 11:27; John 1:9; 6:44; 16:8; Acts 16:14) an unbeliever to repent, or change his mind, about Christ and the gospel, it is difficult to conceive how that same person could so flippantly and instantaneously become a hardened unbeliever to the point of even being an atheist! In order to become a believer in the first place, the Lord must overcome our inherent ignorance, pride, and human and religious viewpoint. Once a person is convinced of the truth of the gospel, the process of reversing course and becoming unconvinced is not so easy. However, the case of the Galatians proves it is still possible. Paul marveled at the fact that false teaching caused the Galatians to stop believing the true gospel "so soon" (Gal. 1:6)—in only a year or two.

Third, the fact that trust and persuasion occur together also shows that faith is not something complicated. It is simply a matter of taking God at His Word whereby in essence our human spirit responds to hearing the gospel with "Amen! I agree, Lord!" Understanding this aspect of faith has very liberating consequences. It means that the type of response God is looking for when a sinner hears the gospel is not a commitment, dedication, covenant, resolution, or pledge on our part to curb sin, try harder, do more, or do better, as is so frequently taught today. Rather, God is simply looking for us to agree with Him concerning His Son, Jesus Christ, and accept

---

18. MacArthur, *Faith Works*, 191.

what He has accomplished for us and what He now freely offers to us. The response of faith that God seeks from us is something objective, where we can know that we have believed and are saved, rather than something subjective, which may leave us in doubt until we have persevered to the end of our Christian lives. Several biblical passages support the conclusion that faith is simply a matter of trusting in Christ's person and work as we are convinced of the truth of the gospel.

> Now when they had passed through Amphipolis and Apollonia, they came to Thessalonica, where there was a synagogue of the Jews. 2 Then Paul, as his custom was, went in to them, and for three Sabbaths reasoned with them from the Scriptures, 3 explaining and demonstrating that the Christ had to suffer and rise again from the dead, and saying, "This Jesus whom I preach to you is the Christ." 4 And some of them were persuaded; and a great multitude of the devout Greeks, and not a few of the leading women, joined Paul and Silas. 5 But the Jews who were not persuaded, becoming envious, took some of the evil men from the marketplace, and gathering a mob, set all the city in an uproar and attacked the house of Jason, and sought to bring them out to the people. (Acts 17:1-5)

Though the word "gospel" is not used here in Acts 17:1-5 to describe the message that was proclaimed to the Thessalonians, the content of the message is summarized in verse 3 as Christ's death and resurrection, which is declared to be the gospel in 1 Corinthians 15:1-4. The response to this message in Thessalonica was that some were "persuaded" (Acts 17:4) and some were "not persuaded" (v. 5). This persuasion about Christ is later described by Paul in 2 Thessalonians as believing the gospel.

> [I]n flaming fire taking vengeance on those who do not know God, and on those who do not obey the gospel of our Lord Jesus Christ. 9 These shall be punished with everlasting destruction from the presence of the Lord and from the glory of His power, 10 when He comes, in that Day, to be glorified in His saints and to be admired among all those who believe, because our testimony among you was believed. (2 Thess. 1:8-10)

This comparison of Acts 17:1-5 with 2 Thessalonians 1:8-10 shows clearly that believing the gospel is synonymous with being persuaded about Christ. A comparison of other passages supports this conclusion. For example, Acts 16:31 says, "Believe on (*epi*) the Lord Jesus Christ, and you shall be saved." The preposition *epi* here is significant since it shows that belief is not merely in (*eis*) a person, as many other passages set forth, but it also rests upon (*epi*) the person of Christ and His work. The preposition *epi* is used frequently in Acts to convey trust, reliance, or dependence on Christ when it occurs together with the verbs "believe" (*pisteuō* + *epi*, i.e., "believe on" – 3:16; 9:35, 42; 11:17, 21; 13:12; 16:31; 22:19; 26:18, 20) and "turn" (*epistrephō* + *epi*, i.e., "turn to" in reliance or dependence – 9:35; 11:21; 14:15; 15:19; 26:18, 20). Therefore, belief in Christ includes trust, reliance, or dependence upon Him while other passages make it evident that being persuaded about Christ is also inherent to faith in Him (Acts 28:23-24).

Acts 2:36 is another key passage showing that faith in Christ for salvation is a matter of being assured, convinced, or persuaded of divinely revealed truth. The same author who wrote the Book of Acts, namely, Luke, states in Luke 1:4 that he wrote his Gospel so that Theophilus would "know the certainty of those things" that he had been taught about Christ. The Greek word for "certainty" in verse 4 is the noun *asphaleian*. This is a rare word, occurring only a few times in the New Testament. But significantly, Luke uses a form of this word twice in Acts: "know assuredly (*asphalōs*) that God has made this Jesus, whom you crucified, both Lord and Christ" (2:36); "because he wanted to know for certain (*asphales*)" (22:30). The basic meaning of this word and its cognate forms is assurance or certainty that something is true. Within the historical narrative of Acts 2:36, Peter commands the unsaved Jews of Jerusalem to not merely "know" that God made Jesus, whom they crucified, both Lord and Christ, but to know this truth "assuredly." Knowing what God has revealed in the gospel does not save anyone, but knowing it "assuredly" (i.e., as true) amounts to agreeing with it, being convinced or persuaded of it, and thus believing it. Therefore, saving faith is nothing less than assurance or certainty that the gospel of Christ is true.

Another example of persuasion being inherent to faith is found in 2 Timothy 1:12: "I know whom I have believed and I am convinced that He is able to guard what I have entrusted to Him until that day" (NASB). Instead of "convinced," other translations say "persuaded" (KJV, NKJV); but the point is the same. Paul had believed in the person of Christ ("whom I have believed") and was convinced of something about that person, namely, that He was "able to guard" Paul's eternal destiny, which he had entrusted to Christ. This verse not only shows that belief involves persuasion, but it provides another clear example of the preservation of the saints by the Savior (eternal security) rather than salvation depending on the saints' perseverance.

One final example where faith means persuasion or certainty is Romans 4:21.[19] There Abraham's faith is described as a matter of him "being fully convinced [*plērophoreō*] that what [God] had promised He was also able to perform." Instead of the phrase "fully convinced" (NKJV, ESV), other versions read "being fully assured" (NASB) or "being fully persuaded" (NIV). While Romans 4:21 clearly illustrates that Abraham's faith meant that he was persuaded, someone might legitimately wonder what it means to be "fully" persuaded. Are there degrees of persuasion where anything less than "full" persuasion is still genuine faith? The one Greek word, *plērophoreō*, rendered "fully convinced/assured/persuaded," is a compound word made up of two words, *plēro*- (to fill, fulfill) and *phoreō*. By itself *phoreō* never means "to convince, assure, or persuade," or if it were stated in the passive voice, "to be convinced, assured, or persuaded." Rather, *phoreō* by itself always means "to carry, wear, or bear habitually."[20] The term *phoreō* takes on the meaning of being persuaded or certain only when it appears with the prefix *plēro*- as in the compound word *plērophoreō*. In addition, the root word *phoreō* never occurs in the New Testament prefixed by other words that might give it the meaning of something less than "full," as in "somewhat convinced," "partially convinced," or "almost persuaded."[21] For these reasons, it is best to interpret the phrase "fully convinced" and its underlying Greek term, *plērophoreō*, in Romans 4:21 as simply a synonym for faith rather than indicating

---

19. Hebrews 11:1 may also demonstrate that persuasion is inherent to faith. While some English versions read "faith is the *substance* of things hoped for, the *evidence* of things not seen" (KJV, NKJV), others say "faith is the *assurance* of things hoped for, the *conviction* of things not seen" (ESV, NASB) and "faith is being *sure* of what we hope for and *certain* of what we do not see" (NIV). Having assurance, being sure, and being certain all speak of persuasion.

20. Walter Bauer, William F. Arndt, and F. Wilbur Gingrich, *A Greek-English Lexicon of the New Testament and Other Early Christian Literature*, 3rd ed., rev. and ed. Frederick W. Danker (Chicago: University of Chicago Press, 2000), 1064.

21. The verb *phoreō* appears as the root of only four other compound words in the New Testament: *karpophoreō*, meaning "to be fruitful" (Matt. 13:23; Mark 4:20, 28; Luke 8:15; Rom. 7:4; Col 1:6, 10); *potomaphorētos* (adjective), "to be born along, swept away by water, a river, or a stream" (Rev. 12:15); *telesphoreō*, "to bear fruit to maturity" (Luke 8:14, 15); and *tropophoreō*, "to bear or put up with someone's manner or moods" (Acts 13:18).

a special, advanced degree of faith (i.e., full faith or persuasion versus partial faith or persuasion).

The use of this same term (*plērophoreō*) later in Romans 14 is significant in showing that faith means being convinced or persuaded of something, with no doubting. In the context of individual liberty of conscience concerning days and diets, Romans 14:5 says, "Let each be fully convinced (*plērophoreisthō*) in his own mind." This use of *plērophoreō* falls in the same chapter and context as Paul's conclusion about liberties, where he writes: "Do you have *faith*? Have it to yourself before God. Happy is he who does not condemn himself in what he approves. But he who *doubts* is condemned if he eats, because he does not eat from faith; for whatever is not from *faith* is sin" (vv. 22-23). Notice the antithesis between faith and doubt. Paul is telling the Romans that if they have any reservation, hesitation, or doubt in their conscience about eating food that has been previously offered to an idol, then they should not eat it because they would not be acting in faith in that case. Therefore, we can conclude that having faith, or being "fully convinced" (Rom. 4:21; 14:5), is not a matter of degrees of certainty or persuasion but is simply another way of expressing faith without doubt.

Faith Without Doubt

Doubt has undergone a spiritual facelift in the twenty-first century. Whereas the Bible *never* speaks positively of doubt, modern pundits and theologians are giving it a new look. Famous Oxford theologian Alister McGrath flatly claims, "*Doubt* is not unbelief. But it can *become* unbelief"; and it "is natural within faith."[22] Likewise, Os Guinness describes doubt neutrally, as merely "a state of mind in suspension between faith and unbelief" and that "there is no believing without some doubting."[23] While these statements give the impression that we need to learn to tolerate doubt within our faith, as though faith and doubt must be held in equilibrium, Gregory Boyd goes even further to extol the spiritual benefits of doubting. He claims that "doubt is necessary and healthy when deciding what we believe is true"[24] and that we should not view it as the "enemy of faith" but rather

---

22. Alister McGrath, "When Doubt Becomes Unbelief," www.ligonier.org/learn/articles/when-doubt-becomes-unbelief (accessed September 9, 2014).

23. Os Guinness, "I Believe in Doubt," www.ligonier.org/learn/articles/i-believe-in-doubt (accessed September 9, 2014).

24. Gregory A. Boyd, *The Benefit of the Doubt: Breaking the Idol of Certainty* (Grand Rapids: Baker, 2013), 215.

learn to "embrace doubt."[25] From the subtitle of his book, Boyd even decries certainty as an "idol" within evangelicalism! Yet according to the plain testimony of the Bible, doubt is not something neutral or even healthy; it is the antithesis of faith—even the nemesis of faith.

If the Bible teaches that faith and doubt are mutually exclusive, then what are the implications for the perseverance view that unbelief can be neither total nor final in one who is truly born again? Are you truly persevering in the faith if you doubt the gospel? If faith excludes doubt, and you purportedly have faith mixed with doubts, is not your belief really unbelief? There is much at stake for the doctrine of perseverance with respect to the relationship between faith and doubt.

Can faith and doubt coexist concerning the gospel? There are simply too many passages in Scripture about faith excluding doubt to conclude that belief in the gospel can simultaneously coexist with doubt about the gospel. The preceding example of Romans 14:22-23 provided a clear example of the mutual exclusivity that exists between faith and doubt. Several other passages firmly support this conclusion as well.

James 1:6 says, "But let him ask in faith (*en pistei*), with no doubting (*mēden diakrinomenos*), for he who doubts is like a wave of the sea driven and tossed by the wind."[26] This is a key verse not only in demonstrating the antithesis between faith and doubt, but even the extent of doubting. The adverb *mēden* can mean "no," "not any," "nobody," or "nothing."[27] Thus, it is a term of exclusion, showing that to no extent can belief and doubt coexist concerning the same thing, such as a prayer request. Consequently, James 1:6 is normally translated in a way that reflects exclusivity: "ask in faith, without any doubting" (NASB); and "ask in faith, with no doubting" (NKJV, ESV). The two words taken together, "doubting" (*diakrinomenos*) + "nothing" (*mēden*) address the extent of doubting and exclude it altogether from faith. According to Greek grammarian A. T. Robertson, the phrase "nothing doubting" (*mēden diakrinomenos*) modifies the

---

25. Ibid., 32.

26. This verse also proves that not all questions about God, the Bible, or the gospel are expressions of doubt, for one can "ask in faith, doubting nothing." This answers the humanistic reasoning of McGrath, Guinness, Boyd, and others who say that all faith must inherently contain some degree of doubt since belief is gained only through the process of first doubting or questioning God, the Bible, or the gospel and then resolving those questions to one's satisfaction.

27. Bauer, Arndt, and Gingrich, *A Greek-English Lexicon of the New Testament and Other Early Christian Literature*, 647.

preceding phrase about asking "in faith" (*en pistei*), so according to Robertson, the phrase about "no doubting" is simply the "negative way of saying *en pistei*."[28] This shows that the phrase "in faith" means "doubting nothing." This is like a teacher saying to his students, "There is a blank space in the upper right corner of your exam where I want you to print your names, not write them." The phrase, "not write them," modifies what it means "to print your names." According to these instructions, the students are not to partially write and partially print their names—they are *only* to print their names. In the same way, James 1:6 says that believing and doubting are opposite or exclusive activities of one another.

Practically speaking, this means that from a divine perspective, believing that the gospel is probably true, or even that it is almost certainly true, still does not qualify as biblical faith in Christ. When King Agrippa said to Paul in Acts 26:28, "You almost persuade me to become a Christian," he was still not a Christian because he had not yet believed the gospel of Christ. Agrippa may have been closer to salvation than he was before he heard Paul because at least now he knew the gospel of Christ, and perhaps he could now agree that it was based in the Old Testament and had a logical consistency. But this does not mean he was now any more willing to believe it. To know the truth and believe it are two separate matters, and there is an eternity of difference between them. For someone to be almost persuaded means that person is still totally lost! The old hymn by Philip Bliss titled, "Almost Persuaded," captures the essence of this truth when it states:

"Almost persuaded," harvest is past!

"Almost persuaded," doom comes at last;

"Almost" cannot avail;

"Almost" is but to fail!

Sad, sad that bitter wail—

"Almost—but lost!"

Besides the previous biblical examples showing that a person cannot be doubting something and be persuaded about it at the same time, there are several other passages in Scripture where faith is set

---

28. A. T. Robertson, *Word Pictures in the New Testament* (Grand Rapids: Baker, n.d.), 6:14.

in opposition to doubt, showing that they are mutually exclusive. This contrast is highlighted below through the use of italics:

> So Jesus answered and said to them, "Assuredly, I say to you, if you have *faith and do not doubt*, you will not only do what was done to the fig tree, but also if you say to this mountain, 'Be removed and be cast into the sea,' it will be done. (Matt. 21:21)

> And He said to them, "Why are you troubled? And why do *doubts* arise in your hearts? 39 "Behold My hands and My feet, that it is I Myself. Handle Me and see, for a spirit does not have flesh and bones as you see I have." 40 When He had said this, He showed them His hands and His feet. 41 But while *they still did not believe* for joy, and marveled, He said to them, "Have you any food here?" (Luke 24:38-41)

> Then the Jews surrounded Him and said to Him, "How long do You keep us in *doubt?* If You are the Christ, tell us plainly." 25 Jesus answered them, "I told you, and you do *not believe*. The works that I do in My Father's name, they bear witness of Me. (John 10:24-25)

While these passages are clear enough in showing the absolute antithesis between faith and doubt, some may still wonder how all of this fits with Mark 9:23-24, which is commonly cited to support the idea that belief and doubt can coexist. In Mark 9, Jesus casts demons out of a man's son. In verse 23, Jesus says to the man, "If you can believe, all things are possible to him who believes." In response, the boy's father cries out to Jesus, "Lord, I believe; help my unbelief" (v. 24). Does this man's statement show that belief and unbelief can simultaneously coexist? Perseverance proponent John Piper thinks so. He writes, "Persevering in faith does not mean that the saints do not go through seasons of doubt and spiritual darkness and measures of unbelief in the promises and the goodness of God. 'I believe; help my unbelief!' (Mark 9:24) is not a contradictory prayer. Measures of unbelief can coexist with a true faith."[29]

However, attempts to harmonize this passage with the doctrine of perseverance lead to the nonsensical conclusion that the boy's

---

29. John Piper, *Five Points: Towards a Deeper Experience of God's Grace* (Ross-shire, Scotland: Christian Focus, 2013), 65.

father really meant, "Lord, I believe you and I doubt you at the same time; so even though I believe in you, help my present unbelief." Instead, it is much better to view the father as simply recognizing and admitting that though he believed Christ at that moment, he was susceptible to unbelief in the future. The man's present belief did not guarantee his belief in Christ thereafter or belief in Him for other matters the Lord would reveal to him in addition to the miraculous healing of his son. Therefore, this passage in no way justifies the unbiblical notion that someone may doubt the gospel and believe it at the same time, and that as long as that person retains some degree of faith (even 99-percent doubt with 1-percent faith), that person's unbelief is not "total" and he or she is still persevering in the faith.

Degrees of Faith

If doubt cannot coexist with true faith, then how do we account for the degrees of faith mentioned in the Bible? Doesn't having "little faith" versus "great faith" mean that believers have lesser or greater degrees of doubt mixed with their faith?

The Bible plainly teaches that a believer's faith can and should continually grow after the new birth, and thus there are varying levels of faith expressed in Scripture. Some believers have "little faith" (Matt. 6:30; 8:26; 14:31; 16:8; Luke 12:28); others have "great faith" (Matt. 8:10; 15:28); while others are said to be "full of the Holy Spirit and of faith" (Acts 11:24). Scripture is also clear that our faith can "increase" (Luke 17:5) and experience "growth" (2 Thess. 1:3). But a person's faith grows after the moment of new birth only in the measure that he or she continues to believe the gospel and consistently learns and applies additional biblical truth. Apart from learning the Word of God, believers will never grow in faith (Heb. 5:12-14; 1 Peter 2:2). But believers may grow by learning more principles, precepts, and promises from the Word of God and appropriating them by faith in their daily walk of fellowship with the Lord. The more divine revelation the believer is exposed to and responds to by faith, the more his faith will expand. It is not that the nature of his faith changes. It is not as though he starts off his Christian life with a little bit of doubt about the gospel mixed with his faith, but then he grows to having less or no doubt about the gospel. Rather, persuasion and trust without doubt at the point of initial faith in Christ remain persuasion and trust without doubt about the gospel after the new birth, as the believer walks by faith. The difference is that the amount of God's truth a person receives and believes continues to grow after regeneration, and therefore that person's faith grows proportionately.

The Lord's earthly ministry among the disciples illustrates this point. Throughout the Lord Jesus' three-year public ministry, He was a walking, talking revelation of God to His disciples (John 1:14, 18; 14:9-11). The Lord's disciples continually witnessed His miracles and heard Him preach the Word of God. Though eleven of the twelve disciples believed Jesus to be the Messiah (John 1:40-42; 2:11; 6:66-71), their concept of the Messiah was deficient and undeveloped. They believed some truth about Him, but the Lord wanted to increase their faith so that they would grow spiritually. Their faith needed to grow as the Object of their faith grew in their own estimation and understanding. Consequently, Christ sought to increase the disciples' faith by progressively revealing to them more truth about Himself throughout His three-year public ministry. Was He, as the Messiah, sovereign over sin, disease, demons, and nature? Could He be trusted to meet every human need in addition to salvation from sin?

In Matthew 14:15-21, the Lord tests the faith of the disciples (John 6:6) by miraculously multiplying five loaves and two fishes to feed over five thousand people, conspicuously leaving twelve baskets of fragments left over—one for each disciple. Later, in Matthew 16:8-9, the Lord reproves the disciples for their lack of faith, reminding them of this earlier miracle, saying, "O you of little faith, why do you reason among yourselves because you have brought no bread? Do you not yet understand, or remember the five loaves of the five thousand and how many baskets you took up?"

Incidents such as this in the Lord's earthly ministry demonstrate that a believer's "little faith" may grow as the content of that believer's faith grows. The more divine revelation the child of God receives and believes, the more that believer's faith increases. Thus, passages dealing with degrees of faith in no way justify the unbiblical conclusion that faith and doubt concerning the saving message of the gospel can simultaneously coexist. A person cannot be believing the gospel and doubting it at the same time, for doubt is unbelief.

At the moment an unregenerate person believes the gospel and is born again, that person is persuaded that the gospel is true. In this respect, faith is not mixed with doubt about the specific truth of the gospel. However, the same person may not yet understand or believe many other divinely revealed truths about Christ. For example, it is not uncommon for new believers, still persuaded by the world's teachings and philosophies, to believe the gospel and get saved while still believing that mankind evolved rather than being direct creations of God. Who among us had full understanding of God's Word when we were saved or even afterwards? Thus, when a person trusts Christ and is born again, he or she may still have doubts about other truths in God's Word but not about the gospel. In this respect, belief in the gospel often coexists alongside doubts about other areas of biblical truth. Though someone may trust Christ for his or her greatest need of eternal salvation from sin, he or she may still fail to trust Him for some lesser need or trial in the Christian life after the new birth. While this may be illogical and inconsistent on the believer's part, it nevertheless happens with all of us. None of us believes every promise or truth in the Word of God all the time throughout our entire Christian lives.

The fact that believers in Christ may still doubt the Lord after salvation is plainly stated in several passages (Rom. 14:23; 1 Tim. 2:8; James 1:6). These verses show that believers may have doubts about certain truths, facts, promises, or propositions from God's Word that often coexist simultaneously with certainty or faith regarding the specific message of the gospel. For that matter, a person who was once convinced of the gospel, and thus is eternally saved, may later develop doubts about the gospel itself and lose certainty about it, resulting in the loss of his or her assurance of salvation (Luke 8:13-14; Gal. 1:6-9; 3:1; 1 Cor. 15:1-2; 2 Cor. 11:1-4; Col. 1:23). Though assurance or certainty of salvation may be lost since it is tied to the saint's ongoing faith, eternal salvation may never be lost since it resides solely with the safekeeping of God.

Doubt & Perseverance

These observations about faith and doubt help to distinguish the biblical teaching of eternal security from the unbiblical teaching of the perseverance of the saints. When the Bible speaks of degrees of faith, it does not mean that faith and doubt can simultaneously coexist concerning the same divinely revealed truth from God's Word. The Bible does not teach what the Calvinist doctrine of perseverance permits, namely, that a person who believes in Christ for salvation can have partial belief of the gospel mixed with partial doubt about the gospel, provided that such doubt or unbelief is not "total" unbelief of the gospel. According to Scripture, there can be no doubting at the moment of new birth since doubt is the antithesis of faith. Doubt of the gospel to any degree is still unbelief of the gospel.

The biblical fact that doubt may exist later within those who once genuinely believed the gospel contradicts the Calvinist claim that genuine believers cannot "totally" lose their faith. When a person has doubts about the gospel, that person does not believe the gospel. Biblically, the presence of doubt means the absence of faith, and the absence of faith means that even children of God can lose their faith in a "total" sense with respect to the saving message of the gospel. Thus, a genuine child of God may not persevere in "saving faith" and may "totally fall from faith."[30] Yet, thankfully, Scripture also teaches that when a born-again person ceases to believe the gospel and totally falls from faith, that child of God will not fall out of the faithful, saving, persevering hand of God but is kept eternally saved from hell and destined for heaven solely by God's grace and fidelity to His promise.

---

30. *Canons of the Synod of Dort*, 3:594.

Chapter 6

Is Final Salvation a Free Gift
or an Earned Reward?

We often go about our day blissfully unaware of life's great contradictions. For instance, have you ever wondered why we push the "Start" button to shut down our computers? Or, why do we say "jumbo shrimp," "dry ice," "pretty ugly," or "Microsoft Works"? Why does Hawaii have an Interstate Highway 1 (H-1)? And isn't asking "May I ask you question?" already a question?

While these contradictions are fairly harmless and humorous, theological contradictions are no laughing matter. Many professing Christians today live with the contradictory belief that eternal life is both a free gift and an earned reward. This contradictory conclusion is arrived at only by mixing human, meritorious works with God's unmerited grace. This lethal combination nullifies grace (Gal. 2:21) since true, biblical grace cannot be mixed with works: "But if it is by grace, it is no longer on the basis of works, otherwise grace is no longer grace" (Rom. 11:6, NASB). Fortunately, God does not expect Christians to live with such contradictions. Nor does His Word contradict itself.

When it comes to eternal salvation, the Bible is clear that there is a significant difference between the *free gift* of *eternal life* for undeserving sinners who place their faith in Christ alone versus *rewards* that are *earned* by the believer's faithfulness and good works. Since God is perfectly righteous (Deut. 32:4; Ps. 7:9; Rom. 3:4-6) and man is inherently sinful (Eccl. 7:20; Rom. 3:10-12), no one will ever be good enough to deserve justification before God (Job 25:4; Rom. 3:19-20). Therefore, eternal salvation from hell to heaven must rest only on the basis of God's grace and the substitutionary work of His Son on behalf of lost, unworthy sinners (Rom. 5:9-10; Eph. 2:8-9; 1 Thess. 5:9-10). All who trust solely in God's saving grace and the finished work of Christ are declared righteous by God and guaranteed eternal life with Him (Acts 13:38-41; Rom. 8:33-39; Titus 3:5-7). Since Christ did all the work to achieve eternal salvation and He alone paid the purchase price for every person to be saved, eternal life is never referred to in the Bible as the believer's "reward" but as God's "gift" to those who trust His Son (John 4:13-14; Rom. 6:23).

Teachings of Men Regarding Rewards

Roman Catholicism openly labels eternal salvation a "reward" for the believer's faith and good works. This is not surprising in light of what Catholicism has historically taught about the necessity of good works for salvation. But it is nothing short of astonishing to hear many Calvinists calling eternal life a reward. For example, A. W. Pink states,

> In Scripture, "eternal life" is presented both as a "gift" and as a "reward" —the reward of perseverance. . . . That eternal life and glory is set forth in God's Word as the reward and end of perseverance which await all faithful Christians is clear from Heb. 10:35, to cite no other passages now: *"Cast not away therefore your confidence which hath great recompense of reward."*[1]

In addition, Reformed scholar and professor Craig Blomberg says that various passages traditionally interpreted as teaching rewards "are not at all talking about degrees of reward in heaven but simply about eternal life."[2] He goes on to say that the crown of rejoicing in 1 Thessalonians 2:19 "appears in synonymous parallelism with the 'hope' and 'joy' of eternal life itself."[3] Regarding the crown of glory in 1 Peter 5:4, he concludes that "it is probably most natural to take this crown too as a metaphor for eternal life."[4] Since Blomberg senses the apparent contradiction between these interpretations and the biblical doctrine of salvation by grace through faith alone, he is naturally constrained to issue the following qualification:

---

1. A. W. Pink, *The Saint's Perseverance* (Lafayette, IN: Sovereign Grace, 2001), 89.
2. Craig L. Blomberg, "Degrees of Reward in the Kingdom of Heaven?" *Journal of the Evangelical Theological Society* 35 (June 1992): 163.
3. Ibid.
4. Ibid., 164.

The greatest danger of the doctrine of degrees of reward in heaven is that it has misled many people into thinking that the very nominal professions that they or their friends have at one time made will be sufficient to save them, even if they fail to receive as high a status in heaven as they might have. This is in no way to argue for works-righteousness. It is merely to remind us of the consistent Biblical theme that true, saving faith does over time lead to visible transformations in lifestyle and to growth in holiness.[5]

Thomas Schreiner is another prominent, contemporary Reformed author and seminary professor who agrees with Blomberg that eternal life is a reward and that practical righteousness in the Christian life is necessary to receive this "reward." When interpreting the crown of 1 Peter 5:4, he says:

It is difficult to know if the crown is equivalent to eternal life itself or if it is a special reward for elders. In the other 'crown' (*stephanos*) texts the reward is entrance into heaven itself (cf. 1 Cor. 9:25; 2 Tim. 4:8; Jas. 1:12; Rev. 2:10; 3:11). The usage in the rest of the New Testament slightly favors the latter notion.[6]

Schreiner elsewhere echoes the disclaimer of Blomberg about works-righteousness when he concludes regarding the readers of Peter's epistle:

They are to refrain from speaking evil and from guile so that they will obtain the eschatological reward, eternal life itself. We must insist again that such a theology is not works righteousness, nor does it compromise the theme that salvation is by grace. Peter believed that those who have received new life from God will live transformed lives and that such lives provide evidence (necessary evidence!) that they have been converted.[7]

---

5. Ibid., 172.
6. Thomas R. Schreiner, *1, 2 Peter, Jude,* New American Commentary (Nashville: Broadman & Holman, 2003), 236.
7. Ibid., 167 (parenthesis and exclamation point original).

Even though these Reformed writers insist their doctrine is consistent with salvation by grace alone, equating eternal life with a reward is truly a form of salvation by works. If a transformed earthly life is truly "necessary" at the final judgment and this transformation of a believer's life depends even to the slightest degree on the believer's responsibility to walk daily in faithful obedience to God's will, then eternal salvation is no longer solely the work of God and it cannot be by faith alone.

Statements from other evangelical, Reformed teachers only confirm this conclusion. John MacArthur speaks of entrance into the Kingdom as being a reward for a saving faith that consists of human suffering, sacrifice, payment, and responsibility.

> Again, that is a perfect picture of saving faith. Someone who truly believes in Christ does not hedge bets. Knowing the cost of discipleship, the true believer signs up and gives everything for Christ. Moses counted the cost (Heb. 11:26). He gave up spectacular worldly wealth in order to suffer for Christ's sake. To the Egyptians in Pharaoh's court, it must have seemed he was trading riches for a reproach. But Moses knew that he was really trading Egypt for a heavenly *reward*. That is the kind of totally committed response the Lord Jesus called for. A desire for Him at any cost. Absolute surrender. A full exchange of self for the Savior. It is the only response that will open the gates of the kingdom. Seen through the eyes of this world, it is as high a price as anyone can pay. But from a kingdom perspective, it is really no sacrifice at all.[8]

Those who teach that believers must persevere in obedient, working faith to obtain final salvation are the very same ones who claim that eternal life is a "reward." Sheer coincidence? I don't think so. If the requirement for salvation is a totally committed response of surrender, exchange of self, giving up everything, and paying the price, then the sole condition for salvation has been radically and tragically transformed from faith alone to faithfulness—from simple trust in Christ's finished work for the believer to what the believer must do for Christ by way of perseverance in faithfulness and good works. If this approach to salvation were true, then eternal life would indeed be the believer's "reward."

---

8. John F. MacArthur, Jr., *The Gospel According to Jesus: What Does Jesus Mean When He Says "Follow Me"?* (Grand Rapids: Zondervan, 1988), 141 (emphasis added).

But in contrast to the preceding claims made by today's Reformed leaders,[9] there are at least seven biblical distinctions in God's Word between rewards and salvation. These are summarized in the following table and explained in the rest of the chapter.

Salvation	Rewards
For unbelievers	For believers
Obtained apart from works	Obtained according to works
By faith at a moment in time	By faithfulness over a lifetime
Can never be lost	Can be lost
Concerns God's acceptance	Concerns God's approval
Eternal deliverance	Eternal privilege and function
No degrees	Degrees

---

9. Though modern adherents of Reformed theology often refer to eternal salvation as a reward, this is certainly not true of all Calvinists. For instance, leading nineteenth century Reformed theologian Charles Hodge states, "Having graciously promised for Christ's sake to overlook the imperfection of their best services, [believers] have the assurance founded on that promise that he who gives to a disciple even a cup of cold water in the name of a disciple, shall in no wise lose his reward. The Scriptures also teach that the happiness or blessedness of believers in a future life will be greater or less in proportion to their devotion to the service of Christ in this life." Charles Hodge, *Systematic Theology*, 3 vols. (Grand Rapids: Eerdmans, 1989), 3:244.

Unbelievers vs. Believers

The first distinction between salvation and rewards is that eternal salvation is offered to *unbelievers* while the recompense of a positive reward is offered only to *believers*. In various evangelistic passages, such as Acts 2:40; 4:12; 5:31; 11:14; 13:23, 26, 38-41, 46-48; 16:30-31 and many others, the appeal is consistently made to unbelieving audiences to believe in Christ for salvation. Existing believers are never implored to believe again or to keep believing in order to receive or maintain their eternal salvation. Conversely, the prospect of receiving a positive reward at the Judgment Seat of Christ (Rom. 14:10; 1 Cor. 3:8-15; 2 Cor. 5:9-10) is given only to believers (Rom. 1:5-8; 1 Cor. 1:2; 2 Cor. 1:1).

The reason for this distinction is due to each person's standing before God. An unsaved person is ineligible for a positive reward because he is spiritually dead to God in his trespasses and sins (Eph. 2:1). All his good deeds are tainted by sin and considered to be filthy rags before God (Isa. 64:6), making it impossible for him to please God (Rom. 8:8; Heb. 11:6). Before any of his deeds can be considered "good," he must first be forgiven of his sins and reconciled to God (Acts 10:43; Rom. 4:6-8; Col. 2:13-14).

When a sinner is eternally saved through faith alone in Christ, God no longer sees that person in his sins but in Christ (Eph. 1:3); and that person receives a new capacity to do good works through the power of the indwelling Holy Spirit (Rom. 8:9-14). Thus the believer has a new foundation to build on—Jesus Christ. For this reason, 1 Corinthians 3:11 states in the context of rewards, "For no other foundation can anyone lay than that which is laid, which is Jesus Christ." Since the unsaved person does not have Christ, he does not have this foundation to build on to gain a positive, eternal reward. According to Scripture, God offers only eternal salvation to unbelievers if they will believe in Jesus Christ, but He offers positive rewards only to believers.

Apart from Works vs. According to Works

The second distinction between salvation and rewards is that salvation is received by grace through faith in Christ *apart from works,* but rewards are obtained by grace through on-going faith, *resulting in Christ-honoring works.* Romans 4:4-6 is a key passage regarding the relationship between works, salvation, and rewards.

Now to him who works, the wages [*misthos*] are not counted as grace but as debt. But to him who does not work but believes on Him who justifies the ungodly, his faith is accounted for righteousness, just as David also describes the blessedness of the man to whom God imputes righteousness apart from works.

Verses 4-5 contrast the one who works for justification in God's sight with the one who does not work for justification but simply believes in Christ. The one who works for justification in God's sight attempts to make God indebted to him as though God were an employer who owes "wages" (NKJV) or a "reward" (KJV) to an employee as a just compensation for his labor. By contrast, the one who does not work for salvation but believes on Christ receives justification from God on the basis of "grace" rather than *misthos* ("wages" or "reward"). Since Romans 4:4-6 contrasts working to receive salvation as a "reward" (*misthos*) and believing to receive salvation by grace, salvation cannot be a reward that is earned by works. Therefore, salvation by grace and earned rewards must be kept distinct.

Reformed theology rejects this distinction, insisting that eternal life is a reward (*misthos*). One Reformed writer claims, "In its most general sense, 'reward' (Greek, *misthos*) is the appropriate consequence or consummation of a course of action. . . . Positively, 'reward' (which is always in the singular in the NT) refers to entering eternal life."[10] Yet the New Testament contains forty-one occurrences of the word *misthos* in its various forms, and not once is eternal life called a reward. In contexts that do not use *misthos* in reference to eschatological reward, it refers to "remuneration for work done" —to literal pay or wages to one who has been hired to do physical work.[11] In more explicitly eschatological contexts, it refers to "recognition (mostly by God) for the moral quality of an action, *recompense*."[12] This is consistent with the biblical teaching that eternal life is a *gift* from God based on *Christ's work for us* (Isa. 55:1-3; John 4:10, 14; Rom. 3:24; 6:23; Rev. 22:17), and *rewards* are compensation from God on the basis of *our work for Christ*.

---

10. John Starke, "You Asked: What Are the Rewards in Heaven Jesus Talks About?" http://thegospelcoalition.org/blogs/tgc/2011/07/18/you-asked-what-are-the-rewards-in-heaven-jesus-talks-about/ (accessed July, 19, 2011).

11. Walter Bauer, William F. Arndt, and F. Wilbur Gingrich, *A Greek-English Lexicon of the New Testament and Other Early Christian Literature*, 3rd edition, rev. and ed. Frederick W. Danker (Chicago: University of Chicago Press, 2000), 653.

12. Ibid.

The distinction between salvation and rewards becomes even clearer by comparing various reward passages to Romans 4:6, which teaches that "God imputes righteousness *apart from works*" whereas other Bible verses teach that rewards are given according to the believer's works. Christ promised His disciples that when He returns, "He will reward each *according to his works*" (Matt. 16:27). Christ also promised in Revelation 22:12, "And behold, I am coming quickly, and My reward [*misthos*] is with Me, to give to every one *according to his work.*" Similarly, 1 Corinthians 3:8 says, "each one will receive his own reward [*misthos*] *according to his own labor.*" Here is a key point: *since salvation cannot be simultaneously "apart from works" and "according to works/labor," there must be a distinction between salvation and rewards.* Eternal life cannot be a reward (*misthos*) that is "according to works/labor" and at the same time be a gift from God (Rom. 6:23) given "apart from works" on the basis of grace (Titus 3:7).

This "apart from" versus "according to" principle must be maintained when reading passages that declare God will judge all people according to their works—whether believers or unbelievers (Job 34:11; Ps. 62:12; Prov. 24:12; Jer. 32:19; Rom. 2:6). Sometimes Scripture speaks of judgment within one's earthly lifetime as being "according to works" (Ezek. 36:19; Zech. 1:6), but more often judgment according to works refers to future negative retribution for evil deeds (Neh. 6:14; Ps. 28:4; Isa. 59:18; Jer. 25:14; 50:29; Lam. 3:64; Ezek. 24:14; Hos. 12:2; 2 Cor. 11:15; 2 Tim. 4:14; Rev. 18:6; 20:12-13). This punitive judgment is reserved strictly for unbelievers—those who did not trust in God's saving grace and the finished work of His Son on their behalf (John 12:46-48; Rom. 2:16; 1 Thess. 1:8-10; 2 Thess. 2:10-12).

This judgment according to unbelievers' works will occur at the end of the Tribulation with the judgment of the nations and at the final sentencing of all lost mankind at the Great White Throne judgment. In contrast, believers, who have been saved by God's grace, will also be judged according to their works (Matt. 16:27; 2 Cor. 5:9-10; 1 Peter 1:17; Rev. 2:23; 22:12) but only for the purpose of determining their positive reward and position of service in God's eternal kingdom. For Church-age believers, this will occur at the Judgment Seat of Christ following the Rapture. This contrast between the eschatological judgment of unbelievers versus that of believers harmonizes with the distinction between salvation and rewards. Salvation is strictly by God's grace and "not according to our works" (2 Tim. 1:9; Titus 3:5), whereas rewards are clearly earned and "according to [our] labor/work" (1 Cor. 3:8; Rev. 22:12).

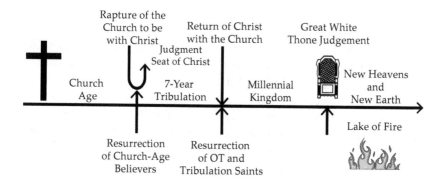

But this also raises several questions about the relationship between grace and rewards. Are rewards given strictly on the basis of good works? Do believers actually "merit" such rewards? And what role, if any, does God's grace play in rewards?

Though rewards are clearly earned, they are also the result of God's gracious generosity. This is true in at least two respects. First, no believer would even be in a position to earn a reward without God's saving grace. Every saint who serves Christ is also a sinner who deserves God's just condemnation. Even after the apostle Paul was saved for many years, he could still speak of himself as the chief of sinners (1 Tim. 1:15). Serving the Savior and earning a reward would be impossible if God simply gave each believer what he or she deserves. Thankfully He gives believers more than they deserve.[13] Rewards are God's overly generous wages rather than a strictly just recompense. Therefore, every believer should be able to say with the apostle Paul, "by the grace of God I am what I am" (1 Cor. 15:10). Even when believers have finished their course and served the Master to the end, the fact remains that each will be unworthy even to stand in the presence of the Savior to receive a reward. Every believer with a grace-perspective should be able to say, "We are unworthy slaves; we have done only that which we ought to have done" (Luke 17:10, NASB). Though believers have no right to expect or demand compensation from God simply for doing what He commands, God

---

13. Matthew 19:29 describes the Lord's generosity in giving future rewards. Christ promises the disciples they "shall receive a hundredfold" for their sacrifices as His followers." He is not saying that eternal life is a reward too. When Jesus adds "and inherit eternal life," He is saying only that the disciples' hundredfold reward "will be in addition to their eternal life in His kingdom" (Louis A. Barbieri, "Matthew" in *The Bible Knowledge Commentary: New Testament*, ed. John F. Walvoord and Roy B. Zuck [Wheaton, IL: Victor, 1983; reprint, Colorado Springs: Cook, 1996], 65).

in His grace and sovereignty has freely chosen to bestow rewards on His servants according to their service for Him. He has even *promised* these rewards to believers in His Word, and what He promises He is obligated (and faithful) to fulfill. For Him to break His promise would be "unjust." This is why the writer of Hebrews exhorts Christians to continue serving Christ, knowing that "God is not unjust to forget your work and labor of love which you have shown toward His name, in that you have ministered to the saints, and do minister" (Heb. 6:10). Though the opportunity even to receive a reward is attributable solely to God's *grace*, His just, promise-keeping character also makes it possible to *earn* a reward.

Second, God's grace plays a role in believers earning a reward because the very means and ability to serve God acceptably are provided freely by His grace (Heb. 12:28). As the Head of the Church, the Lord Jesus Christ distributes to His church the spiritual gifts with which to serve Him (1 Cor. 12:11; 1 Peter 4:10) as well as the power and ability to do so (2 Cor. 9:8; 1 Peter 4:11; 2 Peter 1:3). This is done all by His grace, for "what do you have that you did not receive?" (1 Cor. 4:7). Though Paul could say on the one hand that *he* labored for Christ, he could also say on the other hand, "yet not I, but the *grace of God* which was with me" (1 Cor. 15:10). Even the enablement and ability that must be appropriated to serve the Lord are God's gracious provision since He is not obligated to grant believers such provision. Believers must never forget that though rewards are earned, they are ultimately grounded on the grace of God and even produced by means of His grace.

A Moment vs. a Lifetime

A third biblical distinction between salvation and rewards is that salvation is received in response to faith at a *moment in time* whereas rewards are given in response to faithfulness *over one's lifetime* as a believer. The Lord Jesus testified, "Most assuredly, I say to you, he who hears My word and believes in Him who sent Me has everlasting life, and shall not come into judgment, but has passed from death into life" (John 5:24). Christ makes it clear in this verse that the believer receives eternal life at a point in time. This is highlighted by the three contrasting tenses of salvation in this verse: (1) "he who believes in Me has [*echei*] everlasting life" refers to the *present* possession of salvation; (2) "shall not come into judgment" promises *future* salvation; and (3) "has passed [*metabebēken*] from death to life" refers to *past* salvation.[14] At any point in his life, an unregenerate person may believe in Christ and pass from spiritual death and separation from God to eternal life and reconciliation with Him. This may occur at any point in a person's life, whether he or she is ten years old, forty, or one hundred. By contrast, all believers will have their works judged at the same moment in time—after this life at the Judgment Seat of Christ. While regeneration occurs at a point in time in response to simple faith in Christ and is described in Scripture as a birth (John 3:3-8), rewards will be given in response to the believer's faithfulness over the course of his or her Christian life, which is described as a race that must be finished in order to receive the prize (1 Cor. 9:24-27; Phil. 3:12-14; 2 Tim. 4:6-8; Heb. 12:1-2).

This distinction between salvation and rewards can also be observed in Paul's use of terms relating to "righteousness." At the end of Paul's life, he declared in 2 Timothy 4:7-8, "I have fought the good fight, I have finished the race, I have kept the faith. Finally, there is laid up for me the crown of righteousness, which the Lord, the righteous Judge, will give to me on that Day, and not to me only but also to all who have loved His appearing." The crown of righteousness (*dikaiosynēs*) was laid up for Paul to receive *in the future* (on the day of Christ's coming for His church) because he had kept the faith. By contrast, Paul possessed in his *earthly lifetime* the gift of God's imputed righteousness (Rom. 5:17), not because he kept the faith, but because he believed in Christ at a point in time and was justified, "Therefore, having been justified [*dikaiōthentes*] by faith, we have peace with God through our Lord Jesus Christ" (Rom. 5:1). Since the crown of righteousness and the gift of imputed righteousness are not the same, neither are rewards and salvation. Rewards are a *coronation* from God in the future for the faithfulness and perseverance of the believer who has lived a practically righteous life, and justification is a *declaration* by God of judicial righteousness in this lifetime for the one who at one time placed his or her faith in Christ.

---

14. *Metabebēken* is the perfect-tense, active-voice, indicative-mood form of the verb, *metabainō*. Being in the perfect tense and indicative mood, this verb form in the context indicates that the believer has passed out of death and into life (in the past) with the result that the believer remains in the present out of the realm of death and in the sphere of life (cf. Eph. 2:8).

Never Lost vs. Able to Be Lost

A fourth major distinction between salvation and rewards is that salvation *can never be lost* since believers are eternally secure, but rewards *can be lost*. Christ promised all believers in John 10:28 that they cannot lose their salvation since they are eternally secure: "I give them eternal life, and they shall never perish." Though the gift of eternal life can never be lost, believers may still lose rewards at the Judgment Seat of Christ, as Paul wrote to the Corinthians, "If anyone's work is burned, he will suffer loss; but he himself will be saved, yet so as through fire" (1 Cor. 3:15). If the believer's work is burned up at the Bema, he will still be saved but will experience the loss of a greater reward that he could have had. This must be a real possibility, otherwise Paul could never exhort the Colossian Christians, "Let no one cheat you of your reward" (Col. 2:18). Nor could John admonish, "Look to yourselves, that we do not lose those things we worked for, but that we may receive a full reward" (2 John 8). Nor could the Lord Jesus Himself declare, "Behold, I am coming quickly! Hold fast what you have, that no one may take your crown" (Rev. 3:11). The contrast is evident. Rewards can definitely be lost because they depend on the believer's faithfulness in his walk with the Lord over his lifetime, but salvation can never be lost because it depends solely on Christ's faithfulness and finished work.

Acceptance vs. Approval

A fifth biblical distinction between salvation and rewards is that salvation is a matter of being fully *accepted* by God, but rewards are a matter of God's *approval*. There is a difference between being accepted by God and having His approval. A father may love and accept his son but not approve of his son's foolish and sinful behavior. In this respect, every believer has been fully accepted by God as His own dear child on the basis of His grace and Christ's finished work (Eph. 1:6); but not all believers live in a manner that consistently pleases the Lord. The Corinthians were "saints" and "sanctified in Christ Jesus" (1 Cor. 1:2) in terms of their spiritual position; yet in terms of their condition, they were characteristically "carnal" because they persisted in walking according to their sinful nature rather than the Holy Spirit (1 Cor. 2:14–3:4). Though accepted in Christ, the Corinthians did not have God's approval. Paul wrote to them later saying, "Therefore we make it our aim, whether present or absent, to be well pleasing to Him. For we must all appear before the judgment seat of Christ" (2 Cor. 5:9-10a). Only one who is a believer can please the Lord and earn a reward by a walk of faith (2 Cor. 5:7), as Hebrews 11:6 says that "without faith it is impossible to please Him, for he who comes to God must believe that He is, and that He is a rewarder of those who diligently seek Him." This also means that an unbeliever, by his unbelief, cannot please God (Rom. 8:8). The unbeliever is in need of God's salvation in order to be accepted by Him; but the believer is in need of walking by faith, resulting in Christ-honoring works, that he may please God now in practical sanctification and that his works may be approved at the Bema.

Destiny vs. Privilege and Function

A sixth key distinction between salvation and rewards is that salvation determines a person's eternal *destiny*—the eternal Kingdom rather than the Lake of Fire; whereas rewards determine the believer's *privilege* and *function* in that kingdom. While unbelievers will be separated from God forever in the Lake of Fire (Rev. 20:11-15; 21:8; 22:15), believers in Christ are born again (John 3:3-5) and will enter the coming Kingdom (Matt. 5:20; 7:21; 18:3; 19:23-24; 21:31-32; Rev. 21:27), which begins with the Millennium and continues into the eternal state (Dan. 7:13-14, 18, 26-27). Entering the Kingdom of God is a privilege only for the saved (Matt. 19:25; Mark 10:23-27). Though all who possess salvation will enter the Kingdom, not all will enter it "abundantly" (*plousiōs*) or richly (2 Peter 1:11). According to 2 Peter 1:5, believers who "add" (*epichorēgēsate*) or supply in their faith the positive character traits listed in verses 5-7 will also be "supplied" (*epichorēgēthēsetai*)[15] an entrance by God "abundantly" into His eternal kingdom (v. 11). Faith alone results in entrance into the Kingdom,

---

15. While the verb *epichorēgeō* generally means to provide, furnish, or supply, "it is well to explore the possibility of connection with the Greco-Roman cultural background of generous public service that finds expression in the *chorēg-* family" (Bauer, Arndt, Gingrich, and Danker, *A Greek-English Lexicon of the New Testament and Other Early Christian Literature*, 386-87). The term may indeed have a "generous" connotation (J. H. Moulton and G. Milligan, *Vocabulary of the Greek Testament* [reprint, Peabody, MA: Hendrickson, 1997], 251), since the root word from which *epichorēgeō* derived (*chorēgeō*) originally meant "to bear the expense of a chorus, which was done by a person selected by the state, who was obliged to defray all the expenses of training and maintenance" for the chorus in the Greek tragedies (Marvin R. Vincent, *Word Studies in the New Testament*, 4 vols. [reprint, Peabody, MA: Hendrickson, n.d.], 1:679). The rich entrance promised to faithful believers in 2 Peter 1:11 "will be the generous provision of God" (D. Edmond Hiebert, *Second Peter and Jude: An Expositional Commentary* [Greenville, SC: Unusual Publications, 1989], 61).

but adding to one's faith will result in an entrance coupled with great reward. All believers one day will graduate to heaven, but some will graduate with honors.

Though all believers will reign with Christ in the Kingdom (Rev. 2:26-27; 20:4, 6; 22:5), one's faithfulness as a servant of Christ in this earthly life will determine the degree of reward and privileged service in the Kingdom. This is the meaning of the parable of the talents in Matthew 25 and the parable of the minas in Luke 19. Though these passages apply directly to Israel, they are true in principle even for the Church. In each parable, Christ's servants are rewarded with greater or lesser positions of authority and service in the coming Kingdom. To the one who was given five talents and gained five more, Christ says, "Well done, good and faithful servant; you were faithful over a few things, I will make you ruler over many things. Enter into the joy of your lord" (Matt. 25:21). Christ promises the same for the servant with two talents: "I will make you ruler over many things" (v. 23). Likewise in the parable of the minas, Christ says to His servants, "Have authority over ten cities" (Luke 19:17) and "You also be over five cities" (v. 19).

No Degrees vs. Degrees

A final major distinction between salvation and rewards is that eternal salvation is the *same* for all believers, but there will be varying *degrees* of reward depending on each believer's faithfulness. According to Scripture, it is possible for a believer to miss out on a "full reward" (Ruth 2:12; 2 John 8). Since it is possible to receive less than a full reward, there must necessarily be degrees of reward among the saved, even as there will be varying degrees of punishment among the lost.[16] By contrast, Scripture never speaks of different levels of regeneration, justification, reconciliation, or imputation. Can a believer be any more born-again than he currently is? Can he become more reconciled to God or justified in God's sight than he already is?

---

16. Christ warned the hardened, unbelieving generation of His day who witnessed His miracles and heard His teaching but rejected Him as Israel's messiah, "And you, Capernaum, who are exalted to heaven, will be brought down to Hades; for if the mighty works which were done in you had been done in Sodom, it would have remained until this day. But I say to you that it shall be more tolerable for the land of Sodom in the day of judgment than for you" (Matt. 11:23-24). There will be degrees of punishment among unbelievers in eternity based on the degree to which each one rejected the light he had. Similarly, there will be degrees of positive reward based on faithfulness to God's will and the amount of spiritual light each person possessed.

Every Church-age believer, whether he is the most wretched saint or the most illustrious one, has the same eternal salvation in Christ. This truth is summarized in the great promise of Ephesians 1:3, "Blessed be the God and Father of our Lord Jesus Christ, who has blessed us with every spiritual blessing in the heavenly places in Christ." If believers already possess "every" spiritual blessing in Christ, what further positional salvation-blessings can be gained? Believers are "complete in Him" (Col. 2:10). If Christ is the believer's life (Col. 3:4), and He is unending, perfect life, then how can the believer have any more divine life than he already possesses in Christ? Similarly, if Christ is the believer's righteousness (Jer. 23:6; 1 Cor. 1:30), and He is already perfect, infinite righteousness, then how can the believer be declared any more righteous before God than he already is in Christ?

Though believers cannot change their already perfect salvation, the prospect of receiving a greater degree of reward does provide a tremendous incentive to lead a Christ-honoring life. Throughout history, believers have faced intense persecution and pressure to compromise; but the promise of a potentially greater reward has encouraged them to persevere in faithfulness. This may be the meaning of Hebrews 11:35, which recalls how believers of the past "were tortured, not accepting deliverance, that they might obtain a *better* resurrection." Since believers will be "repaid" for their faithfulness to Christ at the resurrection of the righteous (Luke 14:14), believers can make that day "better" by persevering in faithfulness to God's will.[17] As mentioned previously, some Reformed theologians, such as Blomberg, teach that eternal life is a reward and that there will be no degrees of reward among believers since all will possess eternal life equally.[18] But this effectively negates a powerful biblical incentive to serve Christ and replaces it with the unscriptural motivation of seeking to earn entrance into the Kingdom by one's faithfulness and good works rather than through faith alone in Christ's finished work.

Conclusion

The seven biblical distinctions covered in this chapter demonstrate that there is a definite distinction in God's Word between eternal

---

17. Robert G. Gromacki, *Stand Bold in Grace: An Exposition of Hebrews* (The Woodlands, TX: Kress Christian Publications, 2002), 194; Merrill C. Tenney, *The Reality of the Resurrection* (Chicago: Moody, 1972), 84-85.

18. Blomberg, "Degrees of Reward in the Kingdom of Heaven?" 159.

salvation and rewards. In no way can eternal life be regarded as a reward without creating a contradiction and turning the condition of salvation from faith into faithfulness and works. The biblical condition for salvation is simply to trust in the finished work of Another, Jesus Christ, who persevered to the end in sacrifice for us. Salvation is not a matter of us persevering to the end in sacrifice for Him.

Chapter 7

What Other Biblical Distinctions Clarify Perseverance?

Muddy waters—they're not much good for drinking, bathing, baptisms, washing clothes, or just about any other human function. As human beings, we like our water clean—crystal clean! Yet for some reason many professing Christians seem to tolerate, or even prefer, muddy waters when it comes to theology. Murky theology in the area of perseverance has clouded over several clear and crucial distinctions in the Bible that help resolve the question of whether faith must endure for salvation to be sure.

This chapter is foundational for many of the concepts and passages covered in subsequent chapters. It provides a good dose of Clorox to the muddy waters of perseverance theology as it sets forth several key distinctions in Scripture that have a direct bearing on the topic of perseverance versus preservation. These biblical distinctions include:

- justification vs. sanctification vs. glorification

- eternal salvation vs. discipleship

- being in the family of God vs. having fellowship with God

- the natural man vs. the spiritual man vs. the carnal man

- divine discipline for believers vs. eternal condemnation for unbelievers

- being a professor of salvation vs. a possessor of salvation

Three Tenses of Salvation

The Bible uses the words "save" or "salvation" in reference to three phases or tenses of deliverance from sin and its consequences— past, present, and future deliverance. But when these three distinct phases of salvation get mixed together, not only are passages on each phase of salvation misinterpreted, but the gospel of eternal salvation becomes distorted from a message of God's grace and Christ's finished work to one of ongoing effort and human works. For example, in explaining his perspective on pastoral ministry, notice how John Piper interprets the word "save" in 1 Timothy 4:16 as a reference to future, eternal salvation rather than present sanctification-salvation:

> I used to say my goal as a pastor-teacher was to glorify God by the salvation of sinners and the upbuilding of the body of Christ—winning the lost and edifying the saints. But there was an erroneous assumption behind this goal. The assumption was that my only role in saving people was to preach the gospel to the lost and pray for them. Then after they were converted and joined the church, my instrumentality in their salvation was over, and I was simply God's agent in their relative degree of edification or sanctification.
>
> My error was in thinking that the salvation of only the lost depended on my preaching but not the salvation of the church.
>
> For a time, therefore, it seemed strange to me that the Puritan pastors preached to their flocks as though the people's eternal lives depended on it. . . .
>
> The Puritans believed that without perseverance in the obedience of faith the result would be eternal destruction, not lesser sanctification. Therefore, since preaching and the pastoral ministry in general are a great means to the saints' perseverance, the goal of a pastor is not merely to edify the saints but to *save* the saints. What is at stake on Sunday morning is not merely the upbuilding of the church but its eternal salvation.
>
> But it was not Sibbes and Baxter and Boston and Edwards and Spurgeon who caused me to change my goal. It was the apostle Paul. He wrote to Timothy, "Keep a close watch on yourself and on the teaching. Persist in this, for by so doing you will save both yourself and your hearers" (1 Tim. 4:16).[1]

---

1. John Piper, *Brothers, We Are Not Professionals: A Plea to Pastors for Radical Min-*

As this quote from Piper reveals, there is much at stake in rightly dividing the Word of truth (2 Tim. 2:15) when it comes to the three tenses of salvation. Does your justification as a believer in Christ guarantee your practical sanctification? Must you as a believer in Christ experience a daily, progressive sanctification in order to be guaranteed salvation from the wrath of God? Does the fact of your future glorification and final salvation depend on your walk with Christ and an earthly life of sanctification?

The answer to each of these questions is a resounding "Yes!" according to proponents of the centuries-old Calvinist doctrine of the perseverance of the saints. This unscriptural doctrine teaches that without a general pattern of progressive sanctification in your Christian life you will not be saved from hell.[2] This traditional doctrine of Calvinism is in contrast to the scriptural doctrine of the three tenses of salvation and the eternal security of the believer.

Justification

The Bible teaches that a lost sinner who places his faith in the Lord Jesus Christ alone for eternal salvation is instantaneously saved by God's grace from the *penalty of sin,* namely, eternal separation from God in hell. This is the *past tense* of salvation. It occurs at a *point* in time. It is conditioned on a single *step* of faith, and it results in a person being born again (regeneration), eternally set apart to God in Christ (positional sanctification), and *declared judicially righteous* in the eyes of God (justification). God makes our justification *permanent* from the moment we first believe. This first tense or phase of salvation is found in the following passages: Luke 7:48-50; 18:9-14; John 3:3-16; 5:24; Acts 13:38-39; Romans 3:24-28; 4:1-8; 5:1, 9a, 10a; 8:30; Ephesians 2:5, 8; 2 Thessalonians 2:13-14; 2 Timothy 1:9; Titus 2:11; 3:5-7; Hebrews 10:14; and 1 John 3:1-2a.

---

istry (Nashville: Broadman & Holman, 2002), 105-106.

2. Berkhof describes his view as "a doctrine which assures the believer of a perseverance in holiness" with "the certainty of success in the active striving for sanctification" (Louis Berkhof, *Systematic Theology* [Grand Rapids: Eerdmans, 1991], 548). See also, Edwin Palmer, *The Five Points of Calvinism,* Revised Edition (Grand Rapids: Baker, 1980), 76-79; Curt Daniel, *Biblical Calvinism* (Springfield, IL: Reformed Bible Church, n.d.), 9-10; John Gerstner, *Wrongly Dividing the Word of Truth* (Brentwood, TN: Wolgemuth & Hyatt, 1991), 142-47.

Sanctification

Besides being saved from a hell we deserve to a heaven we don't, God also wants to save and transform us internally before we get to heaven. The Lord desires all believers to be saved by His grace from the *power of sin* and its damaging effects in each person's life. This is the *present tense* of salvation. This occurs at *points* of time as the child of God takes *steps* of faith and walks in daily dependence upon the Lord, resulting in the believer *becoming practically righteous* in the eyes of God and other people (practical sanctification). The second tense or phase of salvation is described in many passages of Scripture, including the following: Matthew 16:24-27; John 8:32; 17:17; Romans 6:1-13; 7:24–8:4; Philippians 2:12; 1 Thessalonians 4:3-7; 1 Timothy 4:16; 6:12, 19; Titus 2:12; Hebrews 10:39; James 1:21; 2:14; 4:12; 5:19-20; and 1 John 3:3.

God makes this practical sanctification *possible* for every believer, but it is not guaranteed, contrary to Calvinism's doctrine of the perseverance of the saints. This is why Romans 8:29-30 describes five unbreakable links in God's chain of salvation, including justification and glorification, but conspicuously there is no mention of practical sanctification. Verse 30 states, "Moreover whom He predestined, these He also called; whom He called, these He also justified; and whom He justified, these He also glorified."

Thus, the presence of good works in the Christian's life should not be considered the necessary evidence of regeneration and justification before God. Instead, good works are the necessary evidence of practical sanctification and justification in the sight of men as the believer walks by faith. The believer who lacks good works in his Christian life has no basis to claim he is walking in the light, though he was genuinely born again and justified in God's sight. The relationship of good works to justification and sanctification is a crucial point explained more thoroughly in the next chapter.

Glorification

Finally, God promises that all who have been justified will also be saved by His grace from the *presence of sin* one day. This is the *future tense* or phase of salvation. It will occur at a *point* in time in the future, either at the moment of death for a believer who dies before the Rapture or at the time of the Rapture when living believers are caught up to meet the Lord in the air and return to heaven (John 14:1-3; 1 Thess.

4:13-18). This future and final salvation is conditioned only on the *step* of faith that occurred at justification, not the believer's walk of faith in the Christian life. Glorification results in the child of God being made *perfectly righteous* (perfect sanctification), in which he no longer possesses a sinful nature, but is permanently and completely transformed into Christ's likeness in body, soul, and spirit, so that he is no longer capable of sinning. This is *promised* to every believer from the moment of initial faith in Christ. This tense or phase of salvation is described in many passages, such as the following: Romans 5:9b, 10b; 8:17-23, 30; 13:11; 1 Corinthians 3:15; 5:5; 1 Thessalonians 1:10; 5:8-9, 23-24; Titus 2:13; Hebrews 9:28; 1 Peter 1:5; 1 John 3:2b; and Revelation 21:3-4.

The distinction between all three tenses or phases of salvation is illustrated in the table below.

Past Salvation	Present Salvation	Future Salvation
Salvation from the *Penalty of Sin* (in hell)	Salvation from the *Power of Sin* (in one's earthly life)	Salvation from the *Presence of Sin* (in heaven)
Justification	Sanctification	Glorification
Point of Time When a person trusts Christ for eternal salvation	*Process of Time* as the believer walks by faith and the Holy Spirit's power	*Point of Time* either at a believer's death or the Rapture
By grace alone, through faith alone, in Christ alone, *apart from works*	By grace alone, through faith alone, *resulting in good works*	By grace alone, through one's initial faith alone at justification

Three Tenses of Sanctification

Among Christians it is common to speak of "sanctification" only in terms of the present process of salvation from sin's power in the believer's daily Christian life. However, the words "sanctify" (*hagiazō*) and "sanctification" (*hagiasmos*) are used in Scripture of all three phases of salvation, just like the words "save" and "salvation." Biblically, sanctification refers to something that is set apart unto God for His own special purposes. The believer in Christ is set apart to God in three phases or tenses, just like the three tenses of salvation.

First, at the very moment of regeneration and justification, every believer has a complete, permanent, *positional* sanctification, in which the believer is placed positionally "in Christ" by the once-for-all baptizing work of the Holy Spirit (1 Cor. 12:12-13). As a result, the believer is set apart unto God in the measure in which Christ is set apart to God the Father (Acts 20:32, 26:18; 1 Cor. 1:30; 2 Thess. 2:13; Heb. 10:10, 14, 29; 1 Peter 1:2) and blessed with all spiritual blessings in the heavenly places in Christ (Eph. 1:3). Based on this positional sanctification, every believer in Christ, whether persistently carnal or spiritual, is constituted a "saint" (*hagios*) before God—a "set-apart one" (Rom. 1:7; 1 Cor. 1:2; 2 Cor. 1:1; Eph. 1:1; Phil. 1:1). This first tense of sanctification is variously referred to as the believer's *position* in Christ, *union* with Christ, or *standing* in Christ.

Second, in distinction to positional sanctification is the believer's *practical* sanctification, also known as the believer's spiritual *condition* in life, *communion* with God, or spiritual *state*. Following positional sanctification, God desires the believer's practical sanctification, in which the saint grows in grace and becomes increasingly set apart from sin's destructive power and influence in his life as he is internally changed by the unhindered power of the Holy Spirit throughout his earthly life (John 17:17; 2 Cor. 3:18, 7:1; 1 Thess. 4:3-7; 2 Tim. 2:21). Therefore, while the position, union, or standing of the believer is perfect and unchanging in God's sight, his present earthly condition, communion, or state varies depending on the consistency of his experiential, daily walk with the Lord (1 Cor. 1:2; 3:1-4; 6:11).

Third, every child of God will one day experience a *perfect* sanctification, when he shall be perfectly and permanently set apart from sin to the Lord in his condition, so that his spiritual condition will finally match his position in Christ. This will occur only when he meets the Lord either at death or the Rapture and is free from the presence of his indwelling sinful nature (1 Thess. 5:23-24; 1 John 3:1-3).

Recognizing the biblical distinction between these three phases of salvation and sanctification is essential in guarding the gospel of God's saving grace and clarifying the condition for eternal salvation. Though all three tenses are accomplished solely by God's grace through faith in Christ, the presence or absence of good works in the believer's life is a barometer of practical sanctification before men, not justification before God. Good works only indicate whether a believer is truly walking by faith and being practically sanctified by the Holy Spirit's inner working. When second-tense salvation passages are interpreted as first-tense salvation passages, good works become the necessary evidence of a person's justification before God. As a result, good works become a requirement for eternal life in addition to faith. However, the possession of eternal life is not conditioned on the *believer's imperfect walk* of faith in holiness and good works done for Jesus Christ; rather it is conditioned solely on faith in *Jesus Christ's perfect work* for the believer.[3]

Eternal Salvation vs. Discipleship

A second key distinction in Scripture that affects one's understanding of perseverance versus preservation is the distinction between eternal salvation and discipleship. Since discipleship involves sacrifice, personal cost, and a continuous pattern of life, it is easy to see why Reformed theology's doctrine of perseverance views discipleship as a requirement for eternal salvation. According to this theology, if someone fails to persevere as a disciple or follower of Christ, then that simply proves he or she was never really born again. Thus, John MacArthur proclaims,

> Let me say again unequivocally that Jesus' summons to deny self and follow Him was an invitation to salvation, not an offer of a "higher life," or a second step of faith following salvation. The contemporary teaching that separates discipleship from salvation springs from ideas that are foreign to Scripture. Every Christian is a disciple.[4]

---

3. For further clarification on the three tenses of salvation, see Dennis M. Rokser, *Salvation in Three Time Zones: Do You Understand the Three Tenses of Salvation?* (Duluth, MN: Grace Gospel Press, 2013).

4. John F. MacArthur, Jr., *The Gospel According to Jesus* (Grand Rapids: Zondervan, 1988), 196.

But is this really true? Are all believers in Christ also disciples of Christ? What does the Bible teach? The word "disciple" (*mathētēs*) occurs 264 times in the New Testament, but only in the Gospels and Acts, and it simply means "a learner or follower." The Pharisees claimed to be followers of Moses (John 9:38); and they had their own disciples who followed their teaching (Matt. 22:15-16), as did John the Baptist with his disciples (Matt. 9:14). In addition, Jesus Christ chose twelve men to be his closest followers (Matt. 10:2; Luke 6:13), who became known as "the twelve disciples" (Matt. 20:17). Among these twelve was an unbeliever (John 6:60-71), Judas Iscariot (Matt. 26:14, 47), who was never born again (John 13:10-11; 17:12). This fact shows that in Scripture not every disciple is considered to be a believer, which means that being a believer and being a disciple are *not* synonymous concepts. According to the Bible, a true disciple is someone who not only believes in Christ but also continues or abides in His Word (John 8:30-31). This distinction between possessing eternal life and being a disciple of Christ is illustrated in the following table.

Eternal Life	Discipleship
Coming to Christ	Following after Christ
Requires Christ's cross	Requires the believer's cross
Condition is initial faith in Christ	Condition is abiding in Christ
Occurs at a point in time	Occurs as a process in time
Is finished	Is not finished
Free to believers	Costly to believers
What God gives believers	What believers give God
Non-meritorious	Merits a reward

There are at least eight major distinctions between possessing eternal life as a believer in Christ versus following Him as a disciple. First, there is a distinction between coming *to* Christ for salvation and coming *after* Christ in terms of following Him as a disciple. This distinction can be observed in Luke 14:25-27, which says:

> 25 Now great multitudes went with Him. And He turned and said to them, 26 "If anyone comes to Me and does not hate his father and mother, wife and children, brothers and sisters, yes, and his own life also, he cannot be My disciple. 27 And whoever does not bear his cross and come after Me cannot be My disciple."

Verses 26-27 set forth two conditions for being Christ's disciple. Notice, Jesus didn't merely say, "If anyone comes to Me" but "If anyone comes to Me and . . .". The first condition to be a disciple is that a person must "come to (*pros*)" Christ by faith for salvation. Second, that person must then love Him more than anyone else and so "come after (*opisō*)" Him in terms of following Him. The way a person comes "to" Christ is simply by faith, as Jesus Himself taught in John 6:35, "I am the bread of life. He who comes to Me shall never hunger, and he who believes in Me shall never thirst." Since never hungering or thirsting are parallel concepts, so are coming to Christ and believing in Him. A person comes "to" Christ by believing in Him. But a person comes "after" Christ by following Him as His disciple.

Both of these concepts can be observed in Matthew 11:28-30, where Christ says, "Come to Me, all you who labor and are heavy laden, and I will give you rest. Take My yoke upon you and learn from Me, for I am gentle and lowly in heart, and you will find rest for your souls. For My yoke is easy and My burden is light." Eternal life is obtained when one ceases to labor and *comes to* Christ by faith in Him and His finished work alone. But Christ also wants believers to *learn* from Him as part of following Him in discipleship.

Besides the distinction between coming "to" Christ versus coming "after" Him, a second distinction between eternal life and discipleship can be seen by the reference to the "cross" in Luke 14:27. There Jesus says, "And whoever does not bear his cross and come after Me cannot be My disciple." The issue in eternal salvation is strictly what Christ accomplished on *His cross* and believing that "message of the cross" (1 Cor. 1:17-18); but the issue in discipleship is the *believer's cross* (Luke 14:27). God does not grant salvation by mingling the blood of our sacrifice with that of His Son. The good works of the believer cannot be added to Christ's finished work on the cross to make a person acceptable to God (John 19:30). Instead, God's salvation formula is simply 3 nails + 1 cross = 4-given!

When people fail to grasp or accept this truth, the gospel is altered from a message about God's saving grace offered freely on the basis of *Christ's* sacrificial death to a message about *the believer's* sacrifice and good works that must be performed as part of daily discipleship. For example, while claiming that Jesus' summons to deny self and follow Him is an "invitation to salvation," John MacArthur then describes discipleship (i.e., salvation) in terms of the believer's sacrifice:

> When Jesus said, "take up your cross" to them, they thought of a cruel instrument of torture and death. . . . They understood He was calling them to die for Him. They knew He was asking them to make the ultimate sacrifice, to surrender to Him as Lord in every sense.[5]

MacArthur concludes his chapter on the cost of discipleship, saying,

> The idea of daily self-denial does not jibe with the contemporary supposition that believing in Jesus is a momentary decision. A true believer is one who signs up for life. . . faith is not an experiment, but a lifelong commitment. It means taking up the cross daily, giving all for Christ each day with no reservations, no uncertainty, no hesitation. . . . A genuine believer *knows* he is going ahead with Christ until death. Having put his hand to the plow, he will not look back (Luke 9:62). That is how it is when you sign up to follow Jesus Christ. That is the stuff of true discipleship.[6]

But if being a disciple is synonymous with being saved, and self-sacrifice is necessary to be a disciple, then how is salvation not by self-sacrifice? This is not the gospel of grace but another gospel—a gospel of good works for salvation.

A third distinction between the possession of eternal life and being Christ's disciple is the condition for each. The condition to receive eternal life is simply to *believe* in Christ (John 3:16); whereas the condition for being a true disciple of Christ is to *abide* or *continue*

---

5. MacArthur, *Gospel According to Jesus*, 201.
6. Ibid., 202.

in His Word (John 15:7-8). In John 6:47, the Lord Jesus states that the condition for eternal life is simply to believe in Him: "Most assuredly, I say to you, he who believes in Me has everlasting life." However, two chapters later in John's Gospel, believing and abiding are distinguished, as it says in John 8:30-32, "As He spoke these words, many believed in Him. Then Jesus said to those Jews who believed Him, 'If you abide in My word, you are My disciples indeed. And you shall know the truth, and the truth shall make you free.'" According to these verses, believing is not the same as abiding or continuing in Christ's Word.

A fourth distinction between receiving eternal life and being a disciple of Christ is the timing of each. Receiving eternal life occurs at a *point in time*; whereas being a disciple is a *process over time*. In John 5:24, Jesus explains that eternal life is received at a point in time: "Most assuredly, I say to you, he who hears My word and believes in Him who sent Me has everlasting life, and shall not come into judgment, but has passed from death into life." The new birth from death into life occurs at a point in time. But being a disciple is a daily process, as the Lord also says in Luke 9:23, "If anyone desires to come after Me, let him deny himself, and take up his cross daily, and follow Me." These verses show that believers are born, but disciples are made over time.

A fifth distinction between eternal salvation and discipleship is similar to the previous one. While receiving eternal life is a completed, *finished* event, daily discipleship is *unfinished* in this lifetime. With each successive person who comes to faith in Christ, a soul is set apart unto God for all eternity as a saint with a new spiritual position in Christ. Hebrews 10:14 states, "For by one offering He has perfected forever those who are being sanctified." Thus the perfect, completed work of new birth and justification before God is distinct from the unfinished business of daily discipleship. This can be seen in the Lord's explanation of the conditions for discipleship in Luke 14:28-30:

> 28 For which of you, intending to build a tower, does not sit down first and count the cost, whether he has enough to finish it—29 lest, after he has laid the foundation, and is not able to finish, all who see it begin to mock him, 30 saying, "This man began to build and was not able to finish."

While eternal salvation is "finished" from the moment a person passes from death into life (John 5:24) because it rests solely upon

Christ's finished sacrifice (John 19:30), discipleship is an unfinished process that involves the believer's own sacrifice throughout his or her Christian life.

A sixth contrast between eternal life and discipleship is that eternal life is *free* to the believer but discipleship is *costly*. Consistent with Paul's declaration that believers are "justified freely by His grace" (Rom. 3:24) is the Bible's final evangelistic invitation in Revelation 22:17: "And the Spirit and the bride say, 'Come!' And let him who hears say, 'Come!' And let him who thirsts come. Whoever desires, let him take the water of life freely." This is not an invitation to those who are already believers, but an invitation to thirsty unbelievers to come to Jesus Christ by faith to receive eternal life and never thirst again (John 4:13-14; 6:35; 7:37-39). As these passages indicate, eternal life is free to the believer (Rom. 6:23). Why? Because it was already paid in full by the Giver (Rom. 8:32). Consequently, God invites the lost to come to Him for eternal salvation "without money and without price" (Isa. 55:1). But in contrast, the Lord's invitation to discipleship cautions believers to "count the cost" (Luke 14:28). Clearly, a sinner who comes to Christ by faith may freely receive eternal life, but following after Him as a disciple may be costly.

Related to this is a seventh distinction. Eternal salvation is what *God gives to believers*, but discipleship is what believers *give up for God*. The direction of giving is exactly the opposite. Ephesians 2:8-9 declares God's grace-gift to believers: "For by grace you have been saved through faith, and that not of yourselves; it is *the gift of God*, not of works, lest anyone should boast." But in Luke 14:33 the Lord Jesus describes what believers must give up to be His disciples: "whoever of you does not forsake all that he has cannot be My disciple."

These clear, biblical distinctions are often obscured and contradicted by those teaching that saints must persevere to be eternally saved. Notice how MacArthur speaks of saving faith in terms of cost and sacrifice to the believer:

> But they had counted the cost, and they knew that what they bought was worthy of the ultimate investment. Again, that is a perfect picture of saving faith. Someone who truly believes in Christ does not hedge bets. Knowing the cost of discipleship, the true believer signs up and gives everything for Christ. . . . That is the kind of totally committed response the Lord Jesus called for. A desire for Him at any cost. Absolute surrender. A full exchange of self for the Savior. It is the

only response that will open the gates of the kingdom. Seen through the eyes of this world, it is as high a price as anyone can pay. But from a kingdom perspective, it is really no sacrifice at all.[7]

Thus in a sense we pay the ultimate price for salvation when our sinful self is nailed to a cross. It is a total abandonment of self-will, like the grain of wheat that falls to the ground and dies so that it can bear much fruit (cf. John 12:24). It is an exchange of all that we are for all that Christ is. And it denotes implicit obedience, full surrender to the lordship of Christ. Nothing less can qualify as saving faith.[8]

If "saving faith" truly required the believer's sacrifice, then salvation would not be an unmerited gift but an earned reward. We do not have to pay the price and exchange our obedience and sacrifice in order for God to open the gates of the Kingdom. Only Christ's work and sacrifice can do that. In the great transaction of salvation, the only thing we exchange with God to get to heaven is our sin for Christ's imputed righteousness, as 2 Corinthians 5:21 says, "He made Him who knew no sin to be sin for us, that we might become the righteousness of God in Him."

One final reason why eternal salvation is distinct from discipleship is because salvation is not by good works and *cannot be merited*, but discipleship requires good works that result in an *earned reward*. In the context of teaching His disciples (Matt. 10:1; 11:1) about discipleship and its compensation (10:24-42), the Lord Jesus spoke of loving Him more than one's closest relative (v. 37), taking up one's cross to follow Him (v. 38), and losing one's life for His sake so that one's life will not be wasted (v. 39). In this context, Christ promises a reward for discipleship:

41 He who receives a prophet in the name of a prophet shall receive a prophet's reward. And he who receives a righteous man in the name of a righteous man shall receive a righteous man's reward. 42 And whoever gives one of these little ones only a cup of cold water in the name of a disciple, assuredly, I say to you, he shall by no means lose his reward.

---

7. Ibid., 141.
8. Ibid., 140.

Later in Matthew's Gospel, Jesus announces to His disciples that He must go to Jerusalem, be killed, and be raised from the dead (Matt. 16:21). While Peter protests this plan (vv. 22-23), Jesus tells His disciples that if they "desire to come after" Him, they must deny themselves, take up their crosses, and follow Him (v. 24). If they choose not to do so, their lives will be wasted or lost; but if they give up their lives for Christ's sake, their lives will have eternal significance and be rewarded when Christ returns. In this context, the Lord promises His disciples, "For the Son of Man will come in the glory of His Father with His angels, and then He will reward each according to his works" (v. 27). Giving up or preserving one's life as a disciple does not determine whether someone will spend eternity in heaven or hell, but it will determine one's reward in the coming Kingdom. Salvation from hell to heaven is a gift of God's grace to sinners who believe in Jesus Christ; but discipleship results in a worthwhile life of good works that will be rewarded when Christ returns.

This grace-versus-works distinction between salvation and discipleship is also evident from the fact that discipleship involves being baptized and keeping Christ's commandments, which are clearly good works. But this is not how one is saved: "Not by works of righteousness which we have done, but according to His mercy He saved us" (Titus 3:5). In the Great Commission passage of Matthew 28:18-20, the church is commanded to literally "disciple all nations" (v. 19), by going, baptizing, and teaching believers to observe all that Christ commanded. Being baptized and taught to observe Christ's commandments are essential to genuine discipleship. However, if discipleship is necessary to be saved, as many perseverance advocates claim, and discipleship entails baptism and obedience to the Lord's commandments, then how can we escape the conclusion that salvation is obtained by good works? The Word of God is clear that being a disciple of Christ is *not* equivalent to being a believer in Christ.

Family of God vs. Fellowship with God

Another vital biblical distinction that clarifies perseverance versus preservation is the one between being a child of God in the family of God versus having fellowship with God. At the moment of new birth, a person goes from being a child of God's wrath, dead in trespasses and sins (Eph. 2:1-3), to being a child of God with eternal life simply through faith in God's Son, Jesus Christ. This is demonstrated in the following verses:

11 He came to His own, and His own did not receive Him. 12 But as many as received Him, to them He gave the right to become children of God, to those who believe in His name: 13 who were born, not of blood, nor of the will of the flesh, nor of the will of man, but of God. (John 1:11-13)

For you are all sons of God through faith in Christ Jesus. (Gal. 3:26)

Once a person enters God's family through spiritual birth, that believer never ceases to be God's child since he or she possesses eternal life that can never be lost (John 10:28-30). But just as children in human families do not always obey their parents and enjoy fellowship with them, neither do children of God always obey their heavenly Father and enjoy spiritual fellowship with Him. Fellowship with God is conditioned on the believer's daily walk. First John 1:5-7 states that since God is holy, He requires practical holiness in the believer's walk in order to have fellowship with Him. The believer experiences fellowship with the Lord by abiding in Christ through a walk of yielded dependence on Him to do His will (John 15:4-5). If the believer ceases to walk in fellowship with the Lord by sinning and walking in the flesh, fellowship with the Lord is broken and must be restored through confession or acknowledgement of sin to the Lord. These Christian life truths are described in 1 John 1:3-9, which states:

3 that which we have seen and heard we declare to you, that you also may have fellowship with us; and truly our fellowship is with the Father and with His Son Jesus Christ. 4 And these things we write to you that your joy may be full. 5 This is the message which we have heard from Him and declare to you, that God is light and in Him is no darkness at all. 6 If we say that we have fellowship with Him, and walk in darkness, we lie and do not practice the truth. 7 But if we walk in the light as He is in the light, we have fellowship with one another, and the blood of Jesus Christ His Son cleanses us from all sin. 8 If we say that we have no sin, we deceive ourselves, and the truth is not in us. 9 If we confess our sins, He is faithful and just to forgive us our sins and to cleanse us from all unrighteousness.

Fellowship with the Lord, just like discipleship, is conditional ("if") for the believer. Not all believers consistently walk in fellowship with the Lord or continue in His Word as an abiding disciple. When believers do not walk in the light as He is in the light (1 John 1:7), the result is carnality or a walk in the flesh rather than the Spirit (Gal. 5:16). Consequently, the child of God may lose fellowship with the Lord, but not salvation, since eternal life is secured through Christ's perfect, finished work rather than the believer's imperfect walk and works.

The distinction between having eternal life as God's child in His family forever versus having fellowship with God as His child on a moment-by-moment basis is illustrated in John 13. In John 13:1-11, on the eve of His crucifixion, Christ fulfills the role of a servant by washing the disciples' feet. His conversation with Peter in verses 6-11 illustrates the distinction between new birth and daily forgiveness.

> 6 Then He came to Simon Peter. And Peter said to Him, "Lord, are You washing my feet?" 7 Jesus answered and said to him, "What I am doing you do not understand now, but you will know after this." 8 Peter said to Him, "You shall never wash my feet!" Jesus answered him, "If I do not wash you, you have no part with Me." 9 Simon Peter said to Him, "Lord, not my feet only, but also my hands and my head!" 10 Jesus said to him, "He who is bathed needs only to wash his feet, but is completely clean; and you are clean, but not all of you." 11 For He knew who would betray Him; therefore He said, "You are not all clean."

If Peter would not let the Lord cleanse him from his sins from day to day, he could have no part in ministry for the Lord and fellowship with Him. But Peter did not need the whole bath of regeneration again. He and the rest of the disciples (with the exception of Judas Iscariot) were already clean from the whole bath of regeneration, which is a once-for-all, non-repeatable event. But Peter and the disciples still needed their feet washed routinely, which pictured daily cleansing from the defilement of sin that breaks fellowship with the Lord in the believer's earthly walk. John 13:10 and 1 John 1:3-9 illustrate the critical distinction between being a child of God in the family of God, which is permanent and eternal, versus having fellowship with God, which depends on the believer's daily walk and willingness to acknowledge his sins to God. These passages on the believer's fellowship with the Lord clearly show that it is possible for a genuine believer to be justified, positionally sanctified, and saved for eternity while also being carnal and not experiencing practical sanctification and abiding fellowship with the Lord, which He desires for all believers.[9]

Natural, Spiritual, and Carnal People

Another crucial biblical distinction that clarifies the subject of perseverance is the distinction between three types of people—the natural person, the spiritual person, and the carnal person. These three types of people are mentioned by the apostle Paul in 1 Corinthians 2:14–3:4, where he writes:

> 14 But the natural man does not receive the things of the Spirit of God, for they are foolishness to him; nor can he know them, because they are spiritually discerned. 15 But he who is spiritual judges all things, yet he himself is rightly judged by no one. 16 For "who has known the mind of the Lord that he may instruct Him?" But we have the mind of Christ. 1 And I, brethren, could not speak to you as to spiritual people but as to carnal, as to babes in Christ. 2 I fed you with milk and not with solid food; for until now you were not able to receive it, and even now you are still not able; 3 for you are still carnal. For where there are envy, strife, and divisions among you, are you not carnal and behaving like mere men? 4 For when one says, "I am of Paul," and another, "I am of Apollos," are you not carnal?

In this passage Paul contrasts three types of people. The "natural" (*psychikos*) person is described as someone who perceives life merely through the physical senses and not by faith in revelation that comes from the Holy Spirit (1 Cor. 2:14). This natural or "soulish" (*psychikos*) man is devoid of the Holy Spirit (Jude 19) and therefore is unsaved (Rom. 8:9). The second person is the "spiritual" (*pneumatikos*) individual (1 Cor. 2:15; 3:1), who is not only saved but also

---

9. This is the very purpose for which the epistle of 1 John was written according to 1 John 1:3-4. For further explanation that 1 John was written to provide believers with tests of their fellowship with the Lord rather than tests of whether they possess eternal life, see Dennis M. Rokser, *How to Interpret 1 John: Fresh Insights & Observations to Consider* (Duluth, MN: Grace Gospel Press, 2015).

characterized by the influence of God's Spirit (*pneuma*) in his life. The "spiritual" believer is filled with the Holy Spirit (Eph. 5:18) and able to understand Spirit-given revelation and apply it to life (1 Cor. 2:16–3:1). The third type of person is the "carnal" (*sarkikos/sarkinos*) individual, whose life is characterized by his flesh (*sarx*) or sinful nature. This person is saved and indwelt by the Holy Spirit, but he walks according to his flesh rather than the Spirit (1 Cor. 3:2-4; Gal. 5:16). Since he is not rightly related to the Spirit of God in his life, he has a diminished capacity for understanding and applying the Word of God (1 Cor. 3:2).

The distinctions between the natural, spiritual, and carnal person are summarized in the following table.

Natural	Spiritual	Carnal
Unregenerate	Regenerate	Regenerate
Void of the Spirit	Indwelt and Filled with the Spirit	Indwelt by the Spirit, but not Filled
Walks by senses	Walks by the Spirit	Walks by the flesh
Regards God's Word as foolish	Discerns all things by God's Word	Minimal discernment of God's Word

Based on 1 Corinthians 2:14–3:4, there is a distinction not only between a lost person (natural man) and a saved person but also between two types of saved people—those who are walking according to the Holy Spirit (spiritual) and those who are walking according to their flesh or sinful nature (carnal). The Bible not only teaches that the baptizing ministry of the Holy Spirit gives church-age believers a unique position in Christ (1 Cor. 12:12-13) but also that every believer in this age has a unique capacity to be "spiritual" or Spirit-filled based on the Holy Spirit's universal, permanent indwelling of all believers in the church age.

Throughout the eras covering the Old Testament and the Gospels, up to the day of Pentecost in Acts 2, the Holy Spirit selectively enabled believers for certain ministry, but His presence within them was not permanent, nor guaranteed to all believers (1 Sam. 10:10; 11:6; 16:14; Ps. 51:11; Luke 11:13). For this reason, the Lord Jesus indicated that the Spirit's ministry would change with the advent of the church age. In the Upper Room on the eve of His crucifixion He promised His disciples, "And I will pray the Father, and He will give you another Helper, that He may abide with you forever—the Spirit of truth, whom the world cannot receive, because it neither sees Him nor knows Him; but you know Him, for He dwells with you and will be in you" (John 14:16-17). Though the Holy Spirit had been "with" the disciples, He would soon be "in" them and would "abide" with them "forever."

Now in the church age, the permanent indwelling of the Holy Spirit in every believer (Rom. 8:9; Eph. 1:13-14; 4:30) makes it possible for all believers to fulfill the commands to continuously "walk in the Spirit" (Gal. 5:16) and "be filled by the Spirit" (Eph. 5:18). In marked contrast to the New Testament epistles, Old Testament saints were never given instructions to continuously walk in the Spirit and be filled by Him because not all believers, at all times, could fulfill such commands. Based on the dispensational change in the Spirit's ministry and the new universal, permanent indwelling of every church-age believer, it was only fitting for Paul to expect all of the Corinthians to be "spiritual" rather than "carnal."

The Reality of the Carnal Christian

Many proponents of the perseverance of the saints deny two categories of believers in 1 Corinthians 2–3. They claim that all believers are "spiritual" simply because they are indwelt by the Holy Spirit (Rom. 8:9) and because Paul supposedly includes the Corinthians in his description of spiritual believers in 1 Corinthians 2:16, "But *we* have the mind of Christ."[10] As a result, one author concludes "that in 1 Cor 2:14–3:4 Paul has only two categories in view: natural and

---

10. William W. Combs, "The Disjunction between Justification and Sanctification in Contemporary Evangelical Theology," *Detroit Baptist Seminary Journal* 6 (Fall 2001): 41; and John F. MacArthur, Jr., *Faith Works: The Gospel According to the Apostles* (Dallas: Word, 1993), 126.

spiritual. The carnal Christian is simply a genuine Christian (Spirit-man) temporarily gone astray."[11] MacArthur goes so far as to speak of "the myth of the carnal Christian"[12] and concludes that "Paul was most certainly *not* defining two classes of Christians, or three classes of humanity. . . . according to Paul, *all* Christians are spiritual. As we shall see, Paul also recognized that all believers behave carnally at times. That is what he was rebuking the Corinthians for."[13] These explanations fail to distinguish the fact that while every believer is *indwelt* by the Holy Spirit in the church age, only a spiritual believer is *filled* with the Holy Spirit.

In addition, when Paul writes in 1 Corinthians 2:16 of those who were spiritual, "But we have the mind of Christ," he does not include the majority of the Corinthians in the first-person plural pronoun, "we." Instead, he is speaking of others who were mature. The context dealing with spirituality and maturity extends back to verse 6 where Paul writes, "However, we speak wisdom to those who are mature." Paul does not include the Corinthians in verse 16 as being wise, discerning, and possessing the mind of Christ because in the next verse he rebukes them: "And I, brethren, could not speak to you as to spiritual people but as to carnal, as to babes in Christ" (3:1). Paul viewed the Corinthians generally and collectively as infants, not as mature.

Furthermore, a few verses later he uses "we" in a manner exclusive of the Corinthians: "For we are God's fellow workers; you are God's field, you are God's building" (v. 9). All believers do not automatically possess the mind of Christ simply because they are indwelt by the Holy Spirit, for Paul previously wrote that these Spirit-indwelt Corinthians were not of "the same mind" and "the same judgment" (1 Cor. 1:10). This explains why Paul elsewhere commands believers to have the mind of Christ (Phil. 2:5). Why would he do so if all believers are automatically "spiritual" and have the mind of Christ?

The context of 1 Corinthians as a whole fits better with the idea that Paul was excluding the Corinthians from those discerning believers who had the mind of Christ in 2:16. If Paul was among the wise, spiritual believers of verse 16 but he viewed the carnal Corinthians as unwise and not able to discern all things because of their carnality, then Paul was in a better position to give an accurate assessment

---

11. Combs, "The Disjunction between Justification and Sanctification in Contemporary Evangelical Theology," 41.

12. MacArthur, *Faith Works*, 124.

13. Ibid., 126.

of the Corinthians' carnal state. Conversely, they would not be in a position to judge him and question his apostolic authority, which they were presently doing (4:3; 9:3).

Finally, the explanation by perseverance proponents that all Christians are spiritual but can "temporarily go astray" and "behave carnally at times" does not do justice to the language of 1 Corinthians 3:1-4. Paul does not merely say that they *behaved* carnally, but that they *were* carnal. In verse 3, Paul makes a declarative statement about their condition, not just their deeds: "For you are still carnal [*eti gar sarkikoi este*]." The verb *este*, from *eimi*, is a stative verb expressing state of being rather than an action.[14] The Corinthians were carnal in their state and not merely in their actions. This is why Paul twice asks rhetorically, "Are you not carnal?" (vv. 3-4). If the standard interpretation of these passages offered by perseverance proponents is correct, then Paul should have said, "Are you not spiritual but behaving carnally?"

The Corinthians' condition was so characterized by the flesh that they appeared indistinguishable from unbelievers. The New King James Version reads in verse 3, "Are you not carnal and behaving like mere men?" The word translated "behaving" does not lend support for the perseverance view since the Greek word is *peripateō*, meaning literally "to walk." Thus the New American Standard Bible reads, "Are you not walking like mere men?" This contradicts the teaching of perseverance proponents who claim that a person's salvation is not genuine unless there is a marked change in one's life when compared to unbelievers. For example, John Piper and his church elders write,

> Obedience, evidencing inner renewal from God, is necessary for final salvation. This is not to say that God demands perfection. It is clear from Philippians 3:12, 13 and 1 John 1:8-10 and Matthew 6:12 that the New Testament does not hold out the demand that we be sinlessly perfect in order to be saved. But the New Testament does demand that we be morally changed and walk in newness of life.[15]

---

14. Daniel B. Wallace, *Greek Grammar beyond the Basics* (Grand Rapids: Zondervan, 1995), 531 n. 50.

15. John Piper and the Council of Elders at Bethlehem Baptist Church Staff, "What We Believe About the Five Points of Calvinism" (March 1998). http://www.desiringgod.org/resource-library/articles/what-we-believe-about-the-five-points-of-calvinism#Perseverance (accessed July 14, 2012).

If the Corinthians needed to manifest inner renewal and walk in newness of life to obtain final salvation, then apparently they were eternally doomed. For Paul explicitly states in 1 Corinthians 3:4 that they walked just like the unsaved. Yet, despite looking like the unsaved in their lifestyle, Paul regards the recipients of his letter to be genuine possessors of eternal life rather than mere professors of salvation. The evidence for this conclusion from 1 Corinthians is abundant and overwhelming.

- The Corinthians were called "brethren" twenty times (1 Cor. 1:10, 11, 26; 2:1; 3:1; 4:6; 7:24, 29; 10:1; 11:2, 33; 12:1; 14:6, 20, 26, 39; 15:1, 50, 58; 16:15).

- They were consistently contrasted with "unbelievers" (6:6; 7:13-14; 10:27; 14:22-23; cf. 14:1).

- They were said to have "believed" the gospel (3:5; 15:11).

- They were "called" by God (1:2, 9, 26).

- They were "chosen" in Christ (1:27-28).

- They were said to be "in Christ" (1:30).

- They had been "baptized" into Christ by the Holy Spirit (12:12-13).

- They were "sanctified in Christ" and "saints" (1:2).

- They were considered to be temples of the Holy Spirit individually (6:19) and His temple corporately (3:16).

- They were spiritually deficient in "no gift" of the Spirit (1:7).

- They were "Christ's" own possession (3:23), and they did not belong to themselves (6:19-20).

- They were instructed by Paul to expect instantaneous transformation at the Rapture, when Christ would come again (15:51-52; 11:26).

- They were told by Paul that they would "judge the world" one day (6:2), even angels (6:3), as part of reigning with Christ (4:8; 15:25).

- They were "begotten" or regenerated (4:15).

- They were "washed," "sanctified" (positionally in Christ, 1:2; but not practically, 3:1-4), and "justified" in Christ (6:11).

A more complete description of a congregations' genuine salvation cannot be found anywhere in the New Testament epistles. Yet despite the Corinthians' evident salvation and perfect standing in Christ, their spiritual state or walk with the Lord was deplorable. The epistle of 1 Corinthians is clear that although the Corinthians were genuine saints, sanctified or set apart in their position in Christ, it is equally clear that they were carnal, worldly, and sinful in their overall spiritual state.

- They were judging the apostle Paul (4:3).

- They were "puffed up" with pride (4:6-7, 18; 5:2).

- They were tolerating a known case of a man committing fornication with "his father's wife" (5:1-2).

- They were going "to law against one another" (6:6-7).

- They were doing wrong and cheating fellow believers (6:8).

- They were likely abusing their spiritual liberties (8:12; 10:23-33).

- They were questioning Paul's apostleship and authority (9:3).

- The women were likely being unsubmissive to the headship of their husbands (11:3-17).

- They were selfishly hoarding food and getting drunk at their fellowship meals before the Lord's Supper (11:20-22).

- They were chastened by the Lord to the point of weakness, sickness, and even death because they would not exercise self-judgment (11:30-32).

- They were likely exercising their spiritual gifts in an unloving way for self-edification (13:1–14:1, 4, 20).

- They were claiming "there is no resurrection of the dead" (15:12).

- They did "not have the knowledge of God" (15:34).

The biblical evidence is unmistakable in the case of the Corinthians. With respect to their *position* they were "sanctified in Christ Jesus" and "called saints" (1:2), but with respect to their *practice* they were sinful rather than saintly. Thus, the walk of the Corinthians neither proved nor disproved the validity of their standing since everyone with a position in Christ's body, the universal church, is truly justified and regenerate.

The Reality of Prolonged & Terminal Carnality

Not only were the Corinthians characteristically "carnal" rather than "spiritual," but they had remained in this condition for a period of approximately three to five years. This is the duration of time from Paul's initial evangelization of Corinth to his writing of the epistle.[16] For this reason Paul states twice that they were "still" (eti) in a state of carnality (1 Cor. 3:2-3). This conflicts with the claim that all believers are spiritual but may "behave carnally at times" and "temporarily go astray." Years ago Benjamin B. Warfield, a notorious Reformed theologian from Princeton, wrote a scathing review of Lewis Sperry Chafer's book He That Is Spiritual. In it he criticized Chafer's distinction between the carnal and spiritual Christian.

> You may find Christians at every stage of this process, for it is a process through which all must pass; but you will find none who will not in God's own good time and way pass through every stage of it. There are not two kinds of Christians, although there are Christians at every conceivable stage of advancement towards the one goal to which all are bound and at which all shall arrive.[17]

One wonders after reading this where Warfield would have placed the Corinthians in their "advancement." Not only were some Corinthians not advancing in their sanctification but some were being disciplined by God to the point of physical death because in their carnal state they refused to exercise self-judgment (1 Cor. 11:30-32). God's discipline was incremental, so that many Corinthians were weak, others sick, and many even slept, which was "a euphemism Paul used to describe death for Christians"[18] (1 Cor. 15:6, 51;

---

16. Dates and ranges vary among commentators. Gromacki and MacArthur see a five-year interval (Robert G. Gromacki, New Testament Survey [Grand Rapids: Baker, 1974], 201-2; John MacArthur, Jr., 1 Corinthians, The MacArthur New Testament Commentary [Chicago: Moody, 1984], 71); Carson and Moo conclude it was four years (D. A. Carson and Douglas J. Moo, An Introduction to the New Testament, 2nd ed. [Grand Rapids: Zondervan, 2005], 451); and Thiselton says it was two and a half years to three and a half years (Anthony C. Thiselton, The First Epistle to the Corinthians, New International Greek Testament Commentary [Grand Rapids: Eerdmans, 2000], 32).

17. Benjamin B. Warfield, as quoted in Chafer, He That Is Spiritual, 68 n.

18. Charles C. Bing, Lordship Salvation: A Biblical Evaluation and Response,

1 Thess. 4:13-15). Though God ended the lives of these carnal Christians prematurely, they were not condemned with the world (1 Cor. 11:32) since God chastens His children for their profit (Heb. 12:5-11) but condemns those outside of Christ (John 3:36; 8:24).

The case of the Corinthians does not justify carnality among Christians since sin always has serious consequences. Based on the reality of terminal carnality and the distinction between spiritual and carnal believers, it is clear that genuine believers may not persevere in faith and good works to the end of their lives. Yet they still remain justified and will be glorified by God's grace.

Divine Discipline vs. Eternal Condemnation

Another key distinction in Scripture that intersects with the question of perseverance versus preservation is the distinction between God's discipline of His own disobedient children versus His eternal condemnation of the lost. The example of the carnal Corinthians shows that perseverance in faith and holiness to the very end of a believer's life does not always occur. Instead, 1 Corinthians 11 makes it clear that it is possible to resist God's chastening and correction even up to the point of physical death. When this occurs, the believer is not punished with eternal, spiritual death in hell, but that believer remains a child of God, preserved in Christ by God's grace.

The Corinthian believers were experiencing physical chastening from the Lord as a result of their continued, willful carnality. Earlier in 1 Corinthians 3:2-3, Paul stated that they had a continual pattern of carnality and their manner of life made them appear indistinguishable from the unsaved. In the immediate context of 1 Corinthians 11, these Corinthians were making a mockery of the Lord's Supper through their selfishness and drunkenness (vv. 17-22). Since they refused to examine their own hearts before the Lord and confess their sin to Him, God had to progressively ratchet up His discipline upon these disobedient children of God. Initially, He caused weakness and sickness among them, and then eventually "sleep" (v. 30), which is a New Testament metaphor for physical death (John 11:11-14; 1 Cor. 15:51; 1 Thess. 4:13-17; 5:10). Thus, 1 Corinthians 11:30-32 says,

30 For this reason many are weak and sick among you, and many sleep. 31 For if we would judge ourselves, we would

GraceLife Edition (Burleson, TX: GraceLife Ministries, 1992), 162.

not be judged. 32 But when we are judged, we are chastened
by the Lord, that we may not be condemned with the world.

God was chastening His disobedient children here for the purpose of restoring them to fellowship with Himself. When His efforts
at restoration are met with such constant resistance, and carnal believers refuse to take heed to themselves and confess their sin to God,
He may choose to call them home by an early death. Like a parent
with a disobedient child, He may say in essence, "Since you're doing
Me no earthly good, come home, my child." In such an instance, the
Lord would protect His own reputation and honor while the believer
would lose all opportunity to further glorify the Lord on earth and
earn an eternal reward.

This passage clearly reveals that there is a difference between
God's treatment of disobedient *unbelievers* versus His treatment of
disobedient *believers*. Verse 32 indicates that His own children receive
His *chastening*, but the unsaved children of this world receive *condemnation*. The Holy Spirit testifies that even these carnal, chastened
Corinthians were genuinely saved, even when chastened to the point
of death.

Some might object to this conclusion and interpret the clause
in verse 32, "that we should not be condemned with the world," as
expressing only the possibility of escaping condemnation along with
the world. In such a case, escaping condemnation with the unsaved
would depend on whether the believer receives God's chastening
and repents by judging himself and acknowledging his sin to the
Lord. However, it must be clarified that this clause is not expressing
any uncertainty as to outcome, as though Paul is saying to the Corinthian Christians, "You might or might not still be condemned with
the world, depending on how you respond to God's chastening."
The *hina* + subjunctive clause, "that (*hina*) we may not be condemned
with the world," should be interpreted at least as expressing result,[19]
just as the NIV has it, "so that we will not be condemned with the

---

19. Friedrich Blass, Albert Debrunner, and Robert Walter Funk, *A Greek Gram-
mar of the New Testament and Other Early Christian Literature* (Chicago: University of
Chicago Press, 1961), 198, §391 (5); A. T. Robertson, *A Grammar of the Greek New Tes-
tament in the Light of Historical Research* (Nashville: Broadman Press, 1934), 997-99;
Nigel Turner, *Prolegomena*, Volume 1 of *A Grammar of New Testament Greek*, by J. H.
Moulton, 4 vols. (Edinburgh: T & T Clark, 1908), 206-9; idem, *Syntax*, Volume 3 of *A
Grammar of New Testament Greek*, by J. H. Moulton, 4 vols. (Edinburgh: T & T Clark,
1963), 102.

world."[20] The sense of certainty of result from the divine perspective is a well-established meaning for this type of syntactical construction in Greek.[21] The particle *hina* followed by a subjunctive mood verb has an additional telic sense in verse 32, expressing both divine purpose and certain outcome. Although some older grammarians once denied that *hina* clauses ever denote "result" in the New Testament,[22] this is now considered to be an overstatement. Wallace writes that this category of usage "indicates *both the intention and its sure accomplishment*" and "what God purposes is what happens and, consequently, *hina* is used to express both the divine purpose and the result."[23] This means that the *hina* clause in 1 Corinthians 11:32 is not a negative warning, saying that believers "might be condemned with the world." Rather, it is a positive declaration of God's purpose and certain result, "that we might *not* be condemned with the world." Paul's whole point in 1 Corinthians 11:28-32 is to show that although believers may be judged by the Lord, even severely to the point of physical death, it is His purpose and certain outcome that they *not* be condemned with unbelievers (John 5:24).

Sometimes the translation of the *hina* + subjunctive clause creates a misimpression in the mind of English readers. The idiomatic English expression, "in order that we might/may/should" often gives the initial impression that some human contingency is being expressed, when in fact the outcome or result is never in doubt from the divine perspective. In this respect, John 3:16 should also be viewed as a promise, not a statement of probability, when it says, "that whoever believes in Him should not perish" (*hina pas ho pisteuōn eis auton mē apolētai*). The use of the subjunctive mood form of the verb for "may . . . perish" in this verse is "all but required" according to common Greek syntax; but semantically John 3:16 does not mean that believers might still perish.[24] Rather it is a *promise* that believers *will not* perish.[25] The same is true of the final clause in 1 Corinthians 11:32.

20. Gordon D. Fee, *The First Epistle to the Corinthians*, New International Commentary on the New Testament (Grand Rapids: Eerdmans, 1987), 566.

21. Walter Bauer, William F. Arndt, and F. Wilbur Gingrich, *A Greek-English Lexicon of the New Testament and Other Early Christian Literature*, 3rd ed., rev. and ed. Frederick W. Danker (Chicago: University of Chicago Press, 2000), 477.

22. Ernest De Witt Burton, *Syntax of the Moods and Tenses in New Testament Greek* (Chicago: University of Chicago Press, 1900; Reprint, Grand Rapids: Kregel, 1976), 94-95, §222-23.

23. Daniel B. Wallace, *Greek Grammar Beyond the Basics: An Exegetical Syntax of the New Testament* (Grand Rapids: Zondervan, 1996), 473.

24. Ibid., 474.

25. For similar significant examples of the *hina* + subjunctive mood clause

All of this shows that 1 Corinthians 11:30-32 presents a serious dilemma for traditional Calvinist doctrine of the perseverance of the saints. Obviously, the Corinthians who were chastened to the point of physical death by the Lord did not persevere in faithfulness and holiness to the end of their lives. They died in a state of carnality; yet they were eternally saved by God's grace. The doctrine of the perseverance of the saints as espoused in Calvinism and Lordship Salvation has no adequate explanation for the scriptural teaching that a genuine believer may commit sin leading to physical death (Acts 5:1-11; 8:13-24; 1 Cor. 5:1-5; 1 John 5:16-17; Rev. 2:20-23) and not continue successfully in the race of the Christian life.

Professors vs. Possessors

Since the dawn of human history when people began to multiply on the earth, there has been a distinction not only between believers and unbelievers, but also between true believers (who belong to God) and those who merely profess to be believers but are in reality still lost unbelievers. In God's sovereign plan, He lets them "both grow together until the harvest" (Matt. 13:30). At His appointed time, He will separate unbelievers from believers, professors from possessors of eternal life, as a farmer separates the wheat from the tares (13:36-43) or the wheat from the chaff (3:12).

Judas Iscariot was one such religious imposter. He was included among the Lord's twelve closest disciples and even entrusted with handling money for the group (John 12:6; 13:29). He was sent out by Christ and given authority to work miracles along with all the other disciples (Matt. 10:1-8); and when Jesus announced that one of them would betray Him, the other disciples did not immediately suspect it was Judas (John 13:21-22; 28-29). Yet Judas was an unbeliever all along. Jesus states this to His disciples in John 6:64, which says, "'But there are some of you who do not believe.' For Jesus knew from the beginning who they were who did not believe, and who would betray Him."

While true believers possess eternal life and are preserved by God's grace, mere professors or religious imposters are not preserved because they have never believed in Christ alone for salvation and thus have never belonged to God. This was the case with Judas. Even after he betrayed the Lord and was "remorseful," admitting, "I have

---

expressing a definite result in salvation contexts, see John 6:39-40; 10:10; 20:31; Galatians 2:16; and 1 Timothy 1:16.

sinned by betraying innocent blood" (Matt. 27:3-4), he still never personally believed in Jesus as the Messiah for his own salvation (John 6:70-71; 13:10-11; 17:12). This demonstrates that simply recognizing one's sin before God will not save anyone. A person must also trust in Christ alone for salvation from sin rather than trust in his or her own good works.

It is a common misconception that people are able to discern whether someone is saved by how that person lives. People would not have known Judas's true inner unbelief by the way he lived most of his life. Nor would people have seen outwardly that the Corinthian saints were saved because their walk was indistinguishable from the lost. This was also the case with the false apostles of Paul's day, who transformed themselves into apostles of Christ and appeared to others as "ministers of righteousness" (2 Cor. 11:13-15), who were received by the church at Corinth despite preaching another Jesus and another gospel (11:1-4). The same may be said of the "false brethren" (*pseudadelphous*) in Jerusalem who stood for law-keeping as a requirement to be justified in God's sight while opposing Paul's gospel of grace (Acts 15:1; Gal. 2:4). Each of these examples show that what a person believes, not how he or she appears to live, makes all the difference between heaven and hell.

The Profession of "Lord, Lord" (Matt. 7:21-23)

One passage often cited as proof for perseverance in faith and good works as a requirement for final salvation is Matthew 7:15-23, where Christ says,

15 Beware of false prophets, who come to you in sheep's clothing, but inwardly they are ravenous wolves. 16 You will know them by their fruits. Do men gather grapes from thornbushes or figs from thistles? 17 Even so, every good tree bears good fruit, but a bad tree bears bad fruit. 18 A good tree cannot bear bad fruit, nor can a bad tree bear good fruit. 19 Every tree that does not bear good fruit is cut down and thrown into the fire. 20 Therefore by their fruits you will know them. 21 Not everyone who says to Me, "Lord, Lord," shall enter the kingdom of heaven, but he who does the will of My Father in heaven. 22 Many will say to Me in that day, "Lord, Lord, have we not prophesied in Your name, cast out demons in Your name, and done many wonders in Your

name?" 23 And then I will declare to them, "I never knew you; depart from Me, you who practice lawlessness!"

Is this passage teaching that the genuineness of a person's faith is proven by a certain amount of good works or practical righteousness since Jesus said, "by their fruits you will know them"? When Christ says at the final judgment, "I never knew you; depart from Me, you who practice lawlessness," will He condemn for all eternity the person who trusted in Him alone as his or her only hope of salvation but who did not do enough good works or have enough practical righteousness in life? Is this passage teaching that a person must live an enduring, obedient, and holy lifestyle to obtain final salvation? The biblical answer to each of these questions is an emphatic, "No!"

Notice carefully that this passage describes false prophets who outwardly look like sheep, or true believers (v. 15). If someone's true colors cannot be determined by that person's external appearance, what did Jesus mean by "fruits"? Two clues in the immediate context indicate that the fruit Jesus had in mind was a person's profession, words, teaching, or testimony. Remember, Jesus is speaking of false *prophets* here. In addition, verses 21-22 record what these people "will say." What people believe in their hearts comes out of their mouths. How can you tell what people believe or who they are trusting? Listen to their profession and see if it agrees with God's Word and the gospel of Christ. In a parallel passage in Matthew 12:33-37, the Lord Jesus defines "fruit" this way, saying,

> 33 Either make the tree good and its fruit good, or else make the tree bad and its fruit bad; for a tree is known by its fruit. 34 Brood of vipers! How can you, being evil, speak good things? For out of the abundance of the heart the mouth speaks. 35 A good man out of the good treasure of his heart brings forth good things, and an evil man out of the evil treasure brings forth evil things. 36 But I say to you that for every idle word men may speak, they will give account of it in the day of judgment. 37 For by your words you will be justified, and by your words you will be condemned.

Immediately prior to these words in Matthew 12, the nation of Israel's religious leaders had just declared that Jesus was not the Messiah and that He performed His miracles through Beelzebub, the ruler of the demons (12:24), rather than through the power of the

Holy Spirit. By saying this, they committed blasphemy against the Holy Spirit (12:31-32). What they believed in their hearts came out of their mouths. This is also true in Matthew 7:15-23. Notice the "fruit" or words spoken by the unbelieving false prophets in verses 21-22: "Not everyone who says to Me, 'Lord, Lord,' shall enter the kingdom of heaven, but he who does the will of My Father in heaven. Many will say to Me in that day, 'Lord, Lord, have we not prophesied in Your name, cast out demons in Your name, and done many wonders in Your name?'"

The problem with the profession of these false prophets was not that they spoke falsely about the works they had done in Jesus' name. Christ never denies that the false prophets did such works in His name. What He denies is that He ever knew them, even while they did such works in His name. But why did Christ never know them? Because they had always trusted in their own works, and at no point had they ever trusted in Him alone. What did they plead before Him as the basis for their acceptance? They pleaded their works of prophesying, casting out demons, and doing many wonders in His name, rather than His work and God's saving grace.

How different this is from the tax collector in Luke 18:9-14, who knew he was unworthy of heaven and "would not so much as raise his eyes to heaven, but beat his breast, saying [literally], 'God, be propitiated toward me the sinner!'" (v. 13). Christ pronounced that this person was truly justified before God (v. 14). The Lord would never turn away someone who humbly approached Him on that basis. While the false prophets in Matthew 7:21-22 believed they were living obediently under the Lordship of Christ, professing "Lord, Lord," they were actually relying on their own religious works instead of having a humble posture of reliance upon Christ alone as their Savior. This reliance upon Christ alone is the Father's will that Jesus referred to in Matthew 7:21. Elsewhere, Matthew's Gospel explains that self-righteousness is insufficient to gain entrance into the Kingdom; instead, one must humble himself and believe in Christ to receive His saving righteousness (Matt. 5:20; 18:1-4; 19:16-26). Matthew 21:31-32 explicitly declares that believing in Christ is the will of the Father for all sinners.

31 "Which of the two did the will of his father?" They said to Him, "The first." Jesus said to them, "Assuredly, I say to you that tax collectors and harlots enter the kingdom of God before you. 32 For John came to you in the way of righteous-

ness, and you did not believe him; but tax collectors and harlots believed him; and when you saw it, you did not afterward relent and believe him."

Regarding the will of the Father, Jesus also states in John 6:40,
"And this is the will of Him who sent Me, that everyone who sees
the Son and believes in Him may have everlasting life." The interpretation that the Father's will for the lost is simply faith in His Son
harmonizes with the rest of Scripture, which teaches that a sinner is
accepted by God solely through faith in Christ, not one's own religious works (Gen. 15:6; Hab. 2:4; Luke 7:50; 18:9-14; Rom. 3:27-28;
4:4-5; 9:30–10:4; Gal. 2:16; Eph. 2:8-9; Titus 3:5). Thus, in response to
the false prophets' plea of "Lord, Lord" and their religious works,
Christ says in Matthew 7:23, "I never knew you; depart from Me, you
who practice lawlessness (*ergazomenoi tēn anomian*)!" He does not
say, "I *once* knew you, but you lost your salvation by lawless living."
Rather, Christ says He "never knew" them. At no time had they ever
trusted in Him alone for their salvation. While they pleaded their
own religious works as the basis for their acceptance, Christ reveals
the true character of their works—that they actually "worked lawlessness" (*ergazomenoi tēn anomian*). The Lord's evaluation of their
works is quite different than their own, as He views man's pre-salvation works as "dung" (Phil. 3:8-9) and "filthy rags" (Isa. 64:6) since
they are tainted by sin and pride and are thus unable to save.

All of this shows that the ultimate reason for the condemnation of these false prophets was not that their lawless works were
too great to be forgiven. No, the Lord knows that man cannot satis-
factorily keep His Law (Ps. 130:3; Gal. 3:10; James 2:10), and that is
why He even graciously promises to forgive man's "lawless (*anomia*)
deeds" (Rom. 4:7). Instead, the real reason these false prophets are
eternally condemned is because they pridefully thought their own
works were sufficient to save them rather than humbly acknowledging their spiritual bankruptcy and need for God's saving mercy and
grace through Christ. Therefore, the difference between a professor
of salvation and a possessor of salvation is that the professor trusts in
his own works while often appearing to live a righteous and worthy
life. The possessor of salvation, however, has trusted solely in Christ
apart from his own works (Rom. 11:6), knowing that he is inherently
unrighteous (Rom. 3:10) and undeserving of salvation (3:19), but still
justified before God freely by His grace (3:24).

Conclusion

When the Bible is consistently interpreted in a normal, literal way, according to context, grammar, cultural and historical background, comparing Scripture with Scripture, the result is a proper recognition of several major distinctions God has placed in His Word. Having spent the last two chapters explaining these crucial distinctions, let's review them now.

- Not all who have received the free gift of eternal life will earn an eternal reward.

- Not all who are justified in God's sight grow in practical sanctification; yet all who are justified will be glorified.

- Not all who possess eternal life as believers in Jesus Christ continue in His Word as true disciples.

- Not all children of God in the family of God have fellowship with God.

- Not all believers in Christ are spiritual since believers can be either spiritual or carnal at any moment, depending on whether they are walking in the Spirit or in the flesh.

- Not all judgment from the Lord is the same: only believers receive chastening from the Lord, and condemnation is reserved for the lost.

- Not all who profess to be saved actually possess eternal salvation.

These clear, biblical distinctions must not be confused, lest our interpretations make the Bible appear to contradict itself—God forbid! Consistently literal interpretation of Scripture must take precedence over traditional systems of theology, even certain theologies inherited from Protestantism that need further reforming to align with the text of God's Word. Only this approach to biblical interpretation and doctrine exalts the inherent authority and consistency of God's truth and allows His Word to speak for itself, letting grace be grace—free (Rom. 3:24) and true (1 Peter 5:12)!

Chapter 8

Does Justification Guarantee Sanctification?

Persevere or perish! Grow spiritually or end up in hell! This is the gospel message being proclaimed by some of the most prominent and popular evangelical Reformed voices in our day. While they say that justification is by faith alone, they go on to teach that your "final justification" also requires you to live a sanctified, holy life of good works. In addition, they say that while your election may have been unconditional, you are still humanly responsible to live a progressively sanctified life if you wish to reach glorification in heaven. While you may believe you are one of God's elect, only a sanctified life will prove it. If you think this description of popular Reformed teaching is just hyperbole or a misrepresentation, then listen to the claims of leading Calvinists themselves.

> Nevertheless, there is an "if" from the human side of things, from the standpoint of our responsibility, in connection with my making sure that I am one of those whom God has promised to preserve unto His heavenly kingdom. Continuance in the faith in the path of obedience, in denying self and following Christ, is not simply desirable but indispensable. No matter how excellent a beginning I have made, if I do not continue to press forward I shall be lost. Yes, lost, and not merely miss some particular crown or millennial honors as the deluded dispensationalists teach. It is persevere or perish: it is final perseverance or perish eternally—there is no other alternative.[1]

---

1. A. W. Pink, *The Saint's Perseverance* (Lafayette, IN: Sovereign Grace, 2001), 77.

Election is unconditional, but glorification is not. There are many warnings in Scripture that those who do not hold fast to Christ can be lost in the end.[2]

As Tom Schreiner says, the book "tackles one of the fundamental questions of our human condition: how can a person be right with God?" The stunning Christian answer is: *sola fide*—faith alone. But be sure you hear this carefully and precisely: He says *right with God* by faith alone, not *attain heaven* by faith alone. There are other conditions for attaining heaven, but no others for entering a right relationship to God. In fact, one must already be in a right relationship with God by faith alone in order to meet the other conditions.[3]

One final word on eternal security. It is a community project. And that is why the pastoral ministry is so utterly serious, and why our preaching must not be playful but earnest. We preach so that saints might persevere in faith to glory. We preach not only for their growth, but because if they don't grow, they perish.[4]

These claims raise many crucial questions concerning the relationship between justification, practical sanctification, and glorification. If you are a believer in Christ, does your justification before God guarantee that you will also live a sanctified life? Is your future glorification and final salvation conditioned on your present, earthly walk? If so, then how sanctified must you be before you can know you have eternal life? Will one good work suffice or must you have a lifelong pattern of good works? If you have been born again, what changes, if any, will inevitably accompany the possession of new life from God? If a sanctified life is necessary to reach glorification and is guaranteed to all who are justified by faith alone, then who is responsible for the believer's sanctification? God? Man? Both? If man is responsible, even in part, then how can sanctification be guaranteed? And how does the grace of God relate to all of this?

---

2. John Piper, *Five Points: Towards a Deeper Experience of God's Grace* (Ross-Shire, Scotland: Christian Focus, 2013), 63.

3. John Piper, Foreword to Thomas R. Schreiner, *Faith Alone—The Doctrine of Justification* (Grand Rapids: Zondervan, 2015), 11.

4. John Piper, *Brothers, We Are Not Professionals: A Plea to Pastors for Radical Ministry* (Nashville: Broadman & Holman, 2002), 110-11.

This chapter shows from Scripture that new birth and justification before God do *not* inevitably result in a practically sanctified life though God desires practical sanctification for every believer. Some degree of outward, practical sanctification *normally* occurs among believers, but a sanctified life is not *guaranteed* for everyone whom God justifies. When sanctification and the good works that accompany it are made a requirement for final salvation in heaven, the gospel of grace becomes corrupted into another gospel. Before considering the many biblical passages that support this conclusion, it is essential to have a solid, biblical foundation regarding the process of practical sanctification.

Biblical Sanctification

An understanding of sanctification begins with God's original creative purpose for man. The first man, Adam, was uniquely created in the image of God with an advanced intellect, emotions, and will, which set him apart from the created animal realm and allowed him to have a special relationship with his Creator (Gen. 1:26-27; 5:1). This image has been retained among all of Adam's descendants despite being marred by sin (Gen. 9:6; 1 Cor. 11:7; James 3:9). As many have correctly said regarding God's image in man today, it is defaced but not erased. This means that man still possesses his intellect, emotions, and volition and is not only capable of a relationship with God by His grace but is also responsible for that. By the grace of God, we as human beings may still fulfill the purpose for which we were created, namely, to serve and glorify God and to enjoy fellowship with Him forever (Isa. 43:7; 1 Cor. 10:31; Col. 1:16; Rev. 4:11).

Being made in the image of God did not automatically make man obedient to God. Adam exercised his volition by choosing to sin, and consequently he died spiritually just as God promised he would if he disobeyed God's command not to eat from the tree of the knowledge of good and evil (Gen. 2:16-17). Since death in the Bible never means nonexistence but rather separation (Rom. 6:23), when Adam sinned he died spiritually in the sense that he became relationally separated from God (Gen. 2:17; 3:6-10). He also became subject to sin's dominion (Rom. 6:14-20) and the power of the Devil (Eph. 2:2; Heb. 2:14-15; 1 John 3:8). As a result, all mankind was plunged into spiritual ruin and separation from God (Rom. 5:12), with the exception of the Man Christ Jesus, who was a human descendant of Adam (Luke 3:23-38) but sinless from the moment of conception (Luke 1:35; 1 Tim. 2:5; Heb.

4:15). By sending His Son to be the Savior of the world, God the Father graciously provided redemption and a new beginning for mankind in the "last Adam" (1 Cor. 15:45). Now salvation and sanctification are a matter of position or identity—being either in Adam or in Christ.

In religious circles it is common to hear people say that man has inherited "original sin," yet few realize that also means all humanity has been identified with the "original sinner"—Adam. From God's perspective, He sees people as either saved or lost (1 Cor. 1:18), either positionally "in Adam" or "in Christ" (1 Cor. 15:22). From the moment of conception, all people start life "in Adam" and are identified with his sin (Rom. 5:12-19). Simply by virtue of being conceived as a descendant of Adam and a member of his race, each person shares Adam's sin and its guilt, being under God's just condemnation and wrath (Rom. 1:18–3:20; 1 Cor. 15:21-22; Eph. 2:1-3). Even Adam's fallen, sinful disposition has been transmitted to the rest of the human race, so that we are "by nature children of wrath" (Eph. 2:3). Consequently, people commit individual acts of rebellion and disobedience against God because they were born sinners and act according to their inherent, sinful nature. Unlike Adam, no one today becomes a sinner by sinning. We sin because we were born sinners and still possess a sinful nature (Rom. 7:15-21). The believer possesses this sin nature until the time of physical death or bodily resurrection at Christ's coming.

Position in Christ & Identification with Him

When most Christians hear the word "sanctification" they think of a change in behavior. Yet the Word of God does not teach that sanctification begins with behavioral change but with a new identity—in Christ. Only a change in identity or position makes it possible for the grace of God to change someone in practice. Though all mankind starts off spiritually dead and lost in Adam, God makes His grace available to all through His Son, Jesus Christ. Where sin abounds, God's grace abounds and prevails much more in Christ (Rom. 5:20-21). When those in Adam hear the gospel of God's grace and place their faith in Jesus Christ and His work alone to save them, at that moment those individuals receive eternal life.

The Holy Spirit also places believers in living union with their new spiritual Head, the Lord Jesus, so that they become members of His body, the universal church (1 Cor. 12:12-13). At that same moment and by that same baptizing ministry of the Holy Spirit, believers are identified with Christ in His death and resurrection. Thus, every believer can say on the authority of God's Word that they have died with Christ and are risen with Him (Rom. 6:2-6; Gal. 2:20; Eph. 2:4-7; Col. 3:1-4). Christ's substitutionary death for sinners and His resurrection made justification available to believers, and identification with Christ's death and resurrection now makes sanctification possible for believers.

Because of the believer's co-crucifixion and co-resurrection with Christ, that believer now stands in a new legal relationship toward his three spiritual foes. Every child of God is now positionally dead to the external foes of the world (Gal. 6:14) and the Devil (Heb. 2:14-15) and to the internal foe of the flesh or sinful nature (Rom. 6:6). But this does not mean that the flesh, the world, and the Devil no longer exist, for every Christian soldier knows all too well the real threat these three adversaries pose. Though they continue to exist and oppose God's will in the believer's life, the believer has died in Christ toward each one of them.

The foe that poses the greatest danger is always the one closest to home, which in the case of the believer is the resident sin nature. When someone is in Adam (prior to salvation), the indwelling sin nature has a position of master over that person so that he obeys the dictates of that sinful nature (Rom. 6:14). Thus, all who are in Adam are currently slaves toward the sin nature (Rom. 6:16-18). But those in Christ stand in a new, changed relationship to God and the indwelling sin nature.

Having died to sin and now being alive to God in Christ, the believer does not need to live in bondage to the sin nature any longer since its legal relationship and position of master over the believer has been judicially broken (Rom. 6:6-10). The believer is now positionally and legally free from the tyranny and dominion of the sinful nature and is now under a new master—the Lord Jesus Christ (Rom. 6:11). Prior to salvation, the lost are alive toward the sin nature but dead toward God (Rom. 6:20a). However, at the moment of new birth, just the opposite occurs. The believer becomes positionally dead toward the sin nature and alive toward God "in Christ Jesus our Lord" (Rom. 6:11). Without this positional sanctification in Christ, practical sanctification by the Spirit's power and spiritual growth in grace would be impossible. While a change in a person's spiritual position from being "in Adam" to "in Christ" makes practical sanctification *possible*, only a change in the believer's spiritual condition makes sanctification *actual*.

The Believer's New Nature

Just as Romans 6 is the key New Testament chapter that reveals the believer's identification and position in Christ, Romans 7 plays a key role in revealing the fact that the believer now possesses a new divine nature that desires to do God's will but has no power in itself to fulfill it. Thus, Paul confesses in Romans 7:18-21,

> 18 For I know that in me (that is, in my flesh) nothing good dwells; for to will is present with me, but how to perform what is good I do not find. 19 For the good that I will to do, I do not do; but the evil I will not to do, that I practice. 20 Now if I do what I will not to do, it is no longer I who do it, but sin that dwells in me. 21 I find then a law, that evil is present with me, the one who wills to do good.

In Romans 7, Paul describes his failure as a believer in seeking to live the Christian life by sheer willpower and self-determination. This passage must be describing Paul's post-salvation experience of failure in the Christian life, rather than his pre-salvation experience, since he repeatedly expresses his will to do good, which reflects the desires of the new divine nature that every believer receives at regeneration.[5] When a believer's human spirit is regenerated at the new birth, he also receives a new nature from God that desires to do the will of God. However, this nature has no power in itself, for the strength and enablement to live the Christian life come from the Holy Spirit, who is the only power source capable of overcoming the indwelling sin nature. While the will of the new nature is set in opposition to the desires of the sin nature, only the Holy Spirit's power provides real spiritual victory over the sin nature and acts of sin.

The Believer's Responsibility in Sanctification

Before explaining the believer's relationship to the Holy Spirit in Romans 8, an important principle from Romans 7 must be underscored: God holds the believer responsible for properly exercising his will to walk by faith in the process of sanctification. In Romans 7, Paul wrongly exercised his will by relying on himself rather than

---

5. Renald E. Showers, *The New Nature* (Neptune, NJ: Loizeaux Brothers, 1986); Andy Woods, "Romans 7 and Sanctification," *Chafer Theological Seminary Journal* 14 (Fall 2009): 4-22.

the Lord and by seeking to live the Christian life by law instead of grace. Thus, the key word repeated throughout Romans 7 is "I" (*egō*). In Romans 8, Paul finds spiritual victory by remembering and reckoning on his position in Christ and walking according to the Holy Spirit. Thus, the key word emphasized in chapter 8 is "Spirit." As will be explained in the following section, this shows that the believer is still responsible to exercise his will by a walk of faith that results in the Spirit's enablement to live a holy and righteous life. The decisive factor of the believer's will in the Christian life is a key reason why sanctification is not automatic, inevitable, or guaranteed for everyone who has been justified.

Proponents of the perseverance of the saints often claim that their doctrine magnifies the sovereignty and grace of God by eliminating man's will entirely from salvation. "Monergism" is often touted (God alone working), as opposed to "synergism" (God and man working together). Calvinism's strongly deterministic view of election leads to the conclusion that final salvation is guaranteed to God's elect because it depends entirely upon His will. Logically, since the will of man plays no decisive role in any phase of salvation, then according to Calvinists even "practical sanctification is guaranteed among all who are justified,"[6] for "the God who requires perseverance in faith and holiness gives the very perseverance he requires."[7]

But keep in mind that Calvinism considers salvation from two different perspectives—God's and man's. From God's perspective, all of salvation—from election to justification to sanctification to glorification—is guaranteed. But from the human perspective, the professing believer must still regard sanctification and final salvation as conditional. This explains why at times Calvinists who believe in the certainty of sanctification and final perseverance can still speak of "an 'if' from the human side of things, from the standpoint of our responsibility."[8] In one sense they say sanctification is guaranteed to all who are justified, but in another sense they say it is still conditional. This is why Louis Berkhof warns, "He who does not live a life of faith is, *as far as his consciousness is concerned*, practically outside of the covenant. If in our purview we include not only the beginning, but also the gradual unfolding and completion

---

6. Herman Witsius, *The Economy of the Covenants Between God and Man* (Grand Rapids: Reformation Heritage, 2010), 2:7.

7. Greg Nichols, *Covenant Theology: A Reformed and Baptistic Perspective on God's Covenants* (Birmingham, AL: Solid Ground, 2011), 135.

8. Pink, *Saint's Perseverance*, 77.

of the covenant life, we may regard sanctification as a condition in addition to faith."[9]

Calvinism's twofold perspective on salvation and sanctification means that if a professing believer lives a sanctified life and perseveres to the end, then it was strictly due to God sovereignly determining and setting the believer's will throughout the entire process. Conversely, if a professing believer fails to live a sanctified life and does not persevere to the end, then it was strictly due to the fact that he was never really one of God's unconditionally elect and he merely had a false, spurious faith.

This raises a fatal problem for the perseverance position. Imagine for a moment if sanctification were strictly monergistic, being determined solely by God's will. If sanctification were strictly a matter of God's will, then why does He not will for all believers to be equally sanctified since no believer is perfect and varying levels of sanctification and spiritual growth are evident among believers? If man's sanctification were purely monergistic and God alone determines each man's will and work, then why doesn't He will for all believers to be perfectly sanctified, never sin, and do good works all the time? Failure in sanctification, even to the slightest imperfection, shows that man is not only responsible for the proper exercise of his will in the process of sanctification, but his volition is also decisive in the outcome.

While it is true, as we will see, that God alone in His grace does the actual work of sanctification, the believer is still responsible to appropriate the grace of God by a walk of faith in order for God's sanctifying work to be fulfilled. But if practical sanctification were truly guaranteed by God for every elect believer, as Calvinism claims, then why is the believer commanded to cooperate with God in the process of sanctification by exercising his volition in response to God's will? For example, both God's will and man's will are present in Philippians 2:12-13, which says,

> Therefore, my beloved, as you have always obeyed, not as in my presence only, but now much more in my absence, work out your own salvation with fear and trembling; for it is God who works in you both to will and to do for His good pleasure.

While God is working in the believer, it is clear that the believer must still comply with God's work by fulfilling the command to

---

9. Louis Berkhof, *Systematic Theology*, 2nd ed. (Grand Rapids: Eerdmans, 1941), 280-81 (emphasis original).

"work out" the salvation that God has already "worked in." This passage is not teaching believers to "work for" their salvation since no phase of salvation, including sanctification, is accomplished by means of human works. The believer must use his volition to rely on the Lord to do His work in and through the yielded, trusting believer. Both the believer's responsibility of dependence and God's work of production are found in Jesus' instruction to His disciples in John 15:4-5.

> 4 Abide in Me, and I in you. As the branch cannot bear fruit of itself, unless it abides in the vine, neither can you, unless you abide in Me. 5 I am the vine, you are the branches. He who abides in Me, and I in him, bears much fruit; for without Me you can do nothing.

In this passage, the Lord Jesus does not tell the disciples to produce fruit; He tells them to bear the fruit that He Himself produces. This realization often comes as a great relief to the burdened believer who has been living under the crushing assumption that he must manufacture what only God can supernaturally produce. This does not mean that the believer's responsibility in the Christian life is to be so passive that he does nothing but wait for the moment that God may sovereignly choose to work through him. Rather, since the Lord wants to continually do His supernatural work in and through the believer, the believer must actively and continually trust God to do His sanctifying work. Dennis Rokser clarifies this point.

> God wants you to recognize and remember that the Christian life is a supernatural way of life, not lived by self-effort but through faith in Jesus Christ by the power of the Holy Spirit. You must come to realize that the Christian life is to be lived in active dependence upon the Lord resulting in passive production on your part![10]

Lewis Sperry Chafer expands on this same point.

> The spiritual life is not passive. Too often it is thus misjudged because of the fact that one, to be spiritual, must cease from self-effort in the direction of spiritual attainments and learn to

---

10. Dennis M. Rokser, *I'm Saved but Struggling with Sin! Is Victory Available? Romans 6–8 Examined* (Duluth, MN: Grace Gospel Press, 2013), 34.

live and serve by the power God has provided. True spirituality knows little of "quietism." It is life more active, enlarged and vital because it is energized by the limitless power of God. Spirit-filled Christians are quite apt to be physically exhausted at the close of the day. They are weary *in* the work, but not weary *of* the work.[11]

Since the believer's will is actively involved in the sanctification process, this means that God in His sovereignty does not "make" the elect do good works; they are done voluntarily in response to His prompting. The manner in which God deals with believers by appealing to their wills can be seen in Paul's appeal to Philemon's volition concerning the runaway slave Onesimus. Paul writes to Philemon, "But without your consent I wanted to do nothing, that your good deed might not be by compulsion, as it were, but voluntary" (Philem. 1:14).

The believer's specific responsibility in sanctification is recorded in Romans 6 by the key words *know, reckon, present/yield,* and *obey.* In order to be practically sanctified, believers are to *know* the truth about their position in Christ and identification with Him (Rom. 6:3, 6, 9) and *reckon* this to be true (Rom. 6:11). In light of each believer's new identity in Christ as one who is legally and positionally alive toward God and dead toward sin, the believer is then to exercise his volition in continually choosing to *present* or *yield* himself to God instead of the sin nature. As the believer does so, he becomes an instrument of God's practical righteousness (Rom. 6:12-13), resulting in holiness and practical sanctification (Rom. 6:19-20). As the believer walks in yielded dependence upon the Lord in light of his position in Christ, he is filled with the Holy Spirit's power, enabling him to have practical victory over his flesh, the world, and the Devil (Rom. 8:1-4, 13; Gal. 5:16; Eph. 5:18).

Just as justification requires *a step* of faith in which a person does not rely on himself or his own good works but trusts solely on the Lord Jesus Christ for salvation, in just the same way sanctification requires the believer to recognize his own insufficiency and weakness to live the Christian life (2 Cor. 1:9-10; 3:5-6) and to take *repeated steps* of faith—a walk of faith (2 Cor. 5:7; Gal. 2:20; Col. 2:6). As the believer continues walking by faith, being repeatedly filled with the Holy Spirit, he is progressively set apart to God, grows in grace, and

---

11. Lewis Sperry Chafer, *He That Is Spiritual: A Classic Study of the Biblical Doctrine of Spirituality,* rev. ed. (Grand Rapids: Zondervan, 1967), 140.

matures into Christlikeness over time (Eph. 4:13, 15; 2 Peter 3:18). As the believer fulfills his human responsibility of beholding Christ by faith as he sees Him in the Word of God, the Spirit of God does the divine, inner work of transformation and sanctification (2 Cor. 3:18). Therefore, sanctification, just like justification, requires the will of man to be exercised in faith while God does the work of justifying and sanctifying. Salvation in all three tenses is always the work of God for man, never the work of man for God. But if we are neither justified nor sanctified by our works, then where do good works fit in the Christian life?

God's Grace & Good Works

We never have to wonder whether God wants believers to do good works since He prepared them beforehand as part of His will for each believer's life (Acts 20:24; Eph. 2:10; 1 Tim. 6:18; Titus 2:14; 3:8). But good works are not the end-all and be-all of the Christian life. God is just as concerned with the *means* to the end as He is with the end itself. This is why an understanding of genuine spirituality is critical. Only as the believer walks by faith and is filled with the Holy Spirit (Rom. 15:13; Eph. 3:16-17) is his service acceptable and pleasing to the Lord (2 Cor. 5:7-9), for "without faith it is impossible to please Him" (Heb. 11:6). Since the believer yields either to his flesh or to the Spirit of God at any given moment, every work in a believer's life is the result of walking either in the flesh or by the Holy Spirit. Therefore, a believer must be spiritual or Spirit-filled (Rom. 8:1-4; 1 Cor. 2:15-16), rather than carnal or yielded to his flesh (1 Cor. 3:1-4), in order to be practically sanctified and do good works that truly glorify the Lord. Contrary to popular religious opinion, the believer is not spiritual *by his works*. Instead, the believer must first be spiritual *in order to do* good works (Gal. 6:1), so that the works done through the yielded, trusting believer stem from the Lord's prior, inner working (1 Cor. 15:10; Col. 1:29; Heb. 13:21).

This means that the Christian is spiritual and sanctified the very same way a lost person becomes justified: by God's grace through faith in Christ, and not by works (Gal. 2:20; 3:3-5). However, when it comes to good works, the critical difference between justification and sanctification is that good works are not the proof of a one-time act of justification before God; they are the proof of the believer's ongoing spiritual condition or walk according to the Spirit (Gal. 5:22-23; Phil. 1:11; Col. 1:10). While God judicially declares righteous in His sight a person who is practically unrighteous and sinful, a person cannot claim to be truly spiritual or practically sanctified while walking in sin. As the apostle John says, a person cannot be walking in the light and in darkness at the same time (1 John 1:5-7). While holiness and good works do not inevitably accompany justification, they must manifest themselves in the life of one who is practically sanctified as the byproduct of a genuine walk of faith.

But this raises another important question about the relationship between God's grace, sanctification, and good works. Why does it contradict grace to conclude that sanctification must inevitably follow justification when both justification and sanctification are wholly by God's grace? The reason is based on the fact that good works do not inevitably accompany justification before God whereas they do accompany sanctification. If good works inevitably accompany sanctification and sanctification is made a requirement to be truly justified, then good works have snuck in the back door as a requirement for salvation. Claiming that sanctification is inevitable and necessary for one who has truly been justified ends up requiring the good works that result from practical sanctification.

Regeneration and the Filling of the Holy Spirit

At this point, some may object that the real issue with inevitable sanctification and change is not justification but regeneration. They may reason that change in one's behavior is technically not caused by a one-time judicial pronouncement of righteousness by God that occurs at justification but by the life-giving effects of regeneration. In other words, they may say that if someone truly has been born again with new life from God, then there will be some fruit, growth, or signs of that new eternal life.

One major problem with this conclusion is that it confuses the Holy Spirit's one-time work of regeneration (John 3:5; Titus 3:5) and the fact of His indwelling (John 14:16-17; Eph. 1:13; 4:30) with His ministry of repeated filling. Practical sanctification and righteous behavior is not the automatic byproduct of regeneration or the Holy Spirit indwelling a believer; rather it is the inevitable result of the Spirit's filling of a yielded, trusting believer. At the moment of justification, the believer is permanently regenerated and indwelt by the Holy Spirit. But the filling of the Spirit may or may not occur in the believer's life, depending on the response of the believer's own volition to either walk in faith toward God or not. This explains why there are passages in Scripture commanding the believer to be continually filled with the Spirit and walk in the Spirit, but there are no passages instructing the believer to be repeatedly justified, regenerated, or sealed by the Spirit.

This need for believers to be routinely filled with Spirit, in contrast to His one-time work of regeneration, sealing, or indwelling, can be observed in four key passages on the believer's responsibility toward the Holy Spirit. In each of these verses, the italicized verbs are in the imperative mood in Greek, indicating a command for the believer.

- And *do not be drunk* with wine, in which is dissipation; but *be filled* with the Spirit. (Eph. 5:18)

- I say then: *Walk* in the Spirit, and you shall not fulfill the lust of the flesh. (Gal. 5:16)

- And *do not grieve* the Holy Spirit of God, by whom you were sealed for the day of redemption. (Eph. 4:30)

- *Do not quench* the Spirit. (1 Thess. 5:19)

Since each of these verses contains commands for believers to continually apply, they demonstrate that the filling of the Spirit and a walk by means of the Spirit are not automatic. If the believer grieves or quenches the Spirit, he cannot be simultaneously filled with the Spirit and walking according to the Spirit. Thus, the believer is either spiritual or carnal at any given moment, for he cannot be walking in yielded dependence upon the Holy Spirit and the flesh or sin nature at the same time.

These verses show that simply because a believer has been regenerated and indwelt by the Holy Spirit does not mean he will automatically and inevitably be filled with the Spirit or walk by means of the Spirit's power. In order to be spiritual or Spirit-filled, the believer must not resist God's will (Phil. 2:13) but walk in yielded dependence upon the Lord in light of his position in Christ. However, when the child of God is obstinate and refuses to do God's will, he grieves the Holy Spirit and walks according to his flesh or sinful nature as a carnal believer (Gal. 3:3; 5:17).

Therefore, regeneration does not automatically result in sanctification because the commands to be filled with the Spirit and to walk by means of the Spirit present ongoing conditions for sanctification that the believer may or may not fulfill. There would be no purpose to such commands if all believers automatically and inevitably lived spiritual lives. Furthermore, the notion of inevitable spirituality and sanctification is contradicted by the case of the carnal Corinthian saints (1 Cor. 3:1-4), some of which were chastened to the point of physical death (1 Cor. 11:30-32).

Divine Discipline

Although regeneration may not lead to practical sanctification, it normally does. When people go from being lost and blind to being convinced of the gospel and regenerated, most do not stop believing immediately afterwards. Most remain persuaded and continue walking by faith, however intermittently. As a result, most genuinely born-again people experience some degree of sanctification. But does this mean that there are *absolutely no* spiritual changes that necessarily and inevitably occur across the board in every regenerated person's life? No, there are some, but probably not the type of changes most people think. For instance, all children of God will receive discipline from God for their spiritual welfare and growth. Since every born-again person is a child of God, the heavenly Father will not be negligent or neutral toward them when it comes to sin in their lives. The writer of Hebrews explains this principle.

> 5 And you have forgotten the exhortation which speaks to you as to sons: "My son, do not despise the chastening of the Lord, nor be discouraged when you are rebuked by Him; 6 for whom the Lord loves He chastens, and scourges every son whom He receives." 7 If you endure chastening, God deals with you as with sons; for what son is there whom a father does not chasten? 8 But if you are without chastening, of which all have become partakers, then you are illegitimate and not sons. (Heb. 12:5-8)

According to this passage, all believers receive God's loving discipline as part of the growth process. While all may not receive this discipline to the same extent, and all may not respond submissively to this chastening, the Lord will not fail to lovingly administer it as needed. Since God does not spank the Devil's children, divine discipline is one inevitable change that is certain for the child of God after justification and regeneration.

Internal Battle

The inside of every regenerated person is like a spiritual boxing ring. In one corner stands the sin nature with its bent towards sin. Across the ring stand the new nature, with its desire for God's will but not the adequate strength to overcome sin, and the Holy Spirit, who has abundant strength to defeat sin every round. Every believer in Christ should be able to relate to this analogy since the addition of the new nature and Holy Spirit create a spiritual dynamic and battleground not experienced by the unregenerate. Galatians 5:16-17 describes this conflict as follows:

16 But I say, walk by the Spirit, and you will not gratify the desires of the flesh. 17 For the desires of the flesh are against the Spirit, and the desires of the Spirit are against the flesh, for these are opposed to each other, to keep you from doing the things you want to do. (ESV)

While the Holy Spirit actively convicts unbelievers of sin, righteousness, and judgment (John 16:8), this is not the same type of conflict as that which occurs inside the believer. For the sinning believer, open warfare rages within his soul (James 4:1; 1 Peter 2:11). There can be no internal peace while he persists in sin, as the Holy Spirit engages in a spiritual tug-of-war against the believer's flesh or sin nature. Since each believer's body is a temple of the Holy Spirit (1 Cor. 6:19), it is impossible for the Spirit to remain neutral and idle while the believer sins, "For the Spirit who dwells in us yearns jealously" (James 4:5).

The internal conflict over sin and divine discipline in the life of every child of God are real and definite changes that take place starting at the moment of new birth. But neither of these necessarily results in practical sanctification and spiritual growth since the Bible plainly states that believers may not heed God's discipline (Acts 5:1-11; 1 Cor. 11:30-31; Heb. 12:5) or yield to the Holy Spirit (Gal. 3:3-5; Eph. 4:30; 1 Thess. 5:19). This is why 1 Thessalonians 4:1-8 declares that while sanctification is God's will for every believer, it may still be rejected by the disobedient Christian: "Therefore he who rejects this does not reject man, but God, who has also given us His Holy Spirit" (1 Thess. 4:8).

Ultimately, personal assurance of eternal salvation does not rest on changes in a person's life but on the finished work of Christ and the unchanging message and promise of the gospel. After all, observable change may be very subjective. Since the extent of sanctification and the rate of spiritual growth and transformation into Christlikeness may vary greatly from saint to saint, how much change must there be in a person's life before he can be sure he has been justified in God's sight? Even if a person's outward behavior appeared to change, this may not mean there has been a corresponding internal change of heart. Religion and legalism miss this point. Those with a bent toward law instead of grace often forget that although carnality may occur in the form of overt licentiousness, it may also be masked through various forms of religion, legalism, asceticism, or mysticism, which may all appear to be externally good. Yet these are all forms of carnality that do not constitute true spirituality and sanctification in God's sight.[12]

Supposed Proof Texts for Guaranteed Sanctification

At this point, some may object and say, "Yeah, but what about such and such a verse? Doesn't it prove the certainty of sanctification?" There are several supposed proof texts commonly used by perseverance proponents as support for the notion of guaranteed sanctification. Each of these is explained in the following section.

New Covenant Promises

Several Old Testament prophecies promise that the nation of Israel will fear and obey the Lord forever when the New Covenant is fulfilled (Jer. 31:31-34; 32:39-40; Ezek. 36:22-38). These passages are often interpreted by those holding to covenant and Reformed theology as support for the certainty of the church-age believer's perseverance and practical sanctification.[13] For example, D. A. Carson

---

12. For further explanation of practical sanctification by God's grace in the Christian life, see Dennis M. Rokser, *I'm Saved but Struggling with Sin! Is Victory Available? Romans 6–8 Examined* (Duluth, MN: Grace Gospel Press, 2013), and Kurt Witzig, "Sanctification by God's Free Grace," in *Freely by His Grace: Classical Free Grace Theology*, ed. J. B. Hixson, Rick Whitmire, and Roy B. Zuck (Duluth, MN: Grace Gospel Press, 2012), 363-418.

13. John Calvin, *Institutes of the Christian Religion*, 2.3.6, 8, 10; William J. Dumbrell, *Covenant and Creation: A Theology of Old Testament Covenants* (Nashville: Thomas Nelson, 1984), 178; Michael Horton, *Introducing Covenant Theology* (Grand Rapids: Baker, 2006), 183; John Piper, *Five Points: Towards a Deeper Experience of God's Grace* (Ross-Shire, Scotland: Christian Focus, 2013), 72; Paul Washer, *The Gospel Call and True Conversion* (Grand Rapids: Reformation Heritage Books, 2013), 175-80; Herman Witsius,

claims, "The assumption in the NT is that saving faith, tied as it is to the new covenant and the power of the Spirit, necessarily issues in good works."[14] The view that good works are inevitable for New Covenant believers leads Bradley Green to profess that they are necessary for salvation.

> In short, "works" are "necessary" for salvation because part of the "newness" of the new covenant is actual, grace-induced and grace-elicited obedience by true members of the new covenant. When the New Testament documents are read against Old Testament texts such as Jeremiah 31:31-34 and Ezekiel 36:22-29 (cf. Ezek. 11:19; 18:31), this obedience is seen as a promised component of the new covenant.[15]

Even a nominal dispensationalist such as John MacArthur cites a New Covenant promise of Jeremiah 32:40 to Israel as support for guaranteed sanctification and perseverance for every church-age believer.

> We've been caused to be born again. We possess new life. That new life is eternal life. Jeremiah 32:40, "And I will make an everlasting covenant with them that I will not turn away from them, to do them good; and I will put the fear of Me in their hearts so that they will not turn away from Me." The covenant of salvation is an everlasting covenant.[16]

In the context of Jeremiah 32:40 and other New Covenant passages in the Old Testament, the recipients of these promises or the parties to the covenant are specifically said to be Israel and Judah (Jer. 31:31, 33; 32:32-37, 41-44; Ezek. 36:22)—not the church. In addition, nowhere in the New Testament are these promises to the nation of Israel said to be transferred to, or fulfilled by, the church. The practice among covenant, Reformed theologians of interpreting

---

The Economy of the Covenants Between God and Man (Grand Rapids: Reformation Heritage, 2010), 2:20, 63.

14. D. A. Carson, "Reflections on Christian Assurance," *Westminster Theological Journal* 54 (Spring 1992): 27.

15. Bradley G. Green, *Covenant and Commandment: Works, Obedience and Faithfulness in the Christian Life*, New Studies in Biblical Theology 33 (Downers Grove, IL: InterVarsity, 2014), 17.

16. John MacArthur, "The Faith That Doesn't Fail," audio recording, GTY155, 2015. See also, John F. MacArthur, Jr., *Faith Works: The Gospel According to the Apostles* (Dallas: Word, 1993), 177.

God's promises originally given to Israel as though they apply to the church is unwarranted and violates the plain, literal, normal meaning of "Israel" and "Judah" in the text of inspired Scripture.

Though the spiritual blessings of the New Covenant in passages such as Jeremiah 32:39-40 are often wrenched from their immediate contexts and made to fit the church, the physical blessings of the same covenant, in the same contexts, are almost always conveniently overlooked. For example, in Jeremiah 32:41, the Lord continues His promises to Judah, saying, "I will rejoice over them to do them good, and I will assuredly plant them *in this land*, with all My heart and with all My soul." What "land" is the Lord referring to? The context of verses 42-44 explain that the "land" is the land of Judah. How can this possibly be made to fit the church?

Other blessings promised in New Covenant passages are often ignored altogether or the original promises to Israel are diminished in order to somehow fit the church. In Ezekiel 36:28, the Lord promises, "Then you shall dwell in the land that I gave to your fathers." In what sense will church-age Gentiles dwell in the land promised to Israel's patriarchs? Ezekiel 36:29-30 promises agricultural prosperity when the covenant is fulfilled. How is this fulfilled by the church? Ezekiel 36:33-38 promises to rebuild the broken down, ruined cities of the land. How is this fulfilled by the church? Ezekiel 36:36-38 promises a population explosion. Again, the only way the fulfillment of this promise can be applied to the church is to radically change the plain, literal meaning of the text.

In instances where some of the spiritual blessings of the New Covenant are interpreted by Reformed, covenant theology as applicable to the church, God's original promises to Israel must be diminished in order to force-fit them to the church. For example, Jeremiah 31:34 promises, "No more shall every man teach his neighbor, and every man his brother, saying, 'Know the Lord,' for they all shall know Me, from the least of them to the greatest of them, says the Lord." The value of this promise is in its universal fulfillment of "all" knowing the Lord and no longer needing to teach one another to know the Lord. But the New Testament plainly states that not all believers in the church know the Lord (John 14:7-9; 1 Cor. 15:34; Gal. 4:9; 1 John 2:3-4) though all are known by Him. If this promise is fulfilled by the church, then why do the apostles write to the church instructing them to know the Lord? Likewise, in Ezekiel 36:25 the Lord promises that the New Covenant recipients will be free "from all your idols." How does this fit with New Testament warnings to church-age believers about idolatry in their lives (1 Cor. 10:7, 14, 20; 2 Cor. 6:14-16; Eph. 5:5-8; Col. 3:5; 1 John 5:21)?

The promises of the New Covenant will be literally and completely fulfilled with the saved, believing nation of Israel, not the church, when the Lord Jesus Christ returns to establish His kingdom on the earth (Rom. 11:26-28). Therefore, the church is not presently fulfilling God's promises to Israel though some of its blessings regarding forgiveness of sins and the indwelling of the Spirit are similar to those promised to Israel. In addition, the church benefits from the blood of Christ that was shed at His first coming to provide the basis for the fulfillment of God's new covenant with Israel. In this sense, the church is related to the covenant's Mediator, Jesus Christ, without being a legal participant in that covenant itself or a party to it. This view is held by an increasing number of traditional dispensationalists, including this author.[17]

But even if the position of other dispensationalists such as MacArthur is correct, that the church currently participates in or partially fulfills the spiritual blessings of the New Covenant while Israel will one day literally fulfill all of the physical and spiritual provisions of the covenant, there is still one glaring problem for the perseverance view. The promises of Jeremiah 32:39-40 and the other New Covenant passages about God sovereignly and deterministically causing Israel to fear and obey the Lord forever are never stated anywhere in the New Testament as being fulfilled by the church today. Why this glaring omission? The fact remains that these passages can only be forced to apply to believers today by imposing a preconceived theology onto the text—a theology which views the church as Israel, disregards context, diminishes the original prom-

---

17. Roy E. Beacham, "The Church Has No Legal Relationship to or Participation in the New Covenant," in *Dispensational Understanding of the New Covenant*, ed. Mike Stallard (Schaumburg, IL: Regular Baptist Press, 2012), 107-44; John Nelson Darby, *Notes on the Epistle to the Hebrews* (Sunbury, PA: Believers Bookshelf, 1970), 85; idem, *Synopsis of the Books of the Bible* (Sunbury, PA: Believers Bookshelf, 1970), 3:181-82, 368; George A. Gunn, "Second Corinthians 3:6 and the Church's Relationship to the New Covenant," *Journal of Dispensational Theology* 13 (December 2009): 25-45; J. B. Hixson and Mark Fontecchio, *What Lies Ahead: A Biblical Overview of the End Times* (Brenham, TX: Lucid, 2013), 139-56; *An Introduction to the New Covenant*, ed. Christopher Cone (Hurst, TX: Tyndale Seminary Press, 2013); *Letters of J. N. D.* [John Nelson Darby], 1879–1882 (n.p.: Stow Hill Bible and Tract Depot, 1970), 3:324-25; Stephen R. Lewis, "The New Covenant," in *Progressive Dispensationalism: An Analysis of the Movement and Defense of Traditional Dispensationalism*, ed. Ron J. Bigalke, Jr. (Lanham, MD: University Press of America, 2005),135-43; John R. Master, "The New Covenant," in *Issues in Dispensationalism*, ed. Wesley R. Willis and John R. Master (Chicago: Moody, 1994), 93-110.

ises of the covenant, and alters the literal meaning of biblical words and names.

2 Corinthians 5:17

In 2 Corinthians 5:17, Paul writes, "Therefore, if anyone is in Christ, he is a new creation; old things have passed away; behold all things have become new." This passage is often misinterpreted as teaching that if a person has been truly born again, he will have a complete turnaround or change in his lifestyle or behavior. Short of this, it is claimed that a person is merely a professor of salvation but not a genuine possessor of it.

However, it should be noted that the phrase "all things" is a textual variant that is not found in the earliest Greek manuscripts. It would be unwise to build a doctrine on this phrase and insist that "all things" in a person's life must change practically in order to qualify as being truly regenerate. After all, who can honestly say that "all things" in their Christian lives now conform to the will of God? Who among us does not still sin? If this verse were describing "all things" changing in terms of a believer's spiritual *condition*, then it would be requiring sinless perfection, which is unbiblical (1 John 1:8, 10). Therefore, it is better to interpret being a "new creation" in the sense of one's *position*, rather than condition, just as the passage itself begins: "if any man be *in Christ*, he is a new creation."

Philippians 1:6

Paul writes in Philippians 1:6, "being confident of this very thing, that He who has begun a good work in you will complete it until the day of Jesus Christ." This is one of the most frequently cited verses to support the doctrine of the perseverance of the saints. It is commonly assumed that this passage is promising all genuine believers that God will sovereignly work in their lives to finish the process of practical sanctification begun at justification, thereby causing believers to persevere in faith and good works to the end of their lives. Despite the popularity of this interpretation, we must ask whether this interpretation fits the context and whether it accords with Paul's use of similar terminology elsewhere in the New Testament and this epistle. Philippians 1:3-7 forms the immediate context for verse 6.

3 I thank my God upon every remembrance of you, 4 always in every prayer of mine making request for you all with joy, 5 for your fellowship in the gospel from the first day until now, 6 being confident of this very thing, that He who has begun a good work in you will complete it until the day of Jesus Christ; 7 just as it is right for me to think this of you all, because I have you in my heart, inasmuch as both in my chains and in the defense and confirmation of the gospel, you all are partakers with me of grace.

Neither the context of verse 6 nor the terminology used in this passage indicates that Paul is referring to the process of practical sanctification. Instead, the good work God was doing in their midst refers to the Philippians' partnership with Paul for the furtherance of the gospel. Several observations support this conclusion.

First, verses 5 and 7 refer to the Philippians' partnership with Paul in the gospel by the expressions "fellowship in the gospel" and being "partakers" of grace with Paul "in the defense and confirmation of the gospel." The word "fellowship" in verse 5 (*koinōnia*) and "partakers" in verse 7 (*sygkoinōnous*) are related terms, showing that Paul viewed the Philippians as sharing in common his gospel ministry. The Philippians were truly partners with Paul in evangelism. This can be seen throughout the epistle. In 1:12, Paul wants them to know how his trials have "turned out for the furtherance of the gospel." In 1:19, Paul tells them that, although he was imprisoned for the gospel, he knew deliverance would come through their prayer and the supply of the Holy Spirit. In 1:27, Paul desires that their "conduct be worthy of the gospel" and that they stand united, "striving together for the faith of the gospel." In 2:22, Paul upholds the example of Timothy, who "served with me in the gospel." In 4:3, Paul describes certain Philippians as "these women who labored with me in the gospel, with Clement also, and the rest of my fellow workers." And in 4:15, Paul reminds them of their original financial gift to his ministry of preaching the gospel, how that "in the beginning of the gospel, when I departed from Macedonia, no church shared with me concerning giving and receiving but you only."

Second, the occasion of Paul's writing his epistle to the Philippians is stated in 4:10-18 where he explicitly acknowledges their most recent financial gift, in addition to their past giving. The epilogue to the epistle in 4:10-18 is widely (and rightly) regarded as forming a parallel to Paul's opening remarks in the prologue of 1:3-7. Since these two sections function like bookends that introduce and restate Paul's primary reason in writing the epistle, the "good work" that Paul must be referring to in 1:6 is the Philippians' financial support of his ministry in furthering the gospel. The manner in which they partnered with Paul in the gospel was not only through their prayers (1:19) but also their financial support. This conclusion is confirmed by the repetition in the epilogue of terms related to *koinōnia* in 1:5 and 1:7. Notice in 4:14-15 how Paul uses these terms twice to show how they shared in common his gospel ministry: "Nevertheless you have done well that you shared (*sygkoinōnēsantes*) in my distress. Now you Philippians know also that in the beginning of the gospel, when I departed from Macedonia, no church shared (*ekoinōnēsen*) with me concerning giving and receiving but you only."

Third, the time references in 1:5-6 and 4:15 further establish the clear parallel theme between the prologue and epilogue concerning the good work of supporting Paul in the gospel. In 1:5, Paul refers to the Philippians' fellowship in the gospel "from the first day until now." In 1:6, he refers to the fact that God had "begun a good work." This thought is repeated in 4:15 by Paul's reference to the Philippians' support "in the beginning of the gospel, when I departed from Macedonia."[18]

Fourth, the possible meaning of *sanctification* for the phrase "good work" in 1:6 has no parallel in the New Testament, whereas the sense of *charitable gift* does occur elsewhere. The combination of the adjective "good" (*agathos*) with the noun "work" (*ergon*) occurs 14 times in the Greek New Testament.[19] In each instance, man is said to be the subject doing the good work rather than God.[20] If the "good work" of Philippians 1:6 refers to God's inner saving work of sanctification, then it is a unique occurrence in the New Testament, making it an unlikely interpretation. By contrast, the adjective "good" (*agathos*), combined with "work" (*ergon*), is clearly used elsewhere by Paul in a context about financial giving (2 Cor. 9:8). In addition, Paul also uses the adjective "good" (*agathos*) with the

---

18. For further parallels between Philippians 1:3-7 and 4:10-18, see John F. Hart, "Does Philippians 1:6 Guarantee Progressive Sanctification? Part 1," *Journal of the Grace Evangelical Society* 9 (Spring 1996): 37-58; idem, "Does Philippians 1:6 Guarantee Progressive Sanctification? Part 2," *Journal of the Grace Evangelical Society* 9 (Autumn 1996): 33-60.

19. See Acts 9:36; Romans 2:7; 13:3; 2 Corinthians 9:8; Ephesians 2:10; Philippians 1:6; Colossians 1:10; 2 Thessalonians 2:17; 1 Timothy 2:10; 5:10; 2 Timothy 2:21; 3:17; Titus 1:16; and 3:1.

20. Hart, "does Philippians 1:6 Guarantee Progressive Sanctification? Part 2," 46 n. 29.

verb form of "work" (*ergeō*) in reference to the good work of giving in 1 Timothy 6:18.

Fifth, when Philippians 1:6 speaks of the good work occurring "in you" (*en hymin*), this prepositional phrase could also be translated "among you." The Greek preposition *en* is often used with a corporate sense, meaning "among" rather than "in."[21] This is how *en* is used in Philippians 2:15, where Paul writes, "among whom you shine as lights in the world." The corporate sense of God beginning a good work "among" the Philippians by financially supporting Paul's gospel ministry fits well with the context of 1:6.

Finally, the Greek word for "complete" in 1:6 (*epiteleō*) is used six other times by the apostle Paul (Rom. 15:28; 2 Cor. 7:1; 8:6, 11 [twice]; Gal. 3:3). Four of these uses are in contexts of believers completing the good work of financial giving as motivated by God's grace (Rom. 15:28; 2 Cor. 8:6, 11). In Philippians 1:6, the meaning is that God will complete the financial support of the gospel until Jesus Christ returns. Though God began doing this among the Philippians (4:15) and continued it on several occasions thereafter through them (4:14), Philippians 1:6 does not necessarily promise that God would use the Philippians as His instruments to complete the work. Notice what the verse does say and what it does not say. It says, "He who has begun a good work in/among you will complete it until the day of Jesus Christ." It does *not* say, "He who has begun a good work in/among you will complete it *in/among you* until the day of Jesus Christ." Philippians 1:6 never promises that God will complete the work in/among the Philippians. It promises only that He *will* complete the work. This means that He may complete this work through others besides the Philippian Christians or through future generations of saints from Philippi who come after them, as is so often said, "God buries His workman but continues His work."

Based on these six exegetical observations, it is best not to interpret Philippians 1:6 as a promise that God will deterministically cause every believer to progress in sanctification and persevere to the end of their lives in faith and good works. Instead, this verse is simply stating Paul's confidence that just as the Lord initiated among the Philippians the good work of partnering with him for the furtherance of the gospel, the Lord would continue working to complete the financial support of the gospel until Christ comes back.

---

21. Walter Bauer, William F. Arndt, and F. Wilbur Gingrich, *A Greek-English Lexicon of the New Testament and Other Early Christian Literature*, 3rd ed., rev. and ed. Frederick W. Danker (Chicago: University of Chicago Press, 2000), 326.

Inheriting the Kingdom Passages

In a few passages in Paul's epistles, he lists various sins and declares that those who do such things will not inherit the kingdom of God (1 Cor. 6:9-11; Gal. 5:19-21; Eph. 5:5-6). These passages are often interpreted as warnings to Christians that if these sins characterize their lives, then their profession of faith in Christ is false and they are unregenerate. However, the evidence from these passages shows that Paul was simply describing the sins that characterize unbelievers and their lost state and using this to exhort believers, who are on their way to heaven, not to live like those who are on their way to hell.

> 9 Do you not know that the unrighteous will not inherit the kingdom of God? Do not be deceived. Neither fornicators, nor idolaters, nor adulterers, nor homosexuals, nor sodomites, 10 nor thieves, nor covetous, nor drunkards, nor revilers, nor extortioners will inherit the kingdom of God. 11 And such were some of you. But you were washed, but you were sanctified, but you were justified in the name of the Lord Jesus and by the Spirit of our God. (1 Cor. 6:9-11)

Who are the "unrighteous" in this passage who will not inherit the kingdom of God? Are they self-deceived professing Christians among the Corinthian congregation who are in reality not even justified saints? No, the "unrighteous" (*adikoi*) of verse 9 are the same "unrighteous" (*adikōn*), unjustified people referred to earlier in the context: "Dare any of you, having a matter against another, go to law before the unrighteous (*adikōn*), and not before the saints?" (1 Cor. 6:1). Since "saints" are contrasted with the "unrighteous" in this passage, and every believer is a saint, including the carnal Corinthians (1 Cor. 1:2), then the "unrighteous" must be a reference to those who are lost and unregenerate. This interpretation of the "unrighteous" is confirmed again in the context by Paul's equation of the "unrighteous" with those of "the world" in 1 Corinthians 6:2 and "unbelievers" in 6:6. These are the same "unrighteous" ones described in verse 9. Thus, in verses 9-10, Paul is describing the sins that characterize unbelievers.

Before a person is justified in God's sight, He sees that unbeliever as being positionally in Adam—spiritually dead in trespasses and sins (Eph. 2:1). Unless an unbeliever places his faith in Jesus Christ for salvation, he will die in his sins (John 8:24). The result of dying in one's sins is that he will remain unforgiven for all eternity. Into eternity, God will see the lost in the lake of fire as still in the various sins that characterized their earthly lives (Rev. 21:8; 22:15). But in contrast to the lost, the Corinthians were washed, sanctified (positionally), and justified in God's sight (1 Cor. 6:11). Even though the Corinthians were carnal and walking like the world around them (1 Cor. 3:1-4), Paul contrasted them with the unsaved or "unrighteous" (6:9), saying, "and such were some of *you*. But *you* were washed, but *you* were sanctified, but *you* were justified" (v. 11). Note carefully that Paul was not warning the Corinthians that some *of them* might not be justified before God (i.e., declared righteous). Instead, he was reminding them that their spiritual *condition* on the earth (practical righteousness) should be consistent with their spiritual *position* in Christ (imputed righteousness). Since they possessed a righteous standing before God, the state of their lives should also be righteous and different from the unrighteous or unsaved.

> 19 Now the works of the flesh are evident, which are: adultery, fornication, uncleanness, lewdness, 20 idolatry, sorcery, hatred, contentions, jealousies, outbursts of wrath, selfish ambitions, dissensions, heresies, 21 envy, murders, drunkenness, revelries, and the like; of which I tell you beforehand, just as I also told you in time past, that those who practice such things will not inherit the kingdom of God. (Gal. 5:19-21)

This passage parallels 1 Corinthians 6:9-11 in exhorting believers who will enter the kingdom to live differently than unbelievers who will not enter the kingdom. Recall from the context of 1 Corinthians 6:1-11 that Paul exhorted the positionally sanctified Corinthian saints, who were destined to reign with Christ (1 Cor. 4:8) and judge the world (1 Cor. 6:2-3), that they were to live differently in their practice than the unrighteous world of unbelievers around them. Galatians 5:19-21 makes the same point.

Since the Galatians were already sons of God in standing (Gal. 4:6) and therefore heirs of the kingdom (Gal. 4:7), they were not to live like children of wrath, who will not inherit the kingdom. For this reason, just prior to Galatians 5:19-21, in verse 16, Paul issues a command for the Galatian believers to walk by means of the Spirit rather than the flesh, showing the real possibility that a justified saint may actually walk in carnality and not by God's Spirit. And if the Galatians were to walk by the flesh, their lives would be characterized by the works of the flesh—the very same fleshly works that characterize the lost, who don't even have the Holy Spirit (vv. 19-21; cf. Rom. 8:9). Thus, Paul tells them before (v. 21, *prolegō*) the kingdom arrives about the fate of unbelievers. He also reminds them of their contrast in positions (heirs vs. not inheriting the kingdom) in order to challenge them to have contrasting conditions (walk by the Spirit [v. 16], resulting in the fruit of the Spirit [vv. 22-23], vs. walk by the flesh [v. 16], resulting in the works of the flesh [vv. 19-21]).

> 5 For this you know, that no fornicator, unclean person, nor covetous man, who is an idolater, has any inheritance in the kingdom of Christ and God. 6 Let no one deceive you with empty words, for because of these things the wrath of God comes upon the sons of disobedience. 7 Therefore do not be partakers with them. 8 For you were once darkness, but now you are light in the Lord. Walk as children of light. (Eph. 5:5-8)

In this passage, Paul is once again describing unbelievers, who are contrasted with the Ephesian believers for the purpose of the Ephesians living differently than the lost. This can be seen from the fact that the phrase "sons of disobedience" (*tous huious tēs apeitheias*) in verse 7 occurs earlier in Ephesians 2:2 (*tois huiois tēs apeitheias*) where it describes the Ephesian believers *before* their regeneration. Paul thereby defines the "sons of disobedience" as unbelievers. Nothing in between Ephesians 2:2 and 5:7 indicates that the phrase "sons of disobedience" changes meaning. The prior usage of the phrase "sons of disobedience" as an unmistakable reference to unbelievers prepares the reader for its use again in Ephesians 5:7 where it also refers to unbelievers, who are still in their sins.

As in Paul's other two passages on inheriting the kingdom, believers and unbelievers are distinguished in Ephesians 5:5-8 by the contrast of pronouns in verses 7-8. The pronoun "them" (*autōn*) in verse 7 refers to the "sons of disobedience" in verse 6, and the word "you" occurs twice in verse 8, once in the being verb "you were" (*ēte*) and once as part of the command to "Walk" (*peripateite* – lit., "You walk").[22] Both uses of "you" in verse 8 refer to the Ephesian believers. This contrast of pronouns follows a consistent Pauline pattern where the believer's position in Christ and eternal destiny are purposely

---

22. Verbs in Greek have person (i.e., first person – I, we; second person – you; third person – he, she, it, they).

set in contrast to the condition and practices of the lost, upon whom God's wrath and judgment is coming (Rom. 13:10-14; 1 Cor. 6:9-11; Gal. 5:21; Eph. 2:1-3; 5:3-8; Col. 3:1-8; 1 Thess. 5:1-8), for the purpose of motivating believers to live godly lives.

Whether it is Ephesians 5:5-8 or Galatians 5:21 or 1 Corinthians 6:9-11, none of these passages on inheriting the kingdom are warnings to professing Christians that if they do not live righteously enough, it will prove that they are merely false professors who are still unregenerate and lost. Instead, each of these passages exhorts those who are saints in position to live saintly in practice or condition. It is as though Paul is saying, "As believers, you are children of God bound for heaven by God's grace, but unbelievers are sons of disobedience facing God's wrath and on their way to hell. So don't you, who are going to heaven, live like those children of wrath with their characteristic sins, who are on their way to hell."[23]

James 2:14-26

> 14 What does it profit, my brethren, if someone says he has faith but does not have works? Can faith save him? 15 If a brother or sister is naked and destitute of daily food, 16 and one of you says to them, "Depart in peace, be warmed and filled," but you do not give them the things which are needed for the body, what does it profit? 17 Thus also faith by itself, if it does not have works, is dead. 18 But someone will say, "You have faith, and I have works." Show me your faith without your works, and I will show you my faith by my works. 19 You believe that there is one God. You do well. Even the demons believe—and tremble! 20 But do you want to know, O foolish man, that faith without works is dead? 21 Was not Abraham our father justified by works when he offered Isaac his son on the altar? 22 Do you see that faith was working together with his works, and by works faith was made perfect? 23 And the Scripture was fulfilled which says, "Abraham believed God, and it was accounted to him for righteousness." And he was called the friend of God. 24 You see then that a man is justified by works, and not by faith

---

23. For further explanation of this interpretation of Paul's inheriting the king-dom passages, see the chapter by Dennis M. Rokser, "Will You Inherit the Kingdom of God?" in *Should Christians Fear Outer Darkness?* by Dennis M. Rokser, Thomas L. Stegall, and Kurt Witzig (Duluth, MN: Grace Gospel Press, 2015), 405-416.

only. 25 Likewise, was not Rahab the harlot also justified by works when she received the messengers and sent them out another way? 26 For as the body without the spirit is dead, so faith without works is dead also.

Few passages in all the Word of God have been as grossly misunderstood as this one. Roman Catholicism has used it to teach that good works are necessary for eternal salvation. Protestants have typically understood James here to teach that faith alone eternally saves, but the kind of faith that saves is never alone; it will always have good works. For example, regarding James 2, MacArthur writes,

> Faith in this context is clearly saving faith (v. 1). James is speaking of eternal salvation. He has referred to "the word implanted, which is able to save your souls" in 1:21. Here he has the same salvation in view. He is not disputing whether faith saves. Rather, he is opposing the notion that faith can be a passive, fruitless, intellectual exercise and still save. Where there are no works, we must assume no faith exists either.[24]

Thus, even many Protestants have subtly and indirectly made works a requirement for eternal salvation, as Piper plainly admits, "Nevertheless, we must also own up to the fact that our final salvation is made contingent upon the subsequent obedience which comes from faith."[25] Similarly, John Gerstner claims, "The question is not whether good works are necessary for salvation, but in what way are they necessary. As the inevitable outworking of saving faith, they are necessary for salvation."[26]

But if James is not teaching that the condition for eternal salvation is faith plus works, or a "working faith" as some would say, then what is his point? James wrote to those who he knew were *already born again* and eternally saved through faith in Christ in order to show that good works are the necessary and inevitable result of a genuine *walk* of faith in the Christian life. James 2:14-26 does not teach that good works are the necessary result of a person initially believing in Christ for justification in God's sight (first-tense salvation). Instead,

---

24. MacArthur, *Faith Works*, 149.

25. John Piper and Pastoral Staff, *What We Believe About the Five Points of Calvinism* (Minneapolis: Bethlehem Baptist Church document, 1998).

26. John H. Gerstner, *Wrongly Dividing the Word of Truth* (Brentwood, TN: Wolgemuth & Hyatt, 1991), 210.

this passage shows that good works are the necessary result of the child of God presently walking by faith, being practically sanctified (second-tense salvation), and therefore justified or declared righteous in the sight of men. To correctly interpret this passage, the audience to whom James was writing must first be identified.

Did James question whether his readers were truly born again? Did he wonder if they were mere professors but not possessors of eternal salvation? Did he write to test the reality of their regeneration and justification before God on the basis of whether they had a "working faith" or not? Or did he believe they were already born again, so that he wrote to test the reality of their second-tense salvation and walk of faith? The entire epistle of James indicates it is the latter.

This can be seen in James's use of the term "brethren." He begins this section in 2:14 by calling them "my brethren." While some New Testament passages use the term "brethren" to describe *ethnic brothers* who were merely fellow Jews (Acts 13:26; 23:6; Rom. 9:3), James uses this term throughout his epistle to describe genuine *brothers in Christ.* In the very first use of "brethren" in his epistle in 1:2-4, James assumes they have "faith" that will undergo trials for the divine purpose of their growth and maturation. In 2:1, he clearly assumes his brethren have "the faith of our Lord Jesus Christ." In 3:1, he instructs his brethren that there should not be many teachers among them, which would be a strange thing to tell unregenerate ethnic brothers! In 5:7-9, he instructs his brethren to be patient in waiting for the coming of the Lord, which is also something James would never instruct an unregenerate person to do. Elsewhere, he refers to them not merely as "brethren" but as "my beloved brethren" (1:16, 19; 2:5). There is every reason to conclude that James considered his audience to be eternally saved. This is also substantiated when we consider his use of the term "saved" in the epistle.

In 2:14, it is commonly assumed that James's use of the word "save" ("Can faith save him?") refers to eternal salvation. However, neither the immediate context of 2:14-26 nor the four other occurrences of "save" (*sōzō*) in the epistle warrant such an assumption. The first occurrence of this term is in James 1:21 where he instructs his readers to "receive with meekness the implanted word, which is able to save your souls." In the immediately preceding verses (1:17-18) he indicated that these same individuals had already received the divine gift of regeneration. So in what sense would these children of God need their souls saved? The use of "save" in 1:21 must be in reference to second-tense salvation—salvation from sin's power and damaging effects in their Christian lives, which we call practical sanctification—not eternal salvation. In fact, in the very next verse (1:22), James commands his readers to be "doers of the word," which is a command only an eternally saved, regenerated individual is capable of fulfilling. In addition, James's three other uses of "save" (*sōzō*) outside of 1:21 and 2:14 are consistent only with a temporal deliverance in this life rather than eternal life (4:12; 5:15, 20).

In 2:14-26, James is not denying the reality of his readers' initial faith in Christ for eternal salvation. He is *not* saying, "You claim to born again, but since you don't have good works as the proof of regeneration, you must never have had genuine, saving faith in Christ." Is it possible for one who has been truly born again, and is a genuine saint, to have a dead faith (2:17, 20)? Yes! That is the very reason why James is addressing such a problem for Christians in 2:14-26. Death in the Bible does not mean *nonexistence*, but *separation*. At death, there is a separation of the spirit from the body, just as James describes in 2:26. When faith is "by itself" (2:17) and separated from works, it is "dead." *That does not mean faith never existed or was never genuine.* You would never say at a funeral while looking at a corpse in a casket, "That must have never been a genuine person." On the contrary, the corpse in the casket is proof that the person was once really alive and a genuine person!

In this passage, James is challenging his regenerated readers to see whether their faith is ongoing, living, and active, as evidenced by their works. Starting in 2:14, he is testing a profession of faith without works when he says, "What does it profit, my brethren, if someone *says* he has faith but does not have works?" Such an inactive, dead faith on the part of a genuine saint does not "save" (2:14c) the Christian in the sense of practical sanctification, nor does it benefit or profit others (2:15-16). Good works do not save us, but they are an essential part of God's plan for the Christian life after a person is regenerated (Eph. 2:8-10; Titus 3:5-8). Technically, a person is also not saved *by* good works in second-tense salvation. Believers are sanctified *by* God's grace and the Spirit's power *through* a walk of faith, which *results in* good works. Good works are not the *means* of sanctification but the inevitable *result* of it. Just as faith without works is a "dead faith" (i.e., a faith "by itself," v. 17), so works without faith are simply "dead works." Work done without faith is simply legalism and cannot please God (Heb. 11:6).[27] Thus, God wills

---

27. The analogy of James 2:26 should not be pressed so far as to teach that works give life to faith, as Hiebert writes, "the one point in the analogy is the fact that the

that every regenerate person walk by faith (2 Cor. 5:7; Gal. 2:20; Col. 2:5-6) in newness of life (Rom. 6:4-6) and the Holy Spirit (Rom. 8:4).

James is perfectly consistent here with what Paul and John teach. The apostle Paul says that a believer cannot be walking according to the Spirit and simultaneously be manifesting the works of the flesh (Gal. 5:16-26). He agrees with James that a Christian's faith should be working through love (Gal. 5:6). Likewise, the apostle John says that believers cannot claim to have fellowship with God while walking in darkness or sin (1 John 1:6). He also says that a child of God cannot truly know God if he does not keep Christ's commandments and walk as He walked (1 John 2:3-6). A genuine believer may not "know" the Lord as he should (John 14:7-9; 1 Cor. 15:34; Gal. 4:9); but if a child of God is walking by faith and keeping Christ's commandments, he can be regarded as a friend of God (John 15:14), which James tells us was the case with Abraham (2:23c).

If believers will walk in faith, the result will be: (1) practical sanctification and good works that are beneficial to others, and (2) justification before men. Abraham was justified or declared righteous *before God by faith alone* (Rom. 4:2-3; Gal. 3:6-11). James 2:23 refers to this moment in Abraham's life by quoting the classic Old Testament passage of Genesis 15:6 on justification before God by faith apart from works. But Abraham was also justified in a second sense—*before men, by faith plus works*—when some forty years later (Gen. 22) he trusted God enough to do the work of offering Isaac (James 2:21). As a result of Abraham's faith working together with his deed (2:22; Heb. 11:17-19), he has been declared righteous by men for the last four millennia. Though God can see the heart, men cannot see what is in the heart of another person except through that person's deeds. God sees a person's faith without their deeds (1 Sam. 16:7). Therefore, justification before God is through faith alone, but justification before men is by faith plus works. James 2:14-26 is not a lesson in how to be justified before God, as many have wrongly assumed; rather it indicates there are two types of justification.

The Greek syntax of James 2:24 supports two kinds of justification. This verse is normally translated, "You see then that a man is justified by works, and not by faith only/alone." This translation assumes that the Greek word for "only" or "alone" (*monon*) functions as an adjective that modifies the noun "faith" (*pisteōs*), as in

---

absence of the second member means sure death, and that it is the aim of James to establish that faith and works are inseparable" (D. Edmond Hiebert, *The Epistle of James* [Chicago: Moody Press, 1979], 200).

the standard translation "faith only." But there is better evidence to support the conclusion that the word for "only" (*monon*) functions as an adverb that modifies the verb "justified," so that the verse is really saying, "You see then that a man is justified by works, and not only (justified) by faith." In Greek, adjectives normally agree with the nouns they modify in case, gender, and number. In James 2:24, *monon* is accusative case, neuter gender, and singular in number. However, the noun *pisteōs* is genitive case, feminine gender, and singular in number. This lack of agreement in both case and gender makes it much more likely that *monon* is functioning adverbially, modifying the verb "justified" (*dikaioutai*), rather than adjectivally, modifying *pisteōs*.[28] This supports the conclusion that in verse 24 James is saying that his readers were not "only justified" by faith alone as in Genesis 15:6 but also potentially justified before man by faith plus works as in Genesis 22. Thus, in 2:14-26, James is seeking to contrast justification *before men by works* (v. 21) with the justification *before God by faith alone* that was mentioned in the previous verse (v. 23) where he quotes Genesis 15:6.

But if James were referring to only one type of justification, namely justification before God, as the passage is usually interpreted, then this presents a blatant contradiction with Paul's teaching. In Romans 4:6, Paul says that God justifies believers "apart from works." But James 2:24 says that man is "justified by works." Justification before God cannot be simultaneously "apart from works" and "by works"!

Traditionally, many Protestant interpreters have assumed that James 2 is speaking of the same type of justification that Paul refers to in Romans 4. But if this were true, then not only would Paul and James contradict one another, but the standard Reformed interpretation would end up essentially agreeing with the Roman Catholic interpretation of James 2 that justification in God's sight cannot be "apart from works." Roman Catholics interpret James 2:24 to say that justification in God's sight is by faith *plus works*. Reformed interpreters, in their attempt to maintain *sola fide* argue that justification before God is by a faith *that works*. Thus, it is common to hear Reformed interpreters equivocate, saying, "Faith alone saves, but

---

28. For further support of this point, see John Niemelä, "Faith Without Works: A Definition," *Chafer Theological Seminary Journal* 6 (April-June 2000): 2-18; idem, "James 2:24: Retranslation Required, Part 1," *Chafer Theological Seminary Journal* 7 (January-March 2001): 13-24; idem, "James 2:24: Retranslation Required, Part 2," *Chafer Theological Seminary Journal* 7 (April-June 2001): 2-15.

saving faith is never alone."[29] In other words, they say good works must always flow from initial faith exercised at justification; otherwise, if a professing Christian's faith is separated from works, then it is considered spurious or non-saving. But how is this substantially different from the doctrine of Roman Catholicism?[30]

Combining Justification and Sanctification

Note the similarity between the teaching of Catholicism and statements made by some of today's Calvinist leaders. Catholicism teaches that *justification includes sanctification:*

The Holy Spirit is the master of the interior life. By giving birth to the "inner man," justification entails the sanctification of his whole being.[31]

Consequently, Catholicism also teaches that *without sanctification there is no justification or salvation:*

Infused into the very essence of the soul, sanctifying grace is a certain supernatural quality granted by God, without which we are not sanctified or assured justification and salvation.[32]

Perseverance advocates say that God only justifies or judicially declares someone to be righteous who is also made practically righteous or sanctified. According to Catholicism, God will not declare someone to be righteous who is not already practically righteous. Similarly, according to some leading Calvinists in our day, there can be no imputed righteousness without infused righteousness, and thus there can be no justification before God without practical sanctification. While Catholicism formally equates justification with sanctification and Calvinists correctly distinguish the two, they sometimes sound very Catholic by making the believer's own practical sanctifi-

29. For a thorough assessment of this common but erroneous cliché, see Fred R. Lybrand, *Back to Faith: Reclaiming Gospel Clarity in an Age of Incongruence* (n.p.: Xulon, 2009).

30. For further explanation of James 2:14-26, see the convincing exegesis and exposition by Dennis M. Rokser in his booklet, *Faith and Works: A Clarification of "Faith Without Works Is Dead" (James 2:14-26)* (Duluth, MN: Grace Gospel Press, 2013).

31. *Catechism of the Catholic Church* (Bloomingdale, OH: Apostolate for Family Consecration, 1994), 483, §1995.

32. *The Catholic Encyclopedia*, ed. Robert C. Broderick (Nashville: Thomas Nelson, 1987), 541.

cation and infused righteousness the reason or cause for God declaring believers righteous, rather than the reason being Christ's perfect righteousness alone (1 Cor. 1:30; 2 Cor. 5:21; Phil. 3:8-9). This can be seen in the following statements by John MacArthur where justification before God and practical sanctification are blended together.

> When a sinner believes in the Lord Jesus Christ, he is declared *to be* righteous, because he now possesses God's own righteousness as a gift of His grace. God does not *consider* a believer to be righteous; He *makes* him righteous.[33]

> Many people believe justified means "just-as-if-I'd-never-sinned." In other words, God says, "I count you righteous even though you're really not." It is true that God makes that declaration, but there is also a reality of righteousness. We are not only declared righteous; we are made righteous. There is not only imputation—the declaration of righteousness—but there is impartation—the granting of real righteousness. God is not guilty of some legal fiction. He is not play acting, that is, saying something is true that isn't.[34]

> I'm convinced that the reason God can declare us righteous is that we are truly made righteous. Otherwise, God is saying something that isn't true about us. I know that there have been many people who have tried to teach that we are only declared to be righteous, and not actually made righteous. They then have this excuse: "Since we are not made righteous, there doesn't have to be the result of righteousness in our lives." But that is not the case.[35]

> There are not two *kinds* of righteousness—only two *aspects* of divine righteousness. Righteousness is a single package; God does not declare someone righteous whom He does not also make righteous. Having begun the process, He will continue it to ultimate glorification.[36]

---

33. John F. MacArthur, Jr., *Romans 1–8*, The MacArthur New Testament Commentary (Chicago: Moody Press, 1991), 208.

34. John F. MacArthur, Jr., *Justified by Faith: Study Notes on Romans 3:20-4:25* (Panorama City, CA: Word of Grace Communications, 1984), 93-94.

35. Ibid., 95.

36. John F. MacArthur, Jr., *Faith Works: The Gospel According to the Apostles* (Dallas: Word, 1993), 110 (italics original).

While Catholicism also teaches that faith and works are necessary to receive salvation, it qualifies the kind of works necessary for eternal life, namely, *grace-enabled good works.*

> We cannot "earn" our salvation through good works, but our faith in Christ puts us in a special grace-filled relationship with God so that our obedience and love, combined with our faith, will be rewarded with eternal life.[37]

Just like Catholicism, Calvinists John MacArthur and Thomas Schreiner attempt to justify the necessity of good works for salvation by appealing to good works that are the product of God's grace and Spirit in the sanctified believer's life.

> Does this mean confession before men is a condition of becoming a true Christian? No, but it means that a characteristic of every genuine believer is that he or she *will* confess Christ before men. . . . The confession is not merely a human work; it is prompted by God, subsequent to the act of believing but inseparable from it.[38]

> First Corinthians 12:3 cannot refer to just saying the words "Jesus is Lord." It must mean more. It includes acknowledging Him as Lord by obeying Him, by surrendering one's will to His lordship, by affirming Him with one's deeds as well as with one's words. . . . This in no way establishes a gospel of human works. Notice that it is the Holy Spirit who enables a person to confess Jesus as Lord.[39]

> Yes, works are necessary to be saved. No, this is not works righteousness, for the works are hardly meritorious. The grace of God is so powerful that it not only grants us salvation apart from our merits, but also transforms us. Christians are not only declared righteous but also experience observable and significant change in their lives.[40]

---

37. *Pillar of Fire, Pillar of Truth* (El Cajon, CA: Catholic Answers, 1997), 23.
38. John F. MacArthur, Jr., *The Gospel According to Jesus* (Grand Rapids: Zondervan, 1988),198-99.
39. Ibid., 209.
40. Thomas R. Schreiner, "Perseverance and Assurance: A Survey and a Proposal," *Southern Baptist Journal of Theology* 2 (Spring 1998): 53.

Regarding Schreiner's statement, Dennis Rokser insightfully responds,

> Yet claiming that God's grace enables good works in no way lessens the believer's personal responsibility to appropriate and act on that grace. The same author even states a few sentences later that we must actively keep ourselves in the love of God to stay saved. He says, "The imperative here reveals that this is our responsibility. To be spared from God's wrath on the last day we must keep ourselves in God's love, and yet such self-keeping is ultimately not our work but God's."[41] This is contradictory. If it is "self-keeping" then it is man's work and the "keeping" is not attributable to God. The same author goes on to conclude, "Though God undergirds all our effort, it is still the case that we must do what the scriptures command."[42] When final salvation is predicated on the believer's cooperation with God in a life of faithfulness and good works (even grace-enabled works), the result is a lack of certainty and security of salvation. Who can know whether they have done enough of "what the scriptures command"?[43]

Simply because believers can be sanctified and enabled to do good works by God's grace does not make our works either sufficient or necessary to save us. If even grace-enabled works were necessary for salvation, then this would contradict the clear teaching of Scripture that salvation is said to be both *by grace* and *not by works*. For example, Titus 3:5 says that believers are saved by God's mercy and "not by works of righteousness which we have done." A work "of righteousness" is not a merely humanistic, worthless, religious work, but one that is truly righteous—one resulting from practical or infused righteousness. Even this kind of work does not save! Likewise, Ephesians 2:8-9 explains how we *are* saved and how we *are not* saved: "For by grace you have been saved. . . . not of works, lest anyone should boast." There is no theological or exegetical justification for concluding that righteous works play any role in saving us when Scripture plainly teaches just the opposite.

---

41. Ibid., 53.
42. Ibid., 54.
43. Dennis M. Rokser, *Shall Never Perish Forever: Is Salvation Forever or Can It Be Lost?* (Duluth, MN: Grace Gospel Press, 2012), 180.

"Future Justification"

Those who teach the necessity of perseverance for salvation are increasingly using phrases such as "future justification," "future salvation," and "final salvation" to require good works for eternal salvation. They admit that justification before God occurs at a point in time, on the condition of faith alone in Christ alone, resulting in the believer being declared righteous by God and receiving His imputed righteousness on the basis of Christ's finished work alone. Initial justification, they say, is conditioned solely on faith. However, since they believe that sanctification and perseverance are also necessary evidence that a person has been truly regenerated and justified, they incorporate sanctification and perseverance as virtual conditions for "future justification." John Piper claims,

> Present justification is based on the substitutionary work of Christ alone, enjoyed in union with him through faith alone. Future justification is the open confirmation and declaration that in Christ Jesus we are perfectly blameless before God. This final judgment accords with our works. That is, the fruit of the Holy Spirit in our lives will be brought forward as the evidence and confirmation of true faith and union with Christ. Without that validating transformation, there will be no future salvation.[44]

Is there one condition for initial, present justification but more than one condition for future justification and salvation? There are serious problems with such a view. The first is eschatological. Immediately after a person dies, that person has the same standing before God as he had immediately before he died. If he believed in Christ and was justified immediately before death, then he remains justified in God's sight immediately after death and into eternity. He does not need to wait until a final, general, universal judgment for validation of whether he is eternally saved or not. Future judgment for believers at Christ's return is not for the purpose of declaring who is saved versus lost in accordance with that person's earthly works, but to determine rewards.

Furthermore, God is omniscient and eternal. No good works need to be "brought forward as the evidence and confirmation of

---

44. John Piper, "The Justification Debate: A Primer," *Christianity Today* (June 2009): 35.

true faith" to a God who is from everlasting to everlasting and knows all things, including the end from the beginning (Ps. 90:2; Isa. 46:10). By the time a believer dies and is in heaven, God will already know whether that person had "true faith" and there will be no need to validate whether that person is saved or not.

Moreover, if "the fruit of the Holy Spirit in our lives" must be "brought forward as evidence . . . of true faith," then won't the basis for "future salvation" shift from Christ's perfect righteousness and work to the believer's imperfect righteousness and works? Since God is infinitely righteous and requires perfect righteousness to be accepted by Him, only His Son's righteousness will be sufficient, which is received as a gift of His grace at the moment of justification by faith alone in Christ alone (Phil. 3:8-9). If man's righteousness is insufficient to justify him in God's eyes at the moment of initial justification (Gal. 3:10; James 2:10), then how can an imperfect earthly life of sanctification be brought forward in the future as necessary evidence to declare him finally justified and saved?

In John 8:11, the Lord Jesus spoke graciously to the woman caught in adultery, saying to her, "Neither do I condemn you. Go and sin no more." Notice, He did not say, "Since I know that you will go and sin no more, therefore I do not condemn you." Nor did Jesus say, "Neither do I condemn you now, but if you go and sin more, then I will condemn you in the future." Justification in this life and in eternity is all by God's grace, based solely on the Savior's own work and righteousness, and conditioned only on faith in Him apart from one's own works.

Justified but Unsanctified Saints

So-called future justification that requires a validating transformation assumes that every justified believer will also live a sanctified life. But is it really possible to be justified in God's sight and not practically sanctified in this lifetime? Historically, this possibility has been denied by those who embrace the doctrine of the perseverance of the saints.[45] This allows some, such as Schreiner, to go so far as to say, "Yes, works are necessary to be saved. . . . Christians are not only declared righteous but also experience observable and signifi-

---

45. See, for example, the Westminster Confession, chapter XIII on Sanctification, points I and III, and chapter XIV on Saving Faith, point III, which not only guarantees practical sanctification but spiritual growth in the Christian life.

cant change in their lives."[46] But this conclusion contradicts the biblical example of the Corinthians who were justified and positionally sanctified yet did not experience "observable and significant change in their lives." Scripture says they literally walked like the unsaved world (1 Cor. 3:4) and some were chastened to the point of physical death (1 Cor. 11:30). They were sanctified positionally in Christ in terms of their *standing* before God as saints, and thus they were justified in His sight, but in terms of their state or practice, they were carnal. But the Corinthians are not the only example of justified yet unsanctified saints in the Bible. Lot and Solomon are also two clear examples.

Righteous Lot

If it were not for the fact that the apostle Peter describes Lot as "righteous" or "just" (i.e., justified), would we ever know he was a believer? One is hard pressed to find even a single deed in Lot's life that was truly righteous. Yet 2 Peter 2:6-9 says he belonged to God as a justified person in contrast to the "unjust" or unjustified with whom he lived.

> 6 and turning the cities of Sodom and Gomorrah into ashes, condemned them to destruction, making them an example to those who afterward would live ungodly; 7 and delivered righteous Lot, who was oppressed by the filthy conduct of the wicked 8 (for that righteous man, dwelling among them, tormented his righteous soul from day to day by seeing and hearing their lawless deeds)—9 then the Lord knows how to deliver the godly out of temptations and to reserve the unjust under punishment for the day of judgment.

Regarding justified Lot, pastor and radio Bible teacher J. Vernon McGee said, "There are going to be some people in heaven who we never even suspected were real born-again children of God. They didn't have very much of a testimony down here. Lot is an example of this—I don't think this man had any testimony for God at all."[47] Is McGee's opinion correct? Did Lot have any testimony for the Lord at all? Was he justified in the sight of men by good works, like his

---

46. Schreiner, "Perseverance and Assurance: A Survey and a Proposal," 53.
47. J. Vernon McGee, *Through the Bible with J. Vernon McGee: 1 Corinthians—Revelation* (Nashville: Thomas Nelson, 1983), 5:737.

relative Abraham? Consider the record of Lot's life according to the book of Genesis:

- Lot leaves Ur of the Chaldeans with his uncle Abram to go to Haran and Canaan, in disobedience to God's revealed instructions for Abram to go without his relatives (11:31; 12:1, 5).

- Lot goes down to Egypt with Abram, which is a picture of the world (12:10–13:1).

- Lot walks by sight instead of faith in coveting the fertile valley of Sodom (13:5-13).

- Lot ends up getting captured by a foreign army, along with the other Sodomites, and must be rescued by Abram (14:12-16).

- Lot's deliverance from God's destruction on Sodom is due to Abraham's intercession for him (18:23-33; 19:29).

- Lot greets the angels as a city official of Sodom and hosts them in his own house (19:1-3).

- Lot offers the wicked men of Sodom his daughters instead of his guests, to do with them as the men of Sodom wished (19:8).

- Lot relays the announcement of Sodom's destruction to his two sons-in-law, who interpret his warning as a joke (19:12-14).

- Lot stalls in leaving Sodom so that the angels must yank him out of the city (19:16).

- Lot declines the angel's command to flee to the mountains, seeking a compromise to flee to the small city of Zoar instead (19:17-22).

- Lot gets drunk two nights in a row and commits incest with his two daughters (19:32-35).

- Lot's two grandsons conceived through his daughters are Ammon and Moab, whose descendants become perennial adversaries of Israel (19:36-38).

Where in Lot's life is the "observable and significant change" that perseverance teachers require? While some people attempt to find a few good works in Lot's life, the examples they come up with are questionable at best. Some say his respectful greeting and hospitality toward the angels are evidence of sanctification. But this may have simply demonstrated the custom of the Middle East, which was much more hospitable to strangers than our modern Western culture. The fact that Lot offers his daughters to the mob instead of his two angel guests shows that Lot may not have been so spiritually minded in hosting them.

In a desperate attempt to find some traces of practical righteousness in Lot's life, MacArthur claims Lot "had respect for holy angels—evidence of his fear of God (19:1-14). He obeyed God by not looking back at Sodom when God's judgment rained down (cf. v. 26)."[48] But if Lot really respected the angels as a reflection of his fear of God, then why did he linger in leaving Sodom after hearing their command to flee, so that the angels had to forcibly remove him and his family from the city? Why did he not heed their instruction to flee to the mountains but pleaded with them for a compromise instead? Even the fact that Lot did not look back as he fled from Sodom (while his wife did) does not necessarily prove that a true fear of the Lord was his motive. He may have been motivated more by fear of dying since a short time after Sodom's destruction he was afraid to stay even in Zoar and fled to a cave in the mountains (19:30).

MacArthur also cites Peter's commentary on Lot's life as evidence for a sanctified life, where 2 Peter 2:8 says, "for that righteous man, dwelling among them, tormented his righteous soul from day to day by seeing and hearing their lawless deeds." MacArthur interprets this as something positive that Lot did,[49] even claiming, "Those who use him as an illustration of someone who is saved but utterly carnal miss the point of 2 Peter 2:8."[50]

But 2 Peter 2:8 is not a positive testimony of practical righteousness in Lot's life. The Greek verb for "tormented" (*ebasanizen*) is in the active voice, meaning Lot was responsible for tormenting his own soul by choosing to dwell among the Sodomites and exposing himself to their wickedness day after day. According to verse 8, this tormenting was not done *to Lot by others*; it was done *by Lot to himself!* There is nothing commendable in this. Lot was not a victim; nor was he innocent. And he certainly was not practically righteous or sanctified. There was absolutely no "observable and

48. MacArthur, *Faith Works,* 128.
49. Ibid.
50. Ibid., 129.

significant change" in his life, such as Schreiner claims is necessary for salvation.[51]

Nor does Lot's life fit the description of "saving faith" required by MacArthur: "It is a total abandonment of self-will, like the grain of wheat that falls to the ground and dies so that it can bear much fruit (cf. John 12:24). It is an exchange of all that we are for all that Christ is. And it denotes implicit obedience, full surrender to the lordship of Christ. Nothing less can qualify as saving faith."[52] By this definition, Lot must have been lost. But the Bible is clear that he was justified, even though he lacked practical righteousness and a sanctified life.

King Solomon

King Solomon represents another case of a justified person who not only was backslidden and led an unsanctified life but who committed idolatry and apostasy (1 Kings 11:1-10).

1 But King Solomon loved many foreign women, as well as the daughter of Pharaoh: women of the Moabites, Ammonites, Edomites, Sidonians, and Hittites—2 from the nations of whom the Lord had said to the children of Israel, "You shall not intermarry with them, nor they with you. Surely they will turn away your hearts after their gods." Solomon clung to these in love. 3 And he had seven hundred wives, princesses, and three hundred concubines; and his wives turned away his heart. 4 For it was so, when Solomon was old, that his wives turned his heart after other gods; and his heart was not loyal to the Lord his God, as was the heart of his father David. 5 For Solomon went after Ashtoreth the goddess of the Sidonians, and after Milcom the abomination of the Ammonites. 6 Solomon did evil in the sight of the Lord, and did not fully follow the Lord, as did his father David. 7 Then Solomon built a high place for Chemosh the abomination of Moab, on the hill that is east of Jerusalem, and for Molech the abomination of the people of Ammon. 8 And he did likewise for all his foreign wives, who burned incense and sacrificed to their gods. 9 So the Lord became angry with Solomon, because his heart had turned from the

---

51. Schreiner, "Perseverance and Assurance: A Survey and a Proposal," 53.
52. John F. MacArthur, Jr., *The Gospel According to Jesus* (Grand Rapids: Zondervan, 1988), 140.

Lord God of Israel, who had appeared to him twice, 10 and had commanded him concerning this thing, that he should not go after other gods; but he did not keep what the Lord had commanded.

Can a man be genuinely saved and yet have a harem of 1,000 women? Can a man be genuinely saved and worship false gods? Can a man be genuinely saved and build temples of worship to such demon-gods? Most Christians today would denounce such a possibility with epithets of "heresy," "antinomianism," and "cheap grace"! Admittedly, it is revolting to consider that a genuinely redeemed child of God would actually stoop to such depths of depravity. Yet the basis for our doctrinal beliefs is not our emotions or personal opinions, but the Word of the Living God—the Bible.

According to the Bible, saved Solomon was not only unequally yoked to an unbelieving wife, which the Bible forbids (2 Cor. 6:14), but he had a thousand unequal yokes upon him! The detrimental effect of such sin was predictable. The man whom God used to write Proverbs, Ecclesiastes, and the Song of Solomon—saved Solomon—turned away from the God of Israel in dreadful idolatry and apostasy. Solomon did not merely passively comply with the false beliefs of his numerous wives, he eventually embraced them as his own; and how great was his fall! The inspired Word tells the woeful story that "his heart was turned from the Lord God of Israel" (1 Kings 11:9), so that "Solomon went after Ashtoreth the goddess of the Zidonians, and after Milcom the abomination of the Ammonites" (v. 5). If this were not enough, verse 7 adds that he followed "Chemosh, the abomination of Moab." Regarding these verses, one commentary states.

> As Solomon grew older he got farther away from God (cf. 1 Kings 11:33). Ashtoreth was a goddess of sex and fertility whose worship involved licentious rites and worship of the stars. She was a vile goddess (cf. 2 Kings 23:13). Molech worship involved human sacrifices, especially children, which was strictly prohibited by the Law (Lev. 18:21; 20:1-5). Chemosh worship was equally cruel and licentious.[53]

Solomon did not merely have his internal affections swayed toward these false gods. He acted upon his heart's idolatrous affec-

---

53. Thomas L. Constable, "1 Kings," in *The Bible Knowledge Commentary*, Old Testament, eds. John F. Walvoord and Roy B. Zuck (Wheaton, IL: Victor, 1985), 508.

tions. He actually had temples and shrines built in honor of these false gods (vv. 7-8). Old Testament scholar John Whitcomb comments regarding Solomon's apostasy:

> Let us attempt to picture the situation that developed around Jerusalem during the last fifteen or twenty years of Solomon's reign. It must have been like Massachusetts Avenue in Washington, D.C., lined with the embassies and legations of many nations—little islands of foreign culture within the borders of the United States. A few years ago I visited this section of our capital city and walked into a fabulously beautiful Moslem mosque crowned with a white limestone minaret piercing the sky above. The costly structure was built with contributions from fifteen predominantly Moslem countries of Africa and Asia, so that there, on that 30,000 square-foot portion of American soil, the god Allah is officially honored! So it was during Solomon's declining years. Shrines to pagan gods with attending priests and guardian queens dotted the hills surrounding Jerusalem.[54]

It is hard to imagine that a true child of God could commit the atrocities done by Solomon—even following a ruthless deity like Milcom, otherwise known as Molech.[55] The Old Testament vividly describes this demon-god (1 Cor. 10:19-21) as requiring child-sacrifice by having babies burned to death upon the fiery arms of his statue (Deut. 12:2-3, 29-31; 2 Kings 23:10; Jer. 32:35). Yet Solomon not only walked after Molech (1 Kings 11:5) but he actually built a house

---

54. John C. Whitcomb, *Solomon to the Exile: Studies in Kings and Chronicles* (Winona Lake, IN: BMH, 1987), 18. It is no wonder that Whitcomb identifies Solomon's transgression as actual "apostasy" when he titles this section of his commentary, "Solomon's Apostasy."

55. Though some scholars maintain a slight distinction between Molech and Milcom (Keil & Delitzsch, *Commentary on the Old Testament* [Peabody, MA: Hendrickson, 1996], 3:119; R. K. Harrison, "Molech," in *The International Standard Bible Encyclopedia*, ed. Geoffrey Bromiley [Grand Rapids: Eerdmans, 1986], 3:401), most acknowledge that they are practically synonymous (John A. Thompson, "Molech," in *The New International Dictionary of Biblical Archeology*, ed. E. M. Blaiklock and R. K. Harrison [Grand Rapids: Zondervan, 1983], 320; Constable, *1 Kings*, 508; John T. Gates, *1 Kings*, in *The Wycliffe Bible Commentary*, ed. Charles Pfeiffer [Chicago: Moody Press, 1987], 322; Robert L. Hubbard, *First & Second Kings*, Everyman's Bible Commentary [Chicago: Moody Press, 1991], 68; Merrill F. Unger, "Molech," in *The New Unger's Bible Dictionary*, ed. R. K. Harrison [Chicago: Moody Press, 1988], 488; Howard F. Vos, *1, 2 Kings*, Bible Study Commentary [Grand Rapids: Lamplighter], 1989, 84; Leon J. Wood, *Israel's United Monarchy* [Grand Rapids: Baker, 1979], 330).

of worship for him (v. 7). In 1 Kings 11:5, the Hebrew text literally says that Solomon "walked after" (*yēlek achărê*) these gods. This is an expression in the Old Testament for the actual worship of idols (Jer. 2:5, 8; 9:14; 16:11; Ezek. 16:47). Thus, the NET Bible translates verse 5, "Solomon worshiped the Sidonian goddess Astarte and the detestable Ammonite god Milcom." Furthermore, 1 Kings 11:33 also implies that Solomon was involved along with his fellow Israelites in "worship" (*shāḥâh*) of these false gods.

Surely all of this constitutes the worst form of apostasy imaginable. Some may object that in Solomon's polytheism he still retained a place for Yahweh, the one, true God of Israel, alongside Ashtoreth, Chemosh, Molech, and other false deities. However, perseverance of the saints proponents should not find any solace in the fact that Solomon did not appear to renounce his faith in Yahweh entirely, at least in a confessional sense. Is there really any virtue in holding only to a creedal belief in Yahweh while simultaneously denying Him in one's heart and committing spiritual adultery with many other gods? Few wives would say to their cheating, philandering husbands, "You mean you still want me too, in addition to your five other women? Oh, what a relief that you still 'love' me along with all those other women!"

Some may claim that the book of Ecclesiastes is evidence that Solomon repented of all these sins at the end of his life and therefore persevered in a state of practical righteousness and sanctification to the end of his life. But this is far from conclusive. While Solomon's perspective in writing Ecclesiastes is certainly retrospective and may have been at the very end of his life, Scripture is silent about his spiritual state at the time of his death. One would think for a believer who apostatized as greatly as Solomon that, if he did end his life with repentance and perseverance in holiness and obedience, Scripture would say so, like it does with the repentance and death of Manasseh (2 Chron. 33:11-20). But it doesn't. Scripture does, however, present Solomon as a frighteningly real example of a person who went apostate yet was truly justified in God's sight and still eternally secure because of God's grace.

Conclusion

The Calvinist doctrine of the perseverance of the saints teaches that every genuine believer will experience progressive sanctification in his or her earthly lifetime, but the apostle Paul in Romans 8:30 conspicuously omits any reference to sanctification between the guarantee of justification and glorification. Though it's true that God in His faithfulness never ceases working within the child of God to bring about greater practical sanctification (Gal. 5:16-17; Phil. 2:13) and most believers do experience some measure of sanctification, this does not automatically guarantee that all believers will become sanctified or even progress in their sanctification since that would require a continual volitional response of faith and yieldedness (Rom. 6:11-13; 12:1; Eph. 4:30; 5:18; Phil. 2:12).

If practical sanctification were strictly a matter of *God's* will, then every child of God would automatically progress in sanctification. But Calvinism's doctrine of perseverance has seriously distorted the teaching of Scripture by claiming that our glorification, or final salvation, is determined partly by our faith in God's work *for us* at Calvary and partly by our collaboration with God's sanctifying work *in us* throughout our Christian lives. However, the terms of eternal salvation as presented in the biblical gospel involve simply trust in Christ's past, finished work, not trust in the Holy Spirit's present work within us. In this sense, the doctrine of the perseverance of the saints practically changes the requirement for eternal salvation from faith alone in Christ alone to faith in Christ *plus* an entire lifetime of sanctified living.

But the biblical gospel of God's grace remains unchanged. Unworthy sinners who place their faith in Christ and are justified at a point in time remain unworthy but justified before God forever, not because they live a transformed life thereafter but because the only basis of their acceptance before God does not change—Jesus Christ and His perfect righteousness. A believer in Christ can never become more accepted by God than he or she is at the initial moment of justification. An entire lifetime of Christian living by the holiest Christian who has ever lived cannot add to the Savior's own saving righteousness imputed to all who simply believe in Him.

Part II

Examining Key Passages on Perseverance

Chapter 9

Perseverance vs. Preservation in the Gospels

If persevering faith is not a requirement for everlasting life, then the teaching of Jesus Christ should reflect this, and it does. But what about all of those passages where Christ says, "he who endures to the end shall be saved," or that certain people only "believe for a while and in time of temptation fall away," or if you "continue in My word, then are you My disciples indeed," or if anyone "does not abide in Me, he is cast out as a branch and is withered; and they gather them and throw them into the fire, and they are burned"? Are these statements requiring perseverance in faith for eternal salvation? This chapter will examine these statements from the Gospels and show that the teaching of Jesus Christ is perfectly consistent with the rest of Scripture, showing that enduring faith is not a requirement for eternal salvation.[1]

---

1. This chapter focuses specifically on perseverance passages. Passages on public confession versus denial of Christ (Matt. 10:32-33) and the unpardonable sin of blasphemy against the Holy Spirit (Matt. 12:9-37) are not covered. In Matthew 10:32-33, public confession of Christ is a requirement for discipleship, resulting in a reward (Matt. 10:34-42), not salvation. John 12:42-43 shows that it is possible to believe in Christ but still not publicly confess Him because of the fear of man. In the case of the unpardonable sin, the Pharisees observed Jesus' many miracles but refused to believe He was the Messiah, believing that He performed miracles by the power of Beelzebub instead of the Holy Spirit (Matt. 12:23-28). The blasphemous words of the Pharisees reflected not only the unbelief of their hearts (Matt. 12:34-37) but a level of hardened unbelief to such an extent that Jesus knew they would never believe in Him, and therefore He said they "will not be forgiven . . . either in this age or in the age to come" (Matt. 12:32). The passage on the unpardonable sin does not present a case of believers failing to persevere in their faith but of people who never believed in Christ. For a detailed explanation of this passage, see Dennis M. Rokser, *Shall Never Perish Forever: Is Salvation Forever or Can It Be Lost?* (Duluth, MN: Grace Gospel Press, 2012), 227-36.

"He Who Endures to the End Shall Be Saved"

Several parallel passages in the Synoptic Gospels contain a form of the statement, "He who endures to the end shall be saved" (Matt. 10:22; 24:13; Mark 13:13; Luke 21:19). This statement is perhaps the mostly commonly cited as support for the doctrine of the perseverance of the saints. In fact, all theological traditions that require the perseverance of a working faith for eternal salvation invariably reference this statement for support, whether it is Catholicism,[2] Lutheranism,[3] Arminianism,[4] or Calvinism.[5] Representing the Reformed, Calvinist tradition, John Piper warns, "It's a mistake to think that perseverance in faith and love is not necessary for final salvation. A deadly mistake. Jesus said in Mark 13:13, 'You will be hated by all for My name's sake. But he who endures to the end shall be saved.'"[6] Is Piper's interpretation warranted? Is Jesus' statement in the parallel passages of Matthew 10:22, 24:13, Mark 13:13, and Luke 21:19 really a warning about persevering to the end of one's life in faith and holiness for eternal salvation from hell? Or has this statement been ripped from its context to teach a doctrine it was never intended to teach?

The notion of every church-age believer's faith persevering to the end of each believer's life for eternal salvation from hell is completely foreign to the context of all four Synoptic Gospel passages. Instead, in each instance, the Lord issues a promise that if those from the

---

2. *Catechism of the Catholic Church* (Bloomingdale, OH: Apostolate for Family Consecration, 1994), 44, §§161-62; Joseph C. Kindel, *What Must I Do to Be Saved?* (Milford, OH: Reihle Foundation, 1995), 79-80; and Robert A. Sungenis, *How Can I Get to Heaven?* (Santa Barbara, CA: Queenship, 1998), 176.

3. John Theodore Mueller, *Christian Dogmatics* (St. Louis: Concordia, 1934), 436; and Francis Pieper, *Christian Dogmatics* (St. Louis: Concordia, 1953), 3:89.

4. Daniel D. Corner, *The Believer's Conditional Security*, 3rd ed. (Washington, PA: Evangelical Outreach, 2000), 249-51; Guy Duty, *If Ye Continue: A Study of the Conditional Aspects of Salvation* (Minneapolis: Bethany, 1966), 65; I. Howard Marshall, *Kept by the Power of God: A Study of Perseverance and Falling Away* (Minneapolis: Bethany, 1969), 74-75; David Pawson, *Once Saved, Always Saved? A Study in Perseverance and Inheritance* (London: Hodder & Stoughton, 1996), 41-42.

5. Anthony A. Hoekema, *Saved by Grace* (Grand Rapids: Eerdmans, 1989), 236, 246; Michael Horton, *Introducing Covenant Theology* (Grand Rapids: Baker, 2006), 185; John Murray, *Redemption: Accomplished and Applied* (Grand Rapids: Eerdmans, 1955), 152; A. W. Pink, *The Saint's Perseverance* (reprint, Lafayette, IN: Sovereign Grace, 2001), 24; John Piper, *The Roots of Endurance* (Wheaton, IL: Crossway, 2002), 20; Thomas R. Schreiner and Ardel B. Caneday, *The Race Set Before Us: A Biblical Theology of Perseverance and Assurance* (Downers Grove, IL: InterVarsity, 2001), 49-50, 147-53; and R. C. Sproul, *Grace Unknown: The Heart of Reformed Theology* (Grand Rapids: Baker, 1997), 198.

6. John Piper, *Stand: A Call for the Endurance of the Saints* (Wheaton, IL: Crossway, 2008), 40.

elect nation of Israel persevere to the end of the most horrific period in human history, known as the great tribulation, they will be physically delivered by Christ's return. While all four contexts support this interpretation, the context of Matthew 24 is the most thorough and is used below to answer the basic contextual questions of where, when, what, and who.

Where does the salvation referred to in Matthew 24:13 take place? The setting of this passage is the land of Israel according to three statements in the context. First, in Matthew 24:15, the Lord Jesus says to those who must endure to the end: "Therefore when you see the 'abomination of desolation' spoken of by Daniel the prophet, standing in the holy place" (v. 15). This is an unmistakable reference to the Antichrist depicted in Daniel 9:27, who one day will set himself up to be worshipped in the temple in Jerusalem (2 Thess. 2:3-4). Second, the Lord goes on to say in the next verse, "then let those who are in Judea flee to the mountains" (Matt. 24:16). Third, in addition to the references to Jerusalem and Judea, the Lord says a few verses later, "And pray that your flight may not be in winter or on the Sabbath" (v. 20). The reference to the Sabbath shows that this warning by Christ applies to the nation of Israel, where travel would be more difficult on the seventh day of the week—a day nationally devoted to rest in recognition of the Mosaic Law.

When does the salvation take place in the statement "he who endures to the end shall be saved"? The Lord specifies the time for this deliverance, saying, "For then there will be great tribulation, such as has not been since the beginning of the world until this time, no, nor ever shall be" (Matt. 24:21). Since this passage speaks of an unprecedented time of tribulation in human history, this can only refer to the future time of God's judgment upon the earth known as the Tribulation. This period of global conflict, persecution, and suffering will be so intense that the Lord must limit its duration. Thus, Christ says in Matthew 24:22, "And unless those days were shortened, no flesh would be saved; but for the elect's sake those days will be shortened."

The entire period of tribulation prior to Christ's return will last seven years. According to the prophecy of Daniel 9:24-27, the 69 "weeks" or periods of seven (*shābûa'*) years have already been fulfilled, but one period of seven years remains. Elsewhere in Scripture this period of tribulation is divided into two halves of 42 months (Rev. 11:2; 13:5) or three and one-half years (Dan. 7:25; 12:7). Though all seven years of this period will involve unprecedented global tribulation (Jer. 30:7; Dan. 12:1), the last half will be particularly severe and is called the "great tribulation" (Matt. 24:21). It is to the "end" of this period that Christ encourages people to endure.

Once again, context clearly establishes what Christ meant by the "end." Starting in Matthew 24:3, the disciples pose a series of questions to the Lord regarding the end times, saying, "Tell us, when will these things be? And what will be the sign of Your coming, and of the *end* of the age?" What follows is Jesus' answer about the *"end* of the age" immediately preceding His return. Thus, a few verses later, after describing the events of the first half of the tribulation, Christ says, "but the *end* is not yet" (v. 6). Then He issues the promise, "he who endures to the *end* shall be saved" (v. 13), followed by the statement, "and then the *end* will come" (v. 14). Clearly, enduring to the "end" refers to the end of the unprecedented time of world history known as the tribulation rather than the end of each individual believer's life during the last 2,000 years of church history. Knowing from the context what the "end" means also helps to clarify what being "saved" means.

What does "saved" mean in Jesus' statement, "he who endures to the end shall be saved"? Is this a reference to spiritual deliverance from eternal suffering in hell? This common false assumption is nowhere to be found in the passage. Instead, the context clearly shows that believers alive during the tribulation are encouraged to endure to the end because they will be physically rescued when the Lord returns. This explains why Christ says in Matthew 24:22, "And unless those days were shortened, no flesh would be saved." The tribulation period will be so devastating that over half of mankind will die by the end (Rev. 6:8; 8:11; 9:15, 18). Therefore, Jesus' statement "he who endures to the end shall be saved" refers to temporal, physical deliverance from the tribulation, not eternal, spiritual deliverance from hell.

Who is meant by the "elect" in Christ's statement, "but for the elect's sake those days will be shortened" (Matt. 24:22)? The elect who must endure to the end to be saved are commonly assumed by Calvinists to be individual Christians from the last 2,000 years of church history who have been unconditionally elected before the foundation of the world for eternal salvation. But this interpretation ignores the context. The "elect" in the passage refers to believers from among God's nationally chosen people—Israel. Thus, Paul in Romans 11 refers to Israel being God's elect people, who will be saved at the time of Christ's return in glory.

26 And so all Israel will be saved, as it is written: "The Deliverer will come out of Zion, and He will turn away ungodliness from Jacob; 27 For this is My covenant with them, when I take away their sins." 28 Concerning the gospel they are enemies for your sake, but concerning the election they are beloved for the sake of the fathers. (Rom. 11:26-28)

At Christ's return, He will rescue His nationally chosen people from the imminent destruction they will face as the armies of the world surround Israel to destroy it (Joel 2:30–3:17; Rev. 16:13-16). The prophecy of Zechariah 12 vividly describes this national salvation.

7 The Lord will save the tents of Judah first, so that the glory of the house of David and the glory of the inhabitants of Jerusalem shall not become greater than that of Judah. 8 In that day the Lord will defend the inhabitants of Jerusalem; the one who is feeble among them in that day shall be like David, and the house of David shall be like God, like the Angel of the Lord before them. 9 It shall be in that day that I will seek to destroy all the nations that come against Jerusalem. 10 And I will pour on the house of David and on the inhabitants of Jerusalem the Spirit of grace and supplication; then they will look on Me whom they pierced. Yes, they will mourn for Him as one mourns for his only son, and grieve for Him as one grieves for a firstborn. (Zech. 12:7-10)

Could the Word of God be any clearer as to the meaning of Christ's statement, "he who endures to the end shall be saved"? The *people* to whom this statement directly applies are not individual, professing Christians but believers from the nation of Israel. The *time* that this passage directly applies to is not the last 2,000 years of church history but the end of the coming tribulation immediately before Christ's return. The *salvation* in view is not deliverance from eternal condemnation in the lake of fire but deliverance from temporal, physical destruction and national annihilation.

All of this means that Christ's statement "he who endures to the end shall be saved" was never intended as a warning to professing Christians throughout the course of the church age that they had better "hang in there" to the end of their Christian lives or else they will face eternal condemnation. Instead, the Lord's statement is intended as an encouragement for Jewish believers to persevere through the most devastating time in human history, knowing the promise of their Messiah to return to rescue them at the end.

The Parable of the Four Soils (Luke 8:11-15)

The parable of the four soils is recorded in Matthew 13:3-9, 18-23; Mark 4:3-9, 14-20; and Luke 8:5-8, 11-15. Only Luke's account explicitly mentions the word "believe," and it is significant in answering the question of whether faith must endure for salvation to be sure. In Luke 8:13, the Lord says that a person may "believe for a while," showing that it is possible to believe but not persevere to the end.

> 11 Now the parable is this: The seed is the word of God. 12 Those by the wayside are the ones who hear; then the devil comes and takes away the word out of their hearts, lest they should believe and be saved. 13 But the ones on the rock are those who, when they hear, receive the word with joy; and these have no root, who believe for a while and in time of temptation fall away. 14 Now the ones that fell among thorns are those who, when they have heard, go out and are choked with cares, riches, and pleasures of life, and bring no fruit to maturity. 15 But the ones that fell on the good ground are those who, having heard the word with a noble and good heart, keep it and bear fruit with patience. (Luke 8:11-15)

In this famous parable, the four soils represent four different responses and conditions of heart toward the seed of God's Word. All interpreters agree on the first and fourth soils, that the person represented by the first soil is an unbeliever who has never been born again and the person represented by the fourth soil is a genuine believer who has been born again. The disagreement is over the classification of the people represented by soils two and three. Arminians view these people as genuine believers who lose their faith and consequently lose their salvation. Calvinists, on the other hand, normally view soils two and three as representative of unbelievers who professed to believe in Christ but were later exposed to be unregenerate unbelievers because they did not endure in the faith and bear fruit for the Lord. Lorraine Boettner explains the typical Calvinist view of the second soil of Luke 8:13.

Some fall away from a profession of faith, but none fall away from the saving grace of God. Those who do fall have never known the latter. They are the stony-ground hearers, who have no root in themselves, but who endure for a while; and when tribulation or persecution arises, straightway they stumble. They are then said to have given up or to have made shipwreck of that faith which they never possessed except in appearance.[7]

Similarly, contemporary Calvinist James White writes,

Many are those who make professions not based upon regeneration, and the "faith" that is theirs will not last. Jesus taught this truth in the parable of the soils in Matthew 13:3-9, 18-23. Some of the seed that was sown resulted in immediate growth. But the growth produced no fruit and did not last. These are those who have false, human faith that does not last. But those with true faith produce fruit and remain.[8]

But do the second and third soils describe unsaved people, who only *profess* faith in Christ but do not *possess* genuine faith? There are two main reasons why soils two and three represent eternally saved people.

First, the people representing soil two fulfill in Luke 8:13 the condition for salvation stated in Luke 8:12. Verse 13 clearly states that the people represented by the second soil "receive the word with joy" and "believe for a while" though they later fall away because of persecution. Regarding soil one in Luke 8:12, the Lord warns of the Devil coming to snatch the Word of God from people's hearts "lest they should believe and be saved." Since soil-two people in Luke 8:13 fulfill the condition for salvation stated in the previous verse to "believe," then logically those in verse 13 who "believe for a while" also receive the result promised in verse 12, namely, that they are "saved."

Perseverance proponents may protest that soil-two people do not really fulfill the condition for salvation given by Jesus in verse 12 since He said to "believe" but in verse 13 the belief of soil-two

7. Lorraine Boettner, *The Reformed Doctrine of Predestination* (Phillipsburg, NJ: Presbyterian & Reformed, 1932), 191.

8. James R. White, *The Potter's Freedom* (Amityville, NY: Calvary Press, 2000), 292.

people is qualified—they "believe *for a while*." Some may argue that the phrase "for a while" nullifies the belief of soil-two people so that they are not really saved. But verse 12 does not say "lest they should *continue to* believe and be saved," as though the real condition for salvation is not merely to believe but to continue to believe. According to verse 13, soil-two people do believe, if only for a while. Temporary faith cannot be dismissed as mere false faith that never really existed, for the Holy Spirit-inspired text says in verse 13 that they "believe." Verse 13 does not say that they merely "professed to believe," or "appeared to believe," or "almost believed." If Jesus is really saying here that they had "false, human faith" simply because they did not persevere or bear fruit, then why didn't He just say so? Why didn't He just say, they "appeared to believe for a while"? Why even bother to say that they *"believed* for a while" if all temporary belief is not actual belief?[9]

A second main reason why the people represented by soils two and three are regenerated is because the Word of God germinates and grows on both soils, which is evidence of new life. Luke's account of the parable presents a significant pattern where the seed of God's Word does not germinate and grow up in soil number one like it does in soils two, three, and four. Compare what Jesus says about each of the four soils:

Soil #1: "And as he sowed, some fell by the wayside; and it was trampled down, and the birds of the air devoured it" (Luke 8:5).

---

9. This is reminiscent of how Reformed commentators often interpret the case of Simon's conversion. Acts 8:13 says, "Then Simon himself also believed; and when he was baptized he continued with Philip, and was amazed, seeing the miracles and signs which were done." Since Simon was later envious of Peter and John's spiritual gift of apostleship and faced possible divine discipline unto death like Ananias and Sapphira (Acts 5) before him, some Reformed theologians conclude Simon must not have really believed. Schreiner and Caneday conclude: "Even though Luke knew that Simon Magus had not received the new birth of the Spirit, he records, 'Simon himself believed and was baptized' (Acts 8:13). Why does Luke tell the story this way? It is because he wants to make it clear that there are varied receptions of the gospel. Simon is an example of one who externally looked like a believer, for he even submitted to baptism. However, his subsequent behavior uncovered his belief to be counterfeit" (Thomas R. Schreiner and Ardel B. Caneday, *The Race Set Before Us: A Biblical Theology of Perseverance & Assurance* (Downers Grove, IL: InterVarsity, 2001), 219 n. 14). This is a clear case of imposing one's theology onto the text, for Luke is directed by the Holy Spirit to write: "Then Simon himself also believed," not "Simon himself *almost* believed" or "Simon himself *appeared* to believe," and so on. Why would Luke say that Simon "believed" if he actually did not?

Soil #2: "Some fell on rock; and as soon as *it sprang up*, it withered away because it lacked moisture" (Luke 8:6).

Soil #3: "And some fell among thorns, and the thorns *sprang up with it* and choked it" (Luke 8:7).

Soil #4: "But others fell on good ground, *sprang up*, and yielded a crop a hundredfold" (Luke 8:8).

Notice that in soils two, three, and four, the seed "sprang up," but conspicuously this is never stated for the first soil, which represents unbelievers. Calvinists sometimes object that soil-two people cannot be saved because they have "no root" in themselves (Luke 8:13). If the root represents the presence of regenerated life from God within the soul of the believer, and Luke 8:13 says they "have no root," then does this mean that these people are unregenerate? The phrase in verse 13 "have no root" (*hrizan ouk exousin*) should not be understood in an absolute sense to preclude the very presence of a root, but rather in the qualified sense of "no *depth of* root." Consequently, the New American Standard Bible translates verse 13: "and these have no *firm* root." This harmonizes better with Christ's teaching about the second soil in the parallel passage of Matthew 13:5, where He says of the second soil, "Some fell on stony places, where they did not have much earth; and they immediately sprang up because they had no *depth* [*bathos*] of earth." Likewise, Christ also taught in Luke 8:6 that "some fell on rock; and as soon as it sprang up, it withered away because it *lacked moisture.*" In both Matthew 13:5 and Luke 8:6, the rocky soil received the seed, it germinated, and then it "sprang up." This certainly indicates the *presence* of new life from the Word of God where no life previously existed.

Too often people wrongly conclude that the absence of fruit in a believer's life means that person does not have real faith and must not be truly regenerated. But if a fruit tree is not bearing fruit as it should, does this mean it is not really a fruit tree? If a football player suits up with the rest of the team but never plays in the game, does this mean he is not a real football player? In just the same way, a person can believe at a moment in time and receive new divine life—regeneration from God—but not bear spiritual fruit like soils two and three. Unfortunately, soils two and three describe an all-too-common condition today among many saints who are saved but unfruitful in the midst of persecution, temptation, and the cares of life. Nevertheless, the parable of the four soils clearly reveals that it is possible for real faith not to persevere and be fruitful for the Lord.

Christ's Intercession for Peter (Luke 22:32)

Luke's Gospel contains another central passage in the debate about perseverance. On the night of His arrest, the Lord Jesus pulls the curtain back to give the oblivious disciples a glimpse into the spiritual battle raging behind the scenes. Turning to Simon Peter, He declares, "Simon, Simon! Indeed, Satan has asked for you, that he may sift you as wheat. But I have prayed for you, that your faith should not fail; and when you have returned to Me, strengthen your brethren" (Luke 22:31-32). Satan's malice here is reminiscent of his approach toward God's servant Job. But in both Job's and Peter's cases, Satan had to get God's permission to do his malicious work. In both cases, the Lord consented with the intention of causing each saint's faith to grow. According to Luke 22:31, Satan had already demanded from God the opportunity to destroy the disciples' faith in anticipation of having Jesus killed. The sovereign God gave His permission but not without Christ also interceding for Peter to counter Satan's attack, so that Peter's "faith should not fail" (v. 32). This statement reveals the Lord Jesus' prayer request to the Father for Peter. On the basis of Christ's prayer for Peter, perseverance proponents claim that Christ prays the same prayer for every believer today, so that every true believer's faith necessarily endures to the end. This conclusion is reflected in the following quotes by perseverance teachers:

> Peter would wrestle with doubt and fear for his life, yet his faith in Christ would never fail. It was guaranteed by the prayer of Christ. It should be remembered that doubt and faith are not mutually exclusive. After Peter denied the Lord, he went out and wept, indicating faith in Christ but shame that he had failed his Lord. We can be assured that this same ministry of Christ is exercised on behalf of believers today.[10]

> And so we are sustained by our supernatural faith given to us by God. And when Jesus said to Peter, "I pray that your

---

10. David Dunlap, "The Battle for Continuing Faith," in *Bible & Life*, Vol. 12, No. 4 (September 2005): 4.

faith fail not," he was saying to him what is true of all of us, the Lord intercedes for us that our faith may endure.[11]

Because of Christ's effective prayer, although Peter's faith flickered, it did not go out. . . . Christ's present ministry of intercession, therefore, preserves the children of God in their faith, even as his prayer for Peter kept him from falling away.[12]

Each of these claims assumes Christ prays the same prayer for all believers that He prayed for Peter in Luke 22:32. But what is this conclusion founded on? While Reformed theology's doctrine of the perseverance of the saints requires this conclusion, there is nothing in the passage itself that warrants this extrapolation to every child of God. In fact, there are several problems with using this passage as a proof text for perseverance.

First, if God sovereignly prevents every believer from losing faith totally and finally, as the fifth point of Calvinism teaches, then why doesn't He also prevent partial, temporary failures? Following Christ's resurrection, Mark 16:11, 13, and 14 state that all of the disciples, including Peter, "did not believe" the Lord had risen from the dead, so that He appeared to them and "rebuked their unbelief and hardness of heart" (v. 14). Luke 24 records that after He appeared in their midst, the disciples "were terrified and frightened" (v. 37) and "still did not believe for joy" (v. 41). If faith is based strictly on God's will rather than man's will, then why would He allow even such temporary lapses of faith? If Peter's faith were strictly a matter of God's sovereign gift, which He alone sustains and causes to persevere, then why would He allow sin at all in the form of temporary unbelief? The Calvinist doctrine that God monergistically determines the will of man to cause perseverance in the faith is seen to be illogical and irreconcilable with the testimony of the Gospels concerning Peter's unbelief.

Second, it says in Luke 22:31-32 that although Satan asked to sift all of the disciples, Christ prayed specifically for Peter. The passage does *not* say what many Calvinists assume it says, namely, that the Lord prayed the same for all the disciples. This distinction can be observed by the shift in pronouns in the Greek text of verses

---

11. John F. MacArthur, "The Perseverance of the Saints, Part 1," *Grace to You*, August 29, 2004.

12. Robert A. Peterson and Michael D. Williams, *Why I Am Not An Arminian* (Downers Grove, IL: InterVarsity, 2004), 68.

31-32 from plural (regarding all the disciples) to singular (regarding Peter): "Simon, Simon! Indeed, Satan has asked for you [plural], that he may sift [you] as wheat. But I have prayed for you [singular], that your [singular] faith should not fail; and when you [singular] have returned to Me, strengthen your [singular] brethren." If this passage were teaching that Christ prays for all Christians to persevere in faith, then why doesn't Jesus say as much in the passage? Why doesn't He say that He prays for each disciple's faith not to fail? This would have been a golden opportunity to explicitly reveal what Reformed theology assumes and requires of this passage. To conclude that Christ's prayer for Peter has also been His ongoing prayer for every believer throughout the church age is an assumption[13] that appears to be theologically driven since the passage actually says that Christ prayed for Peter, not all the disciples. So why did Jesus pray specifically for *Peter's* faith not to fail?

A third major problem with using this passage as a proof text for perseverance is that it concerns leadership, not eternal salvation.[14] Many Calvinists and Arminians err by assuming Luke 22:31-32 is a salvation passage. Marshall, an Arminian commentator, misses the main point of the passage, saying that Satan's attack "is not directed so much against Jesus as against the disciples themselves in order to lead them to apostasy and loss of salvation."[15] But where is the concept of salvation even implied in the passage? Instead, the passage itself makes clear that the Lord's purpose in praying for Peter's faith not to fail is so that he can be a vessel for God to use in strengthening the other disciples, not so that he could remain saved. The whole notion of Peter's faith being prevented from failing for his salvation to be preserved is completely foreign to the context. On the other hand, since Peter was the outspoken leader among the other disciples as a "first among equals"[16] in apostolic authority, the Lord prayed directly for his faith, so that he could be restored to fellowship with the Lord and in turn minister to his brethren—his fellow disciples (v. 32).

---

13. Joel B. Green, *The Gospel of Luke*, New International Commentary on the New Testament (Grand Rapids: Eerdmans, 1997), 773 n. 114.

14. Gene A. Getz, *Elders and Leaders: A Biblical, Historical, and Cultural Perspective* (Chicago: Moody, 2003), 217-20.

15. I. Howard Marshall, *Commentary on Luke*, New International Greek Testament Commentary (Grand Rapids: Eerdmans, 1978), 820.

16. Darrell L. Bock, *Luke 9:51–24:53*, Baker Exegetical Commentary on the New Testament (Grand Rapids: Baker, 1996), 1742.

Believers Who Must Still Believe (John 2:23-25)

The Gospel of John is known as the Gospel of belief since the word "believe" occurs in it nearly 100 times. Thus, John's Gospel provides ample opportunity for the Lord to demonstrate the claim that belief must endure to the end of one's life to obtain final salvation. Yet as one reads all twenty-one chapters, one is struck by the complete absence of statements requiring ongoing belief for eternal life. However, this has not stopped many perseverance advocates from attempting to support their doctrine from this book.

According to the purpose statement of John's Gospel, this book was written primarily with an evangelistic intent of turning its unbelieving readers into believers in Christ in order that they might possess eternal life. John 20:30-31 says, "And truly Jesus did many other signs in the presence of His disciples, which are not written in this book; but these are written that you may believe that Jesus is the Christ, the Son of God, and that believing you may have life in His name." While many perseverance advocates agree that the purpose of John is evangelistic, they also see the book as being evangelistic in the sense of testing the genuineness of people's profession of faith — that John is concerned with a special *kind* or *quality* of faith, a committed, enduring, fruitful, and working faith.[17] Without such faith, a person is considered not to be truly regenerated.[18]

This conclusion is based, in part, upon the observation that John's Gospel records several appeals to the original, believing disciples within the historical narrative to still believe (13:19; 14:1, 11, 29; 16:27, 30). The disciples are challenged to "believe" even though they are already believers! This has often been misconstrued as teaching

---

17. James Montgomery Boice, *The Gospel of John* (Grand Rapids: Zondervan, 1985), 543-47; D. A. Carson, *The Gospel According to John*, Pillar New Testament Commentary (Grand Rapids: Eerdmans, 1991), 347-48; Gerald F. Hawthorne, "The Concept of Faith in the Fourth Gospel," *Bibliotheca Sacra* 116 (April 1959): 122n8, 126; Phillip Hook, "A Biblical Definition of Saving Faith," *Bibliotheca Sacra* 121 (April 1964): 139; Craig A. Keener, *The Gospel of John: A Commentary* (Peabody, MA: Hendrickson, 2003), 1:277; Andreas J. Köstenberger, *John*, Baker Exegetical Commentary on the New Testament (Grand Rapids: Baker, 2004), 115-17, 261; J. Carl Laney, *John*, Moody Gospel Commentary (Chicago: Moody Press, 1992), 20-22, 371; Leon Morris, *Jesus is the Christ: Studies in the Theology of John* (Grand Rapids: Eerdmans, 1989), 180; Merrill C. Tenney, *John: The Gospel of Belief* (Grand Rapids: Eerdmans, 1976), 83, 85, 146-47; idem, "Topics from the Gospel of John: Part IV: The Growth of Belief." *Bibliotheca Sacra* 132 (October 1975): 357; George Allen Turner and Julius R. Mantey, *The Gospel According to John* (Grand Rapids: Eerdmans, n.d.), 401.

18. Laney, *John*, 162-63; William MacDonald, "John" in *Believer's Bible Commentary, New Testament*, rev. ed. (Nashville: Thomas Nelson, 1990), 333.

that John is requiring believers to persevere in their belief in order to possess final salvation. The major problem with this view, however, is that although the faith of the disciples needed development, it was not spurious or non-saving in terms of its nature. Rather, it was genuine; and the disciples were truly regenerate (except for Judas Iscariot), as Jesus Himself testified in John 6:68-71, 13:8-11, and 15:3. Though the disciples believed in Jesus as the Christ, their concept of the Messiah or Christ was deficient and needed development.

For this reason we see throughout the progression of John's Gospel that the disciples' faith developed in proportion to the progress of revelation about Jesus being the Christ. Since biblical faith is always a response to God's revelation and since Jesus in His earthly ministry was an unfolding revelation of God before the eyes of the disciples (John 1:14-18; Heb. 1:1-2), their faith developed or progressed in the measure that the Object of their faith progressively revealed Himself. This progress occurred throughout His earthly ministry until it culminated in the Cross and Resurrection as the climactic sign or revelation of Him being "the Christ, the Son of God" (20:31).

Certain signs in the Gospel of John not only elicit faith within unbelievers, but they also lead to the development of faith among Christ's believing disciples. This can be observed in several passages. For example, before the miraculous multiplication of the five loaves and two fish, John informs the reader that this sign was done "to test" the disciples—presumably to test their faith. John 6:5-6 says, "Then Jesus lifted up His eyes, and seeing a great multitude coming toward Him, He said to Philip, 'Where shall we buy bread, that these may eat?' But this He said to test him, for He Himself knew what He would do." It is no coincidence that when the fragments of the loaves were gathered up *by the disciples* after the crowd of 5,000 had eaten (6:12), there were exactly 12 baskets left over. Conspicuously, there was one basket for each disciple. This clearly demonstrates that Jesus was testing the faith of His own disciples and that the original historical occurrence of this sign was for their developing faith.

Similarly, in John 11 with the sign of the raising of Lazarus from the dead, Jesus tests both the believing disciples and the unbelieving Jews who are present. Even though John had earlier recorded the fact of the disciples' belief in Jesus (John 2:11; 6:69), we are also informed prior to the actual raising of Lazarus that this miracle was intended to expand the existing belief of the disciples. After Lazarus dies, John 11:14-15 states, "Then Jesus said to them plainly 'Lazarus is dead. And I am glad for your sakes that I was not there, that you may believe. Nevertheless let us go to him.'" If the disciples were already believers, then why would Christ raise Lazarus from the dead in order that the disciples "may believe" (11:15)? It was evidently intended for the development of their belief in Him, not the inception of their faith.

This was true not only for the faith of the twelve, but also for the development of the faith of the female disciple Martha, the sister of Lazarus. In its original context, John 11:27 contains Martha's profession of faith and is, therefore, a passage describing the faith of one who was already regenerate. In contrast to John 20:30-31, John 11:27 is not describing how to become a new believer, though it is often used that way. Prior to the raising of her brother Lazarus, it is not clear whether Martha had a correct understanding of Jesus being the Christ, the Son of God, as she professed in 11:27 since later she expressed doubt about Jesus' ability to raise Lazarus from the dead (v. 39) even though she possessed an orthodox belief in the resurrection of the dead (v. 24). Therefore, Jesus exhorts her in the very next verse (v. 40) to "believe" that she would yet "see the glory of God" demonstrated through Him (John 1:14).

But the raising of Lazarus in its historical context was intended not only for the twelve disciples and Martha, it was also intended for unbelievers. Thus, in John 11:42, Christ speaks to the Father, exclaiming, "And I know that You always hear Me, but because of the people who are standing by I said this, that they may believe that you sent Me." The bystanders included both believing disciples and unbelievers. This is evidenced by John 11:45, which says, "Then many of the Jews who had come to Mary, and had seen the things Jesus did, believed in Him." The sign of the raising of Lazarus resulted in many Jews becoming believers in Jesus (John 12:11). The Lazarus-sign thus becomes representative of John's purpose as a whole. It was intended for a dual purpose—to develop the faith of already existing disciples and to lead people to initial belief in Jesus as the Christ for eternal life.

Another passage in John's Gospel sometimes used to assert the necessity of perseverance in belief for eternal life is John 2:23-25. In the New American Standard Bible this passage reads as follows:

> 23 Now when He was in Jerusalem at the Passover, during the feast, many believed in His name, observing His signs which He was doing. 24 But Jesus, on His part, was not entrusting Himself to them, for He knew all men, 25 and because He did

not need anyone to testify concerning man, for He Himself knew what was in man.

According to John Piper, the people who believed in Christ's name in John 2:23 did not really believe in Christ and were not saved. Piper claims,

> John 2:23-25 has an unsettling effect. What it says, in essence, is that Jesus knows what is in every heart, and so he can see when someone believes in a way that is not really believing. In other words, Jesus' ability to know every heart perfectly leads to the unsettling truth that some belief is not the kind of belief that obtains fellowship with Jesus and eternal life. Some belief is not saving belief.[19]

Another perseverance advocate, John MacArthur, explains in greater detail why the belief of those in verse 23 was supposedly not the right "kind of belief."

> They believed in His name, beholding His signs which He was doing. But Jesus on His part was not entrusting Himself to them for He knew all men and because He did not need anyone to bear witness concerning man for He Himself knew what was in man and He knew their faith was not true faith. They believed but their believing was not adequate . . . it was not genuine. There was not saving faith. To put it simply, He had no faith in their faith. He didn't believe in their believing. They believed that He was the Messiah, that doesn't mean they surrendered their souls to His lordship. That doesn't mean they were willing to turn from their sin. He knew their belief was shallow. He knew it was not the genuine work of the Spirit of God. And if He talked of sacrifice and when He talked of repentance, and when He talked of a cross, they would be gone. And Jesus would not accept the moment's emotional decision. He would not accept a faith born of selfishness.[20]

---

19. John Piper, "He Knew What Was in Man," January 11, 2009; www.desiring-god.org/sermons/he-knew-what-was-in-man (accessed May 22, 2014).

20. John MacArthur, *The Nature of Saving Faith*, GC 90-21.

Even though the apostle John records in verse 23 that "many believed" in Christ's name, perseverance proponents flatly contradict Scripture, claiming they really didn't believe—at least not savingly. However, John had recorded earlier in his Gospel, in John 1:12, that belief in Christ's name would result in new birth or becoming a child of God. Likewise, in John 3:18, belief in Christ's name is equivalent to belief in the person of Christ, resulting in salvation from God's condemnation. John 2:23 is effectively sandwiched between two declarations that belief in Christ's name is sufficient for eternal salvation. So, are we really to believe that John had a different meaning for belief in Christ's name in chapter 2 than he did in chapters 1 and 3? This conclusion is clearly theologically forced upon the passage.

When passages such as John 2:23-25 appear to contradict the doctrine of the perseverance of the saints, its proponents often resort to the standard reply that although the text says they had "believed" or had "faith," it must not have been "real" faith. But this begs the question, why then does Scripture actually say they "believed" or had "faith"? Why didn't the writer of Scripture just plainly say that they "didn't *really* believe," or they had "false faith," or "non-saving faith" so as not to mislead the reader into thinking they actually did "believe"? Why must a Calvinistic inference always be made in such cases?

Some perseverance advocates interpret the belief of those in John 2:23 as inadequate faith because the people believed based on the signs Christ performed. "Sign faith" is viewed as something less than faith in Christ Himself. But this overlooks the fact that in the very purpose statement for the entire book, John 20:30-31, John explains that he intentionally employed Christ's signs in order to lead people to belief in Christ for eternal life. Isn't this "saving faith"?

The mere fact that Christ didn't entrust Himself (2:24) to those who believed in His name (v. 23) doesn't mean these people had non-saving faith. Eternal life is never conditioned on Christ trusting us, as though we must be trustworthy objects of Christ's faith to receive eternal life! Rather, salvation is conditioned on our trust in Christ as the only reliable, trustworthy object of faith. The fact is, at the beginning of Christ's public ministry in John 2, there were very few reliable believers, for many genuine believers were more concerned for their own reputation than His (John 12:42-43).[21]

---

21. Debbie Hunn, "The Believers Jesus Doubted: John 2:23-25," *Trinity Journal* 25 (Spring 2004): 15-25.

Continuing in Christ's Word as a True Disciple (John 8:30-32)

The Bible clearly teaches that it is possible not to continue in the word of Christ as His disciple. John 8:30-32 is commonly misinterpreted by advocates of the doctrine of the perseverance of the saints. They understand this passage as a warning to some people who only appear to believe in Christ (v. 30) but who are really unbelievers (vv. 33-59) since they may not "continue" in Christ's word and follow Christ as His disciples (vv. 31-32).[22] J. Carl Laney expresses this typical, theologically driven interpretation when he writes,

> John records that as a result of this interaction Jesus won some adherents. Whereas the statement is rather straightforward, the concept of "belief" is more complex. Did the adherents really come to trust in His Person as Messiah and Son of God. Were they saved? Regenerated? It is suggested that those people had an intellectual understanding rather than personal trust. They had begun believing but did not continue in the faith. Those same Jews would later seek to kill Him. Their "belief" seems to have come short of regenerating faith.[23]

Likewise, James Montgomery Boice writes concerning John 8:30-32,

> Specific warnings are given to those who heard the gospel and appeared to trust in Christ, and yet were not truly saved. For example, Jesus said, "If you continue in my word, you are truly my disciples" (John 8:31). This seems to say that perseverance on the part of the believer is the final proof of whether he or she is truly born again.[24]

Similarly, A.W. Pink indicates based on this passage that more than believing is necessary for salvation, claiming that one must also walk in obedience as a disciple of Christ to be eternally secure.

---

22. Carson, *Gospel According to John*, 347-48; Leon Morris, *The Gospel According to John* (Grand Rapids: Eerdmans, 1971), 454-56; Tenney, *John: The Gospel of Belief*, 146-49.

23. Laney, *John*, 162-63.

24. James Montgomery Boice, *Foundations of the Christian Faith*, rev. ed. (Downers Grove, IL: InterVarsity, 1986), 520.

It is therefore incumbent upon us to take not of those passages which press upon us the necessity of continuance,
for they constitute another of those safeguards which God
has placed around the doctrine of the security of His saints.
On a certain occasion "many believed on Him" (John 8:30),
but so far from Christ assuring them that Heaven was now
their settled portion, we are told "Then said Jesus to those
Jews which believed on Him, IF ye continue in MY word
then are ye My disciples indeed" (v. 31). Unless we abide
in subjection to Christ, unless we walk in obedience to Him
unto the end of our earthly course, we are but disciples in
name and semblance.[25]

These common misinterpretations are, first of all, the result of
utterly disregarding the context of this passage. Jesus was speaking
to large crowds in the temple (8:20, 59) in Jerusalem who had gathered for the feast of tabernacles (7:2, 37). The crowds were already
divided in their opinions about the identity of Jesus (7:43). Among
the audience whom Christ addressed, there were scribes and Pharisees present (8:2, 12-13) who were unbelievers and thus unsaved
(7:48; 8:24). These unbelievers are distinguished in 8:33-59 from those
in 8:30-32 who came to believe in Christ as He was teaching.

In the mixed crowd of believers and unbelievers, it was the
unbelievers whom Christ addressed in 8:33-36, who mistakenly
thought Christ was addressing them in verses 31-32. This is why they
responded in their self-deception by testifying that they were free, but
in fact they were still in bondage to sin. These are the ones who sought
to kill Christ (8:37-40). These are the ones whose father was the Devil
(8:41-44). These are the ones whom Christ, twice, explicitly declares
were *not* believers (8:45-46). Therefore, to interpret these unbelieving
men described in John 8:33-59 as being the same men who were twice
described by the apostle John as believers in 8:30-31 not only does
violence to the context, but it creates an unnecessary and unscriptural contradiction between the testimony of John in verses 30-31 and
the testimony of Christ in verses 45-46. It must also be emphasized
that the conclusion that the people of verses 30-31 truly "believed"
in Christ comes from the apostle John as the writer, not the people's
own profession or inaccurate estimation of themselves.

---

25. A. W. Pink, *The Saint's Perseverance* (Lafayette, IN: Sovereign Grace, 2001), 76.

Second, some commentators have misinterpreted this passage based on an artificial syntactical distinction.[26] They say the people who "believed on Him" (*episteusan eis auton*) in 8:30 were truly saved but distinct from those people in 8:31 who were unsaved because they merely "believed Him" (*pepisteukotas*[27] *auto*). The claim is made that the presence or absence of the Greek preposition *eis* makes all the difference between a belief that is genuine and a belief that is false. Supposedly the people in verse 30 believed "on" (*eis*) the very person of Christ, whereas the people in verse 31 merely believed Christ's words and thus had something less than a "saving" kind of faith.

However, the need to distinguish true believers in verse 30 from pseudo-believers in verse 31 appears to be driven by a theological bias for the doctrine of the perseverance of the saints rather than by Greek syntax. The word "believe" (*pisteuō*) often appears in the Gospel of John without the preposition *eis* or any preposition for that matter, yet clearly in some cases the context indicates that genuine salvation is meant. John 5:24 is one example of this. There "believe" is used without any preposition, where Christ literally says, "he who hears My word and *believes in Him* who sent Me has everlasting life, and shall not come into judgment, but has passed from death into life."[28]

Third, John 8:30-32 is often misinterpreted because of the erroneous theological assumption that all believers in Christ must necessarily be disciples of Christ. However, continuance in the word of Christ proves only that someone is actively following Christ as His disciple, in addition to possessing eternal life. Scripturally, every true disciple of Christ is also a believer in Christ, but not every believer follows Christ as His disciple. For this reason, Christ uses a conditional statement in verse 31 to address those who were already believers: "*If* you continue in My word, then you are truly disciples of Mine"[29] (NASB).

---

26. Edwin Blum, *Gospel of John*, The Bible Knowledge Commentary, New Testament, ed. John Walvoord & Roy Zuck (Wheaton, IL: Victor Books, 1983), 304-305; Frederic L. Godet, *Commentary on John's Gospel* (Grand Rapids: Kregel, 1978), 665-66; Elmer Towns, *The Gospel of John: Believe and Live* (Old Tappan, NJ: Revell, 1990), 173; W. E. Vine, *The Collected Writings of W. E. Vine*, Vol. 1 (Nashville: Nelson, 1996), 267; B. F. Westcott, *The Gospel According to St. John* (Grand Rapids: Eerdmans, 1967), 132-33.

27. *Pisteuō* in verse 31 is a perfect tense, active voice, participle.

28. "He who . . . believes Him who sent Me" (*pisteuon to pempsanti mē*). It may be further emphasized that if the people of verse 31 were distinct from those in verse 30, the use of the perfect tense, active voice of *pisteuō* in verse 31 hardly seems appropriate since this indicates a personally held and settled belief, rather than a fleeting one. For other New Testament examples of the perfect tense, active voice, participle of *pisteuō* without a preposition which also indicate "true" faith, see Acts 15:5; 16:34; 18:27; 19:8; 21:20, 25; and Titus 3:8.

29. This is a third-class conditional "if" statement in Greek, meaning it is the

The issue in John 8:30-32 is discipleship, not salvation—and there is a vast difference between the two, as explained in chapter 7. To muddle this distinction between a believer and a disciple is to change the requirement for salvation from simple *faith* in Christ to *faithfulness* towards Christ, issuing in good works. The end result is a perverted gospel of faith plus works rather than the simple gospel of salvation by grace alone, through faith alone, in Christ alone (Gal. 1:6-9).

Cast Out Branches That Do Not Abide (John 15:1-6)

The Gospel of John not only declares that it is possible to not continue as a disciple of Christ, it is also possible to not abide in Him (John 15:1-8).

> 1 I am the true vine, and My Father is the vinedresser. 2 Every branch in Me that does not bear fruit He takes away; and every branch that bears fruit He prunes, that it may bear more fruit. 3 You are already clean because of the word which I have spoken to you. 4 Abide in Me, and I in you. As the branch cannot bear fruit of itself, unless it abides in the vine, neither can you, unless you abide in Me. 5 I am the vine, you are the branches. He who abides in Me, and I in him, bears much fruit; for without Me you can do nothing. 6 If anyone does not abide in Me, he is cast out as a branch and is withered; and they gather them and throw them into the fire, and they are burned. 7 If you abide in Me, and My words abide in you, you will ask what you desire, and it shall be done for you. 8 By this My Father is glorified, that you bear much fruit; so you will be My disciples.

This passage is similar to the previous discipleship passage in John 8:30-32. Here the emphasis is on continuing in fellowship with Christ as the source of spiritual life, which will result in fruitfulness and evidence of being Christ's disciple. Not surprisingly, many commentators misunderstand Christ here to be issuing a warning to this effect: "Bear fruit or perish forever!" Some have misinterpreted Christ here as saying that salvation can be *lost* if Christians do not abide or stay connected with Christ. On the other hand, Calvinists who do not believe salvation can be "lost" typically interpret these

---

condition of possibility; i.e. these believers might or might not have continued in Christ's word.

verses as presenting a *test of the reality* of one's faith in Christ. If your faith is genuine, they say, it will be proven by a fruitful, persevering, or abiding faith. Their doctrine of the perseverance of the saints necessitates this interpretation.

J. Carl Laney represents this view. He writes regarding John 15:1-6, "the fruitless branches represent disciples who have had an external association with Christ that is not matched by an internal, spiritual union entered into by personal faith and regeneration."[30] Laney continues,

> The Gospel of John also presents the reader with an enigma of "belief" that is not belief. In the progress of belief there is a stage that falls short of genuine or consummated faith resulting in salvation (2:23-25; 7:31; 8:31, 40, 45-46; 12:11, 37). Tenney refers to the "belief" that falls short of genuine faith as "superficial." Morris calls it "transitory belief" that is not saving faith. Many were inclined to believe something about Jesus but were not willing to yield their allegiance to Him or trust Him as their personal sin-bearer.[31]

But do the branches that are unfruitful and do not abide in Christ represent unsaved, unbelievers who have only a pseudo-faith in Christ? Or can genuine believers be capable of not abiding in Christ and thus be spiritually unfruitful? Before any theological or doctrinal conclusions can be reached, we must first carefully examine what this passage *is* saying and what it *is not* saying.

In the context of John 13–17, the Lord Jesus was preparing His disciples for spiritual service in an unbelieving, hostile world following His imminent departure. He would leave His disciples in this world, but that was no reason for the disciples to abandon their faith in Him. In the context, Christ was specifically addressing only the eleven, saved, believing disciples, who would form the apostolic foundation of Christ's universal church (Eph. 2:20) and through whom God would change the world forever by the preaching of the gospel. Judas Iscariot, the unsaved, unbelieving disciple had previously departed from their company (John 13:30). Consequently, Christ was not concerned here with testing the genuineness of the salvation of His eleven remaining disciples. Instead, He instructed them in the new spiritual relationships they would have with Him,

---

30. Laney, *John*, 272.
31. Ibid, 272-73.

the Holy Spirit, each other, and the world following His ascension to the Father and the descent of the Holy Spirit on the day of Pentecost. Christ's purpose in John 15 was *to encourage* His disciples through the analogy of a Vine and its branches, not to admonish them toward self-examination by measuring the genuineness of their profession, thereby *warning* them of possible divine judgment.

In verse 1, Christ is the true Vine, and the Father is the vine-dresser. In verse 2, believers are represented by branches. While there is universal agreement among commentators that the *fruitful* branches represent regenerated believers in Christ, there is great difference of opinion regarding the identity of the *unfruitful* branches and the implications of the Greek word *airō* in verse 2, translated "He takes away." This word can be translated variously as either "He takes away," "He lifts up," "He picks up," "He carries away," or "He removes."

Many perseverance advocates interpret *airō negatively* as a *warning*, meaning that God "takes away" unbelieving professors in eternal judgment. But this word can also be interpreted *positively* as an *encouragement* to fallen branches that God the Father, as the heavenly vinedresser, will tenderly care for His vineyard and "lift them up" to be in a position where they can be exposed to the sun and have the potential to be more fruitful. This interpretation is consistent with real viticultural practices of first-century vinedressers.[32]

The takes-away-in-judgment view has several other problems. First, it doesn't accord with the flow of the passage. There is a progression in this passage from a branch that "does not bear fruit" (v. 2), to branches that "bear fruit" (v. 2), to branches that "bear more fruit" (v. 2), to branches that "bear much fruit" (v. 5). This progression indicates that it is the Father's objective to foster greater growth and productivity, not to stymie potential future growth with a fatal act of condemnation. Most plant life in the natural realm actually begins life without fruit, and it develops until it has grown sufficiently enough to sustain fruit. It would seem absurd for the Father to "cut off" (NIV) all branches in His eternal judgment that were not bearing fruit; otherwise few branches in Christ would ever *even begin* bearing fruit!

Another major problem that the takes-away-in-judgment view faces is the actual description of the unfruitful branches in verse 2. Christ describes them as "Every branch *in Me* that does not bear

---

32. For a detailed explanation of such practices, see Gary Derickson and Earl Radmacher, *The Disciplemaker* (Salem, OR: Charis Press, 2001), 326-29.

fruit." If such unfruitful branches represent unsaved professors whose pseudo-faith is revealed by their unfruitfulness and failure to abide in Christ, then in what sense were these mere professors ever "in Christ" if they were never saved to begin with? It will not suffice to use the example of Judas Iscariot, as Carson does,[33] claiming that Judas represents a branch that had "real contact with Jesus" and thus fulfilled Christ's description of a "branch *in Me* that does not bear fruit" (v. 2). Nor is it convincing to cite similar examples of people who had "some degree of connection with Jesus, or with the Christian church."[34] The phrase "in Me" is used in the Gospel of John to describe *only* a true, positive, spiritual relationship Christ has with someone, such as with the Father or believers. *Not once* is this phrase used of someone who professed to have a spiritual relationship with Christ but did not.[35]

Finally, the takes-away-in-judgment view creates a logical conundrum whereby believers are commanded to do what will certainly be true of them anyway. The disciples are commanded by Christ to "Abide in Me"[36] (v. 4) even though according to the doctrine of the perseverance of the saints, it is already guaranteed that they will abide in Christ since the eleven disciples in this context possessed true, "saving" faith. However, with the conditional "if" statements in verses 6-7, abiding in Christ is presented only as a *possibility*, not a *certainty!*[37] If abiding in fellowship with Jesus Christ by yieldedness and dependence were not guaranteed for the eleven apostles, then it is certainly not guaranteed for you and me as Christians today.

But perhaps you are wondering at this point about the consequence for not abiding in Christ as stated in verse 6, "If a man abide not in me, he is cast forth as a branch, and is withered; and men gather them, and cast them into the fire, and they are burned" (KJV). Is this a reference to judgment in hell as many commentators assume? Among commentators, there are at least four different interpretations of this verse.

View #1: First, some interpret this to be a reference to judgment in hell for believers who *lose* their *salvation* because they do not abide

---

33. Carson, *Gospel According to John*, 515.

34. Ibid.

35. See John 6:56; 10:38; 14:10 (2x), 11, 20, 30; 15:2, 4 (2x), 5, 6, 7; 16:33; 17:21, 23.

36. "Abide" (*meinate*) in v. 4 is a verb in the aorist tense, active voice, and imperative mood; thus it's a command.

37. Both verses 6 and 7 begin with a third class conditional "if" statement in Greek, meaning here, "If you abide in Me . . . and you may or may not."

in Christ.[38] However, this interpretation contradicts Christ's previous affirmations of eternal security in John 5:24, 6:37, and 10:28, as well as the entire doctrine of salvation by grace.

View #2: The second interpretation is that of Calvinism's doctrine of the perseverance of the saints.[39] This view also interprets burning and fire in verse 6 as a reference to judgment in hell; but instead of a believer losing his or her salvation, these branches represent those who were *never saved* in the first place because they did not have a true, "saving" faith that is fruitful and enduring. However, it is unlikely that the reference in verse 6 to being "gathered" and "cast into the fire" is a reference to *God's* judgment of unbelievers in *hell*. There are five reasons why this interpretation is incorrect based on the words and grammar of the text.

First, the passage does not say that it is *God* who does the gathering, casting, and burning of unfruitful branches. Verse 6 says it is *men*.[40]

Second, the timing of these activities is in the *present*, not the *future*, since all three verbs ("gather," "cast," and "burned") are in the present tense and used of present, rather than future, time.[41]

---

38. This view is espoused by Roman Catholics and Arminians: Robert Sungenis, *Not By Faith Alone: The Biblical Evidence for the Catholic Doctrine of Justification* (Santa Barbara, CA: Queenship, 1996), 278; I. Howard Marshall, *Kept by the Power of God: A Study of Perseverance and Falling Away* (Minneapolis: Bethany House, 1969), 183-84; Grant R. Osborne, "Soteriology in the Gospel of John," in *The Grace of God and the Will of Man*, Clark Pinnock, gen. ed. (Minneapolis: Bethany House, 1989), 258; Robert Shank, *Life in the Son: A Study of the Doctrine of Perseverance* (Springfield, MO: Westcott, 1961), 40-47.

39. Carson, *Gospel According to John*, 517; Laney, *John*, 274-75; John F. MacArthur, Jr., *Saved without a Doubt* (Wheaton, IL: Victor, 1992), 31-34.

40. Though technically the word for "men" does not appear in the Greek text, both the verbs "gather" (*synagousin*) and "cast" (*ballousin*) are plural in number, meaning that those who do the gathering and casting are plural; i.e., "*they* gather them," hence the KJV rendering, "men gather them." If God were the One judging, these verbs would be singular; i.e., "*He* gathers them." Some have suggested that the plural is used in reference to God's angels. But the holy angels are entirely foreign to the context of John 15 and the Upper Room Discourse, never being mentioned even once in John 13–17.

41. This cannot be a reference to holy angels gathering unsaved humanity to be cast into hell at the end of either the future tribulation (Matt. 13:39-42; 24:31; 25:31-46) or millennial kingdom (Rev. 20:11-15) since the verbs in verse 6 for "gathered" (*synagousin*), "cast" (*ballousin*), and "burned" (*kaietai*) are all *present tense* actions, not *future tense*. While it is true that the Gospel of John contains present tense verbs used with a future sense (e.g., *erchomai* in 14:3), such is not the case with the terms *synagō*, *ballō*, and *kaiō*.

Third, it is technically not *people* who are said to be gathered for burning, but *branches*.[42]

Fourth, if the casting forth of fruitless branches and their being cast into the fire represents God's eternal judgment of unbelievers in hell, then there is no adequate explanation for the process of withering or drying up that is also mentioned in verse 6. The withering occurs *after* being cast forth but *before* being gathered for the fire. Are proponents of the judgment-in-hell interpretation really prepared to accept the conclusion that God first passes eternal judgment on fruitless branches in this lifetime, with the result that this causes them to wither while they are yet alive on the earth, and then after they die He casts them into hell? This would be the required order of events in John 15:6. According to this judgment-in-hell interpretation, the reference in verse 6 to withering as a branch seems unnecessary and even out of place.

Fifth, when the term "fire" is used in Scripture as a reference to eternal judgment in hell, it is normally accompanied by some modifying word or words in the immediate context to indicate this, such as "unquenchable fire," "everlasting fire," or "lake of fire." But this is not the case in verse 6.

For these reasons, the first two interpretations of John 15:6 that conclude the branches are people being burned up in hell cannot be correct.

View #3: A third major view of John 15:6 interprets the phrase "cast out" to be a reference to temporal judgment upon a genuine but disobedient believer as part of God's earthly discipline rather than as a reference to eternal judgment in hell. According to this view, God's discipline *may* lead to a premature physical death, but the child of God will still enter heaven eternally saved.[43] Others modify this view somewhat, believing that the branches in verse 6 are disciplined by

---

42. The verse begins with *people* not abiding but ends with *branches* that are gathered and burned. Verse 6 begins with a person, "If a man abide not in me" (KJV). The word for the one who does not abide in Christ ("a man" in the KJV) is the Greek pronoun *tis*, a masculine (or feminine) singular. It definitely is not a neuter pronoun. However, verse 6 uses the neuter plural pronoun (*auta*) to describe the things that are gathered for burning: "and men gather *them* (*auta*)." The antecedent to the neuter pronoun "them" is logically the neuter noun "branch" (*to klēma*). Therefore, technically the things which are actually said to be gathered for burning are not *people* who don't abide in Christ but *branches*. Christ never actually states that men are burned.

43. Lewis Sperry Chafer, *Systematic Theology*, 8 vols. (Grand Rapids: Kregel, 1993), 3:298-300, 7:4; Joseph Dillow, "Abiding is Remaining in Fellowship: Another Look at John 15:1-6," *Bibliotheca Sacra* 147 (January 1990): 52-53.

God but not necessarily to the point of physical death. This view sees the "burning" of verse 6 as a reference to the burning of believers' worthless works at the judgment seat of Christ (1 Cor. 3:10-15) in which they will lose potential reward but not their salvation.

View #4: The fourth and correct view, in this author's opinion, is a modification of the third view. This view acknowledges that a genuine believer can be "cast forth" as a branch, spiritually "wither," and even be fruitless in the Christian life. However, instead of viewing the reference to being "burned" in verse 6 as something that *God* does as an act of judgment upon *people* (such as causing sickness or even physical death), it is simply a concluding statement regarding what *human* vinedressers in the first century were doing with unfruitful, unproductive, useless *branches*.

Humanly speaking, such branches were no longer good for anything except to be used as kindling for fire. This is likely the reason why verse 6 ends with *men* rather than God gathering the unfruitful branches and casting them into the fire. This also explains the consistent use of the present tense for the verbs *gather, cast,* and *burn.* It was a human process presently going on in Jesus and the disciples' day. This also best explains why in verse 6 the withering occurs *after* being cast forth but *before* being burned. Finally, this also explains best why Christ doesn't actually say it is *men* who are cast into the fire but *branches*. In John 15:6, Christ is illustrating spiritual fruitlessness and uselessness for believers who do not abide in Him; He is not illustrating divine judgment in hell. One commentary summarizes this fourth view well.

> Rather than being a warning of discipline or judgment, verse six is an illustration of uselessness in light of post-harvest, dormancy inducing, pruning. . . . Everything purged in early spring was either growing from a branch (sprigs and suckers), the branch not being removed, or from an undesired location on the trunk. Only at the end of the season would there be "branches" removed, piled up, and burned. In fact, Jesus may have chosen to allude to post harvest cultural practices specifically because He did not want His disciples to mistakenly link fruitfulness or fruitlessness to divine discipline. Rather He wanted them to see the importance of abiding itself. In the vineyard, anything not attached to the vine is useless and discarded. A part of the discarding process at the

end of the productive season is the burning of dry materials. The burning need not describe judgment, but is simply one of the steps in the process being described. It is simply what happens to pruned materials. Their uselessness, not their destruction, is being emphasized.[44]

What John 15:1-8 is teaching, along with John 2:23-25 and 8:30-32, is that genuine believers in Christ may *not* abide in a relationship of *communion* or fellowship with Christ and thus not grow as they should if they do not walk in daily dependence upon the Lord. Nevertheless, a believer's *union* with Christ is permanent and eternally secure. But if believers consistently fail to abide in Christ, the result will be unfruitfulness and spiritual uselessness, according to John 15:4-6. Though it is true that this may be accompanied by divine discipline and loss of potential reward, as stated in view #3 and as other Scripture passages reveal, this is not the point of Christ's Vine and branches lesson in John 15.

Conclusion

Did Jesus Christ Himself teach that perseverance in faith and good works is necessary for eternal life? There simply are no passages in the Gospels that actually teach this widely held but erroneous view. Instead, the teaching of Jesus Christ in the Gospels is that eternal life is granted on the basis of a single step of faith in Him (John 3:14-16; 4:13-15; 6:31-35), as demonstrated earlier in chapter 4 and confirmed by Christ's teaching that it is possible to be regenerated but only "believe for a while" (Luke 8:13). Even when believers do not abide in Christ and cease to be fruitful as His disciples, the gracious but iron-clad promises of Christ toward them remain true: "the one who comes to Me I will by no means cast out" (John 6:37) and "I give them eternal life, and they shall never perish; neither shall anyone snatch them out of My hand" (John 10:28).

---

44. Gary Derickson & Earl Radmacher, *The Disciplemaker* (Salem, OR: Charis Press, 2001), 178.

Chapter 10

Perseverance vs. Preservation
in Paul's Church Epistles

The apostle Paul is often called the "apostle of grace" because the Lord gave him an abundance of revelation and under-standing about His grace unparalleled among the other writ-ers of Scripture. If perseverance in faith and good works to the end of one's life were truly a requirement for salvation that is consistent with God's grace, then we should expect to find this doctrine taught in the Pauline Epistles. But we don't. Instead, we see in Paul's writ-ings the value and necessity of perseverance for the present Chris-tian life, but not to reach heaven. When each key Pauline passage is considered in terms of its context and content, and then compared to parallel passages, it is evident that Paul's epistles do not teach the perseverance of the saints for eternal life, but the preservation of the saints by the Savior.[1]

Eternal Life to Those Who Patiently Continue (Romans 2:7)

5 But in accordance with your hardness and your impeni-tent heart you are treasuring up for yourself wrath in the day of wrath and revelation of the righteous judgment of God, 6 who "will render to each one according to his deeds": 7 eter-nal life to those who by patient continuance in doing good seek for glory, honor, and immortality; 8 but to those who are self-seeking and do not obey the truth, but obey unrighteous-

---

1. It bears repeating that many Pauline passages clearly and repeatedly teach the truth of eternal security for every child of God (e.g., Rom. 5:9-10; 8:38-39; Eph. 1:13-14; 4:30), but the focus of this book and chapter is on the topic of perseverance.

ness—indignation and wrath, 9 tribulation and anguish, on every soul of man who does evil, of the Jew first and also of the Greek; 10 but glory, honor, and peace to everyone who works what is good, to the Jew first and also to the Greek.

Romans 2:7 should be considered a perseverance passage since the term in Greek for the phrase "patient continuance" (*hypomonē*) elsewhere in Scripture often means "endurance" or "perseverance," as it does in the context of Romans 2. The question is not whether Romans 2:7 is a Pauline passage on perseverance but whether Paul meant to teach that people are actually required to fulfill the condition of perseverance in good works for eternal life, or whether Paul is presenting this hypothetically, like the possibility of people perfectly keeping God's law. Certain Reformed commentators conclude that this verse is indeed setting forth perseverance in good works as an attainable condition for the elect to receive the "reward" of final justification and eternal life. John Murray interprets the passage this way, stating:

> The word rendered "patience" is perhaps better translated by "perseverance" or "endurance". We are reminded of the truth that it is he who endures to the end that will be saved (Matt. 24:13) and that "we are made partakers of Christ, if we hold fast the beginning of our confidence firm unto the end" (Heb. 3:14; cf. Col. 1:22, 23).[2]

Thomas Schreiner shares the same interpretation of Romans 2:6-10.

> It seems fair to conclude that eternal life will be granted to those who persevere in doing good works. There is little doubt, then, that vv. 7-10 constitute a fuller explanation of the traditional statement cited in v. 6. And it should be noted that Paul does not focus only on the negative, but he also brings in the positive: those who do good works will receive an eschatological reward, namely, eternal life.[3]

Calvinists Murray and Schreiner reject the majority view among Protestant commentators, who interpret Romans 2:6-10 as present-

---

2. John Murray, *The Epistle to the Romans,* New International Commentary on the New Testament (Grand Rapids: Eerdmans, 1959), 64.
3. Thomas Schreiner, "Did Paul Believe in Justification by Works? Another Look at Romans 2,"*Bulletin for Biblical Research* 3 (1993): 142-43.

ing a merely hypothetical, rather than an actual, possibility. In other words, Paul is teaching that if someone could persevere in doing good, then he or she would be justified on that basis and receive eternal life as a reward—but the reality of man's condition is such that no one can accomplish this, which is the point Paul is seeking to prove. While Schreiner admits the hypothetical interpretation is possible, he rejects it, claiming it is not evident in the passage: "The promise of eternal life for those who do good works could possibly be hypothetical, but there is no evident indication in the text that Paul is speaking hypothetically. Thus, a better conclusion is that Paul believes some people do good works and thereby receive eternal life."[4] Schreiner goes on to say that "the burden of proof is on those who defend the hypothetical view since the presumption is that Paul affirms with Judaism and the Old Testament that good works are necessary for eternal life."[5]

Putting aside for a moment Schreiner's false assumption that the Old Testament required good works for eternal life, is there support for the hypothetical view of Romans 2:6-10 from the text itself, or are these verses really requiring perseverance in good works for eternal life? There are several indications from the passage that Paul is presenting only a hypothetical possibility. First, the main point of the entire section from 1:18–3:20 is that all mankind stands legally and justly condemned in the sight of a perfectly righteous God, whether that person is a Jew with the Law, or a Gentile without the Law, or whether that person is immoral, moral, or religious. When it comes to justification and eternal life, these distinctions among people do not matter in the sight of a perfectly righteous God. The verdict from heaven is the same—"they are all under sin" (3:9); "there is none righteous, no, not one" (3:10); "there is none who does good, no, not one" (3:12). The point Paul establishes in chapters 1–3 is that no one can be justified in God's sight by works since all lack the righteousness God requires and all stand justly condemned before Him. Therefore, chapters 3–5 teach that God must give righteousness and justification to man freely, as a gift of His grace, through faith, and apart from works. The point of the larger context of Romans 1:18–3:20 is that man cannot be justified by his works; while the point of the following section of Romans 3:21–5:11 is that man must be justified by God's grace through faith apart from works. Since Romans 2:6-10 occurs in a section of the epistle that explains the *need* to be justified,

---

4. Ibid., 137.
5. Ibid., 143.

not *how* to be justified, the statement about "patient continuance in doing good" must contribute toward the main point of showing man his need for justification, rather than explaining how to be justified.

Second, each verse in the following section of Romans 2:11-14 begins with the explanatory conjunction "for" (*gar*), showing that these verses are inseparably connected to the preceding thought of verses 6-10. And what is the content or Paul's main point in verses 11-14? He concludes that "not the hearers of the law are just in the sight of God, but the doers of the law will be justified" (v. 13). Clearly, Paul must be speaking hypothetically here; otherwise, he would be contradicting himself within Romans since he concludes in the very next chapter that "by the deeds of the law no flesh will be justified in His sight, for by the law is the knowledge of sin" (3:20) and "that a man is justified by faith apart from the deeds of the law" (3:28). The point of Romans 2:6-10 is not to show how a man *can* be justified before God, but how he actually *cannot* be justified—by perseverance in good works. Paul's point cannot be that a man is justified before God "by patient continuance in doing good" and "seek[ing] for glory, honor, and immortality" (2:7) when in fact his whole point is to show that "there is none who does good, no, not one" (3:12) and "none who seeks after God" (3:11). Schreiner turns Romans 2:6-10 on its head, making it say exactly the opposite of what it was intended to say.

Third, while Schreiner denies that the context of Romans 2 supports hypothetical language, that is exactly what we find in verses 25-27, where several third-class conditional "if" statements occur in the Greek text—the condition of possibility. This can be observed in the italicized words of the English text below:

> 25 For circumcision is indeed profitable *if* you keep the law; but *if* you are a breaker of the law, your circumcision has become uncircumcision. 26 Therefore, *if* an uncircumcised man keeps the righteous requirements of the law, will not his uncircumcision be counted as circumcision? 27 And will not the physically uncircumcised, *if* he fulfills the law, judge you who, even with your written code and circumcision, are a transgressor of the law?

According to Romans 2:25-27, circumcision would indeed be counted for righteousness if a man were to keep or fulfill the rest of the Mosaic Law. If he does not keep or fulfill the entire Law, he is considered a "breaker of the law." So, can people actually keep the law and justify themselves before God on the basis of their works? Galatians 3:10 teaches that a man is cursed if he "does not continue in all things which are written in the book of the law, to do them," and James 2:10 says that "whoever shall keep the whole law, and yet stumble in one point, he is guilty of all." This means that if a man were circumcised and kept all of the law except for only one occasion over his entire lifetime, he is still condemned and not justified before God.

Fourth, Schreiner's interpretation of Romans 2:6-10 as an actual, rather than a hypothetical, prescription from God for eternal life results in a contradiction with Paul's teaching elsewhere. Schreiner seeks to legitimize works as a requirement for eternal life by distinguishing between two kinds of works—merely legal works versus truly good works. He claims that doing "works of law" will not justify a person, but doing "good works" will result in eternal life.

> Apparently, Paul believed that works in some sense were necessary for eternal life. The statement in Gal 5:21 is especially significant because in this letter he has emphasized that no one can be justified by "works of law" (Gal 2:16; cf. 3:2, 5, 10). He still maintains, nevertheless, that good works are essential for entrance into the kingdom of God (cf. 2 Cor 5:10).[6]

Schreiner's statement confuses two separate events—the judgment seat of Christ in heaven following the Rapture of the church prior the Tribulation versus entrance into the kingdom when Christ returns to the earth at the end of the Tribulation. Only church-age believers, who have already been justified, will be present at the judgment seat of Christ; and the issue there will be the judgment of their works to determine a possible eternal reward (2 Cor. 5:10), not to determine whether these raptured and already-justified saints in heaven qualify to enter the kingdom. Unfortunately Schreiner, like many other Reformed writers, mixes these two events, and in the process turns the condition for an eternal reward only for believers into the condition for eternal salvation for all mankind.

Furthermore, Schreiner completely contradicts Paul's teaching elsewhere about salvation being by grace through faith *apart from the believer's works*. Titus 3:5 and Romans 4:5-6 do not merely discount so-called "works of law" but even truly "good" and "righteous" works as being necessary for justification. In Titus 3:5, Paul says, "not

---

6. Ibid., 138.

by works of righteousness which we have done, but according to His mercy He saved us." In Romans 4:5, Paul teaches that justification in God's sight is "to him who does *not work*, but believes." *Any work,* whether "good," "righteous," or "legal," cannot justify a person in God's sight. That is why Paul says in Romans 4:6 that "God imputes righteousness *apart from works.*" Justification cannot be given simultaneously "apart from works" (4:6) and to those "who persevere in doing good works" (2:7), as Schreiner claims, without Paul contradicting himself. Paul cannot be teaching in Romans 2:6-7 that eternal life is granted "according to works" since he says just the opposite in 2 Timothy 1:9—that eternal salvation is "not according to our works, but according to His own purpose and grace." It is a hopeless contradiction to assert that eternal life is given on the one hand "by patient continuance in doing good" (Rom. 2:7), while on the other hand it is "not according to our works" (2 Tim. 1:9)!

While Romans 2:7 deals with perseverance, it does not prove that perseverance in good works is a requirement for eternal life, as taught by the fifth point of Calvinism. Instead, this verse teaches just the opposite—that man *cannot* receive eternal life by perseverance.

Justification in View of a Life of Faith (Romans 4:22)

> 19 And not being weak in faith, he did not consider his own body, already dead (since he was about a hundred years old), and the deadness of Sarah's womb. 20 He did not waver at the promise of God through unbelief, but was strengthened in faith, giving glory to God, 21 and being fully convinced that what He had promised He was also able to perform. 22 And therefore "it was accounted to him for righteousness."

This passage is occasionally cited as support for perseverance in faith being a requirement for justification.[7] For example, Leon Morris states, "It was this constancy in faith that was the reason for Abraham's being reckoned as righteous."[8] Was it really Abraham's perseverance that God saw and reckoned him righteous as a result?

---

7. Daniel P. Fuller, "Another Reply to Counted Righteous in Christ," *Reformation & Revival Journal* 12 (Fall 2003): 117-18; idem, *The Unity of the Bible* (Grand Rapids: Zondervan, 1992), 271-72, 310-16; Thomas R. Schreiner and Ardel B. Caneday, *The Race Set Before Us: A Biblical Theology of Perseverance and Assurance* (Downers Grove, IL: InterVarsity, 2001), 273-75.

8. Leon Morris, *The Epistle to the Romans*, Pillar New Testament Commentary (Grand Rapids: Eerdmans, 1988), 213.

Does Paul really teach in Romans 4:19-22 that only a certain kind of faith justifies—a persevering, productive, obedient faith? Leading Reformed author John Piper and his former pastoral staff have cited Romans 4:22 to support the requirement for perseverance, claiming that God not only justifies people based on their first act of faith but also on the basis of their subsequent acts of faith over the course of their Christian lives.

> Nevertheless, we must also own up to the fact that our final salvation is made contingent upon the subsequent obedience which comes from faith. The way these two truths fit together is that we are justified on the basis of our first act of faith because God sees in it (like he can see the tree in an acorn) the embryo of a life of faith. This is why those who do not lead a life of faith with its inevitable obedience simply bear witness to the fact that their first act of faith was not genuine.
>
> The textual support for this is that Romans 4:3 cites Genesis 15:6 as the point where Abraham was justified by God. This is a reference to an act of faith early in Abraham's career. Romans 4:19-22, however, refers to an experience of Abraham many years later (when he was 100 years old, see Genesis 21:5, 12) and says that because of the faith of this experience Abraham was reckoned righteous. In other words, it seems that the faith which justified Abraham is not merely his first act of faith but the faith which gave rise to acts of obedience later in his life. (The same thing could be shown from James 2:21-24 in its reference to a still later act in Abraham's life, namely, the offering of his son, Isaac, in Genesis 22.) The way we put together these crucial threads of Biblical truth is by saying that we are indeed justified on the basis of our first act of faith but not without reference to all the subsequent acts of faith which give rise to the obedience that God demands.[9]

Is Paul really teaching in Romans 4 from the example of Abraham that persevering, obedient faith is the kind of faith that justifies a sinner before God? No, Paul's point is not about perseverance

---

9. John Piper and Pastoral Staff of the Bethlehem Baptist Church, "What We Believe About the Five Points of Calvinism" (Minneapolis: Bethlehem Baptist Church, 2002). See also, John Piper, "The Purpose and Perseverance of Faith" (Rom. 4:22-25), www.desiringgod.org/messages/the-purpose-and-perseverance-of-faith (accessed April 26, 2016).

or productiveness, but about the nature of justifying faith as belief in God's promise and life-giving ability (4:13, 14, 16, 20, 21, 24, 25), rather than reliance upon the works of the law (especially circumcision) for justification.

The two quotations of the classic Old Testament text on justification by faith alone (Gen. 15:6) in Romans 4:3 and 4:22 serve as bookends to frame Paul's argument about Abraham's justification by faith. In Romans 4, Paul uses Abraham as the premiere Old Testament example of how a person is justified in God's sight. Here Paul shows that Abraham is the "father" or archetype of all who believe (4:11, 12, 16, 17, 18), whether Gentiles, who are without the Law and circumcision, or Jews, who have the Law and circumcision (4:9-16). Paul quotes Genesis 15:6 about Abraham believing God's promise of an heir. This initial faith was "accounted to him for righteousness." Significantly, in Genesis 15, Abraham was not yet circumcised (4:9-10). So, Paul presents proof from the life of Israel's chief patriarch that Gentiles, who do not have circumcision and the Law, can be justified by faith alone, just like Abraham before his circumcision. Next, Paul provides evidence from a context dealing with circumcision in Genesis 17 to show that Abraham once again believes God's promise of an heir. In Genesis 17, the Lord prescribes circumcision for Abraham and his descendants, who in Paul's argument typify Jews, who possess circumcision and the Law. Thus, in Romans 4:19-21, Paul uses the example of Abraham's faith in God's promise of an heir from Genesis 17–18 in order to prove that justification is by faith alone, whether a person is a circumcised Jew with the Law or an uncircumcised Gentile without the Law. Both are justified the same way—by grace alone, through faith alone, apart from works.

In addition, Paul refers to the example of Abraham's faith in Genesis 17–18 in order to emphasize that the nature of justifying faith involves belief in God's promise of life. Genesis 17–18 is where Abraham and Sarah receive God's promise of an heir from their own bodies even though Sarah is 90 years old and past childbearing age ("the deadness of Sarah's womb," Rom. 4:19), and Abraham is almost 100 (Gen. 17:17; Rom. 4:19). By referring to Genesis 17–18 in Romans 4:19-21, Paul is not only illustrating the nature of justifying faith as belief in God's promise of life, but he also sets the stage for his concluding point in the chapter about the Christian's belief in the resurrection of Christ: "Now it was not written for his sake alone that it was imputed to him, but also for us. It shall be imputed to us who believe in Him who raised up Jesus our Lord from the dead, who was delivered up because of our offenses, and was raised because of our justification" (4:23-25).

There are glaring problems with the view that Romans 4:19-22 requires a persevering, working faith for justification. If it were true that we are justified only by a "faith that works," then wouldn't faith plus works still be required for justification? Wouldn't this flatly contradict Paul's whole point stated earlier in Romans 4 that justification is "to him who does *not work but believes*" (4:5) and that justification is *"apart from works"* (4:6)? Furthermore, if Paul's point in 4:19-22 is to demonstrate the kind of persevering, productive, obedient faith that justifies, then why did he select Genesis 15 and 17–18 as the pair of passages to prove his point? Why not contrast Genesis 15:6 with a later event, such as Genesis 22, where Abraham offers his son Isaac upon the altar as a great act of faith (Heb. 11:17; James 2:21-23)? While Genesis 22 would appear to be the optimal passage Paul could have cited to prove his supposed point about genuine faith for justification always resulting in good works, this still would not prove that justifying faith perseveres to the end of one's life. If Paul chose to cite Genesis 15:6 as the starting point of Abraham's justifying faith, then why did Paul choose Genesis 18 as the end point? In Genesis 18, Abraham is "only" 100 years old. In Genesis 22, Isaac is called a "lad" (v. 5), possibly being a teenager, making Abraham around 115 years old. But Abraham lived to the age of 175, according to Genesis 25:7. So, if Paul intended to show in Romans 4:19-22 the perseverance of Abraham's faith as the kind of faith that justifies, then why did he cite Genesis 17–18, leaving 75 more years of Abraham's life?

Paul's point in quoting Genesis 15:6 in the introductory verse of Romans 4:3 and the concluding, summarizing statement of Romans 4:22 is simply to show from the example of Abraham that it is *faith* which justifies, not whether a person is circumcised with the Law or uncircumcised without the Law. Genesis 15:6 shows that Abraham had faith while uncircumcised, and thus a person can be justified without the works of the Law. Conversely, Paul's reference to Genesis 17–18 also shows that Abraham had faith in God's promise while circumcised, so that he might be the father of all who believe, whether Jews, who are circumcised and possess the Law, or Gentiles, who are uncircumcised and do not possess the Law. In either case, God justifies people today the same way He justified Abraham—the Genesis 15:6 way. Thus, Genesis 15:6 is quoted twice in

Romans 4, once to introduce Abraham as an example of justification by faith alone (4:3) and once at the end of the chapter to summarize, restate, and conclude the example of Abraham's justification by faith (4:22), not to prove that one's faith must also work and persevere in order for God to justify someone. This simple interpretation harmonizes best with the details of Romans 4 and Paul's overarching point in Romans 1–4 about God justifying Jews and Gentiles today exactly the same way—by grace, through faith in Jesus Christ, apart from works (Rom. 1:16; 2:10, 14, 17, 24; 3:1, 9, 29-30).

Olive Trees and Branches Cut Off
for Unbelief (Romans 11:16-24)

16 For if the firstfruit is holy, the lump is also holy; and if the root is holy, so are the branches. 17 And if some of the branches were broken off, and you, being a wild olive tree, were grafted in among them, and with them became a partaker of the root and fatness of the olive tree, 18 do not boast against the branches. But if you do boast, remember that you do not support the root, but the root supports you. 19 You will say then, "Branches were broken off that I might be grafted in." 20 Well said. Because of unbelief they were broken off, and you stand by faith. Do not be haughty, but fear. 21 For if God did not spare the natural branches, He may not spare you either. 22 Therefore consider the goodness and severity of God: on those who fell, severity; but toward you, goodness, if you continue in His goodness. Otherwise you also will be cut off. 23 And they also, if they do not continue in unbelief, will be grafted in, for God is able to graft them in again. 24 For if you were cut out of the olive tree which is wild by nature, and were grafted contrary to nature into a cultivated olive tree, how much more will these, who are natural branches, be grafted into their own olive tree?

This passage is often interpreted as teaching that perseverance in faith to the end of one's life is necessary for one's eternal salvation. This interpretation is shared by a host of theologians and commentators from Catholicism,[10] Lutheranism,[11] Arminianism,[12] and Calvinism,[13] none of whom accept a dispensational, premillennial point of view on this passage. Once again, Thomas Schreiner represents the view of Reformed theology with his comments on Romans 11:22.

> The necessity of continuing in the faith is hammered home in the closing words in verse 22: "if you remain in his kindness; otherwise you also will be cut off". . . . This threat cannot be dismissed as an idle one. Paul often warns his readers of the necessity of continuing in the faith in order to be saved. . . . One should never conclude from Paul's teaching on divine election that he downplayed the necessity of human beings continuing to exercise faith in order to obtain eschatological salvation.[14]

Is this passage really teaching that unless individuals continue in their faith, they will not obtain final salvation from God but will be condemned in hell? This passage cannot be understood correctly apart from recognizing the dispensational distinction between national Israel and the largely Gentile church in God's prophetic program, which forms the larger context of Romans 9–11. Many non-dispensational interpreters approach this passage with the assumption that Israel has lost forever its separate ethnic, national identity in the plan of God and has been "replaced" by the church or subsumed into the church to form one people of God.[15] Yet Romans 11 speaks of

---

10. Karl Keating, *Catholicism and Fundamentalism* (San Francisco: Ignatius, 1988), 174; Joseph C. Kindel, *What Must I Do to Be Saved?* (Milford, OH: Reihle Foundation, 1995), 80; and Robert A. Sungenis, *How Can I Get to Heaven?* (Santa Barbara, CA: Queenship, 1998), 178.

11. John Theodore Mueller, *Christian Dogmatics* (St. Louis: Concordia, 1934), 439; Francis Pieper, *Christian Dogmatics* (St. Louis: Concordia, 1953), 3:96.

12. Daniel D. Corner, *The Believer's Conditional Security*, 3rd ed. (Washington, PA: Evangelical Outreach, 2000), 399; James D. G. Dunn, *Romans 9-16*, Word Biblical Commentary (n.p.: Word, 1988), 674-75; Guy Duty, *If Ye Continue: A Study of the Conditional Aspects of Salvation* (Minneapolis: Bethany, 1966), 98-99; I. Howard Marshall, *Kept by the Power of God: A Study of Perseverance and Falling Away* (Minneapolis: Bethany, 1969), 99-105; David Pawson, *Once Saved, Always Saved? A Study in Perseverance and Inheritance* (London: Hodder & Stoughton, 1996), 54-55.

13. Charles Hodge, *Commentary on the Epistle to the Romans* (reprint, Grand Rapids: Eerdmans, 1994), 370; Morris, *Epistle to the Romans*, 416-17; Murray, *Epistle to the Romans*, 2:88; A. W. Pink, *The Saint's Perseverance* (reprint, Lafayette, IN: Sovereign Grace, 2001), 77.

14. Thomas R. Schreiner, *Romans*, Baker Exegetical Commentary on the New Testament (Grand Rapids: Baker, 1998), 608.

15. Douglas J. Moo, *The Epistle to the Romans*, New International Commentary on

Israel as a distinct corporate body being restored (v. 12) at the future time of the resurrection (v. 15) when Christ returns (v. 26).

Romans 11:16-24 warns Gentiles collectively to continue in belief and God's goodness lest they be cut off from God's olive tree. This raises a critical question—what does the olive tree represent? Individual salvation or a corporate position of service? Though salvation is unquestionably part of the peripheral context (vv. 11, 14-15, 26), *individual salvation* is not the focus of the passage. Gentiles and Israelites *as corporate entities* are the focus.[16] Dispensationalist Lewis Sperry Chafer correctly explains, "This message is addressed to Gentiles as contrasted to Israel, and is a distinction between God's dealing with Israel in one dispensation and with the mass of Gentiles in another dispensation, rather than a warning to saved individuals."[17]

This corporate emphasis of Romans 11:16-24 can be observed from the fact that Paul speaks of only two trees—a "wild olive tree" versus the "cultivated olive tree." The "wild olive tree" represents Gentiles, as strangers to God's covenants and promises to Israel (Eph. 2:11-12); while the "cultivated olive tree" represents Israel, as occupying the privileged position of being God's representatives (Exod. 19:3-6; Rom. 9:3-5). Significantly, Paul speaks only of these two trees. If Paul were teaching that the cultivated olive tree, which the Gentiles were grafted into, represents the place of individual salvation, then this would conflict with the rest of Scripture since the Bible is clear that Gentiles have always been able to be justified before God while still being Gentiles. The Old Testament is clear that Gentiles were saved *as Gentiles* and *remained Gentiles* without becoming Israelites or part of the cultivated olive tree (Exod. 18:9-12; Jonah 3:5; Matt. 12:41; Luke 11:32). Therefore, the olive tree in Romans 11 cannot picture the place of individual salvation; instead, it must picture the corporate position of either Israel or the Gentiles being the privileged channel through whom God presently works.

Though individual branches are mentioned in Paul's tree analogy in Romans 11, they are mentioned only as they relate to the two trees. The purpose of this passage is to show that although Israel had a place of privilege as God's channel of blessing to the Gentile world

---

the New Testament (Grand Rapids: Eerdmans, 1996), 709.

16. Lewis Sperry Chafer, *Systematic Theology* (Dallas: Dallas Seminary Press, 1948; reprint, Grand Rapids: Kregel, 1993), 3:306; H. A. Ironside, *Lectures on the Epistle to the Romans* (Neptune, NJ: Loizeaux, 1927), 140-41; and Alva J. McClain, *Romans: The Gospel of God's Grace* (Chicago: Moody, 1973), 201.

17. Chafer, *Salvation: A Clear Doctrinal Analysis*, 76.

(Rom. 9:3-5),[18] the nation temporarily lost this privilege because of its unbelief. Therefore, Gentiles should not become proud and self-confident lest they also lose this "place of favor or privilege"[19] as God's representatives to the world. Even though God is collectively working through the largely Gentile church in the present age, in the future millennial kingdom when "the times of the Gentiles are fulfilled" (Luke 21:24) and "the fullness of the Gentiles has come in" (Rom. 11:25), Israel will be reconciled to God as a corporate, national entity (Rom. 11:26-28) and restored to its place of privilege above Gentile nations (Deut. 28:13; Zech. 8:23).

Confirmed Blameless to the End (1 Corinthians 1:8)

4 I thank my God always concerning you for the grace of God which was given to you by Christ Jesus, 5 that you were enriched in everything by Him in all utterance and all knowledge, 6 even as the testimony of Christ was confirmed in you, 7 so that you come short in no gift, eagerly waiting for the revelation of our Lord Jesus Christ, 8 who will also confirm you to the end, *that you may be* blameless in the day of our Lord Jesus Christ. 9 God is faithful, by whom you were called into the fellowship of His Son, Jesus Christ our Lord.

This passage is teaching pure preservation. In verses 4-9, Paul does not express gratitude for the Corinthians' spiritual response to God, for it was not commendable. Instead, he is thankful for what God alone had graciously done among the Corinthians. Even the statement in verse 6 that the testimony of Christ "was confirmed" in or among the Corinthians speaks of God confirming the divine authority of Paul's gospel preaching to the city of Corinth (1 Cor. 2:1-4) by accompanying miraculous signs from God.[20] Thus, in the midst of this series of statements of divine accomplishment in 1 Corinthians 1:4-9, Paul makes a magnificent promise of God's grace in verse 8, namely, that the Lord would maintain the judicial and positional forgiveness of each Corinthian saint in Christ until the end of their earthly lives.

---

18. W. H. Griffith Thomas, *Commentary on Romans* (Grand Rapids: Eerdmans, 1946; reprint, Grand Rapids: Kregel, 1974), 297.

19. McClain, *Romans*, 201.

20. The Greek word for "confirm" (*bebaioō*) in verses 6 and 8 also occurs in Mark 16:20 and Hebrews 2:3, which describe miraculous signs done through the apostles in order to confirm or authenticate their message.

In light of the Corinthians' notorious carnality, the blamelessness Paul speaks of in verse 8 must refer to the positional, judicial forgiveness every child of God possesses today in Christ, which is received at the moment of justification and new birth. The Lord promises judicial forgiveness in several passages of Scripture, saying that He will no longer remember the believer's sins (Ps. 103:12; Isa. 38:17; Micah 7:19; Heb. 8:12; 10:17). Of course, God is omniscient and does not forget sin, so this figure of speech must be indicating that He does not hold the believer's sins against him in the sense of condemning or punishing him. While believers lose fellowship with God by committing sin, they also remain "blameless" in God's sight in the sense of judicial forgiveness. Robert Gromacki clarifies this concept of blamelessness in 1 Corinthians 1:8.

> The word "blameless" does not mean that the believers were without sin or blame in their practice. The epistle clearly shows their faults. Rather, it is a legal term. No charge of condemnation nor sentencing to eternal death would ever be brought against them in the court of divine justice. Literally, the word here translated "blameless" means "not called in" (*anegklētos*). It is the answer to Paul's rhetorical questions: "Who shall lay anything to the charge of God's elect? It is God that justifieth. Who is he that condemneth? It is Christ that died . . ." (Rom. 8:33-34).[21]

Since Paul has very little positive to say to the Corinthians about their own walk with the Lord, he chooses in the introductory section of 1:4-9 to emphasize God's work on behalf of the Corinthians and their standing or position in Christ. The Corinthians were characteristically carnal and not walking in fellowship with God (1 Cor. 3:1-4). Some were so persistently carnal that they were chastened by God with weakness, sickness, and even maximum divine discipline—death (11:30-32). Even though they were not persevering in faithfulness to God, the promise of divine preservation still applied to these carnal Christians—that Christ "will also confirm you to the end, *that you may be* blameless in the day of our Lord Jesus Christ" (1 Cor. 1:8). The italicized words *"that you may be"* are not in the Greek text but are supplied to make the English read more smoothly. Thus, verse 8 is not stating a mere possibility for the Corinthians; it is issu-

---

21. Robert G. Gromacki, *Called to Be Saints: An Exposition of 1 Corinthians* (Grand Rapids: Baker, 1977), 8.

ing an ironclad promise from God. The Corinthians could be certain that the Lord would preserve them judicially blameless to the end despite their carnality. But what does the phrase "to the end" mean? Was this promise of preservation only for a limited time or until the end of their lives?

The phrase "to the end" refers twice in the immediate context to the return of Christ at the Rapture. The end of verse 7 says that the Corinthians were "eagerly waiting for the revelation of our Lord Jesus Christ." The following verse speaks of "the day of our Lord Jesus Christ." Since Paul and the first-century church lived with the expectation that Jesus Christ could come back at any moment, believers' earthly lives were expected to end at the time of Christ's coming, when they would be instantaneously resurrected and glorified to meet the Lord in the air at the Rapture.[22] Thus, Paul's promise that the Lord will "confirm you to the end, blameless in the day of our Lord Jesus Christ" should be viewed as a promise of divine preservation to the end of each believer's life throughout the church age. When the promise of 1 Corinthians 1:8 is compared to the Corinthians' track record of carnality, it is clear that verse 8 is promising preservation without the manmade requirement of perseverance for final justification.

Competing for a Crown vs. Disqualification
(1 Corinthians 9:23-27)

23 Now this I do for the gospel's sake, that I may be partaker of it with you. 24 Do you not know that those who run in a race all run, but one receives the prize? Run in such a way that you may obtain it. 25 And everyone who competes for the prize is temperate in all things. Now they do it to obtain a perishable crown, but we for an imperishable crown. 26 Therefore I run thus: not with uncertainty. Thus I fight: not as one who beats the air. 27 But I discipline my body and bring it into subjection, lest, when I have preached to others, I myself should become disqualified.

---

22. Instead of using third-person pronouns (they, them) to describe a later generation living to see the Lord's coming, New Testament writers uniformly employ first- and second-person pronouns (I, we, us, you, your) for their expectation of seeing the Lord's imminent appearing within their own lifetimes (John 14:1-3; 1 Cor.1:7-8; 15:51-52; Phil. 1:6, 10; 3:20; Col. 3:4; 1 Thess. 4:15-17; 2 Thess. 2:1; 1 Tim. 6:14; Titus 2:12-13; James 5:7-9; 1 Peter 1:13; 1 John 2:28; 3:2-3). This shows that God has desired the church throughout its entire history to live with this same expectancy.

Do you have to compete for your eternal salvation like a boxer and runner training for the Olympic Games? Was the apostle Paul in jeopardy of going to hell if he didn't finish the race of his Christian life? Should believers be motivated to live their Christian lives by the possibility of becoming disqualified for final salvation? The answer to each of those questions is "yes" according to those who teach that salvation can either be lost or must be proven by perseverance to the end. Those who say that salvation can be lost, such as Arminians, often appeal to this passage in 1 Corinthians 9 to support their false teaching, as do Calvinists who hold to the doctrine of the perseverance of the saints. In either case, whether it is Arminianism or Calvinism, both theological viewpoints teach that you must approach the race of the Christian life with a boxer's or runner's mindset of needing to compete to the end in order to guarantee that you will ultimately possess the prize of eternal life. This perspective can be seen in the following comments on 1 Corinthians 9:23-27 by Calvinists Thomas Schreiner and Ardel Caneday.

> Paul explains in verse 23 that his own salvation is bound up with how he ministers the gospel to others: "I do all this on account of the gospel, in order that I may become a fellow beneficiary of it." His passion to save others calls for tending carefully to himself. All that he does to win others is guided by his objective to be sure that he also receives the blessing of eternal life promised in the gospel. Paul's own race that leads to eternal life runs directly through the faithful execution of his apostolic mission: to proclaim the gospel of Jesus Christ (cf. 1 Tim. 4:16). Therefore, Paul's use of the athletic motif—whether the runner or the boxer—illustrates the kind of faith that he must exercise in order to receive the salvation his own gospel promises. . . . The prize or wreath is resurrection to eternal life; the running and boxing is obedient faith.[23]

Similarly, Calvinist Samuel Storms concludes:

> Failing to finish the race because of injury or perhaps veering off course and crossing over into another runner's lane will, in the world of track and field, lead to almost certain disqualification. Paul appears to be drawing on this analogy to make his case that if we hope to receive the prize of full and

---

23. Schreiner and Caneday, *The Race Set Before Us*, 113-14.

final salvation, we too must endure to the end; we too must not run so as to suffer expulsion.[24]

If you are a believer in Jesus Christ, is 1 Corinthians 9:23-27 teaching that you must compete in your Christian life like a boxer or a runner to receive the prize of eternal salvation? Is it teaching that if you don't compete in this manner you will be disqualified or expelled from final salvation? Neither the surrounding context nor the content of these five verses support such an anti-grace, works-oriented approach to final salvation.

Any attempt at correctly interpreting 1 Corinthians 9:23-27 must first account for the surrounding context and explain why this section falls in between chapters 8 and 10 on Christian liberties. Both the immediate and broader contexts reveal that Paul is not concerned at all about his final salvation but about using his freedom of conscience in areas of Christian liberty to most effectively serve others, especially in preaching the gospel and reaching the lost. In the broader context of chapters 8 and 10, Paul teaches the Corinthians how they may use their Christian liberties wisely so as not to wound the conscience of fellow brethren or give offense to Jews and Gentiles who need to be saved.

In the context of chapter 9, Paul shifts to his own personal use of his freedoms in Christ to serve others most effectively as an apostle and preacher of the gospel. Though he has the right to eat and drink, to travel in ministry with a believing wife, and to refrain from his trade of tentmaking (Acts 18:3) to support his ministry (1 Cor. 9:1-6), he curtails each of these personal rights for the sake of furthering the gospel (9:12) and avoiding even the appearance of abuse of his apostolic authority (9:18) so that by all means he might lead more Jews and Gentiles to salvation (9:19-22). The context and flow of thought emphasize Paul's passionate concern for the salvation of others, not himself. This was the race and prize that Paul so purposefully pursued in the athletic metaphor of 9:24-27. Paul spoke of his purpose and pursuit of winning in 9:19-22 by the repeated use of the conjunction *hina*, which expresses purpose, and the word "win," which is italicized below for emphasis.

19 For though I am free from all men,
    I have made myself a servant to all,

---

24. Sam Storms, *Kept for Jesus: What the New Testament Really Teaches About Assurance of Salvation and Eternal Security* (Wheaton, IL: Crossway, 2015), 140.

that (*hina*) I might *win* the more;
20 and to the Jews I became as a Jew,
    that (*hina*) I might *win* Jews;
    to those who are under the law, as under the law,
    that (*hina*) I might *win* those who are under the law;
21 to those who are without law,
    as without law (not being without law toward God,
    but under law toward Christ),
    that (*hina*) I might *win* those who are without law;
22 to the weak I became as weak,
    that (*hina*) I might *win* the weak.
    I have become all things to all men,
    that (*hina*) I might by all means save some.

Clearly for Paul, *winning* in his gospel ministry as an apostle meant utilizing his liberties most effectively in leading *others to salvation*, not striving for his own personal salvation. This is the context of the Olympic Games illustration in verses 24-27. But what about the hinge statement of verse 23? If Paul's personal, eternal salvation is not at issue anywhere in the immediate context of chapter 9 or the larger context of chapters 8 and 10, then what does he mean by being a "partaker" in 9:23 when he says, "Now this I do for the gospel's sake, that I may be partaker of it with you"? Was his "objective to be sure that he also receives the blessing of eternal life promised in the gospel," as Schreiner and Caneday claim? The answer is found in the preceding context, where Paul explains the concept of being a "partaker" in 9:10-14.

10 Or does He say it altogether for our sakes? For our sakes, no doubt, this is written, that he who plows should plow in hope, and he who threshes in hope should be partaker of his hope. 11 If we have sown spiritual things for you, is it a great thing if we reap your material things? 12 If others are partakers of this right over you, are we not even more? Nevertheless we have not used this right, but endure all things lest we hinder the gospel of Christ. 13 Do you not know that those who minister the holy things eat of the things of the temple, and those who serve at the altar partake of the offerings of the altar? 14 Even so the Lord has commanded that those who preach the gospel should live from the gospel.

The context of 1 Corinthians 9 shows that being a "partaker" of the gospel has nothing to do with guaranteeing personal salvation by one's perseverance to the end. Rather, the context deals with financial and material support for ministers of the gospel. Paul is teaching that though he has the right to be financially and materially supported in the gospel ministry by others, he chooses instead to support himself in the gospel ministry because he views himself as a servant to others (9:19-23). He abstains from using his rights as an apostle so that he might reinvest his rights, so to speak, in reaching even more people with the gospel. Thus, verse 23 may be translated, "Now this I do for the gospel's sake, that I may be a fellow partaker thereof." Greek scholar A. T. Robertson comments on the translation of verse 23, saying, "Literally, *That I may become co-partner with others in the gospel*. The point is that he may be able to share the gospel with others, his evangelistic passion."[25] Paul is not saying in verse 23 that he must still make sure he personally has partaken of the eternal life that he preaches to others!

Instead, the context indicates that Paul is speaking of getting a "reward" for preaching the gospel (9:17-18). For Paul in verses 16-18, his alternatives are either preaching the gospel willingly and receiving a reward, or not preaching the gospel willingly but still having the obligation from the Lord to preach it. Note that Paul does not present his alternatives as either preaching the gospel willingly and going to heaven, or not preaching the gospel willingly and ending up in hell, disqualified from salvation. On the contrary, his argument is that if he faithfully perseveres in his God-appointed race of gospel ministry, then he will not be disqualified from receiving the reward of a "prize" (v. 24) or a "crown" (v. 25; cf. 1 Cor. 3:10-15; 4:1-5). Since crowns in the New Testament invariably speak of rewards for believers' faithful service to the Lord (2 Tim. 4:8; 1 Peter 5:4; Rev. 3:11; 4:4, 10), the "crown" Paul sought in 1 Corinthians 9:25 cannot refer to God's grace-gift of salvation. The free gift of salvation is never described as a "prize"; but the word "prize" is a fitting description for a reward.

Furthermore, the word "competes" (v. 25) is not appropriate as a description of the condition for salvation. The word "competes" (*agōnizomai*) is where we get our English word "agonize." Louw and Nida define this term: "to compete in an athletic contest, with

---

25. A. T. Robertson, *Word Pictures in the New Testament*, 6 vols. (Grand Rapids: Baker, n.d.), 4:148 (emphasis added).

emphasis on effort."[26] How does strenuous athletic effort fit with salvation being solely by God's grace and not of works? Do believers really have to fight like an Olympic boxer and train like an Olympic runner to stay on track to reach heaven?

But if Paul is not referring to training for final salvation like an athlete in the first-century Greek Olympic Games, then what does he mean in verse 27 when he says: "But I discipline my body and bring it into subjection, lest, when I have preached to others, I myself should become disqualified"? The Greek word for "disqualified" (*adokimos*) is the negative form of the same word that means "approved" (*dokimos*). While *adokimos* is sometimes used as a description for the unsaved, *dokimos* also occurs elsewhere in the context of believers using their liberties wisely for the edification of others (Rom. 14:18) and in the context of rewards for perseverance through trials (James 1:12). Therefore, in 1 Corinthians 9:27, Paul is simply saying that, like an athlete who trains for the purpose of winning the competition, he seeks to use his liberties and rights as an apostle in order to maximize, rather than jeopardize, the effectiveness of his gospel preaching to the lost. By becoming disqualified in the race, he would lose this ministry opportunity and reward, not lose or disprove his salvation.

You Are Saved, If You Hold Fast (1 Corinthians 15:2)

1 Moreover, brethren, I declare to you the gospel which I preached to you, which also you received and in which you stand, 2 by which also you are saved, if you hold fast that word which I preached to you—unless you believed in vain. 3 For I delivered to you first of all that which I also received: that Christ died for our sins according to the Scriptures, 4 and that He was buried, and that He rose again the third day according to the Scriptures

Great confusion surrounds the meaning of the term "saved" in verse 2. Does this refer to the believer's temporal, practical sanctification in the Christian life? Or, does it refer to the justification and eternal salvation of every believer? If "saved" refers to eternal salvation, then is this passage teaching that believers must hold fast to the gospel in order to maintain eternal life, as Arminians typically inter-

---

26. Johannes P. Louw and Eugene A. Nida et al., *Greek-English Lexicon of the New Testament Based on Semantic Domains*, 2 vols. (New York: United Bible Societies, 1988), 2:528, §50.1.

pret this passage?[27] Or, if "saved" refers to eternal salvation, then is this passage teaching that believers must hold fast to the gospel in order to prove that one's initial faith was genuine, saving faith, which is the normal Calvinism view?[28] The Calvinist, perseverance interpretation of 1 Corinthians 15:2 is stated by nineteenth-century theologian Charles Hodge, who writes:

> Their salvation, however, is conditioned on their persever-ance. If they do not persevere, they will not only fail of the consummation of the work of salvation, but it becomes mani-fest that they never were justified or renewed. . . . Here it is evident that the condition of salvation is not retaining in the memory, but persevering in the faith. "The gospel saves you," says the apostle, "if you hold fast the gospel which I preached unto you."[29]

A more contemporary statement of the Calvinist view is found in John MacArthur's commentary on 1 Corinthians, where he writes regarding 15:2:

> Paul's qualifying phrase—*if you hold fast the word which I preached to you, unless you believed in vain*—does not teach that true believers are in danger of losing their salvation, but it is a warning against non-saving faith. So a clearer render-ing would be, ". . . if you hold fast what I preached to you, unless your faith is worthless or unless you believed with-out effect." The Corinthians' holding fast to what Paul had preached (see 11:2) was the result of and an evidence of their genuine salvation, just as their salvation and new life were an evidence of the power of Christ's resurrection. It must be

---

27. Daniel D. Corner, *The Believer's Conditional Security: Eternal Security Refuted* (Washington, PA: Evangelical Outreach, 2000), 240-42; Guy Duty, *If Ye Continue: A Study of the Conditional Aspects of Salvation* (Minneapolis: Bethany House, 1966), 113; I. Howard Marshall, *Kept by the Power of God: A Study of Perseverance and Falling Away* (Minneapolis: Bethany House, 1969), 118; David Pawson, *Once Saved, Always Saved? A Study in Perseverance and Inheritance* (London: Hodder & Stoughton, 1996), 57-58; Robert Shank, *Life in the Son* (Springfield, MO: Westcott Publishers, 1961), 239, 299.

28. For a more extensive treatment of the various interpretations of 1 Corinthi-ans 15:1-2 in evangelicalism, see Thomas L. Stegall, *The Gospel of the Christ: A Bibli-cal Response to the Crossless Gospel Regarding the Contents of Saving Faith* (Milwaukee: Grace Gospel Press, 2009), 479-528.

29. Charles Hodge, *Commentary on the First Epistle to the Corinthians* (reprint, Grand Rapids: Eerdmans, 1950), 311.

recognized, however, that some lacked the true saving faith, and thus did not continue to obey the Word of God.[30]

There are several reasons why this interpretation cannot be correct. First and foremost, the apostle Paul knew that those to whom he was writing in Corinth were genuine believers. This fact can be readily observed from Paul's descriptions of these Corinthians throughout this epistle. They were referred to by Paul twenty times as his "brethren" (1:10, 11, 26; 2:1; 3:1; 4:6; 7:24, 29; 10:1; 11:2, 33; 12:1; 14:6, 20, 26, 39; 15:1, 50, 58; 16:15). The term "brethren" speaks of kinship in Christ. This term goes beyond mere ethnic brotherhood, as in Romans 9:3, since Paul was ethnically Jewish and the Corinthians were largely Gentile (1 Cor. 12:2). In addition, nowhere in 1 Corinthians 15 does Paul even infer that the Corinthians might be "false brethren" (*pseudadelphous*), as he does elsewhere for mere professors of Christ (Gal. 2:4).

Paul also knew that he was writing to those who possessed genuine faith in Christ and eternal salvation since he regarded the Corinthians as "called" (1:2, 9, 26), "chosen" (1:27-28), "in Christ" (1:30), "baptized" into Christ by the Holy Spirit (12:12-13), and therefore "sanctified in Christ" and "saints" (1:2). The Corinthians were also considered to be temples of the Holy Spirit individually (6:19) and His temple corporately (3:16). They were spiritually deficient in "no gift" of the Spirit (1:7). They are said to be "Christ's" own possession (3:23), who did not even belong to themselves anymore (6:19-20). They were instructed by Paul to expect instantaneous transformation when Christ comes back and the church is caught up to meet Him (15:51-52 cf. 11:26). They were told by Paul that they would "judge the world" one day (6:2), even angels (6:3), as part of reigning with Christ (4:8; 15:25). And far from speculating as to whether these Corinthians were truly "justified" or "renewed" as Hodge claims, Paul declares quite clearly that they were already "begotten" or regenerated (4:15), already "washed," "sanctified" (positionally in Christ, 1:2; but not practically, 3:1-4), and "justified" in Christ (6:11).[31]

In addition, nowhere in 1 Corinthians does Paul issue "a warning against non-saving faith," as MacArthur claims that Paul is

---

30. John F. MacArthur, 1 *Corinthians*, MacArthur New Testament Commentary (Chicago: Moody Press, 1984), 399.

31. Each of these four verbs in 1 Corinthians 4:15 and 6:11 are in the aorist tense and indicative mood in Greek, indicating that these things had already become true of the Corinthians sometime in their past.

doing in 15:2. Far from questioning whether these Corinthians had originally, truly believed in Christ for their eternal salvation, Paul repeatedly, explicitly indicates that they had believed. They were consistently contrasted with "unbelievers" (6:6; 7:13-14; 10:27; 14:22 cf. 14:1). They were commanded by Paul to "stand fast in the faith" (16:13), something that would be impossible to do for someone without faith. In addition, the immediate context of 15:2 says the Corinthians already believed: "Therefore, whether it was I or they, so we preach and so you believed" (15:11). The fact that Paul regarded the Corinthians as having already believed is also seen earlier in the epistle where Paul wrote, "Who then is Paul, and who is Apollos, but ministers through whom you believed" (3:5). Far from issuing "a warning against non-saving faith" in 1 Corinthians 15:2, no more definite and complete depiction could be presented of a people that had genuinely believed in Christ for eternal salvation than that which is presented in 1 Corinthians.

A second reason the Calvinist, perseverance view of 1 Corinthians 15:2 cannot be correct is because it misconstrues the meaning of the phrase "unless you believed in vain." By believing "in vain" (*eikē*), Paul does not mean "that some lacked true saving faith" and that this "is a warning against non-saving faith" as MacArthur asserts. For the Corinthians to have believed "in vain" did not mean that they didn't genuinely believe in the first place, or that they didn't have the supposedly right *kind* of faith—an obedient, persevering, working kind of faith. Rather, believing "in vain" meant that their faith might fall short of its God-intended purpose or goal of a productive, fruitful Christian life that would glorify the Lord. Paul was not questioning whether they had genuinely believed in the past, but whether their past faith would fall incomplete and come to a deficient end practically. For this reason, the phrase "unless you believed in vain" should be understood to mean "unless you believed *without success or effect.*"[32] The phrase "in vain" throughout the New Testament consistently does *not* call into question the authenticity of the action (when used adverbially) or thing (when used adjectivally) it modifies.[33] Consider a few Pauline examples:

---

32. J. H. Thayer, ed., *The New Thayer's Greek-English Lexicon* (Peabody, MA: Hendrickson, 1981), 176.

33. This is true whether "in vain" is *eikē* in the Greek (1 Cor. 15:2), or other terms used synonymously, such as *kenoō/kenos* or *dōrean*.

- "We then, as workers together with Him also plead with you not to receive the grace of God in vain (*kenos*)" (2 Cor. 6:1). Paul is not questioning here whether the Corinthians in their past had truly received the grace of God, but whether they would do so without fulfilling the divinely intended purpose of that grace. Commentator Ralph Martin states regarding this verse, "But we concur with Hughes (217) that it is doubtful in 6:1 that Paul is considering either counterfeit faith or the concept of perseverance."[34]

- "lest by any means I might run, or had run, in vain (*kenos*)" (Gal. 2:2). If there was not unity on the gospel between Paul and the "pillars" in Jerusalem (Peter, James, John), would Paul's previous running in the gospel ministry not have been genuine and authentic? Was Paul wondering if he had the right kind of running? Or was he simply saying that if they were not united on the gospel after all, their disunity would divide Jewish and Gentile believers and his running would not yield the divinely intended result or purpose of unity? If such were the case, Paul's running would be "without success" and "to no avail."

- "lest I have labored for you in vain (*eikē*)" (Gal. 4:11). By using the modifying expression, "in vain," was Paul questioning whether he had genuinely labored for the

---

34. Ralph P. Martin, *2 Corinthians*, Word Biblical Commentary (Dallas: Word Publishing, 1986), 166. See also, Philip E. Hughes, *The Second Epistle to the Corinthians*, New International Commentary on the New Testament (Grand Rapids: Eerdmans, 1962), 217-19. Both commentators argue from the context that 6:1 is a plea for the Corinthians to let the grace of God transform their lives, resulting in greater reward at the judgment seat of Christ (2 Cor. 5:10). Martin says, "Therefore, it appears that the meaning behind Paul's understanding of receiving the grace of God in vain is. . . . to fail to grow and mature in the Christian life, as evidenced by a life under the control of the one who died for believers" (Ibid., 167). Hughes states, "For them to receive the grace of God in vain meant that their practice did not measure up to their profession as Christians, that their lives were so inconsistent as to constitute a denial of the logical implications of the gospel, namely, and in particular, that Christ died for them so that they might no longer live to themselves but to His glory (5:15). This is a matter of which Paul had written more fully and graphically in his earlier letter: as recipients of the grace of God they were securely placed upon Jesus Christ, the only foundation, but they were in danger of building on that foundation with wood, hay, and stubble—a structure which would be made manifest and destroyed in the day of the Lord, though they themselves will be saved (1 Cor. 3:10-15). It is in this sense that the grace of God may be received in vain" (ibid., 218-19).

Galatians in the past? Did he have the right kind of labor? We see that his genuine labors for the Lord would be "without success" and "to no avail" if the Galatians capitulated to the pressure from the legalists. Here again, as with the Corinthians, by possibly laboring "in vain" for the Galatians, Paul was not calling into question the authenticity of their eternal salvation, for he regarded them as children of God (Gal. 3:26-28; 4:6-7, 9).

- "so that I may rejoice in the day of Christ that I have not run in vain (*kenos*) or labored in vain (*kenos*)" (Phil. 2:16). Again, Paul was not doubting the fact that he had actually and truly run and labored for the Lord with the Philippian Christians. But his running and laboring would not reach their divinely intended goal or purpose if the Philippians did not continue to "work out" their own salvation (Phil. 2:12) via practical sanctification until the Lord returned (2:16). It can readily be seen that Paul did not intend his "in vain" comments to question the genuineness of the Philippians' regeneration or justification since he regarded them as being fellow recipients of the grace of God (1:7), citizens of heaven (3:20), and as having their names written in the Book of Life (4:3).

In Paul's writings, the expression "in vain" never calls into question the genuineness or reality of the original action or thing modified. This fact makes it highly unlikely that Paul is calling into question the authenticity of the Corinthians' faith by the statement in 1 Corinthians 15:2, "unless you believed in vain." Instead, Paul is questioning whether their justification will fall short of God's intended goal of practical sanctification in their Christian lives.

A third reason 1 Corinthians 15:2 is not requiring perseverance for final salvation or to prove initial justification is because it is addressing present-tense salvation, or sanctification. The word "saved" (*sōzō*) in verse 2 is in the present tense, so that Paul is saying, "by which also you are being saved." Paul is not addressing the question of whether the Corinthians would attain the future "consummation of the work of salvation" by holding fast to the gospel, as Hodge maintains. Such a view misinterprets Paul's exhortation to "hold fast" as the necessary proof of initial salvation (justification) and as the condition for final salvation (glorification). In 1 Corinthians 15:2, Paul is not doubting either the Corinthians' past justification or future glorification, but he is challenging them about their present salvation, or practical sanctification, in their Christian lives. Dennis Rokser correctly explains, writing:

> These Corinthians via the Gospel were being presently saved from the POWER OF SIN in their Christian lives as long as they remained steadfast to the Gospel, just like they had been saved from the PENALTY OF SIN (Hell) when they had trusted in Christ. In other words, the Gospel they had received would continue to have saving effects from spiritual damage upon their lives *"if you hold fast the word which I preached to you."*[35]

This view correctly interprets Paul to be teaching that the gospel was necessary for the Corinthians to believe initially for justification and it was necessary for them to continue believing for their practical sanctification. This interpretation provides the best explanation for the tenses of the verbs used throughout the passage. If Paul was telling the Corinthians that in order to experience a present-tense salvation they must continually hold fast to the same gospel they originally believed, then we should expect to see a combination of past- and present-tense verbs indicating this in the passage. And we do. Verse 2 says,

by which also you are *saved* [present tense – "being saved"],

if you *hold fast* [present tense – "are holding fast"] that word

which I *preached* to you [past tense – when I first preached
                                                    the gospel to you],

unless you *believed* [past tense – at justification] in vain.

Appropriately, Paul's gospel preaching and the Corinthians' believing are both stated to be *past-tense* events, and their being saved and their holding fast to the word are said to be ongoing, *present-tense* processes. This fits perfectly with Paul teaching that Christians

---

35. Dennis Rokser, *Let's Preach the Gospel* (Duluth, MN: Duluth Bible Church, n.d.), 22. See also, J. Hampton Keathley III, *ABCs for Christian Growth: Laying the Foundation*, 5th edition (n.p.: Biblical Studies Press, 1996-2002), 441-42; David K. Lowery, "1 Corinthians," in *The Bible Knowledge Commentary*, New Testament, ed. John F. Walvoord and Roy B. Zuck (Wheaton, IL: Victor Books, 1983), 542; Lloyd A. Olson, *Eternal Security: Once Saved; Always Saved* (Mustang, OK: Tate, 2007), 100-1.

are practically sanctified by holding to the same gospel that we initially believe for our justification.

The tenses of the Greek verbs indicate a shift from the past to the present tense, showing that Paul is focusing on the Corinthians' present sanctification-salvation in verse 2. These verbs are italicized in 1 Corinthians 15:1-2 as follows to show Paul's transition from the past to the present: "Moreover, brethren, I declare to you the gospel which I preached to you, which also *you received* and in which *you stand,* 2 by which also *you are saved,* if you *hold fast* that word which I preached to you—unless you believed in vain." According to verses 1-2, the Corinthians related to the gospel in three ways. First, they "received" (aorist tense, active voice, indicative mood of *paralambanō*) it. Second, Paul says that the gospel was the message upon which, literally, "you have stood" (perfect tense, active voice, indicative mood of *histēmi*).[36] Third, it was the message by which they were also presently being "saved," as long as they would "hold fast" to it.

Note carefully the progression indicated by the three verb tenses in verses 1-2. With "received" (aorist tense, indicative mood) in verse 1, there is an emphasis upon how the Corinthians *initially* responded to the gospel. With "stand" or "have stood" (perfect tense, indicative mood) at the end of verse 1, there is a bridge between their initial *past* response and their *present* response.[37] With "are saved" and "hold fast" (both present tense, indicative mood) in verse 2, there is an emphasis upon their *present* response to the gospel and their present salvation. This progression from the aorist tense for "received" to the perfect tense for "have stood" to the present tense for "are saved . . . hold fast" underscores once again that the empha-

---

36. The perfect tense of "stand" (*histēmi*) in verse 1 indicates an action in the past with the results continuing into the present, all from the standpoint of the writer. It indicates that from Paul's perspective, the Corinthians had stood upon the gospel after receiving it and this had continued up to the time of Paul's writing. Verse 1 does not necessarily need to be translated "in which you have stood" since the emphasis of the perfect tense is upon the abiding results in the present; and thus the translation, "in which you stand" (present tense emphasis) is perfectly valid in the KJV, NKJV, and NASB. It is only noted here because it could easily be assumed to be a simple present tense with the past tense of the Greek text going unrecognized by the English reader.

37. The progression from an aorist, to a perfect, to a present tense verb should not be viewed as merely stylistic variation, or arbitrary and thus inconsequential. Paul's use of the perfect tense of "stand" in verse 1 is intentional. Regarding the perfect tense in Greek, Daniel Wallace writes, "The perfect tense is used less frequently than the present, aorist, future, or imperfect; when it is used, there is usually a deliberate choice on the part of the writer" (*Greek Grammar Beyond the Basics* [Grand Rapids: Zondervan, 1996], 573).

sis of *sōzō* in verse 2 is upon the present sanctification-salvation of the Corinthians.

Following the present tense of "are saved" and "hold fast" in verse 2, Paul then switches back to the past tense of "believed" at the end of verse 2 and "delivered" in verse 3 as he recalls his initial evangelization of the Corinthians. Paul says, "unless you *believed* in vain. 3 For I *delivered* [both aorist tense, indicative mood, i.e. past tense] to you first of all that which I also received: that Christ died." By going back to the past tense for the message of Christ crucified and risen (vv. 3-4) as the message he first "delivered" and that they also "believed" (v. 2c), Paul is underscoring that the Corinthians must continue in this same gospel in order to be presently saved, or sanctified.

A fourth reason Paul is addressing the present-tense salvation or sanctification of the Corinthians in verse 2 is based on the intermediate context. Later in chapter 15, Paul addresses the practical effects upon their Christian lives of abandoning belief in Christ's resurrection. In 1 Corinthians 15:30-34, Paul writes:

> 30 And why do we stand in jeopardy every hour? 31 I affirm, by the boasting in you which I have in Christ Jesus our Lord, I die daily. 32 If, in the manner of men, I have fought with beasts at Ephesus, what advantage is it to me? If the dead do not rise, "Let us eat and drink, for tomorrow we die!" 33 Do not be deceived: "Evil company corrupts good habits." 34 Awake to righteousness, and do not sin; for some do not have the knowledge of God. I speak this to your shame.

In verses 30-31, we see the positive effects in the Christian life of holding to the truth of Christ's resurrection. This guarantee of bodily resurrection personally motivated the apostle Paul to be willing to stick his neck on the line for the Lord on a daily basis! And in verse 32, Paul says that if there were no resurrection, instead of being willing to die for Christ, he may as well "live it up" hedonistically in this world. Then in verses 33-34, he admonishes the Corinthians for letting the evil company of resurrection-deniers affect their own knowledge of God and their conduct. For the Corinthians to deny the gospel truth of the resurrection would certainly have had an adverse effect upon their Christian lives and their practical sanctification.

A fifth reason present sanctification-salvation is in view in 1 Corinthians 15:2 is because of the use of *histēmi* ("stand") at the end of verse 1: "Moreover, brethren, I declare to you the gospel which I preached to you, which also you received and in which you *stand.*" In 1 Corinthians 15:1-2, Paul is saying that the Corinthian believers had stood upon the gospel in the past and up to the present. But this standing, like their sanctification-salvation, would continue only if they held fast to the gospel Paul initially preached to them. This usage of the verb *histēmi* in 1 Corinthians 15:1 is consistent with how the term is employed elsewhere in the Pauline Epistles, where it is used routinely of some *present* aspect of the Christian life. It is *never* a descriptive term for eternal salvation itself, nor as a term describing the condition for eternal salvation. However, this term is used quite frequently to describe the present Christian life (Rom. 5:2; 11:20; 14:4; 1 Cor. 7:37; 10:12; 2 Cor. 1:24; Eph. 6:11, 13-14; Col. 4:12). Since the term *histēmi* is never used in the New Testament as a synonym for eternal salvation or as a synonym for saving faith, it is doubtful that Paul is using it in 1 Corinthians 15:2 as a condition for final salvation or as proof of initial salvation.

A final reason 1 Corinthians 15:2 addresses present-tense salvation is because it is perfectly consistent with other Pauline passages where continuing in the truth of the gospel is necessary for sanctification, growth, and a state of spiritual readiness in anticipation of Christ's imminent return for His church. A constant theme of the Pauline Epistles is that the cross and resurrection of Christ, along with the believer's identification with Christ in His work, form the foundation for the entire Christian life (Rom. 6:3-6; 1 Cor. 6:14, 19-20; 15:1-4; 2 Cor. 4:10-11; 5:14-16a; 13:4; Gal. 2:20; 6:12-16; Eph. 1:20; 5:25; Phil. 1:21; 2:5-8; 3:10-11; Col. 2:6, 20; 3:1-4; 2 Tim. 2:11). If the Corinthians did not continue to hold fast to that word about Christ's resurrection that Paul originally delivered to them in the gospel (1 Cor. 15:1-2), then an important plank upon which to live their Christian lives would be removed. The truth of the gospel directly affects the believer's practical sanctification. This fact is corroborated by at least four parallel Pauline passages (Gal. 3:1-4; Phil. 2:12-16; Col. 1:22-28; 1 Thess. 2:1–3:13) where the Christian's continuance in God's Word, particularly the gospel, results in practical sanctification, spiritual growth, and a Christian life that is not "in vain." Only by holding fast to the gospel of God's grace will believers grow in grace and be ready for the imminent coming of the Lord Jesus Christ (Phil. 2:16; 1 Thess. 2:19; 3:13).

When every detail of 1 Corinthians 15:1-2 is carefully considered, these verses show that Paul was urging the Corinthian saints to persevere in the gospel for their ongoing spiritual growth and sanctification, not to either *retain* eternal life (Arminianism) or *prove* that they possessed it in the first place (Calvinism).

Being in the Faith vs. Disqualified (2 Corinthians 13:5)

> 2 I have told you before, and foretell as if I were present the second time, and now being absent I write to those who have sinned before, and to all the rest, that if I come again I will not spare—3 since you seek a proof of Christ speaking in me, who is not weak toward you, but mighty in you. 4 For though He was crucified in weakness, yet He lives by the power of God. For we also are weak in Him, but we shall live with Him by the power of God toward you. 5 Examine yourselves as to whether you are in the faith. Test yourselves. Do you not know yourselves, that Jesus Christ is in you?—unless indeed you are disqualified. 6 But I trust that you will know that we are not disqualified. 7 Now I pray to God that you do no evil, not that we should appear approved, but that you should do what is honorable, though we may seem disqualified.

Second Corinthians 13:5 is often used as support for questioning whether someone is saved on the basis of how that person lives. If someone professes to believe but does not persevere in faithfulness, that person is supposedly "disqualified" from salvation. According to Arminianism, this means that person has lost his or her salvation. According to Calvinism, this means that person has disproven the genuineness of his or her faith. But is Paul really calling into question the reality of the Corinthians' faith and salvation in verse 5? This interpretation cannot be correct, for it conflicts with Paul's testimony of the Corinthians' faith elsewhere in the epistle and with the context of chapter 13.

Paul had no doubt whether the Corinthians initially believed in Christ for salvation. Notice in 2 Corinthians 1:21-24 how Paul speaks to the Corinthians as though they have faith: "Now He who establishes us with you in Christ and has anointed us is God, who also has sealed us and given us the Spirit in our hearts as a guarantee. Moreover I call God as witness against my soul, that to spare you I came no more to Corinth. Not that we have dominion over your faith, but are fellow workers for your joy; for by faith you stand." Only genuine believers can be fellow workers with Paul who are able to stand by faith.

The apostle Paul led the Corinthians to Christ (Acts 18:1-11; 1 Cor. 4:15; 2 Cor. 10:14-15), and he pointed to them as proof of the genuineness of his apostolic ministry. Therefore, he writes in 2 Corinthians 3:1-3, "Do we begin again to commend ourselves? Or do we need, as some others, epistles of commendation to you or letters of commendation from you? You are our epistle written in our hearts, known and read by all men; clearly you are an epistle of Christ, ministered by us, written not with ink but by the Spirit of the living God, not on tablets of stone but on tablets of flesh, that is, of the heart." Would Paul ever say such things to unbelievers?

In fact, Paul even goes on to contrast the Corinthians with unbelievers in 2 Corinthians 6:14-16: "Do not be unequally yoked together with unbelievers. For what fellowship has righteousness with lawlessness? And what communion has light with darkness? And what accord has Christ with Belial? Or what part has a believer with an unbeliever? And what agreement has the temple of God with idols? For you are the temple of the living God." Just like in 1 Corinthians, Paul views the recipients of 2 Corinthians as true believers in Christ.

Though Paul has no question about the genuineness of their initial, saving faith, he challenges them for concluding that his apostolic authority is not from Christ. Thus, he writes, "Do you look at things according to the outward appearance? If anyone is convinced in himself that he is Christ's, let him again consider this in himself, that just as he is Christ's, even so we are Christ's" (10:7). To their shame, the Corinthians sought proof of Christ working through Paul (2 Cor. 13:3). Should an apostle have to prove himself to the very believers he led to the Lord and who are themselves the very fruit and proof of his ministry?

This context of Paul defending his own apostleship to the Corinthians (2 Cor. 10–12) is often ignored by those who interpret 2 Corinthians 13:5 as teaching the real possibility of being "disqualified" for heaven on the basis of carnality and disobedience in the Christian life. To assume that Paul was actually in doubt about the Corinthians' salvation misses the point of the passage. Paul's whole argument is predicated on the fact that he knew they were saved and that they also knew they were saved. Paul states in verse 5, "Examine yourselves as to whether you are in the faith. Test yourselves. Do you not know yourselves, that Jesus Christ is in you? — unless indeed you are disqualified." The reason Paul says this is not to show that the Corinthians were not saved but to prove or confirm that they were saved, so as to affirm the genuineness of Paul's apostleship.

When Paul says, "unless indeed (*ei mēti*) you are disqualified," there is no doubt in his mind that they are saved, for he uses the second-class condition in Greek (*ei mēti*) to express something that is contrary to fact or assumed *not* to be true.[38] In other words, according to the grammar of the verse, Paul assumes that the Corinthians are *not* "disqualified" but are truly "in the faith" and "Christ is in [them]." Paul's whole argument is that if the Corinthians are "in the faith" (and they are), then Paul's apostleship is valid because he is the one God used to lead them to their faith. Though the Corinthians sought to examine Paul, he tells them to examine themselves so that, ironically, the proof of Paul's apostleship would come from a source they were not expecting—themselves![39]

Second Corinthians 13:5 does not mean what many professing Christians assume it means. This passage does not support the practice of examining our faithfulness, perseverance, and good works to assure ourselves that we are saved, for how much obedience is enough to know with certainty that we are fully accepted by God? Assurance of salvation never comes from looking at our imperfect walk but at the objective truth of the gospel. Salvation is sure only to those who look away from self and toward Jesus Christ by faith, believing that He is the Son of God, who died for all our sins, rose from the dead, and promises eternal life to all who receive His salvation solely by grace.

If You Continue in the Faith & Hope
of the Gospel (Colossians 1:23)

19 For it pleased the Father that in Him all the fullness should dwell, 20 and by Him to reconcile all things to Himself, by Him, whether things on earth or things in heaven, having made peace through the blood of His cross. 21 And you, who once were alienated and enemies in your mind by wicked works, yet now He has reconciled 22 in the body of His flesh through death, to present you holy, and blameless, and above reproach in His sight—23 if indeed you continue

---

38. Friedrich Blass, Albert Debrunner, and Robert Walter Funk, *A Greek Grammar of the New Testament and Other Early Christian Literature* (Chicago: University of Chicago Press, 1961), 221; Nigel Turner, "Syntax," Vol. III, *A Grammar of New Testament Greek*, ed. James Hope Moulton (Edinburgh: T & T Clark, 1963), 284.

39. For a fuller explanation and defense of this interpretation, see Perry C. Brown, "What Is the Meaning of 'Examine Yourselves' in 2 Corinthians 13:5?" *Bibliotheca Sacra* 154 (April 1997): 175-88.

in the faith, grounded and steadfast, and are not moved away from the hope of the gospel which you heard, which was preached to every creature under heaven, of which I, Paul, became a minister.

Colossians 1:23 is one of the most common verses used by Calvinists and Arminians to require perseverance to make it to heaven. It is often assumed that the presentation before God spoken of in verse 22 refers to being in heaven one day. Calvinist Sam Storms says of verses 22-23:

> Paul seems clearly to say that if you don't persevere by continuing in the faith, you will not be presented before God holy and blameless and without reproach. Whether "the faith" is a reference to one's personal trust in Jesus or the objective body of truths we call "the Christian faith," the fact remains: if you don't continue in it, you will not experience the inestimable joy of standing forever in the presence of God. So, yes, there is truly a conditional element involved ("if indeed"). The condition for final presentation is faithful perseverance. The notion espoused by some that one "act of faith" in Jesus Christ eternally secures final salvation, irrespective of how one lives, is unbiblical.[40]

But what if the presentation spoken of in verse 22 ("to present you holy, blameless, and above reproach in His sight") refers to God's goal for each believer *in the present,* while the believer awaits and prepares for the Lord's return? What if the phrase "in His sight" in verse 22 refers to what God sees in the believer *right now* rather than the believer's future standing in glory in heaven? This changes the entire interpretation.

It is critical to note that the reconciliation of verse 21 refers to a past event that has already transpired. The verb "reconciled" is in the aorist tense and indicative mood, indicating that Paul viewed the Colossian believers as having already been reconciled to God. But would they go on to fulfill God's purpose of sanctification for

---

40. Storms, *Kept for Jesus*, 150. For a similar view, see also Judith M. Gundry Volf, *Paul & Perseverance: Staying In and Falling Away* (Louisville: Westminster/John Knox, 1990), 197 n. 231; Robert A. Peterson, "The Perseverance of the Saints: A Theological Exegesis of Four Key New Testament Passages," *Presbyterion* 17 (1991): 95-99; John Piper, *Five Points: Towards a Deeper Experience of God's Grace* (Ross-shire, UK: Christian Focus, 2013), 64; Schreiner and Caneday, *The Race Set Before Us*, 74, 192-93.

their Christian lives?[41] This purpose is stated in the infinitive clause of verse 22: "to present you holy, and blameless, and above reproach in His sight." Based on this grammatical shift from the past tense accomplishments of verses 20-21 to the Lord's present purposes for each believer, C. I. Scofield explains that verses 22-23 refer to the believer's present state or condition before God rather than his spiritual standing or settled position in Christ.

> Verse 23 has troubled some believers: "If ye continue in the faith grounded and settled, and be not moved away from the hope of the gospel...." The thought of this whole passage is that reconciliation through Christ's death is now accomplished for the believer in Him; but the Christian's *state*, as "holy . . . without blemish and unreprovable," depends on his continuance in the faith. . . . "The hope of the gospel" (Col. 1:23) is not the hope to be saved; for the believer that is always regarded as accomplished.[42]

The evidence to support this conclusion comes not only from observing the grammatical shift from the past tense (vv. 20-21) to the present tense (vv. 22-23), but also from three additional observations: (a) Paul already regarded the faith and salvation of his Colossian readers to be genuine; (b) the phrase "in His sight" in verse 22 refers to the present, not the future; (c) the infinitival purpose clause "to present you" in verse 22 also refers to a presentation transpiring in God's sight in the present rather than at glorification in the future.

How did Paul view the Colossians—as true believers, or mere professors, or a mixture of both? By saying in verse 23, "if you continue in the faith, grounded and steadfast, and are not moved away from the hope of the gospel," was Paul viewing their perseverance in the faith as proof or confirmation of whether they truly believed in the past when they first heard the gospel? Calvinist theologian Wayne Grudem believes so.

> It is only natural that Paul and the other New Testament writers would speak this way, for they are addressing groups of people who profess to be Christians, without being able to

---

41. Lewis Sperry Chafer, *Systematic Theology*, 8 vols. (Dallas: Dallas Theological Seminary, 1948), 3:308.

42. C. I. Scofield, *Scofield Bible Correspondence Course*, 6 vols. (Chicago: Moody Bible Institute), 4:792, 794.

know the actual state of every person's heart. There may have been people at Colossae who had joined in the fellowship of the church, and perhaps even professed that they had faith in Christ and had been baptized into membership of the church, but who never had true saving faith. How is Paul to distinguish such people from true believers? How can he avoid giving them false assurance, assurance that they will be saved eternally when in fact they will not, unless they come to true repentance and faith? Paul knows that those whose faith is not real will eventually fall away from participation in the fellowship of the church. Therefore he tells his readers that they will ultimately be saved, *"provided that you continue in the faith"* (Col. 1:23). Those who continue show thereby that they are genuine believers. But those who do not continue in the faith show that there was no genuine faith in their hearts in the first place.[43]

This common Calvinist interpretation of verse 23 completely contradicts Paul's statements about the Colossians elsewhere in this epistle. For example, in his opening greeting in Colossians 1:3-4, Paul gives thanks to God for the Colossians "since we heard of your faith in Christ Jesus and of your love for all the saints." Is this the way you would greet someone whose faith was in question? In verse 5, Paul describes the hope that was already laid up for them in heaven. In verse 6, Paul says the Colossians were already bearing spiritual fruit. In verses 9-11, Paul prays for their spiritual walk, which he would never do for unbelievers, who have no walk with the Lord. Instead, he would pray for their salvation. Then in verses 12-14, Paul uses the past tense to describe several aspects of their salvation that were already accomplished, such as their being "qualified . . . to be partakers of the inheritance of the saints in the light" (v. 12), having already been "delivered . . . from the power of darkness and conveyed . . . into the kingdom" of God's beloved Son (v. 13), and already having "redemption" in Christ and "the forgiveness of sins" (v. 14).

Furthermore, in chapter 2, Paul even explicitly states that these Colossian believers had received Christ: "As you therefore have received Christ Jesus the Lord, so walk in Him" (v. 6). Since they had already received Christ by faith, they were now to continue walking by faith. Thus, Paul explicitly refers to their "faith" in chapter 2 by expressing his desire to see "the steadfastness of your faith in

---

43. Wayne Grudem, *Systematic Theology* (Grand Rapids: Zondervan, 1994), 793.

Christ" (v. 5), and that they would be "established in the faith" (v. 7). The genuineness of the Colossians' initial faith in Christ for salvation was not in question; but what Paul was legitimately concerned about was whether they would continue walking by faith and that their faith would be steadfast and established, which would occur only by holding fast to the gospel (1:23) and the sufficiency of Christ (2:2-3, 9-13; 3:1-4, 11), instead of embracing the philosophy of the world (2:8), legalism (2:14-17), mysticism (2:18-19), or asceticism (2:20-23). The portrait of the Colossians in this epistle clearly portrays the Colossians as genuine saints with eternal salvation because they initially believed in Christ. But their walk of faith through the dangerous minefield of this world was still in question and a cause of concern and prayer for the apostle Paul.

A second major reason why Colossians 1:22-23 is not requiring perseverance in faith for final salvation is because the phrase "in His sight" refers to how God sees believers in the present, not the future.[44] The phrase "in His sight" (*katenōpion*) in Colossians 1:22 is often assumed to be a reference to the believer standing in God's future, heavenly presence, but it actually refers to what God sees in men now, in the present. This term *katenōpion* occurs only 3 times in the New Testament, with Jude 1 being a definite reference to the future in glory, but with Ephesians 1:4 being a debated passage just like Colossians 1:22. However, the cognate root word *enōpion* occurs 17 times in Paul's epistles and in only one passage (1 Cor. 1:29) does it even *possibly* refer to the future, immediate presence of God in heaven. In all 16 remaining occurrences, it refers to being *presently* in the sight of either God (Rom. 3:20; 14:22; 2 Cor. 4:2; 7:12; 8:21; Gal. 1:20; 1 Tim. 2:3; 5:4, 20; 6:13; 2 Tim. 2:14; 4:1) or men (Rom. 12:17; 2 Cor. 8:21; 1 Tim. 5:20; 6:12). When a study is done in both the Old and New Testaments of such general concepts and phrases as being "in His sight," the "sight of God," and the "sight of the Lord," it is overwhelmingly evident that these phrases nearly always refer to what God sees right now in the present, not the future.

Likewise, to be presented "holy, and blameless (*amōmous*), and above reproach (*anegklētos*)" in God's sight does not necessarily refer to future glorification, as is commonly assumed. The believer is to be experientially holy now, in the present (1 Cor. 7:34; 2 Cor. 7:1; Titus 1:8; 1 Peter 1:15-16). Though Paul uses the term *amōmous* to refer to future glory (Eph. 5:27), he also uses it to refer to the present life of the believer, as in Philippians 2:15: "that you may become blameless

---

44. Chafer, *Systematic Theology*, 3:307-8.

(*amōmous*) and harmless, children of God without fault in the midst of a crooked and perverse generation, among whom you shine as lights in the world." Similarly, though Paul uses the term *anegklētos* to refer to future glorification at Christ's coming (1 Cor. 1:8), he also uses it of the present (1 Tim. 3:10; Titus 1:6, 7).

Some who condition final salvation and glorification on holding fast to the gospel until the end of one's life claim that Ephesians 5:27 must be a parallel passage to Colossians 1:22 because Ephesians and Colossians are parallel epistles. But there is a significant difference in wording between Ephesians 5:27 and Colossians 1:22 that sets them apart. In Ephesians 5:27, there is the addition of the word "glorious" ("that He might present her to Himself a glorious church"), which speaks of glorification and thus the future. In addition, Ephesians 5:27 goes on to say, "a glorious church, not having spot or wrinkle or any such thing." This also indicates future glorification since no Christian could honestly say on this side of heaven that he or she is spiritually "without spot or wrinkle or any such thing." These significant additions are not found in Colossians 1:22.

Besides the evident fact of the Colossians' genuine, initial faith and the present-tense meaning of "in His sight" (1:22), a final reason why Colossians 1:22-23 is addressing practical sanctification and not glorification is based on the meaning of the infinitive phrase "to present" in verse 22. When Paul says, "to present you holy, and blameless, and above reproach" in God's sight, he is referring to God's purpose for the believer's present earthly life. The root word for "present" (*paristēmi*) in Colossians 1:22 and 28 is elsewhere used by Paul predominantly in reference to the present Christian life (Rom. 6:13, 16, 19; 12:1; 16:2; 1 Cor. 8:8; 2 Cor. 11:2; 2 Tim. 2:15; 4:17), rather than a future glorification (Rom. 14:10; 2 Cor. 4:14; Eph. 5:27). Though it is God's stated purpose for every reconciled believer to be presented holy before Him (Col. 1:22), the believer's volitional response of presenting himself to God is also necessary in order for actual sanctification to occur (Rom. 6:13, 16, 19; 12:1).

This interpretation of "present" (*paristēmi*) is confirmed by the way this term is used in the immediate context, where Paul continues in Colossians 1:27-29:

27 To them God willed to make known what are the riches of the glory of this mystery among the Gentiles: which is Christ in you, the hope of glory. 28 Him we preach, warning every man and teaching every man in all wisdom, that we may

present (paristēmi) every man *perfect (teleios)* in Christ Jesus.
29 To this end I also labor, striving according to His working
which works in me mightily.

When Paul says in verse 28, "that we may *present* every man *perfect* in Christ Jesus," he is not speaking of final salvation at glorification, but of a state of spiritual growth and maturity in one's Christian life. This is how the term "perfect" *(teleios)* is used elsewhere by Paul (1 Cor. 2:6; 14:20; Eph. 4:13; Phil. 3:12, 15; Col. 4:12). Though God's stated objective is to "present" *(paristēmi)* every reconciled believer to Himself in a holy, sanctified condition (Col. 1:22-23), and Paul labored in his teaching ministry to "present" *(paristēmi)* every Christian this way (Col. 1:28-29), the believer must still volitionally choose to "present" *(paristēmi)* himself to God in order for sanctification and spiritual growth to actually occur (Rom. 6:13-19).

The apostle Paul had a shepherd's heart to see each and every believer not only justified before God but also sanctified, mature, and "perfect" in His sight. To this end he labored (Col. 1:29), along with others (Col. 4:12). The apostle Paul was not satisfied just to see sinners saved from hell; he shared the Lord's desire for every child of God to grow into Christ-likeness (Gal. 4:19). If this did not occur, he viewed his labors as being "in vain" (Gal. 4:11; Phil. 2:16). Since Paul lived with the eager expectation of Christ's return for the church at any moment, he labored in ministry with the great objective of seeing every believer grow in Christ and be "perfect" (Col. 1:28), to be continuously ready for the Lord Jesus to appear at any moment. Thus the believer's presentation in holiness to God is not speaking of glorification itself, which is after this life, but of a present, continuous state of practical sanctification in anticipation of Christ's any-moment coming. Colossians 1:22-29 confirms the teaching of 1 Corinthians 15:1-4 that Christians must hold fast to the gospel in order to be spiritually sanctified and "perfect" or complete.

Preserved Blameless by the Lord (1 Thessalonians 5:23-24)

23 Now may the God of peace Himself sanctify you completely; and may your whole spirit, soul, and body be preserved blameless at the coming of our Lord Jesus Christ. 24 He who calls you is faithful, who also will do it.

Here is another clear passage, like 1 Corinthians 1:8, that promises the preservation of believers in Christ. The reason third-tense sanctification and preservation can be guaranteed is because all the work is done by the Lord (v. 24). Once again, Paul is writing to people who he knew were true believers (1 Thess. 1:3, 7-8; 2:10, 13; 3:2, 5-7, 10; 2 Thess. 1:3-4, 10). To these believers in Thessalonica, Paul expresses his prayerful desire (reflecting the Lord's desire), saying "may the God of peace . . . may your whole spirit, soul, and body" (v. 23). The twofold occurrence of the optative mood in Greek for "may" does not mean that Paul merely wished for the Thessalonians' complete sanctification and preservation and that it was only a possibility. The next verse contains the indicative mood statement, "He who calls you is faithful, who also will do it," guaranteeing that the request of verse 23 will be fulfilled. Note that the complete sanctification and preservation of verse 23 is not guaranteed in verse 24 on the basis of the Thessalonians' faithfulness but on the Lord's faithfulness. If preservation were dependent even in the slightest on the faithfulness and perseverance of believers, Paul could never make this promise. But since the Lord is the one who does all the work of keeping, preserving, and perfectly sanctifying in heaven everyone who has believed the gospel, we can rest assured that the Lord will not fail to keep His promise and preserve all those who have believed in His Son.

Conclusion

The only way certain passages in Paul's epistles can be interpreted as requiring perseverance in faith and good works for final salvation is by ignoring context, grammar and syntax, and parallel Pauline usage. It is unfortunate that a system of theology is routinely imposed onto passage after passage in Paul's writings, instead of letting the text of God's Word speak for itself. The Reformed doctrine of the perseverance of the saints can be propped up from Paul's epistles only by stringing together select, individual statements that are wrenched from their contexts and assumed to be proof texts. But when passages on perseverance and preservation in Paul's letters are allowed to speak for themselves, the result is a beautiful balance between God's promise of preservation for every believer in Christ and His pastoral desire for every believer to be transformed into Christ's likeness through a walk of yielded dependence on Him.

Chapter 11

Perseverance vs. Preservation
in Paul's Pastoral Epistles

The nineteenth-century humorist and author, Samuel Lang-
horne Clemens (aka Mark Twain), is perhaps best known for
his classic novels, *The Adventures of Tom Sawyer* and *The Adventures of Huckleberry Finn.* What is not so well-known is the fact that
he married a Christian woman named Olivia Langdon. While Mark
Twain himself was not a believer, early in their marriage he joined his
wife in prayer over their meals and in Bible reading. But this practice
soon waned. Eventually Twain's irreverent attitude, coupled with
fame, fortune, worldwide travels and exposure to the philosophies
of men, wore down her sincere faith.

Later in life Olivia confided in her sister that she had given up
her earlier beliefs. When personal tragedy struck the couple, Mark
Twain, whom she affectionately called "Youth," attempted to console
her, saying, "If it comforts you to lean on the Christian faith, do so."
She replied, "But I can't, Youth. I haven't any."[1] Besides providing
a poignant lesson on the danger of believers becoming unequally
yoked in marriage to unbelievers (2 Cor. 6:14-18), this sad and tragic
account illustrates the reality that someone with faith in Jesus Christ
may actually reach a point of faithlessness.

While those who hold to Reformed theology are forced to conclude that Olivia Langdon Clemens must not have ever truly believed
in Christ, Paul's two pastoral epistles to Timothy contain nine passages that explicitly warn about the real possibility of genuine faith

---

1. Clarence E. N. Macartney, *Macartney's Illustrations: Illustrations from the Sermons of Clarence Edward Macartney* (New York: Abingdon-Cokesbury Press, 1946),
225.

not persevering to the end of one's life. In these epistles, Paul informs Timothy that genuine believers may stray from the faith, shipwreck their faith, fall away from the faith, deny the faith, cast off initial faith, become faithless, stray from the truth, and have faith overthrown. Few books in all of Scripture speak as directly to the issue of perseverance in faith as do Paul's epistles to Timothy.

Straying from Sincere Faith (1 Timothy 1:3-7)

> 3 As I urged you when I went into Macedonia—remain in Ephesus that you may charge some that they teach no other doctrine, 4 nor give heed to fables and endless genealogies, which cause disputes rather than godly edification which is in faith. 5 Now the purpose of the commandment is love from a pure heart, from a good conscience, and from sincere faith, 6 from which some, having strayed, have turned aside to idle talk, 7 desiring to be teachers of the law, understanding neither what they say nor the things which they affirm.

According to 1 Timothy 1:3-7, it is possible to stray from a sincere faith. Here the apostle Paul instructs Timothy as a pastor in Ephesus to command certain individuals in the Ephesian church not to teach the errors they apparently had already come to embrace. Paul could say that such individuals had strayed from a sincere or genuine faith and had turned away from the truth. Several relevant factors should be noted in this passage.

First, the individuals in verse 3 whom Timothy was to command to "teach no other doctrine" (*heterodidaskalein*, i.e. heterodoxy) were undoubtedly the same ones referred to in verses 6-7, of whom it is said that they had already turned aside to fables regarding the Law. There were already Christians present in Ephesus who had embraced error and were now to be commanded by Timothy not to teach such false doctrine. The content of their false doctrine revolved around matters of the "law" (v. 7), specifically "fables" (*mythos*, i.e. myths) and "genealogies" (v. 4). This legalistic, Judaistic influence was ever-present in the apostolic era, even as there is ever a tendency toward legalism today (Acts 15; 2 Cor. 11; Gal. 1–6; Phil. 3:2; Col. 2:16; 1 Thess. 2:14-17; Titus 1:9-11; 3:9-11). First Timothy 1:3-7 teaches the sobering reality that it is possible for one who is genuinely saved to embrace false doctrine, which Paul calls "fables" and "idle talk."

Second, there is no indication from the context that these people were simply professors who never possessed genuine faith in Christ. If such were the case, then in addition to commanding them not to teach their heterodoxy concerning the Law, we would also expect Timothy to be commanding them to "believe on the Lord Jesus Christ" and be saved (Acts 16:31). According to verse 6, these individuals strayed from the things mentioned previously in verse 5, including love from a pure heart, a good conscience, and a sincere faith.[2] They did not merely stray from love but also from a good conscience and a sincere faith. This indicates that these people initially possessed faith. If these individuals were only professors who never truly believed in Christ, then this passage would be saying that they strayed from a faith they never possessed in the first place, which is a logical absurdity.

Third, the Greek term in verse 6 for "having strayed" (*astochēsantes*) has the root meaning of "missing the mark." It essentially means "to miss, fail, deviate, depart."[3] No matter how you look at it, none of these definitions bode well for the doctrine of the perseverance of the saints. Whether one has failed, deviated from, departed from, or missed the mark of sincere faith, they certainly have not persevered in the faith! One outstanding Greek scholar named Henry Alford stated that the translation should read "some having failed" since the idea of missing the mark by swerving or turning aside "seems hardly precise enough."[4] In one ancient, secular use of this Greek term, a man bewails the loss of his pet fighting rooster, stating that it had "failed" him by dying in the fight.[5] If the idea behind the Greek term *astocheō* is indeed that of "having failed," then 1 Timothy 1:6 is explicit that it is possible for someone with faith in Christ not to persevere in that faith.

---

2. In verse 6, the term for "which" (*hon*) is a feminine, plural pronoun modifying the preceding four feminine singular nouns in verse 5—love, heart, conscience, and faith.

3. Walter Bauer, William F. Arndt, and F. Wilbur Gingrich, *A Greek-English Lexicon of the New Testament and Other Early Christian Literature*, 3rd ed., rev. and ed. Frederick W. Danker (Chicago: University of Chicago Press, 2000), 146. See also H. G. Liddell and R. Scott, *A Greek-English Lexicon*, rev. and augmented by H. S. Jones and R. McKenzie, with a Revised Supplement by P. G. W. Glare and A. A. Thompson (New York: Oxford University Press, 1996), 262.

4. Henry Alford, *The Greek Testament*, Vol. III, with revision by Everett F. Harrison (Chicago: Moody Press, 1958), 304.

5. J. H. Moulton and G. Milligan, *Vocabulary of the Greek Testament* (Peabody, MA: Hendrickson, 1997), 87.

Shipwrecked Faith (1 Timothy 1:18-20)

18 This charge I commit to you, son Timothy, according to the prophecies previously made concerning you, that by them you may wage the good warfare, 19 having faith and a good conscience, which some having rejected, concerning the faith have suffered shipwreck, 20 of whom are Hymenaeus and Alexander, whom I delivered to Satan that they may learn not to blaspheme.

Paul exhorts Timothy here to fight the "good fight" of faith, as he does later in this same epistle (1 Tim. 6:12). One means of doing so is to continually hold on to faith and a good conscience, which Hymenaeus and Alexander had failed to do and the result was disastrous—their faith was ruined. Here is another clear scriptural example of genuine faith not persevering.

There are several items in this passage that are not consistent with the doctrine of genuine faith always persevering. First, the fact that Paul commands Timothy to hold on to his faith implies that Timothy's faith would not automatically persevere. Why command someone to do something that you are certain he is going to do anyway? According to Paul in 2 Timothy 1:5, Timothy had genuine faith. If the apostle Paul believed the Calvinist doctrine that genuine faith always perseveres, and he knew that Timothy had genuine faith, then it would be unnecessary to command Timothy to continually hold on to his genuine faith in 1 Timothy 1:19.

Second, this passage mentions two false teachers, Hymenaeus and Alexander. Who were these men? Hymenaeus is probably the same individual mentioned later in 2 Timothy 2:17-18 who taught that the resurrection already occurred in some sense, and thus he overthrew the faith of some. The identity of Alexander and his false doctrine is more difficult to determine since several people bore the name Alexander in the New Testament (Mark 15:21; Acts 4:6; 19:33; 2 Tim. 4:14); yet 1 Timothy 1:20 may be the only reference to this particular individual.

However, one thing is certain regarding both Hymenaeus and Alexander—their faith was definitely shipwrecked against the rocks of heresy. The Greek term for "shipwrecked" (*nauageō*) in verse 19 essentially means "to break a ship to pieces" (from *naus*, meaning "ship," and *agnumi*, meaning "to break").[6] The term itself is used only here and in 2 Corinthians 11:25 where Paul states that he had been shipwrecked three times. One such instance of Paul being shipwrecked is described in Acts 27:1-44. There it says Paul's ship was "broken up" (v. 41) so that the passengers had to swim to the shore of a nearby island on "boards" and parts of the ship (v. 44). Clearly the prospect of shipwreck was the dread of every ancient mariner since it meant the complete cessation of their ship functioning as a ship, with the likely prospect of either being marooned or dying at sea. The term "shipwreck" depicts a sense of complete destruction. Just as ships suffered shipwreck and ceased to function as ships, so the faith of Hymenaeus and Alexander ceased to function as genuine faith. This fact cannot be reconciled with the doctrine that "those who have true faith can lose that faith neither totally nor finally."[7]

Seeing this predicament, some perseverance advocates acknowledge that Hymenaeus and Alexander never lost their *personal faith* but merely shipwrecked *the faith*—the body of Christian doctrine to be believed. One commentator explains this view when he writes, "By their teaching they were making shipwreck of the faith, that is, the body of truth which comprises the Christian faith. Since 'faith' has the article (*tēn pistin*) it is best to understand it objectively, rather than 'their faith.'"[8] This interpretation sees a distinction between "the faith" (Christian doctrine) and "faith" (personal belief) based upon the presence of the definite article "the" before the word "faith" in 1 Timothy 1:19. However, Greek scholars also recognize that the presence of the article "the" (*tēn*) before "faith" (*pistin*) is a common Greek idiom where the article is used as a possessive pronoun, so that verse 19 could also be translated, "concerning *their* faith have suffered shipwreck."[9] Consequently, several English Bibles translate the phrase as "their faith."[10]

---

6. George W. Knight, *Commentary on the Pastoral Epistles*, New International Greek Testament Commentary (Grand Rapids: Eerdmans, 1992), 110; A. T. Robertson, *Word Pictures in the New Testament*, Vol. IV (Grand Rapids: Baker, n.d.), 566.

7. Anthony A. Hoekema, *Saved by Grace* (Grand Rapids: Eerdmans, 1989), 234.

8. Homer A. Kent Jr., *The Pastoral Epistles*, rev. ed. (Winona Lake, IN: BMH, 1982), 92-93. See also Kenneth Wuest, "The Pastoral Epistles in the Greek New Testament" in *Word Studies in the Greek New Testament* (Grand Rapids: Eerdmans, 1952), 32.

9. Robert G. Gromacki, *Stand True to the Charge: An Exposition of 1 Timothy* (Schaumburg, IL: Regular Baptist Press, 1982), 44; J. N. D. Kelly, *The Pastoral Epistles*, Black's New Testament Commentary (Peabody, MA: Hendrickson, 1960), 57-58; Knight, *Commentary on the Pastoral Epistles*, 109-10; Robertson, *Word Pictures in the New Testament*, 4:566.

10. These include the English Standard Version (ESV), New American Standard Bible (NASB), New International Version (NIV), Revised Standard Version (RSV),

Whether the Greek phrase *tēn pistin* should be understood as "the faith" or "their faith" should not ultimately matter because the personal "faith" of an individual who falls away from "the faith" must still be considered vain and displeasing from God's perspective (Mark 16:14; Heb. 11:6).[11] Later in this same epistle in 6:10-12, this sharp theological distinction between personal "faith" and "the faith" becomes blurred. There, verse 10 has "the faith," verse 11 has simply "faith," and verse 12 in Greek has "the faith." In this passage, some had strayed from "the faith" by pursuing riches (v. 10), and thus Timothy was to pursue "faith" (v. 11) as part of the good fight of "the faith" (v. 12). In terms of Paul's usage, and in God's mind, there is no virtue in a personal "faith" that simultaneously rejects "the faith." Some Bible scholars recognize this point and declare regarding 1 Timothy 1:19 that the Greek expression *tēn pistin* is practically *both* "their faith" and "the faith." The actual apostasy of Hymenaeus and Alexander cannot be denied by appealing to a distinction between personal "faith" and "the faith."

Regarding apostasy, 1 Timothy 1:20 indicates that Hymenaeus and Alexander had been turned over "to Satan" because of their blasphemy. In this passage, the apostle Paul exercised his authority to put them out of the fellowship of the local church and into Satan's destructive domain of the world. This was not done for the purpose of restoring their salvation, for they had never lost their regeneration or eternal salvation. Rather the passage explicitly states that this action was taken so that they might "learn" something in their earthly lifetime, namely, not to blaspheme. The Greek term for "learn" (*paideuō*) is where we get our English word "pedagogue." This chastening action was temporal and pedagogical for the purpose of correction with a view toward restoring their fellowship with God and the rest of the church (1 Cor. 5:5; 11:30-32).

The fact that Hymenaeus and Alexander were turned over to Satan and his realm for chastening also indicates that they had actually apostatized. If being turned over to Satan is not a case of apostasy, then what is? Even though Hymenaeus and Alexander are an obvious example of genuine believers who apostatized, advocates of the Calvinist doctrine of perseverance claim that apostasy is not possible for a genuine believer. John MacArthur

---

New American Bible (NAB), and New Jerusalem Bible (NJB).

11. Gordon D. Fee, *1 and 2 Timothy, Titus*, New International Biblical Commentary (Peabody, MA: Hendrickson, 1988), 58; W. E. Vine, *The Collected Writings of W. E. Vine*, Vol. 3 (Nashville: Thomas Nelson, 1996), 154.

explains this view when he writes, "No matter how convincing a person's testimony might seem, once he becomes apostate he has demonstrated irrefutably that he was never saved."[12] If spiritual apostasy is not possible for the genuine Christian, and Hymenaeus and Alexander did apostatize, then the only apparent resolution of this passage with the Calvinist doctrine of perseverance is to conclude that these men did not have genuine faith to begin with and thus they were never saved.

However, perseverance advocates will not be helped by this explanation either since there is nothing in the context of 1 Timothy 1:18-20 to indicate that these men were never originally saved. Two facts from the passage indicate that these men originally did have "genuine" faith. First, the fact that these men were turned over to Satan indicates that they had originally escaped the domain of Satan in some sense, either positionally (Gal. 2:14; Eph. 2:2) or practically (Job 1:8-11; Luke 22:31; 1 Peter 5:8). This cannot be said of someone who has never been saved. The Word of God knows nothing of unregenerate people who are already children of the Devil (John 8:44; 1 John 5:19) suddenly being "turned over" to him. That would be illogical as well as unscriptural. Moreover, the fact that the faith of Hymenaeus and Alexander was shipwrecked indicates that it once genuinely existed. You cannot shipwreck a ship that never even existed. If you were to see the broken pieces of a ship upon a seashore, you would not deny the genuineness of the ship that once existed; you would simply acknowledge that the broken ship is no longer operational as a ship. So it is with the faith of some saints who venture to sail upon the seas of false doctrine.

There is no evidence that Hymenaeus and Alexander ever returned to fellowship with God or died with their "ship of faith" intact. Though their correction and restoration may have been *desired* by Paul in 1 Timothy 1:20, it was by no means *certain*, as the Calvinist doctrine of perseverance requires for someone with genuine faith. What God's Word does reveal is that approximately four to six years later, when Paul wrote his second epistle to Timothy, Hymenaeus still had not repented (2 Tim. 2:17-26). There is absolutely no indication from Scripture that either Hymenaeus or Alexander ever repented or returned to "the faith."

---

12. John F. MacArthur, Jr., *The Gospel According to Jesus* (Grand Rapids: Zondervan, 1988), 98.

Falling Away from the Faith (1 Timothy 4:1-3)

1 But the Spirit explicitly says that in later times some will fall away from the faith, paying attention to deceitful spirits and doctrines of demons, 2 by means of the hypocrisy of liars seared in their own conscience as with a branding iron, 3 men who forbid marriage and advocate abstaining from foods, which God has created to be gratefully shared in by those who believe and know the truth.

Here is yet another passage that teaches that the possibility of one who is saved to depart from his or her faith. The New American Standard Bible is quoted above, because in this instance it translates the passage with greater precision. There are three parties[13] described in this passage: (1) the demonic spirits, who are the source of false doctrine; (2) the human false teachers, who are called "liars" in verse 2 and are the mediums for the demonic false teaching; and (3) the human victims of false doctrine, who are actually the ones who fall away from the faith in verse 1. This passage issues a sobering warning that genuine believers may apostatize as a result of heeding false doctrine and false teachers (in this case probably unsaved false teachers), which all stems from demonic deception.

This passage also provides an illustration of apostasy since the Greek word for "fall away" in verse 1 is *apostēsontai*, which is the form of a Greek word from which our English word "apostasy" is derived.[14] The term literally means to stand off, go away, withdraw, depart, desert, or fall away.[15] Though the term occurs fourteen times in the Greek

---

13. The KJV and NKJV give the impression in verse 2 that there are just two parties involved, namely, the demons and the false teachers, who themselves fall away from the faith. However, most scholars agree that the human "liars" of verse 2 are separate from their victims who fall away from the faith in verse 1. See Alford, *The Greek Testament*, 3:335; Fee, *1 and 2 Timothy, Titus*, 97; Kent, *The Pastoral Epistles*, 143-45; Knight, *Commentary on the Pastoral Epistles*, 189; Robertson, *Word Pictures in the New Testament*, 4:578; Eugene Stock, *Practical Truths from the Pastoral Epistles* (Grand Rapids: Kregel, 1983), 227; Marvin R. Vincent, *Vincent's Word Studies in the New Testament*, Vol. IV (Peabody, MA: Hendrickson, n.d.), 244; Vine, *The Collected Writings of W. E. Vine*, 3:175; and Wuest, *Word Studies in the Greek New Testament*, 2:66.

14. The Greek word in v. 1, *apostēsontai*, is the third person, plural, future tense, middle voice, indicative mood form of *aphistēmi*. The word *aphistēmi* is a compound word made up of two Greek words, the prepositional prefix *aph-* from *apo*, which means "away," and the root word *histēmi*, which means "to stand." Literally, apostasy is "standing away" from a position once held or occupied.

15. W. Bauer, *A Greek-English Lexicon of the New Testament and Other Early Christian Literature*, translated by W. F. Arndt and F. W. Gingrich; revised and augmented

New Testament, it is used only in the context of spiritual departure or apostasy in three passages (Luke 8:13; 1 Tim. 4:1; Heb. 3:12).

The apostasy or falling away mentioned in this passage is predicted to occur in the later times (v. 1), and it will be characterized by legalism and asceticism, which forbids marriage and abstains from certain foods (v. 3). The "later times" does not refer only to the very last segment of the 2,000 years of church history, as some might be prone to think. Rather, a careful study of Scripture reveals that the later times, or "last days," span from the apostles' generation all the way to Christ's return (2 Tim. 3:5; 4:3-5; Heb. 1:1-2; 1 Peter 1:18-20; 1 John 2:18). The last days or "later times" encompass the entire church age.

The apostles lived with the expectation of Christ's imminent return in their own lifetime.[16] They did not live with the belief that the church age would last 2,000 years and that Christ would not return for two entire millennia. They believed they were living in the last times. Therefore, the fulfillment of the Holy Spirit's prophecy in 1 Timothy 4:1-3 could have occurred either within Paul and Timothy's generation or any time subsequent to them.

Though this passage has application toward any asceticism throughout the church age, it is so specific in citing the precise form of false doctrine that its identification with Roman Catholicism seems hard to miss. What other professing Christian body has made it a matter of church policy and doctrine to forbid marriage and require holy days of fasting? This prophecy undoubtedly describes the rise of that great apostate form of Christianity, Roman Catholicism, within the first few centuries of church history.

Within the early church, genuine believers were falling away in apostasy through demonically inspired false doctrines, until there was a departure from "the faith" on such a grand scale that the "Mother Church" could no longer be identified as the true body of Christ, consisting of His own regenerated members. With succeeding generations of professing Christians, the percentage of those who

---

by F. W. Danker (Chicago: University of Chicago Press, 1979), 126-27; Liddell and Scott, *A Greek-English Lexicon*, 291; Thayer, *New Thayer's Greek-English Lexicon of the New Testament*, 89.

16. After the time of Christ's death, the apostles and first-century believers are always described in the Epistles as expecting the Rapture to occur in their own lifetime. This is especially evidenced by the use of 1st and 2nd person pronouns (I, we, us, you, your) in prophetic passages dealing with Christ's return. See 1 Cor. 1:7-8; 15:51-52; Phil. 1:6, 10; 3:20; Col. 3:4; 1 Thess. 4:15-17; 2 Thess. 2:1; 1 Tim. 6:14; Titus 2:12-13; James 5:7-9; 1 Peter 1:13; 1 John 2:28; 3:2-3. There is no sense from these passages that the return of Christ was a far-off event in the understanding of these first-generation Christians.

at one time actually possessed "the faith" grew smaller and smaller. Eventually Christendom became engulfed with unsaved professing Christians who never had "the faith" to begin with, so as to depart from it. As the ranks of succeeding generations swelled with people who had never once believed the truth of the gospel but were reared on "doctrines of demons," the institutionalized church gradually became the receptacle of so much that is "antichrist." It eventually became the habitation for every foul and unclean spirit (Matt. 13:24–32; Rev. 17:1–18:4). Such is the heritage of Romanism.

This brings us back to the matter of the perseverance of the saints. In 1 Timothy 4:1 it says that "some" will fall away or apostatize from "the faith." Do the people in verse 1 who fall away from the faith constitute genuine believers or mere professors? Since losing genuine faith and committing apostasy is impossible according to the Calvinist doctrine of perseverance, then the only explanation left to the Calvinist is to conclude that these individuals were never genuine believers. Anthony Hoekema holds this interpretation of 1 Timothy 4:1.

> The word "faith," however, as is common in the Pastoral Epistles, is here used in the objective sense, as meaning the truth which is believed (*fides quae creditur*) rather than the act which appropriates Christ and his merits (*fides qua creditur*). What Paul is saying here is that in later times many will fall away from a profession of the Christian religion. Such a defection would not imply that these defectors had true faith to begin with.[17]

Against this interpretation stand several factors that lead to the opposite conclusion, namely, that these were indeed genuine believers who fell from the faith. First, while it is true, as some Calvinists have correctly noted, that there is a technical distinction between personal faith ("faith") and the objective body of Christian truth ("the faith"),[18] it is not true that one who merely holds to "the faith" must possess something less than genuine, personal "saving faith." In the 243 occurrences of the word for faith (*pistis*) in the Greek New

---

17. Hoekema, *Saved by Grace*, 249. For a similar explanation, see Norman L. Geisler, *Four Views on Eternal Security*, ed. J. Matthew Pinson (Grand Rapids: Zondervan, 2002), 91.

18. Gordon H. Clark, *Faith and Saving Faith* (Jefferson, MD: Trinity Foundation, 1990), 32.

Testament,[19] the word occurs with the article ("the faith") 129 times. Of the 128 occurrences of "the faith" outside of 1 Timothy 4:1, *not once* does this phrase describe someone who is not a believer or one with something less than genuine faith in God! In fact, in numerous passages the phrase "the faith" in Greek does not refer to the objective body of Christian doctrine at all but seems to refer only to personal faith![20] Therefore, one should not be so insistent that unsaved, unbelievers fell away from merely the body of Christian doctrine rather than genuine believers falling away from personal faith.

Second, it should be noted that later in this same epistle, in 1 Timothy 6:10-12, the fine theological distinction between personal "faith" and "the faith" cannot be maintained. As mentioned earlier, verse 10 has "the faith," verse 11 has simply "faith," and verse 12 in Greek has "the faith." In this passage, some had strayed from "the faith" (v. 10) by pursuing riches, and thus Timothy was to pursue "faith" (v. 11) as part of the good fight of "the faith" (v. 12). Clearly, holding to "the faith" cannot be differentiated from having personal "faith."

Third, the expression "the faith" occurs just one chapter later in this same epistle in 1 Timothy 5:8, where it says, "if anyone does not provide for his own, and especially for those of his household, he has denied the faith and is worse than an unbeliever." Here, the one who initially has "the faith" and ends up practically denying "the faith" is contrasted with an *unbeliever!* This means that the ones who had "the faith" were regarded by Paul (and the Lord) as actual believers, not unbelievers who only had "mental assent" but not "saving faith."

Fourth, the fact that the individuals in 1 Timothy 4:1 *fall away* from the faith reveals that they once had the faith, for you cannot *fall away* from something you never had. The word in 1 Timothy 4:1 for "fall away" (*aphistēmi*) consistently conveys the idea of departure from a position once occupied. In all eleven occurrences of this word in the Greek New Testament where faith is not at issue like it is in Luke 8:13, 1 Timothy 4:1, and Hebrews 3:12, the meaning of this word is clearly that of a spatial departure from a position once held.[21]

---

19. Using the Nestle-Aland 27th edition Greek New Testament.

20. See for example, Matthew 23:23; Luke 18:8; Acts 3:16; 15:9; 16:5; Romans 3:30; 4:14, 19-20; 10:17; 11:20; 12:6; 14:1; 1 Corinthians 13:2; 2 Corinthians 1:24; 4:13; Galatians 2:20; 3:14, 23, 25, 26; Ephesians 3:17; 6:16; Philippians 1:25; 3:9; Colossians 2:12; 1 Thessalonians 1:3; 2 Thessalonians 3:2; Hebrews 4:2; 6:12; 11:39; James 2:14, 17, 18, 20, 22, 24, 26; and 1 Peter 5:9.

21. See Luke 2:37; 4:13; 13:27; Acts 5:37-38; 12:10; 15:38; 19:9; 22:29; 2 Corinthians 12:8; and 2 Timothy 2:19. Even in 2 Timothy 2:19, where believers are told to "depart from iniquity," the context deals with the subject of *separation* from false teachers. It reveals that Timothy was to "shun" (2:16) the false teaching of Hymenaeus and

Therefore, it is most logical to conclude that in 1 Timothy 4:1, those who apostatized fell away from the faith they once possessed.

Finally, Paul instructs Timothy in 1 Timothy 4:6 and 4:11 to continually remind the "brethren" of "these things" recorded in 4:1-5. By doing so, he is effectively issuing a warning to these genuine believers not to fulfill the apostasy that the Holy Spirit predicts in 4:1. There is nothing in the context of this passage to indicate that genuine believers in Christ are immune to the apostasy mentioned in 4:1.

Denying the Faith (1 Timothy 5:8)

> But if anyone does not provide for his own, and especially for those of his household, he has denied the faith and is worse than an unbeliever.

According to this verse, not every denial of the faith is through doctrinal defection or heresy. Here it is through hypocrisy when our deeds do not befit our doctrine. If a Christian in practice does not provide for the needs of his own family, he is worse than an unbeliever because even unbelievers naturally care for their own. Many true children of God have not persevered in the faith in this sense. The term for "deny" (*arneomai*) in 1 Timothy 5:8 is used repeatedly in all four Gospels of Peter's denial of Christ (Matt. 26:70-72; Mark 14:68-70; Luke 22:57; John 18:25-27). The same term is used in the Epistles to describe the unsaved false teachers who deny Christ (2 Tim. 3:5; Titus 1:16; 2 Peter 2:1; 1 John 2:22-23; Jude 1). This demonstrates that it is possible for a genuine child of God to be like the unsaved in denying the faith; and in a practical sense, it is possible to be even worse than an unbeliever by not providing for the needs of one's own family.

Casting Off Faith (1 Timothy 5:11-15)

> 11 But refuse the younger widows; for when they have begun to grow wanton against Christ, they desire to marry, 12 having condemnation because they have cast off their first faith. 13 And besides they learn to be idle, wandering about from house

---

Philetus and to "cleanse" himself from these dishonorable vessels in God's house (2:21). Undoubtedly, Timothy was once in the proximate company and fellowship of these two men, but now he was commanded to "depart" from them and the iniquity associated with them (2:19).

to house, and not only idle but also gossips and busybodies, saying things which they ought not. 14 Therefore I desire that the younger widows marry, bear children, manage the house, give no opportunity to the adversary to speak reproachfully. 15 For some have already turned aside after Satan.

There is no implication in this passage that Paul is addressing the conduct of young women in the church who merely professed faith in Christ but never truly possessed faith in Christ. In order for these young women to have cast off their initial faith,[22] they must have had faith in the first place in order to cast it off! Paul would never tell an unbeliever not to cast off his or her "first faith" since that person would have no faith to cast off! With their physical and emotional desires unyielded to the Lord, these young women put their desire for a husband ahead of their desire for Jesus Christ. In this sense, as is all too common today, they cast off their initial faith. Like 1 Timothy 5:8, this is another example of apostasy for non-doctrinal reasons.

Moreover, these young women are described as having turned aside to follow after Satan. The term for following "after" Satan (*opisō*) is used throughout the four Gospels in the positive sense of following Christ as His disciple (Matt. 10:38; 16:24; Mark 1:17; 8:34; Luke 9:23, 62; 14:27). No doubt these young women were unwittingly following after the adversary of God. While many deny that genuine believers can do this, Scripture elsewhere testifies (Matt. 16:23; 1 Tim. 3:6-7; 2 Tim. 2:25-26) that this is a frighteningly real possibility. Why should we consider it strange for genuine believers to sometimes follow two enemies of God, namely, one's own flesh (indwelling sin nature) and the world, yet preclude the possibility of following after the third enemy of God?

Elsewhere, the apostle Paul warned about this possibility in 1 Corinthians 10:14, where he commands believers to "flee from idolatry." A little later in verses 20-22, he plainly states that "the things which the Gentiles sacrifice they sacrifice to demons and not to God, and *I do not want you to have fellowship with demons.* You cannot drink the cup of the Lord and the cup of demons; you cannot partake of the Lord's table and of the table of demons. Or do we provoke the Lord

---

22. "First faith" in verse 12 is the literal translation of the Greek expression *prōtēn pistin,* which is why the ESV accurately translates it "former faith." The NASB and NIV have "previous pledge" and "first pledge," which are highly interpretive, dynamic translations that actually convey the erroneous and unscriptural idea that faith is a pledge to God.

to jealousy?" If we could see for one moment as God sees the true spiritual state of affairs that exists in the church today among genuine believers, we would probably be shocked by the amount of fellowshipping with demons and following after Satan that is actually taking place. When this occurs, we can be sure that it also invites the chastening hand of God, as Paul also warned about in 1 Corinthians 10:8-11, 22, and 11:29-32.

Straying from the Faith (1 Timothy 6:9-10, 20-21)

> 9 But those who desire to be rich fall into temptation and a snare, and into many foolish and harmful lusts which drown men in destruction and perdition. 10 For the love of money is a root of all kinds of evil, for which some have strayed from the faith in their greediness, and pierced themselves through with many sorrows.

Just as some denied the faith in 1 Timothy 5:8 by neglecting to provide for the physical needs of their own family, here in an opposite sense it is also possible to stray from the faith by loving money and making our ambition the pursuit of it, rather than serving the Lord Jesus. The word for "strayed" in the Greek text of verse 10 (*apoplanaō*) occurs only one other time in the New Testament. In Mark 13:22, this term is used of antichrists and false prophets in the future tribulation who will lead people astray by their deception. Many genuine believers have been led astray from their faith in Christ by the love of money. This truth is also depicted by the third soil in Luke 8:14 in Christ's parable of the seed and four soils.

> 20 O Timothy! Guard what was committed to your trust, avoiding the profane and idle babblings and contradictions of what is falsely called knowledge—21 by professing it some have strayed concerning the faith. Grace be with you.

This passage reiterates the previous warnings in 1 Timothy 1:5-6 and 4:1-3 about the dangers of doctrinal deviation. It should be noted from this passage that Paul considered Timothy personally susceptible to apostasy and warned him accordingly. There is no assumption here that since Timothy had genuine faith (2 Tim. 1:5) he was guaranteed to persevere in that faith to the end. Straying from the faith was a real possibility for Timothy.

Being Faithless (2 Timothy 2:11-13)

11 This is a faithful saying: For if we died with Him, we shall also live with Him. 12 If we endure, we shall also reign with Him. If we deny Him, He also will deny us. 13 If we are faithless, He remains faithful; He cannot deny Himself.

Two initial observations must be noted to interpret this passage correctly and to see how it applies to the question of perseverance. First, Paul consistently uses the first-person plural pronoun "we" in all four parallel sentences. He does not say "you," "he," "she," "they," "them," and so forth, referring to someone else. He includes himself and Timothy consistently throughout the passage. This means that from Paul's perspective, it was possible for Timothy and even himself to deny Christ and become faithless (vv. 12-13). Second, in the preceding context, Paul had just addressed both salvation (v. 10) and rewards (vv. 5-6), and therefore it is reasonable to see both subjects continuing to be addressed in verses 11-13.

2 Timothy 2:11

In verse 11 it says, "If we died (aorist tense) with Him, we shall (future tense) also live with Him." Dying with Christ should not be interpreted as a reference to possible future martyrdom for Paul and Timothy because the aorist tense in its culminative or perfective aspect is used here to indicate something that had already transpired in the past and resulted in something that was still true of both Paul and Timothy (and all believers). What did Paul mean by the believer's death "with Him"? This is a reference to one's co-crucifixion with Christ. At the very moment a believer is justified, the Holy Spirit baptizes that person positionally into Christ so that he is identified forevermore with Christ in His death, burial, and resurrection (Rom. 6:3-11; 1 Cor. 12:12-13; Gal. 2:20; 5:24; 6:14; Col. 2:11-13; 3:1, 3; 1 Peter 2:24). In Galatians 2:20, Paul refers to this supernatural work of God when he writes, "I have been crucified with Christ; it is no longer I who live but Christ lives in me." Just as Jesus Christ once died but lives forevermore, so the fact that all true believers have once died with Christ is coupled with the guarantee that all will live with Him as well. Second Timothy 2:11 is a reference to one aspect of the saint's guaranteed salvation. But the passage now shifts to the subject of rewards.

2 Timothy 2:12a

In verse 12, it says, "If we endure, we shall also reign with Him." Reigning here should not be understood as a reference to eternal salvation but to a future reward for faithful, enduring service on the part of those who have already been saved by God's grace (Matt. 19:28; 25:20-23; 1 Cor. 3:10-15; 2 Tim. 4:6-8; Rev. 2:10; 20:4-6). In Revelation 2:25-27, Christ promises His church, "But hold fast what you have till I come. And he who overcomes, and keeps My works until the end, to him I will give power over the nations—'He shall rule them with a rod of iron; they shall be dashed to pieces like the potter's vessels'—as I also received from My Father." Christ promises this co-rulership to those who fulfill two conditions—being an overcomer and keeping Christ's works to the end.[23] First John 5:1-5 defines the overcomer simply as one who has been born again by faith in the Lord Jesus Christ. Thus, the first condition for receiving a future reward is that one must be saved. Second, one must not only be saved but must keep Christ's "works until the end." If a saint perseveres in faithfulness and good works, he or she will be rewarded with rulership in Christ's future kingdom. This is what 2 Timothy 2:12 means when it says, "If we endure, we shall also reign with Him." This passage teaches that the perseverance of the saints does not result in eternal salvation but in a better resurrection and reign with Christ in His kingdom, which is a reward.

2 Timothy 2:12b

Second Timothy 2:12b represents the opposite of verse 12a. What happens if we do not endure but end up denying Christ? Verse 12b says, "If we deny Him, He also will deny us." At first glance, this passage may appear to teach that salvation can be lost, which is the standard Arminian interpretation of this statement.[24] On the other hand, the Calvinist interpretation says that if a person ever denies Christ, then that person's faith is proven to be spurious and non-saving since genuine faith always endures to the end. Thus, John MacArthur writes,

---

23. Revelation 2:26 is explained in greater detail in chapter 15.

24. Stephen M. Ashby, *Four Views on Eternal Security*, J. Matthew Pinson, gen. ed. (Grand Rapids: Zondervan, 2002), 161-62; I. Howard Marshall, *Kept by the Power of God: A Study of Perseverance and Falling Away* (Minneapolis: Bethany House, 1969), 132-33; Robert Shank, *Life in the Son: A Study of the Doctrine of Perseverance* (Springfield, MO: Westcott Publishers, 1961), 281.

The Greek verb rendered *deny* is the future tense, and the clause is therefore more clearly rendered, "If we ever deny Him" or "If in the future we deny Him." It looks at some confrontation that makes the cost of confessing Christ very high and thereby tests one's true faith. A person who fails to endure and hold onto his confession of Christ will *deny Him,* because he never belonged to Christ at all.[25]

However, the verb for "deny" in verse 12 is *arneomai,* and it is the same word used repeatedly in the Gospels to describe Peter's denial of Christ (Matt. 26:70, 72; Mark 14:68, 70; Luke 22:57; John 13:38; 18:25, 27). Did the apostle Peter "never belong to Christ at all"? Possibly realizing this predicament, MacArthur goes on to explain, "So perhaps the answer to the issue of Peter's denial is that his was a momentary failure, followed by repentance. . . . There is a settled, final kind of denial that does not repent and thereby evidences an unregenerate heart."[26] But is this really what Paul meant in 2 Timothy 2:12b?

The term "deny" (*arneomai*) in 2 Timothy 2:12b is better interpreted as a failure to follow Christ as His disciple and consequently not receive a reward. The word *arneomai* is also used in Matthew 10:33, where Christ says, "But whoever denies Me before men, him I will also deny before My Father who is in heaven." Immediately following Matthew 10:33, Christ discusses the cost of following Him as His disciple, even taking up one's cross if necessary (Matt. 10:38). He is not referring to salvation in this context since we are not saved by carrying *our* crosses but by the work Christ accomplished on *His* cross! The discourse of Matthew 10:33 then concludes in 10:41-42 with three references to a "reward" that is promised to those who do not deny Christ but faithfully follow Him as disciples.

In another parallel passage to 2 Timothy 2:12, Christ says to His disciples, "If anyone desires to come after Me, let him deny himself, and take up his cross, and follow Me" (Matt. 16:24). Just three verses later, Christ concludes His short lesson on the cost of discipleship by saying, "the Son of Man will come in the glory of His Father with His angels, and then He will *reward* each according to his *works*" (Matt. 16:27, italics added). Clearly, not denying Christ and openly following Him as His disciple is described as a "work" that Christ will one day

25. John MacArthur, *2 Timothy,* MacArthur New Testament Commentary (Chicago: Moody Press, 1995), 64.

26. Ibid, 65.

"reward." In contrast, salvation is received by simple faith in Christ as a free gift and is not a reward according to our works (Rom. 4:4-5).

So 2 Timothy 2:12b is not addressing either the loss of salvation by denying Christ, as Arminianism teaches, or the disproving of our salvation, as Calvinism claims. Instead, it is teaching the flip-side of verse 12a, namely, that if we deny Christ He also will deny us one day in the future at His judgment seat by not giving us a reward (1 Cor. 3:10-15; 2 Cor. 5:9-10). By so teaching in verse 12b, Paul has returned to the theme of rewards discussed in the immediately preceding context of 2 Timothy 2:4-6 and elsewhere throughout the epistle (1:18; 4:1, 7-8, 14).

2 Timothy 2:13

Following the strong warning about denial in verse 12b, this passage ends in verse 13 with a promise of reassurance and comfort: "If we are faithless, He remains faithful; He cannot deny Himself." The terms "faithless" (*apistoumen*) and "faithful" (*pistos*) are set in contrast to one another. For His part, Christ remains faithful to His salvation promises (John 3:16, 36; 5:24; 6:39; 10:28) because faithfulness is essential to His very nature (Heb. 2:17; 10:23; Rev. 1:5; 3:14; 19:11). However, for our part as Christians, this passage admits the real possibility that we may be "faithless." Much is riding on the correct interpretation of this verse. If indeed verse 13 is teaching that people who are eternally saved can be "faithless," then this one verse alone refutes the entire Calvinist doctrine of the perseverance of the saints.

At this point, it should be recalled how Calvinist perseverance proponents view faith and apostasy. According to this view, the perseverance of the saints means that "those who have true faith can lose that faith neither totally nor finally."[27] Loraine Boettner further explains, "This doctrine of Perseverance does not mean that Christians do not temporarily fall the victims of sin, for alas, this is all too common. Even the best of men backslide temporarily. But they are never completely defeated; for God, by the exercise of His grace on their hearts infallibly prevents even the weakest saint from final apostasy."[28] If apostasy is precluded by Calvinism's doctrine of perseverance, then there must be some explanation for those who at one

---

27. Hoekema, *Saved by Grace*, 234.
28. Loraine Boettner, *The Reformed Doctrine of Predestination* (Phillipsburg, NJ: Presbyterian & Reformed, 1932), 187.

time seemed to be genuine believers but who later appear "faithless" as 2 Timothy 2:13 says. Edwin Palmer, another leading Calvinist, provides the solution: "So, one answer to this problem of apparent defections from the Christian faith is that some of the backslidings that we see may be only temporary setbacks of a stumbling Christian, who by the grace of the Holy Spirit, will eventually come back fully to the faith he seems to have denied."[29] According to the Calvinist doctrine of the perseverance of the saints, a genuine child of God may temporarily stumble in sin, backslide, and even appear to deny the faith, but in reality he will never apostatize or cease believing.

Because 2 Timothy 2:13 clearly states the possibility that "we" as Christians may be "faithless," some Calvinists seek to harmonize this passage with their theology by interpreting this as a reference to mere professors of Christ who have a spurious faith that falls short of true, saving faith. For example, John MacArthur comments regarding verse 13:

> *If we are faithless,* Christ *remains faithful.* In this context, *apisteō* (*are faithless*) means lack of saving faith, not merely weak or unreliable faith. The unsaved ultimately deny Christ, because they never had faith in Him for salvation. But *He remains faithful,* not only to those who believe in Him but to those who do not, as here. . . . Just as Christ will never renege on His promise to save those who trust in Him, He also will never renege on His promise to condemn those who do not.[30]

Amazingly, because MacArthur believes that genuine Christians are incapable of being "faithless," he interprets this passage as a negative promise of God's condemnation of unbelievers rather than a positive promise to "faithless" saints. However, it is doubtful that 2 Timothy 2:13 was ever intended by the Lord to be a threat, conveying the idea that He is "faithful" (*pistos*) to punish the unsaved. The Greek word *pistos* is used a total of fifteen times in the New Testament when applied to God, and in all fourteen occurrences outside of 2 Timothy 2:13, God's faithfulness is always the basis of something *positive* toward believers (1 Cor. 1:9; 10:13; 2 Cor. 1:18; 1 Thess. 5:24; 2 Thess. 3:3; Heb. 2:17; 3:2; 10:23; 11:11; 1 Peter 4:19; 1 John 1:9; Rev. 1:5; 3:14; 19:11).

---

29. Edwin H. Palmer, *The Five Points of Calvinism* (Grand Rapids: Baker, 1980), 77.
30. MacArthur, *2 Timothy*, 66 (emphasis original).

There is a second interpretation of 2 Timothy 2:13 offered by Calvinists that seeks to reconcile their doctrine of perseverance with the fact of some saints being "faithless" (*apistoumen*). This interpretation views *apistoumen* as meaning "unfaithfulness" in the general sense of disobedience toward God rather than faithlessness or the absence of faith. In this sense, genuine believers can be "unfaithful" to God without actually going apostate or reaching a state of being "faithless." A critical question to answer is whether *apistoumen* in verse 13 means "faithless" or "unfaithful"? Should verse 13 be translated "If we are faithless" or "If we are unfaithful"?[31]

Since the theological implications of either interpretation are so significant, it is necessary to examine the meaning of *apistoumen* in 2 Timothy 2:13 very carefully. The word *apistoumen* is simply a form of the Greek word *apisteō*.[32] While the standard Greek lexicons list both possible meanings for *apisteō*, some seem to favor the meaning "faithless"[33] in the case of 2 Timothy 2:13 while others seem to favor the translation "to be unfaithful."[34] Similarly, commentators are ranged on both sides, with some interpreting *apistoumen* as "faithless"[35] and some favoring the reading "unfaithful."[36] Still others see the correct translation of *apistoumen* as "faithless" but say that this means something less than apostasy.[37] Yet another source says *apistoumen* may mean either "faithless" or "untrue" to God.[38] With such difference of opinion, the only way to resolve the matter is to carefully examine

---

31. Most English Bibles translate *apistoumen* as "faithless." These include the New King James Version, New American Standard Bible (1977 and 1995), American Standard Version, New International Version, English Standard Version, Revised Standard Version, New Revised Standard Version, and the New Jerusalem Bible.

32. *Apistoumen* is the first person, plural, present tense, active voice, indicative mood form of *apisteō*.

33. Liddell and Scott, *Greek-English Lexicon*, 189; Johannes P. Louw and Eugene Nida, eds. *Greek-English Lexicon of the New Testament Based on Semantic Domains*, Vol. 1 (New York: United Bible Societies, 1988), 378.

34. Bauer, Danker, Arndt, and Gingrich, *A Greek-English Lexicon of the New Testament and Other Early Christian Literature*, 103; Thayer, *New Thayer's Greek-English Lexicon of the New Testament*, 57.

35. Alford, *Greek Testament*, 3:382; Gordon D. Fee, *1 and 2 Timothy, Titus*, New International Biblical Commentary (Peabody, MA: Hendrickson, 1988), 251; D. Edmond Hiebert, *Second Timothy*, Everyman's Bible Commentary (Chicago: Moody Press, 1958), 64; Robertson, *Word Pictures in the New Testament*, 4:619; Stock, *Practical Truths from the Pastoral Epistles*, 61; Vine, *Collected Writings of W. E. Vine*, 3:214.

36. Knight, *Commentary on the Pastoral Epistles*, 406-7; Newport J. D. White, *The Expositor's Greek Testament*, Vol. IV, ed. W. Robertson Nicoll (Grand Rapids: Eerdmans, 1990), 164.

37. Kelly, *Pastoral Epistles*, 180-81; Kent, *Pastoral Epistles*, 264-65.

38. Vincent, *Vincent's Word Studies in the New Testament*, 4:300.

how this word is used in the primary context of 2 Timothy 2:13 and then how it is used in the rest of the New Testament.

Those who interpret this as general "unfaithfulness" see a direct, parallel contrast between people and God in verse 13 when it says, "If we are faithless [*apistoumen*], He remains faithful [*pistos*]." They reason that since God does not "believe" or "have faith" per se but can only be "faithful" (*pistos*) in terms of His character, then *apistoumen* should be translated as the opposite of "faithful," namely, "unfaithful." In this case the verse would be translated, "If we are *unfaithful*, He remains *faithful*." This interpretation initially appears to have strong support from the immediate context since the parallel structures of all three preceding sentences involve directly opposing concepts. For example, in verse 11, the opposite of dying is living. In verse 12a, the opposite of enduring under (*hypomenō*) suffering and adversity is reigning as a king (*symbasileuō*). In verse 12b, the opposite of us denying Christ is Christ denying us. Therefore, it certainly appears quite logical to conclude that the opposite of God's faithfulness in verse 13 is our unfaithfulness.

However, though this exegesis is true to a point, it does not go far enough. We still must understand what is involved in the Greek concept of "unfaithfulness" (*apisteō/apistoumen*). In English, the term "unfaithful" normally denotes the idea of "disloyal," without any reference necessarily to the presence or absence of individual belief. In Greek, however, a person was described as "unfaithful" primarily because that individual lacked "faith" or "belief."[39] In 2 Timothy 2:13, *apistoumen* is simply a form of the root word *apisteō*, just like our English word "running" is simply a form of the word "run." When the term *apisteō* is used elsewhere in the New Testament, it consistently means "faithless" in the absolute sense of "lack of belief" and not merely "unfaithful" in the sense of "disloyalty."

Apisteō occurs a total of seven times in the Greek New Testament outside of 2 Timothy 2:13 (Mark 16:11, 16; Luke 24:11, 41; Acts 28:24; Rom. 3:3; 1 Peter 2:7 [Critical Text]). In three of these instances *apisteō* is clearly used of the unsaved, who are "faithless" in the absolute sense (Mark 16:16; Acts 28:24; 1 Peter 2:7). Romans 3:3 is also most likely describing the faithlessness of unsaved Jews since the imme-

---

39. In the vast preponderance of occurrences of *apisteō* in extra-biblical Greek literature, the term contains the idea of unbelief rather than disloyalty without regard to belief. See the references in Bauer, Danker, Arndt, and Gingrich, *Greek-English Lexicon of the New Testament and Other Early Christian Literature*, 103; Liddell and Scott, *Greek-English Lexicon*, 189.

diately preceding context (Rom. 2:28-29) deals with regenerate Jews who had faith versus unregenerate Jews who lacked faith. In the three remaining instances of *apisteō* in the New Testament, Christ's disciples were without faith or were "faithless" regarding the fact of His resurrection. These saved men simply did not believe that Christ had risen (Mark 16:11; Luke 24:11, 41). In this respect, they had an absolute "lack of belief" regarding Christ's resurrection and were not merely "unfaithful" in the general sense of "disloyalty."

Another technical matter is well worth considering at this point—the true meaning of *apistoumen* in 2 Timothy 2:13. In terms of semantics, the direct opposite of *pistos* in the second clause of 2 Timothy 2:13 would be *apistos*, which is a word related to *apisteō* and nearly identical in meaning with it.[40] When *apistos* is used all 16 times by Paul in his epistles, in *every* instance it refers to the *unsaved* who were "faithless," never merely an "unfaithful" Christian (1 Cor. 6:6; 7:12, 13, 14 [2x], 15; 10:27; 14:22 [2x], 23, 24; 2 Cor. 4:4; 6:14, 15; 1 Tim. 5:8; Titus 1:15). Likewise, in the remaining seven non-Pauline occurrences of *apistos* in the New Testament, it always refers to *unsaved* unbelievers who are "faithless" (Matt. 17:17; Mark 9:19; Luke 9:41; 12:46; Acts 26:8; Rev. 21:8), with the singular exception of Thomas' unbelief following Christ's resurrection (John 20:27). These facts serve as further confirmation that in 2 Timothy 2:13 *apisteō* most likely means "faithless" rather than just "unfaithful."

What all of this demonstrates is that even those who have been genuinely and eternally saved by God's grace may become "faithless" in their Christian lives. It is entirely possible for a genuine Christian to lose his faith after he has once believed in Christ and been instantaneously and eternally saved by God.[41] Though some advocates of the Calvinist doctrine of the perseverance of the saints have mocked the conclusion that there could exist such a thing as an "unbelieving believer," that is precisely what we see in the case of the disciples after Christ's resurrection. Similarly, the Galatians were truly saved (Gal. 4:6-7), but they did not continue to believe the true gospel of grace since they embraced a false gospel of works (Gal. 1:6-9; 3:1-3; 4:9-11; 5:1-4). In addition, the Exodus generation of Israelites, which certainly consisted of more regenerated souls than just

---

40. Louw and Nida, *Greek-English Lexicon of the New Testament Based on Semantic Domains*, 1:378; Moulton and Milligan, *Vocabulary of the Greek Testament*, 58; Robertson, *Word Pictures in the New Testament*, 2:291.

41. Charles C. Ryrie, *So Great Salvation: What It Means to Believe in Jesus Christ* (Wheaton, IL: Victor, 1989), 141.

"faithful" Joshua and Caleb, was described as having "an evil heart of unbelief" (Num. 14:11; Deut. 1:32; 9:23; Heb. 3:7-19).

Whether it is the case of the eleven disciples, the Galatians, or the Israelites, these biblical examples cannot be reconciled with the Calvinist claim that "those who have true faith can lose that faith neither totally nor finally." In each case, these biblical saints were, at least for a time, completely unbelieving with respect to some of the most fundamental and cardinal doctrines of the faith. The Calvinist may object here with respect to the *totality* of unbelief, claiming that the disciples and Galatians still retained at least their faith in the deity of Christ while the Israelites retained their belief in Yahweh as the one, true God. Yet whatever semblance of faith remained in these saints was actually considered "vain" by the Lord (1 Cor. 15:14, 17; Gal. 3:4; 4:11), as evidenced by the fact that each group was sternly rebuked by the Lord for their unbelief (Num. 14:26-35; Mark 16:14; Gal. 3:1). The Lord reproved them for their unbelief but not while simultaneously valuing or commending what vestige of doctrinal correctness remained in them.

The same must be said regarding the *finality* of unbelief. It makes no difference to an omniscient God, who knows the end from the beginning, whether a Christian is unbelieving in the middle of his Christian life or at the very end of his life while upon his deathbed. Ultimately, we are not kept saved by the amount, quality, or constancy of our faith, but by the grace and finished work of the Savior whom we initially trusted. God always remains faithful to His Word and promises, so that even when we sin as believers and our faith fails:

- God's grace still abounds much more toward us (Rom. 5:20),

- there is still no condemnation for us (Rom. 8:1),

- there is still the guarantee of our future glorification (Rom. 8:30),

- He is still for us (Rom. 8:31),

- we are still justified in His sight (Rom. 8:33),

- the saving work of Christ still applies toward us (Rom. 8:34),

- He still loves us for Christ's sake (Rom. 8:35-39),

- and He will not revoke His gift of eternal life (Rom. 6:23; 11:29).

"If we are faithless, He remains faithful, for He cannot deny Himself" (2 Tim. 2:13).

Faith Overthrown (2 Timothy 2:14-18)

14 Remind them of these things, charging them before the Lord not to strive about words to no profit, to the ruin of the hearers. 15 Be diligent to present yourself approved to God, a worker who does not need to be ashamed, rightly dividing the word of truth. 16 But shun profane and idle babblings, for they will increase to more ungodliness. 17 And their message will spread like cancer. Hymenaeus and Philetus are of this sort, 18 who have strayed concerning the truth, saying that the resurrection is already past; and they overthrow the faith of some.

This passage shows once again that a person's faith may be overthrown through the fatal effects of false teaching. An unbiased reader of this passage would never come away with the impression that the faith of God's elect will certainly and necessarily persevere, as Calvinism teaches. Here is another clear warning that the endurance of our faith is not guaranteed.

While Calvinism has historically taught that genuine Christians may falter and even fall in their walk of faith, it has also taught that a genuine Christian will never fall completely and finally into sin and unbelief. According to the Synod of Dort, where the five points of Calvinism were first delineated, genuine saints may be "carried away by the flesh, and the world, and Satan, unto grievous and atrocious sins . . . which the mournful falls of David and Peter . . . demonstrate,"[42] but they cannot "totally fall from faith . . . nor finally continue in their falls."[43] This is supposedly guaranteed because God "assuredly and efficaciously renews them to repentance" so that they "finally work out their salvation more earnestly with fear and trembling."[44] Is this how we are to understand the "overthrow" of one's faith in 2 Timothy 2:18? Is Paul merely warning about a temporary, partial, and incomplete lapse of faith?

---

42. Thomas Scott, *The Articles of the Synod of Dort* (Harrisonburg, VA: Sprinkle, 1993), 316.

43. Ibid, 318.

44. Ibid, 317.

As we will see, once again this Reformed doctrine cannot be reconciled with either the biblical terminology employed or the contextual sense of finality and completeness in 2:14-18. The word for "overthrow" in 2:18 is *anatrepō*. Thayer's lexicon defines this word as meaning "to overthrow, overturn, destroy."[45] Louw and Nida's lexicon says *anatrepō* means "to cause something to be completely overturned."[46] Yet another standard lexicon includes the English translation "ruin" as one possible meaning.[47] To have one's faith *completely overturned, destroyed,* or *ruined* indicates a complete reversal or negation of faith.

Anatrepō is also used just two other times in the Greek New Testament. In John 2:15 it is used of Christ violently overturning the corrupt money-changers' tables and driving them out of the Temple. This word is also used in Titus 1:11 of "whole houses" being overturned by false teachers. In both occurrences of *anatrepō* outside of 2 Timothy 2:18 there is nothing partial or incomplete about the "overthrow." The meaning of these passages is clear enough to be taken at face value. The only way someone can have his faith overthrown is if he had a genuine faith to be overthrown. Something cannot be overthrown that does not genuinely exist. Tables in the Temple (John 2:15) and households (Titus 1:11) were overthrown because they were genuine tables and households!

The definition and usage of *anatrepō* in 2 Timothy 2:18 as a complete overthrow is also consistent with the immediate context in which it occurs. A few verses earlier in verse 14, Paul warns about "the ruin of the hearers." The Greek word for "ruin" is *katastrophē,* which transliterates into our English word "catastrophe."[48] In verse 16, Paul also warns that a failure to separate from false doctrine will cause that false teaching to "increase to more ungodliness." This is certainly no guarantee of progressive sanctification for all the redeemed, which is another tenet of Calvinism. In 2:17, Paul warns that false teaching will eat at believers like "cancer" (NKJV). The term in Greek is *gangraina,* which is literally "gangrene." The disease of gangrene cannot be dealt with partially or incompletely. It must be dealt with immediately and decisively. The deadly infection must

---

45. Thayer, *New Thayer's Greek-English Lexicon of the New Testament*, 43.

46. Louw and Nida, *Greek-English Lexicon of the New Testament Based on Semantic Domains*, 1:214.

47. Liddell and Scott, *Greek-English Lexicon*, 124.

48. The only other occurrence of the noun *katastrophē* in the Greek New Testament is in the Majority Text of 2 Peter 2:6, where it is used to describe God's judgment upon Sodom and Gomorrah. It was complete, not partial, devastation.

be stopped completely in its tracks, with the infected bodily tissues completely removed (often through amputation), or the result will be certain death. Left untreated, the victim of gangrene will develop a shock-like syndrome with decreased blood pressure, kidney failure, coma, and finally death.

The apostle Paul was fully aware of the effects of *gangraina* in his day and intentionally employed this term under the direction of the Holy Spirit as a fitting metaphor of what will happen in the spiritual life of a believer who treats false doctrine casually. If the Word of God is not accurately interpreted and taught (vv. 14-15) and false doctrine is not separated from (vv. 16-17), the Lord warns believers in 2 Timothy 2:14-18 that their faith can actually be overthrown.[49]

Conclusion

When the testimony of Paul's two pastoral epistles to Timothy is taken collectively concerning the question of faith's perseverance, a clearer picture could not be painted. According to the voice of the Holy Spirit Himself, genuine but secure saints may indeed:

- stray from the faith,

- shipwreck their faith,

- fall away from the faith,

- deny the faith,

- cast off initial faith,

- become faithless,

- and have faith overthrown.

---

49. Some may object that either the false teachers (2 Tim. 2:16-17) or those who were affected by the false teachers (v. 18) did not have "genuine" faith based on what follows in verses 19 and 25-26. In verse 19, Paul quotes from Numbers 16:5, "The Lord knows those who are His." In the episode in Numbers 16, the question was not about the Lord knowing who was justified in His sight and who was not. Rather, as the context shows in Numbers 16 with rebellious Korah and here in 2 Timothy 2 with false teachers Hymenaeus and Philetus, the issue was God knowing who were His duly appointed leaders and spokesmen truly ministering on His behalf versus those who were not. The reference in 2 Timothy 2:25-26 to those (presumably Hymenaeus and Philetus) who needed repentance, being in the Devil's "snare," is most likely describing the condition of genuine but fallen saints since Paul had previously warned about this specific possibility for a "new convert" in regards to the qualifications for an overseer in 1 Timothy 3:6-7.

The language of 1 and 2 Timothy does not remotely resemble Calvinism's doctrine of the perseverance of the saints. In fact, more diametrical descriptions could not be made, showing that one set of descriptions comes from God and one comes from man. Which will you choose to accept? The time has long since come for the Reformed tradition of the perseverance of the saints to undergo another round of biblical reformation.

Chapter 12

Perseverance vs. Preservation in Hebrews

The subjects of perseverance and preservation in the book of Hebrews have been a theological battleground for centuries. Arminians appeal to the warning passages in Hebrews as proof that faith can be lost and therefore salvation itself can be lost. Calvinists, on the other hand, teach that eternal salvation and genuine faith can never be lost, so that the warnings of Hebrews are directed at unbelieving, false professors of faith in Christ, who never really possessed genuine faith and salvation in the first place. So which interpretation is correct? Could they both be wrong? Is there an element of truth in both views? Is there a third interpretative option that makes better sense of the context and content of Hebrews?

This chapter shows from the book of Hebrews that genuine faith in Christ can be lost and is not guaranteed to persevere to the end of one's life. However, Hebrews also teaches that though one's faith may be lost, eternal salvation can never be lost and the child of God remains eternally secure from the prospect of condemnation in hell (Heb. 7:25; 10:14; 13:5-6). The Epistle of Hebrews was written to genuine Hebrew Christian believers, who possessed eternal life and were saved from hell but who were also in danger of returning to the religious system of Judaism and not continuing in the Christian faith. If they were to apostatize in this way, they would not be eternally condemned but there would be definite consequences for their refusal to persevere, such as: losing fellowship with God (3:7-19) and spiritual rest of soul (4:1-11), not growing to spiritual maturity (5:11–6:1), receiving divine discipline (12:5-11) possibly to the point of physical death (10:26-29), and losing their eternal reward (10:35; 11:6, 35).

Background & Context of Hebrews

Correct interpretation of Scripture only comes by first considering the immediate and larger context of a verse or passage. For the book of Hebrews, this involves asking and answering a few basic questions. To whom was Hebrews written—believers or unbelievers? Where did the recipients or readers of this epistle live—in Israel or outside the land? When was this epistle written—before A.D. 70 or afterwards?

Readers of Hebrews

Evidence from within Hebrews establishes the fact that its intended recipients were genuine believers, meaning they were genuinely saved. For example, the readers are addressed as "brethren" (3:1, 12; 10:19; 13:22-23). While "brethren" sometimes means merely having a physical, ethnic kinship like Paul with his fellow Israelites (Rom. 9:3), in Hebrews the term must refer to the spiritual kinship of brothers or sisters in Christ and in the family of God since the recipients of this letter are specifically addressed as "holy brethren" (3:1).

Second, the readers of Hebrews are assumed to have believed already (Heb. 4:3; 10:39), without any qualification to the effect that they "almost" believed, stopped short of believing, or initially believed in some deficient manner. They are said to presently possess "confidence" in Christ (3:14; 10:35) and are instructed to "hold fast" (3:14; 4:14; 10:23) and endure (10:36). The inspired writer of Hebrews would never speak in positive terms about the "confidence" of an unbeliever. Nor would the writer exhort unbelieving professors of salvation to "hold fast" in their false faith. Instead, an unbelieving, professing reader would be exhorted to believe in Christ and be saved, just like Paul and Silas exhorted the Philippian jailer: "Believe on the Lord Jesus Christ and you shall be saved" (Acts 16:31). Of the 38 exhortations to the readers in the book of Hebrews,[1] why is there not a single exhortation to trust Christ for salvation, if indeed Hebrews is warning its readers about the possible unreality of their professed faith?[2]

---

1. J. Dwight Pentecost, *A Faith That Endures: The Book of Hebrews Applied to the Real Issues of Life* (Grand Rapids: Discovery House, 1992), 24-25.

2. Andy M. Woods, "The Paradigm of Kadesh Barnea as a Solution to the Problem of Hebrews 6:4-6," *Chafer Theological Seminary Journal* 12 (Spring 2006): 51.

Third, the readers are addressed as those who have been born again. Nowhere in the epistle is there a single exhortation for the readers to become children of God or be born again. Instead, they are reproved for their lack of spiritual growth, not their unregenerate status. "For though by this time you ought to be teachers, you need someone to teach you again the first principles of the oracles of God: and you have come to need milk and not solid food. For everyone who partakes only of milk is unskilled in the word of righteousness, for he is a babe" (5:12-13). If the readers had never been born again, why is the writer reproving them for their lack of growth, saying, "by this time you ought to be teachers"? By what "time"? Obviously, from the time of their new birth since a person cannot be expected to grow and be a teacher of others unless he has been born first. Clearly, the recipients of Hebrews were regenerate and therefore genuine believers in Christ, though they needed to go on to maturity (6:1).

Fourth, the readers are consistently addressed using first-person, plural pronouns. This shows that the writer, who is obviously a believer himself as an inspired writer of Scripture, identifies with his readers as fellow believers. For the use of the pronoun "we," see Hebrews 2:1, 3; 3:14, 19; 4:3; 10:26, 30, 39; and 12:28. For the pronoun "us," see 4:1, 2, 11; 6:1, 3; 10:26, 30, 39; and 12:28.

Fifth, the writer of Hebrews reminds his readers that though they had their earthly goods plundered as a result of persecution (10:34), they had a better and enduring possession in terms of their salvation with the Lord (10:34). This can only be true of a genuine believer. Some Greek manuscripts even have the prepositional phrase "in heaven" in verse 34, so that it reads: "you have a better and an enduring possession for yourselves in heaven." In the next verse, the readers are exhorted to continue in the faith for the sake of earning a reward: "Therefore do not cast away your confidence, which has great reward" (v. 35). Only believers in Christ are capable of earning a future, eternal reward for perseverance in the race of the Christian life, which shows that the readers of Hebrews had true faith in Christ. So what was the identity of the recipients of this epistle? Commentator M. R. De Haan concludes they were definitely believers.

To begin the study of Hebrews with the traditional preconceived idea that it was written to religious, unconverted professors who came short of salvation, is to be in a dense fog all the rest of the way, facing irreconcilable obstacles. These people addressed did not come short of salvation, but were in danger of coming short of a life of service and victory and rewards at the Judgment Seat of Christ.[3]

Date, Place, and Circumstances of Hebrews

The spiritual conditions described in the epistle depict Hebrew Christians living in Israel prior to the destruction of Jerusalem by the Romans in A.D. 70. This epistle describes Jewish priests presently ministering (5:1-4; 7:21, 27-28; 8:3-4) and offering sacrifices for the people (9:9; 10:1-3, 11; 13:10-11). This conclusion is not based merely on the use of the present tense in these verses but on a combination of factors. First, the writer uses the present tense for the present ministry of the priests (5:1-4; 13:10-11) *in contrast to* the aorist tense when summarizing Christ's past work (5:5; 13:12). Second, there is no mention in the epistle of the A.D. 70 destruction, which so significantly altered the course of Jewish history and Jewish-Christian relations that it certainly would have been mentioned had it occurred already. Third, the urgency of the writer's warnings against turning back to the Temple, Jewish priesthood, and sacrificial system hardly seems fitting if these were all destroyed in A.D. 70 and no longer functioning.

The location where the priests were sacrificing must have been the city of Jerusalem where the Temple was located. There is a clear contrast in the epistle between the spiritual "city of the living God, the heavenly Jerusalem" (11:10, 16; 12:22) versus the current geographical "camp" (13:13) or "city" (13:14) of Jerusalem. The camp or city of Jerusalem contained the permanent form of the "tabernacle" (i.e., Temple) spoken of in 13:10, from which the readers were commanded to separate or disassociate themselves by going "forth to [Christ], outside the camp, bearing His reproach. For here we have no continuing city, but we seek the one to come" (13:13-14). Undoubtedly, the writer of Hebrews is exhorting his readers not to return to the Jewish temple and system of worship that was headquartered and still operational in the city of Jerusalem.[4]

This setting for the epistle sheds significant light on its warning and perseverance passages. The readers were facing persecution from their unbelieving Jewish peers in the land of Israel (10:32-34; 12:3-4; 13:3, 7, 23), so that they considered abandoning their faith in

---

3. M. R. De Hann, *Studies in Hebrews* (Grand Rapids: Kregel, 1996), 50.
4. Peter Walker, "Jerusalem in Hebrews 13:9-14 and the Dating of the Epistle," *Tyndale Bulletin* 45 (1994): 39-71.

Christ and taking the easier path of returning to Judaism (2:1; 3:12; 4:11; 6:6; 10:39; 12:15, 25). The readers were susceptible to this temptation, having already stagnated in their spiritual growth (5:11–6:1). Thus, the writer of Hebrews issues five warnings, which incrementally intensify, regarding the consequences of turning back (2:1-4; 3:7–4:13; 6:1-8; 10:26-39; 12:25-29). In addition, the readers needed to be reminded and exhorted that Jesus Christ and His new economy of grace is far "better" than the Mosaic Law with its Levitical priesthood and offerings (1:4; 7:7, 19, 22; 8:6; 9:23; 10:34; 12:24).

Based on these observations, it is evident that the writer of Hebrews is exhorting genuine believers to persevere in their faith, not so they can go to heaven one day, or prove that they exercised genuine faith in Christ in the past at their justification, but to continue having fellowship with the Lord and serving Him acceptably.

Whose House We Are If . . . (Hebrews 3:6)

1 Therefore, holy brethren, partakers of the heavenly calling, consider the Apostle and High Priest of our confession, Christ Jesus, 2 who was faithful to Him who appointed Him, as Moses also was faithful in all His house. 3 For this One has been counted worthy of more glory than Moses, inasmuch as He who built the house has more honor than the house. 4 For every house is built by someone, but He who built all things is God. 5 And Moses indeed was faithful in all His house as a servant, for a testimony of those things which would be spoken afterward, 6 but Christ as a Son over His own house, whose house we are if we hold fast the confidence and the rejoicing of the hope firm to the end.

Hebrews 3:6 uses the word "confidence" (*parrēsia*, Heb. 4:16; 10:19, 35) coupled with the thought of perseverance to the end. As such, verse 6 is often cited as a proof text for the necessity of perseverance in faith to enter heaven. Arminians conclude that this verse is setting forth perseverance in faith as a condition for reaching heaven. Calvinists conclude that verse 6 is a declarative statement proving the reality of one's faith and saved status. According to Calvinists, verse 6 teaches that all true believers will continue firmly in the faith to the end because they are Christ's house.

Before explaining what verse 6 is teaching, it will be helpful to consider several reasons why Hebrews 3:6 cannot be teaching that perseverance in faith proves a person belongs to Christ's church and is saved. First, the writer of Hebrews knew already that his readers were saved, which is why in verse 1 he calls them "holy brethren" and "partakers of the heavenly calling." The description "holy brethren" does not refer to the readers' practical sanctification but to their separated position in Christ as "saints" or those who were "sanctified" (Heb. 10:14). Philip Hughes explains.

> To the designation "brethren" the writer joins the adjective *holy*, thus linking it with another frequent synonym for Christians in the New Testament (particularly in the Pauline writings) which, when it stands by itself, means "holy ones" or "saints." The description of the brethren as "holy" does not imply that they are holy in themselves, but rather "sanctified" or "consecrated" as those who have been chosen and set apart by God.[5]

The additional description of the readers in Hebrews 3:1 as "partakers of the heavenly calling" refers to the origin, nature, and purpose of their calling. Just as Jesus Christ was their "apostle" sent by God the Father from heaven, even so their calling by God came from heaven. The heavenly calling in the context of verse 1 is not necessarily a calling *to* heaven but *from* heaven. Since God Himself is holy, each believer is called to live a holy life of service to God (1 Peter 1:15-16), and in the context of Hebrews, to live for the better, "heavenly" things that pertain to Christ rather than the earthly things of the Law (8:5; 9:23-24; 11:16; 12:22). The description of the readers of Hebrews as "holy brethren" and "partakers of the heavenly calling" can apply only to true believers in Christ.[6] Therefore, the genuineness of the readers' faith and eternal salvation was not in doubt.

Second, the Greek text of Hebrews 3:6 contains a third-class conditional statement ("if we hold fast"), making it doubtful that this verse is declaring what all believers *will* do, namely, persevere to the end. If the writer of Hebrews assumed his readers would persevere in faith to the end, he would more likely have used a first-class conditional statement, which is the type of conditional statement normally used to set forth the condition of *assumed reality* from the writer's per-

---

5. Philip Edgcumbe Hughes, *A Commentary on the Epistle to the Hebrews* (Grand Rapids: Eerdmans, 1977), 125.

6. Dennis M. Rokser, *Shall Never Perish Forever: Is Salvation Forever or Can It Be Lost?* (Duluth, MN: Grace Gospel Press, 2013), 294.

spective (i.e., "Since we will hold fast to the end, we are His house"). However, in verse 6, the writer uses the third-class condition, which is normally the type of conditional statement used to set forth a condition of *uncertainty* in which something might or might not be true (i.e., "If we hold fast to the end, and we might or might not, then we are His house"). While some Calvinists have pointed to instances where the third-class condition can still function like a first-class condition in setting forth the condition of assumed reality,[7] this is an appeal to its rare and less likely usage. Furthermore, the disputed third-class conditional statements in Hebrews 3:6 and 14 are both immediately followed by third-class conditional statements in verses 7 and 15, which clearly have the sense of uncertainty that a condition might or might not be true: "Today, if you will hear His voice, do not harden your hearts as in the rebellion." The writer of Hebrews was saying that the readers might or might not choose to continue hearing God's Word (Heb. 12:19-20, 24-25; 13:22).

Third, in Hebrews 3:1-6, Christ and Moses represent exceptional examples of faithfulness in service to God. They are by no means the norm for all believers when it comes to faithful perseverance. If believers must follow their example to ultimately arrive in heaven and escape hell, then believers have no chance of being saved. Are any of us as faithful as the Lord Himself, who "was in all points tempted as we are, yet without sin" (4:15), or even as faithful as Moses, the man who spoke with God face to face (Ex. 33:11) and was the most humble man on the face of the earth (Num. 12:3)?

Fourth, Hebrews 3:5 sets forth Moses as an example of a faithful "servant." If Hebrews 3:1-6 is teaching that believers must follow the example of Moses to be saved from hell, then it is requiring *service* for salvation. This would mean that salvation is by works and not by grace, which is a clear contradiction of Scripture (Rom. 3:27-28; 4:4-6; 11:6). Believers do not serve God to be accepted by Him. We are already accepted (Eph. 1:6), sanctified, and set apart to Him on the basis of Christ's perfect, finished work (Heb. 10:10-14). While we as believers are already accepted in Christ, our service now as believer-priests may or may not be acceptable to God (12:28; 13:15-16, 21).

Fifth, if Christ is set forth in Hebrews 3 as the example of faithfulness that church-age believers must follow for their salvation, then how does the example of Christ form a suitable pattern to follow for our eternal salvation? Christ was not faithful over God's house in

---

7. Buist M. Fanning, "A Classical Reformed View," in *Four Views on the Warning Passages in Hebrews*, ed. Herbert W. Bateman, IV (Grand Rapids: Kregel, 2007), 206-15.

order to be saved or to prove that He was saved. Therefore, the point of correspondence in Hebrews 3:1-6 between Christ and believers is not salvation from hell but being a faithful vessel for God in each person's sphere of priestly service and ministry. Just as Christ has been faithful as our High Priest in the sphere of service where God the Father placed Him, even so Christians must also persevere in faithfulness in our sphere of service as believer-priests.

Lastly, Calvinists and Arminians typically assume that the statement in Hebrews 3:6 "whose house we are" speaks of belonging to Christ's body, the church, and thus being eternally saved. But verse 6 does not say "whose we are if we hold fast," but "whose *house* we are if we hold fast." The meaning of "house" in verse 6 is critical for a correct understanding of the passage. Does being part of Christ's "house" mean being a member of the church?

While the term "house" (*oikos*) refers to the church in the epistles of Peter and Paul (1 Tim. 3:15; 2 Tim. 2:20 [*oikia*]; 1 Peter 2:5; 4:17), it never has this meaning in its 11 occurrences in Hebrews. Outside of chapter 3, the word "house" (*oikos*) occurs five times in the epistle. In Hebrews 11:7, "house" refers to the immediate family of Noah. In its three occurrences in Hebrews 8:8 and 10, "house" refers to the nation of Israel. Its use in Hebrews 10:21 deserves special consideration since it parallels Hebrews 3:1-6, as seen in the comparison on the opposite page.

The word "house" is used in Hebrews 10:21 in reference to the figurative tabernacle, in which Jesus Christ serves as "High Priest" (v. 21) and to which believers are urged to "enter" (v. 19) and "draw near" (v. 22). The description in verse 22 of the manner in which believers are to draw near pictures the ministry of a priest serving in the tabernacle. In the Old Testament, both the tabernacle where the priests ministered (Ex. 29:16; Lev. 1:5; 8:19, 24; 9:12, 18; Num 19:4) and the priests themselves (Ex. 29:20-21; Lev. 8:30) were "sprinkled" with blood (Heb. 10:22). In addition, the priests were to wash their bodies with "pure water" (Heb. 10:22) as they ministered in the tabernacle (Ex. 29:4; 30:19-21; 40:12, 30-32; Num. 19:7). Therefore, the word "house" in Hebrews 10:21 is clearly used in a context dealing with the sphere of priestly service to God. But what about the context of Hebrews 3:6?

The statement in Hebrews 3:2 and 5 that "Moses was faithful in all His house as a servant" is not a picture of eternal salvation or justification, but of the believer's sphere of priestly service to God.

Hebrews 3:1–6	Hebrews 10:19–23
1 Therefore, holy **brethren**, partakers of the heavenly calling, consider the Apostle and **High Priest** of our **confession**, Christ Jesus, 2 who was **faithful** to Him who appointed Him, as Moses also was **faithful** in all His **house**. 3 For this One has been counted worthy of more glory than Moses, inasmuch as He who built the **house** has more honor than the **house**. 4 For every **house** is built by someone, but He who built all things is **God**. 5 And Moses indeed was **faithful** in all His **house** as a servant, for a testimony of those things which would be spoken afterward, 6 but Christ as a Son over His own house, whose house we are if we **hold fast** the **confidence** [*parrēsia*] and the rejoicing of the **hope** firm to the end.	19 Therefore, **brethren**, having **boldness** [*parrēsia*] to enter the Holiest by the blood of Jesus, 20 by a new and living way which He consecrated for us, through the veil, that is, His flesh, 21 and having a **High Priest** over the **house** of **God**, 22 let us draw near with a true heart in full assurance of faith, having our hearts sprinkled from an evil conscience and our bodies washed with pure water. 23 Let us **hold fast** the **confession** of our **hope** without wavering, for He who promised is **faithful**.

This statement is a clear reference to Numbers 12:7-8, where the Lord says of Moses, "Not so with My servant Moses; He is faithful in all My house. I speak with him face to face." In the context of Numbers 12:7-8, Moses, Aaron, and Miriam are all stationed at the door of the tabernacle to hear God speak. At the tabernacle of meeting, Moses spoke with God face to face as with a friend (Ex. 33:7-11; Deut. 34:10). While it is true that Moses was faithful in the "house" of Israel, it is also true that he was faithful in the narrower sense of ministering in the "tabernacle," even in a priestly manner. David Allen explains well Moses' role as a priest and its connection to Hebrews 3:2 and 5.

> The context of Num 12:7 points to a priestly interpretation of "house" where the tabernacle was the center of worship and priestly duties. Moses was called a priest explicitly only once in the Old Testament (Ps 99:6), and he was from the tribe of Levi (Exod 2:1-10). The Pentateuch affirms Moses' acting as the priest at both the inauguration of the nation and Aaron as priest (Exod 19-20; 28-29). Moses' actions were often priestly even though Aaron and the Levites performed the priestly duties. For example, Moses sanctified Aaron and the tabernacle, served at the altar, and made atonement for the people (see Exod 29:1; 24:6; 32:20 respectively). And Moses, not Aaron, passed on the high priesthood to Eleazar on Mount Hor (Num 20:22-29).[8]

In addition to the word "house" in Hebrews 3:2 and 5 pointing to Moses' faithfulness as a priest in the tabernacle, the context surrounding Hebrews 3:2-6 points to Christ's faithfulness as the believer's High Priest, which further establishes the meaning of "house" as the sphere of the believer's priestly service to God. Christ's High Priesthood is explicitly referred to in Hebrews 2:17-18, which immediately precedes Hebrews 3:1-6. Then in Hebrews 3:1, the writer of Hebrews appeals to his readers to "consider the Apostle and High Priest of our confession, Christ Jesus." This focus on Christ in His High Priesthood was the key to these Hebrew-Christian readers persevering in their faith and not succumbing to the temptation to turn back to Judaism in apostasy (Heb. 12:1-4).[9] Rather, Christ was able to sympathize with their weakness and grant His mercy and grace to help those facing temptation (4:14-16). The references to Christ's High Priesthood (2:17-18; 4:14-16) enclose the extended exhortation in 3:7-4:13 about receiving the Word of God with faith rather than unbelief like the generation of Israelites who died in the wilderness.

---

8. David L. Allen, *Hebrews*, New American Commentary (Nashville: Broadman & Holman, 2010), 242.

9. De Hann, *Studies in Hebrews*, 52-53.

The following columns show how Hebrews 3:1-6 is bounded by references to Christ's High Priesthood.

Hebrews 2:17–3:1	Hebrews 3:2–4:13	Hebrews 4:14–16
17 Therefore, in all things He had to be made like His brethren, that He might be a **merciful** [*eleēmōn*] and **faithful High Priest** in things pertaining to God, to make propitiation for the sins of the people. 18 For in that He Himself has suffered, being **tempted** [*peirazō*], He is able to **aid** [*boētheō*] those who are **tempted** [*peirazō*]. 1 Therefore, holy brethren, partakers of the **heavenly** calling, consider the Apostle and **High Priest** of our **confession**, Christ Jesus	7 Therefore, as the Holy Spirit says: "Today, if you will hear His voice, 8 Do not harden your hearts as in the rebellion, In the day of **trial** [*peirasmos*] in the wilderness, 9 Where your fathers **tested** [*peirazō*] Me, **tried** Me, And saw My works forty years."	14 Seeing then that we have a great **High Priest** who has passed through the **heavens,** Jesus the Son of God, let us hold fast our **confession.** 15 For we do not have a **High Priest** who cannot sympathize with our weaknesses, but was in all points **tempted** [*peirazō*] as we are, yet without sin. 16 Let us therefore come **boldly** [*parrēsia*] to the throne of grace, that we may obtain **mercy** [*eleos*] and find grace to **help** [*boētheia*] in time of need.

The evidence from the parallel reference to "house" in Hebrews 10:21 and the immediate context of Hebrews 3:1-6 does not support the conclusion that the phrase "whose house we are" (v. 6) means belonging to Christ's body, the church, and thus being saved. Verse 6 is not exhorting believers to either stay saved or prove that their faith was genuine from the start. Instead, this often misunderstood and misused passage is exhorting believers to persevere in their faith in order to remain in the sphere or place of privileged priestly service to God. The Lord had promised Israel at Mount Sinai that they would be "a kingdom of priests and a holy nation" (Ex. 19:6) to Him if they would obey His Word (Ex. 19:5). But that generation hardened their hearts in unbelief toward God (Num. 14; Heb. 3:7-19) and were judged by Him for 40 years in the wilderness, thereby losing the privilege of entering the Promised Land and functioning as "a kingdom of priests." Being in the sphere of priestly service to God is a privilege that can be lost in the lives of genuine believers who do not hold fast to Christ, though salvation itself can never be lost.[10]

In this regard, Hebrews 3 sounds a warning to Hebrew Christians that is similar to the warning issued to Gentile believers in Romans 11:17-24, where Gentile believers were exhorted to remain in God's "olive tree"—the place of usefulness, privileged service, and testimony for the Lord—by continuing in faith. In the same way, the readers of Hebrews were to remain in God's "house" of priestly service by holding fast their confidence in Christ and not turning back to the Jewish temple and priesthood (Heb. 12:28; 13:10-16).

We Have Become Partakers of Christ If . . . (Hebrews 3:14)

12 Beware, brethren, lest there be in any of you an evil heart of unbelief in departing from the living God; 13 but exhort one another daily, while it is called "Today," lest any of you be hardened through the deceitfulness of sin. 14 For we have become partakers of Christ if we hold the beginning of our confidence steadfast to the end, 15 while it is said: "Today, if you will hear His voice, Do not harden your hearts as in the rebellion." 16 For who, having heard, rebelled? Indeed, was it not all who came out of Egypt, led by Moses? 17 Now with whom was He angry forty years? Was it not with those who sinned, whose corpses fell in the wilderness? 18 And to whom did He swear that they would not enter His rest, but to those who did not obey? 19 So we see that they could not enter in because of unbelief.

---

10. Thomas L. Constable, *Expository Notes on Hebrews* (Garland, TX: Sonic Light, 2016), 40-41.

This passage, and verse 14 in particular, is often counted as another proof text for perseverance in faith as a requirement for possessing Christ and salvation. But this interpretation widely misses the mark, for the passage deals instead with genuine believers partaking of fellowship with Christ and entering into the present experience of spiritual rest that God promises to the Christian who walks by faith. W. H. Griffith Thomas explains this interpretation of verse 14:

> Once more the believers are reminded of the need of patient continuance if they are to enjoy the fellowship of Christ. It is not enough to commence the Christian life; it must be continued "firm" unto the end. This does not mean the loss of salvation, but it undoubtedly signifies the certain loss of spiritual blessing if we are unfaithful and do not "hold fast" the beginning of our confidence.[11]

Meaning of "Partakers"

The statement in verse 14 that "we have become partakers of Christ" does not refer to partaking of eternal salvation as proved by a persevering faith, but to fellowship and partnership with Christ, especially in suffering. The word "partaker" is *metochos* and has the meaning of a companion, sharer, or partner in verse 14. The masculine form of this word occurs six times in the New Testament (Luke 5:7; Heb. 1:9; 3:1, 14; 6:4; 12:8), the feminine form (*metochē*) occurs once (2 Cor. 6:14), and the verb form (*metechō*) eight times (1 Cor. 9:10, 12; 10:17, 21, 30; Heb. 2:14; 5:13; 7:13). The standard Greek-English lexicon says the verb *metechō* means "to have a part or share in something, share, have a share, participate" or "to partake of something in common with someone."[12] Likewise, the noun/adjective forms *metochos* and *metochē* mean "sharing, participating in" or being a "(business) partner, companion."[13] This sense of "sharer" or "partner" is also common in secular Koine Greek papyrus manuscripts outside of the New Testament.[14]

---

11. W. H. Griffith Thomas, *Let Us Go On: The Secret of Christian Progress in the Epistle to the Hebrews* (Grand Rapids: Zondervan, 1944), 45.

12. Walter Bauer, William F. Arndt, and F. Wilbur Gingrich, *A Greek-English Lexicon of the New Testament and Other Early Christian Literature*, 3rd ed., rev. and ed. Frederick W. Danker (Chicago: University of Chicago Press, 2000), 642.

13. Ibid., 643.

14. J. H. Moulton and G. Milligan, *Vocabulary of the Greek Testament* (London: Hodder & Stoughton, 1930; reprint, Peabody, MA: Hendrickson, 1997), 406.

The fact that these words are synonymous with the concept of fellowship or communion can be seen in three New Testament passages, where *metochos/metochē* or *metechō* occur together with the words normally translated "fellowship" (*koinōnia*) or "to have fellowship" (*koinōneō*).[15]

> So they signaled to their partners [*metochois*] in the other boat to come and help them. And they came and filled both the boats, so that they began to sink. . . . and so also were James and John, the sons of Zebedee, who were partners [*koinōnoi*] with Simon. And Jesus said to Simon, "Do not be afraid. From now on you will catch men." (Luke 5:7, 10)

> 16 The cup of blessing which we bless, is it not the communion [*koinōnia*] of the blood of Christ? The bread which we break, is it not the communion [*koinōnia*] of the body of Christ? 17 For we, though many, are one bread and one body; for we all partake [*metechomen*] of that one bread. 18 Observe Israel after the flesh: Are not those who eat of the sacrifices partakers [*koinōnoi*] of the altar? 19 What am I saying then? That an idol is anything, or what is offered to idols is anything? 20 Rather, that the things which the Gentiles sacrifice they sacrifice to demons and not to God, and I do not want you to have fellowship [*koinōnous*] with demons. 21 You cannot drink the cup of the Lord and the cup of demons; you cannot partake [*metechein*] of the Lord's table and of the table of demons. (1 Cor. 10:16-21)

> Do not be unequally yoked together with unbelievers. For what fellowship [*metochē*] has righteousness with lawlessness? And what communion [*koinōnia*] has light with darkness? (2 Cor. 6:14)

The writer of Hebrews also uses this word *metochos* with the sense of fellowship, communion, or partnership in 3:14. Believers share fellowship, communion, or partnership with Christ by continuing to walk by faith in Him and do His will. This also involves sharing in His sufferings, which is a prominent theme running throughout the book of Hebrews (2:10; 5:8; 10:32-34; 11:25-26, 35-38; 12:2-4; 13:3, 23). The apostle Peter wrote, "For to this you were called, because Christ

---

15. Ibid., 405.

also suffered for us, leaving us an example, that you should follow His steps" (1 Peter 2:21). The apostle Paul fully embraced this calling, exclaiming, "that I may know Him and the power of His resurrection, and the fellowship of His sufferings, being conformed to His death" (Phil. 3:10). Suffering for and with Christ is emphasized repeatedly in the New Testament (Luke 14:27; John 15:18-20; Acts 14:22; Rom. 8:17; Phil. 1:29; Col. 1:24; 2 Tim. 3:12). The readers of Hebrews needed to embrace this aspect of God's clearly revealed will, but they would only partake of fellowship with Christ and suffering for Him if they continued to walk in daily dependence on Him as their strength (Heb. 2:16, 18; 4:16).

Israel's Unbelief at Kadesh Barnea

The writer of Hebrews knew that genuine believers, such as his readers, were not immune to spiritual arterial sclerosis—a hardening of the heart toward God in unbelief. Thus, he warned them in Hebrews 3 not to become like the Exodus generation, whose belief turned into unbelief when they rejected God's will at Kadesh Barnea and refused to enter the Promised Land by faith (Num. 14). The fact that the writer of Hebrews applies this example from Israel's past history to his first-century readers presents a serious problem for the Calvinist doctrine of the perseverance of the saints.

According to the typical Reformed, Calvinist interpretation of Hebrews 3:14, believers demonstrate the genuineness of their faith by persevering to the end. If anyone has "an evil heart of unbelief in departing from the living God" (v. 12) like Israel at Kadesh Barnea, then this supposedly proves that person never truly believed. However, the example of the Exodus generation of Israelites does not fit the Calvinist paradigm, for Scripture states that these Israelites initially had genuine faith but then they departed from that faith at Kadesh Barnea. Israel's example actually confirms the truth of eternal security rather than the doctrine of the perseverance of the saints for salvation.

Scripture clearly testifies that the Exodus generation to whom Moses ministered believed in the Lord (Ex. 4:5). When Moses came to them to announce God's deliverance of them out of Egypt, they responded in faith. "So the people believed; and when they heard that the Lord had visited the children of Israel and that He had looked on their affliction, then they bowed their heads and worshiped" (Ex. 4:31). Later, when Israel left Egypt, Scripture says they believed the

Lord. "Thus Israel saw the great work which the Lord had done in Egypt; so the people feared the Lord, and believed the Lord and His servant Moses" (14:31). Lest there be any doubt as to the genuineness of Israel's faith, the inspired commentary of this account in Hebrews 11 testifies that Israel was redeemed from Egypt by faith: "By faith they passed through the Red Sea as by dry land, whereas the Egyptians, attempting to do so, were drowned" (Heb. 11:29).

But even that generation of Israelites, who are recorded in God's "hall of fame of faith" in Hebrews 11, later departed from the living God in unbelief. At Kadesh Barnea, the nation made a fateful decision to reject the report of Joshua and Caleb and to accept the recommendation of the ten unbelieving spies not to go into the Promised Land. Scripture plainly states the real problem—at the core of their refusal to enter Canaan was unbelief in the Lord (Num. 14:11; 20:12; Deut. 1:32; 9:23; Ps. 106:24; Jude 5). Consequently, the carcasses of that generation fell in the wilderness over the next forty years (Num. 14:29-35). So, did these Israelites, who initially believed, lose their salvation? Did their apostasy reveal that their faith was a false, spurious, non-saving faith after all? No, they were still God's redeemed people, saved out of Egypt, but unable to advance spiritually, being under divine discipline. Pentecost summarizes well their spiritual status.

> The unbelief of that generation did not cancel God's eternal, unconditional covenant promises. Their rebellion did not change the relation of the nation to God; they were still His redeemed people (Isa. 43:1-3). What they forfeited by their unbelief was the enjoyment of their blessings as a redeemed covenant people. They surrendered the joys of the land and the life of peace and rest. After forty years a new generation would respond to God's promises in faith and would enter and possess the land (Num. 14:31). Rebellion neither canceled God's promises nor changed the status of the nation before God. However, that generation did lose the blessings that God promised to provide. . . . The Kadesh experience teaches the necessity of believing God and of obeying God in all circumstances in spite of the obstacles. God is faithful and is to be believed and obeyed at all costs. Disobedience will not bring about loss of position, but certainly will result in the loss of blessings.[16]

---

16. J. Dwight Pentecost, "Kadesh Barnea in the Book of Hebrews," in *Basic Theology Applied: A Practical Application of Basic Theology in Honor of Charles C. Ryrie and His*

Entering God's Present "Rest"

The standard Calvinist interpretation of Hebrews 3 faces an additional problem. If Hebrews 3 is indeed a warning passage regarding genuine belief and eternal salvation, then were Joshua and Caleb the only Israelites with true saving faith? Hebrews 3:16-18 says, "For who, having heard, rebelled? Indeed, was it not all who came out of Egypt, led by Moses? Now with whom was He angry forty years? Was it not with those who sinned, whose corpses fell in the wilderness? And to whom did He swear that they would not enter His rest, but to those who did not obey?" The only Israelites who persevered in faith and escaped God's temporal judgment according to Numbers 14 were Joshua and Caleb. But if the point of Hebrews 3 is escaping God's eternal condemnation, then to be consistent, the Reformed position logically must argue that there were only two regenerated, justified, eternally saved people in the entire nation! Even Moses must not have been saved since he was also prohibited from entering the Promised Land because of his own unbelief (Num. 20:12)!

Instead, it is more reasonable and fitting with Scripture to conclude that although Israel was redeemed, justified, and eternally saved, they were under temporal discipline by God. Joshua and Caleb represent two positive examples of believers who accepted God's will by faith and had fellowship with Him in His plan of service by entering and conquering the promised land of Canaan. In a similar way, New Testament believers can become "partakers of Christ" (Heb. 3:14) by continuing steadfastly in their faith despite antagonism from those in unbelief. If believers will continue believing, they will experience the peace and rest of soul that God offers to all believers in the present.[17] This is the type of "rest" spoken of in Hebrews 3–4 that believers must still "enter" into daily ("today") by faith (Heb. 3:18-19; 4:1, 3, 5, 6, 10, 11). Once again, Pentecost summarizes well the type of "rest" in Hebrews 3–4 God promises to those who walk by faith.

This is not the rest of salvation, for they are recognized as believers already (3:1). Nor is it the future millennial rest in which all persecution will cease. Such a future expecta-

---

Work, ed. Wesley and Elaine Willis, and John and Janet Master (Wheaton, IL: Victor, 1995), 130.

17. For support of the rest in Hebrews 3–4 being the believer's present experience rather than an eschatological reward, see Rodney J. Decker, "The Warnings of Hebrews Three and Four," *Journal of Ministry and Theology* 5 (Spring 2001): 5-27.

tion would neither provide a solution to their present problems, nor follow the imagery of the rest laid before Israel at Kadesh, which was a faith/life rest to be entered in their present experience. Thus we conclude that the rest referred to in Hebrews 4:1 is that faith/life rest into which a believer enters by faith, and in which he enjoys the promised blessings that God gives to those who believe and obey Him.[18]

Those Who Fall Away (Hebrews 6:4-6)

1 Therefore, leaving the discussion of the elementary principles of Christ, let us go on to perfection, not laying again the foundation of repentance from dead works and of faith toward God, 2 of the doctrine of baptisms, of laying on of hands, of resurrection of the dead, and of eternal judgment. 3 And this we will do if God permits. 4 For it is impossible for those who were once enlightened, and have tasted the heavenly gift, and have become partakers of the Holy Spirit, 5 and have tasted the good word of God and the powers of the age to come, 6 if they fall away, to renew them again to repentance, since they crucify again for themselves the Son of God, and put Him to an open shame. 7 For the earth which drinks in the rain that often comes upon it, and bears herbs useful for those by whom it is cultivated, receives blessing from God; 8 but if it bears thorns and briars, it is rejected and near to being cursed, whose end is to be burned. 9 But, beloved, we are confident of better things concerning you, yes, things that accompany salvation, though we speak in this manner. 10 For God is not unjust to forget your work and labor of love which you have shown toward His name, in that you have ministered to the saints, and do minister. 11 And we desire that each one of you show the same diligence to the full assurance of hope until the end, 12 that you do not become sluggish, but imitate those who through faith and patience inherit the promises.

This portion of chapter 6 is perhaps the most well-known and hotly-contested section in the entire epistle. Arminians see in these verses evidence that genuine believers may lose their faith and in the process also lose salvation. But if verses 4-6 were really teaching that

---

18. Pentecost, "Kadesh Barnea in the Book of Hebrews," 131-32.

salvation can be lost, then they must also be saying that eternal salvation can only be lost once in a Christian's lifetime and thereafter a person's fate is sealed since verse 4 says it is "impossible" renew that person to repentance. Calvinists typically see in verses 4-6 a description of people whose false faith is exposed by their apostasy, who prove they were never saved in the first place. But neither the typical Calvinist nor Arminian views accurately handle the details of the passage. So what is this passage saying? Hebrews 6:1-12 describes the spiritual crossroads to which the immature, Hebrew Christians had come. They were faced with two options. Either they could go on to spiritual maturity by continuing in their faith amidst great opposition and thus receive God's present blessings and future reward, or they could return to Judaism with its "dead works" of temple worship and priestly sacrifices, resulting in God's temporal judgment, loss of blessing, and loss of future reward.

Context of Maturity

The context of this disputed passage concerns spiritual maturity, not eternal condemnation and salvation. Though people often focus only on verses 4-6, these verses are set within a context dealing with the subject of maturity. This section begins in 5:11 where the writer says the Hebrew-Christian readers had become "dull [*nōthroi*] of hearing." The section ends in 6:12 with the writer admonishing the readers "not [to] become sluggish [*nōthroi*]." These two uses of *nōthroi* function like bookends, forming an inclusio, where Hebrews 5:11–6:12 constitutes a cohesive literary unit. Thus, the writer implores his readers in 6:1, "let us go on to perfection [*teleiotēta*]," where the word for "perfection" conveys the idea of completeness (Col. 3:14) or "maturity in contrast to the stage of elementary knowledge."[19]

Then, in Hebrews 6:1-2, the writer mentions six areas of doctrine that were foundational, which he did not wish to teach again. Pentecost says that these "were all doctrines stressed in Pharisaic Judaism. These certainly were not wrong; but they were elementary and were not the foundation for maturity."[20] In verse 3, the writer returns to the thought of verse 1 about going on to perfection, saying, "and this we will do if God permits." But, if God commands every believer to grow spiritually (2 Peter 3:18), then why would He not allow these

---

19. Bauer, Danker, Arndt, and Gingrich, *Greek-English Lexicon of the New Testament*, 996.

20. Pentecost, *Faith That Endures*, 104.

Hebrew Christians to go on to perfection? The context shows that they could not go on to maturity if they became unrepentant and fell away from the faith (Heb. 6:6).

Identity of Those Who Fall Away

Is it really possible for genuine believers to "fall away" from faith in Christ and as verse 6 says, "crucify again for themselves the Son of God, and put Him to an open shame"? Calvinists would typically say no, interpreting those in verses 4-6 as unbelievers, who manifest their unbelief by not persevering. Calvinists also claim that the switch from first-person pronouns in verses 1-3 ("us," "we") to third-person pronouns in verses 4-6 ("those," "they") proves that the writer is distinguishing between true believers and unbelievers. But it is better to conclude that the writer knew his readers had not yet fallen into a hardened state of unbelief and unrepentance, so that the description in verse 6 did not apply to them yet, though it could in the future if they did not continue steadfastly in their Christian faith. Otherwise, if the warning of verse 6 did not apply to the readers as a realistic possibility, why bother stating it? In fact, the readers were previously warned about the possibility of falling spiritually in Hebrews 4:11: "Let us therefore be diligent to enter that rest, lest anyone fall according to the same example of disobedience."

Scripture elsewhere warns about the possibility of genuine believers falling away. In Jesus' parable of the four soils, He describes the first soil as unbelievers, but the second soil are believers who fall away: "Those by the wayside are the ones who hear; then the devil comes and takes away the word out of their hearts, lest they should believe and be saved. But the ones on the rock are those who, when they hear, receive the word with joy; and these have no root, who believe for a while and in time of temptation fall away" (Luke 8:12-13). Likewise, the apostle Paul warned the saved but carnal Corinthians, "Therefore let him who thinks he stands take heed lest he fall" (1 Cor. 10:12). Even though the child of God may fall from faith, he can never fall out of the hand of God (John 10:28-29) or fall away from eternal salvation, as the psalmist says, "The steps of a good man are ordered by the Lord, and He delights in his way. Though he fall, he shall not be utterly cast down; for the Lord upholds him with His hand" (Ps. 37:23-24).

The inspired writer of Hebrews understood well that true believers, including himself, were capable of falling from their faith. Thus, he describes this possibility in Hebrews 6:4-6. The description given in these verses can only apply to a genuine child of God. Since one article in the Greek precedes the five descriptive participles in verses 4-6, these verses must be describing the same person.[21] In other words, the positive description of a genuine believer in verses 4-5 cannot be separated from the negative description in verse 6. This means that the genuine believer of verses 4-5 is capable of the condition described in verse 6. But does the description in verses 4-5 really describe genuine believers?

Participle 1: "those who were once enlightened" (v. 4). The root word for "enlightened" (*phōtizō*) is the same word used to describe the believing readers of this epistle: "But recall the former days in which, after you were illuminated [*phōtizō*], you endured a great struggle with sufferings" (10:32). This illumination was a once-for-all enlightenment since the word "once" (*hapax*) is used repeatedly by the writer of Hebrews to convey finality (9:7, 26, 27, 28; 10:2; 12:26-27).[22]

Participle 2: "and have tasted of the heavenly gift" (v. 4). The root word for "tasted" (*geuomai*) does not refer to something less than full consumption, as though false professors merely sampled the gospel of Christ, but then spit it out in unbelief. "Tasted" refers to a true experience of something, to appropriate or ingest the heavenly gift. The word *geuomai* is used in Hebrews 2:9 of Christ's death on the cross: "But we see Jesus, who was made a little lower than the angels, for the suffering of death crowned with glory and honor, that He, by the grace of God, might taste [*geuomai*] death for everyone." Since Christ obviously did not come short of truly dying, neither did those in 6:4 come short of receiving the heavenly gift.

Participle 3: "and have become partakers of the Holy Spirit" (v. 4). The word for "partakers" (*metochoi*) was used previously in 1:9 for Christ's "companions," and in 3:1 for believers participating in the heavenly calling, and in 3:14 for believers

---

21. Hal Harless, "Fallen Away or Fallen Down? The Meaning of Hebrews 6:1-9," *Chafer Theological Seminary Journal* 9 (Spring 2003): 6-9; Daniel B. Wallace, *Greek Grammar Beyond the Basics: An Exegetical Syntax of the New Testament* (Grand Rapids: Zondervan, 1996), 632-33.

22. Woods, "The Paradigm of Kadesh Barnea as a Solution to the Problem of Hebrews 6:4-6," 54.

partnering or communing with Christ in terms of fellowship. Only those who have received the Holy Spirit and are being led by Him (i.e., believers) are capable of the Spirit's fellowship (Rom. 8:9; 2 Cor. 13:14).

Participle 4: "and have tasted the good word of God and the powers of the age to come" (v. 5). The same word for "tasted" (*geuomai*) is used here as in verse 4 for tasting the heavenly gift. In other words, those described here in verse 5 had not merely sampled and spit out the Word of God, they had received it and been born again (Titus 3:5-7; James 1:18; 1 Peter 1:23).

Participle 5: "if they fall away" (v. 6). Several English Bibles give the impression that the falling away (*parapesontas*) here is only hypothetical, as if those described in verses 4-5 might or might not fulfill the description of this fifth participle in verse 6 of falling away. But there is no conditional "if" statement in the Greek. Daniel Wallace says that the participle *parapesontas* "should be taken as adjectival"[23] rather than adverbial, resulting in the translation "and then have fallen away" (ESV, NASB, NRSV).

If those described in verses 4-6 are true believers who are capable of falling away, this leads to two other crucial questions. Why would it be "impossible" (v. 4) to "renew them again to repentance" (v. 6)? And in what sense can true believers who fall away "crucify again for themselves the Son of God, and put Him to an open shame" (v. 6)? Dennis Rokser gives a clear answer and explanation to these questions:

The phrase "since they crucify again" is just one word in the Greek text *anastauroō*. It is a present active temporal participle, which is contemporaneous in time to the action of the main verb and that carries the idea of *while doing*, especially when it is related to the main verb. This could then be translated, "If they fall away, [it is impossible] to renew them again to repentance, *while* they crucify again for themselves the Son of God, and put Him to an open shame." The

---

23. Wallace, *Greek Grammar Beyond the Basics*, 633. See also, J. A. Sproule, "*Parapesontas* in Hebrews 6:6," *Grace Theological Journal* 2 (Fall 1981): 327-32.

writer of Hebrews is not shutting the door forever upon these believers experiencing spiritual growth again. But he is making it clear that this spiritual renewal will not occur *while at the same time* they persist in going back to the defunct Temple and its needless sacrifices.[24]

Hal Harless concurs, adding,

By the transgression of returning to the sacrificial system, they placed themselves beyond repentance. However, their state need not be enduring. The impossibility of renewing them to repentance remains while they continue to *again crucify to themselves the Son of God, and put Him to open shame. . . .* Returning to the sacrificial system was tantamount to crucifying Christ *to themselves (heautois).* This *put Him to open shame* because it implies that the death of Christ, instead of being *one sacrifice for sins for all time* (Hebrews 10:1-12), was no better than the repeated Levitical offerings.[25]

Regarding those in Hebrews 6:4-6 who turn back to Judaism, we may conclude that it would be impossible to renew them again to repentance (a change of mind) as long as they remained in a state of willful rebellion. Believers cannot (v. 3) go on to maturity (v. 1) if they do not allow their minds to be renewed daily (Rom. 12:2).

Blessing vs. Cursing

In Hebrews 6:7-12, two different outcomes are described—one negative, namely, God's judgment, and one positive, namely, His blessing. Verses 7-8 provide an illustration about God either blessing or cursing the land, depending on how it responds to His provision of rain: "7 For the earth which drinks in the rain that often comes upon it, and bears herbs useful for those by whom it is cultivated, receives blessing from God; 8 but if it bears thorns and briars, it is rejected and near to being cursed, whose end is to be burned."

These verses are not describing two different plots of land as Calvinists claim—one representing the true believer (v. 7) and the other representing the false believer (v. 8). The translation of these verses in the New International Version gives this misimpression: "7 Land

---

24. Rokser, *Shall Never Perish Forever,* 239-40.
25. Harless, "Fallen Away or Fallen Down? The Meaning of Hebrews 6:1-9," 15.

that drinks in the rain often falling on it and that produces a crop useful to those for whom it is farmed receives the blessing of God. 8 But land that produces thorns and thistles is worthless and is in danger of being cursed. In the end it will be burned." However, the Greek text uses the singular article (*hē*) in verse 7 for "the earth" (*hē gē*). The conditional participle that begins verse 8 (*ekpherousa*), translated "if it bears," is also singular and corresponds to the singular "earth" in verse 7. Grammatically, this shows that there is only one plot of land being referred to, which is capable of yielding two different crops. There is no justification for interpreting verses 7-8 as two separate lands with different crops. But what "land" is being referred to in verses 7-8? And what does it mean for the land to be "rejected and near to being cursed, whose end is to be burned"?

Naturally, some of have assumed that the language of rejection, cursing, and burning must refer to God's eternal condemnation of unbelievers in hell. But this assumption doesn't necessarily follow from the details of the text and the larger first-century context of the epistle. Verses 7-8 may be describing either individuals who fall away or the unbelieving nation of Israel or both.

Understood individually, verse 8 may be describing Hebrew Christians who reject the "rain" of God's Word that comes down upon them (Isa. 53:10-11), who fall away and return to Judaism, thereby "crucify[ing] again for themselves the Son of God, and put[ting] Him to an open shame" (Heb. 6:6). In such a case, all of their religious works would be vanity, or useless "thorns and thistles" (v. 8), since they would amount to nothing more than "dead works" in God's sight (9:14). Works done in a religiously carnal Christian's life, which may appear "good" before men, will be put to the fire test at the judgment seat of Christ. In the words of 1 Corinthians 3:15, "If anyone's work is burned, he will suffer loss; but he himself will be saved, yet so as through fire." This fits with the word "rejected" in Hebrews 6:8, which is *adokimos*. This is the same word used by Paul in 1 Corinthians 9:27 in the context of possibly being disallowed a reward from the Lord. The basic meaning of *adokimos* is disapproved. At the judgment seat of Christ, the Lord will not approve of any works done apart from His will. All thorns and thistles will be burned up. Besides the words "rejected" (*adokimos*) and "burned," the phrase "near to being cursed" is a third description in Hebrews 6:8 that people often assume refers to hell. The adverb "near" (*eggys*) qualifies the cursing and indicates a condition short of cursing—the ground is close to being cursed but not yet actually cursed. This is not a reference to eternal condemnation in hell but of God's temporal judgment in the form of discipline upon either individuals who fall away or the unbelieving covenant nation of Israel or both.

The "land" reference in Hebrews 6:7-8 should be understood nationally as a reference to the land of Israel and the city of Jerusalem to which apostatizing Hebrew Christians would return for worship in the Temple. If the Hebrew-Christian readers of the epistle fell away and returned to Judaism, then they must be forewarned that "the land" (*hē gē*) was facing God's imminent temporal judgment in the form of cursing. The theme of blessing and cursing is prominent throughout the Old Testament and would have surely struck a chord with these Hebrew-Christians. Deuteronomy 28–30 stipulated obedience to receive God's blessing, while disobedience brought down His curse. Randall Gleason clarifies the meaning of blessing and cursing in verses 7-8.

> The combination of blessing and curse fits more closely with Deuteronomy 11:26-28. There God offered the survivors of the wilderness generation two options: blessing for obedience or a curse for disobedience. These are further elaborated in Deuteronomy 28–29 with lists of blessings and curses. The final curse is on the land, which will be "a burning waste, unsown and unproductive, and no grass grows in it" (29:23). Disobedience would result in the devastation of the land. Since the blessings of obedience were experienced in relationship to the land (28:1-6), the destruction of the land meant the withholding of those blessings. Likewise in Hebrews 6:7-8 the author referred to the land of promise by the word *gē*. Rather than an undefined piece of "ground" as indicated by most translations, the word *gē* declares that the sacred land of the Jews will be a place of cursing and judgment rather than safety for those Jewish believers who desired to return to Judaism. In light of the Old Testament blessing-curse motif, the judgment in view in Hebrews 6:7-8 is best understood as the forfeiture of blessing and the experience of temporal discipline rather than eternal destruction.[26]

When Hebrews 6:8 says the land which bears thorns and thistles is "near [*eggys*] to being cursed," it is doubtful that the writer intends

---

26. Randall C. Gleason, "The Old Testament Background of the Warning in Hebrews 6:4-8," *Bibliotheca Sacra* 155 (January 1998): 86.

a meaning akin to "close to being cursed but will never actually experience cursing." When the same term is used later in the epistle, it carries the idea of something eventual and certain to happen. The only other use of *eggys* in Hebrews is in 8:13, which says in reference to the old covenant giving way to the new covenant, "Now what is becoming obsolete and growing old is ready [*eggys*] to vanish away." From God's standpoint, the impending destruction upon "the land" was certain and near.

When Hebrews was written, likely in the 60s A.D., the Jewish nation was in full-fledged rebellion toward God. The first-century Jewish historian Josephus explains the spiritual condition of those in Jerusalem shortly before its destruction by the Romans in A.D. 70:

> I believe that, had the Romans delayed their punishment of these villains, the city would have been swallowed up by the earth, or overwhelmed with a flood, or like Sodom, consumed with fire from heaven. For the generation which was in it was far more ungodly than the men on whom these punishments had in former times fallen. By their madness the whole nation came to be ruined.[27]

Not only the pagan, Gentile world, but Israel in particular was ripe for God's severe discipline as His covenant people (Lev. 26:31-33; Deut. 28:49-64). This judgment was known and taught by Christ and the apostles (Matt. 12:39-45; 23:35-36; 27:25; Luke 21:20-24; Acts 2:40)[28] and would soon come to fruition when the Roman armies arrived to burn and raze the land and its temple in A.D. 70. Gleason sheds light on the significance of this judgment alluded to in Hebrews 6:7-8.

> Though the eschatological outlook of this judgment may refer to the future judgment seat of Christ, it may also have in view the impending destruction of Jerusalem. The author may have been warning his audience not to return to Judaism because "the land" of Israel had produced "thorns and this-

---

27. Quoted in Philip Schaff, ed., *Ante-Nicene Christianity*, vol. 1 of *History of the Christian Church*, 5th ed. (Charles Scribner's Sons, 1910; reprint, Grand Rapids: Eerdmans, 1967), 399.

28. J. Dwight Pentecost, "The Apostles' Use of Jesus' Predictions of Judgment on Jerusalem in A.D. 70," in *Integrity of Heart, Skillfulness of Hands: Biblical and Leadership Studies in Honor of Donald K. Campbell*, ed. Charles H. Dyer and Roy B. Zuck (Grand Rapids: Baker, 1994), 134-43.

tles" and was now "worthless." Hence the land was "close to being cursed" because the Roman army was threatening an invasion of Judea to crush the Jewish revolt. As foreseen by the author, Jerusalem was burned and leveled by the Romans. This corresponds to the curse on the land in Deuteronomy 29:22-27. Consequently the author intended his readers to view the land as a place of judgment rather than blessing. This fits the force of the author's argument, for to return to Judaism would mean entering the realm of God's physical judgment. If the readers sided with Judaism rather than the people of Jesus, they would experience the same "fury of fire" intended to "consume the adversaries" —their Jewish persecutors (Heb. 10:27).[29]

The details surrounding the horrific events of Judah and Jerusalem's destruction in A.D. 70 are reserved for the next section of this chapter on Hebrews 10:26-29. But in regards to Hebrews 6:7-8, the writer of the epistle is likely alluding to the impending national cursing, burning, and rejection that will come upon those who reject the Word of God—a theme resumed with greater vividness and intensity in 10:26-29. The land illustration of blessing and cursing in 6:7-8 speaks of national divine discipline, not God's eternal condemnation in hell. But it also serves as a warning to the spiritually lethargic and immature Hebrew Christians not to fall away and realign themselves with an unbelieving nation that was headed for utter destruction. Instead, if they wanted to reap God's blessings, they needed to hold fast to their confession of faith in Christ and go "outside the camp, bearing His reproach" (13:13).

Better Things that Accompany Salvation

Despite the strong language and warning of verses 4-8, the writer of Hebrews was hopeful and confident that his readers would respond positively to his exhortations. Rather than the "thorns and thistles" and temporal divine discipline mentioned in verse 8, he was "confident of better things concerning [them], . . . things that accompany salvation" (v. 9). Verse 9 is often misread by Calvinists as if to say, "We are confident of your salvation" or more precisely "We are confident of something [singular] better concerning you, that thing

---

29. Gleason, "The Old Testament Background of the Warning in Hebrews 6:4-8," 88-89.

[singular] being salvation." But observe that verse 9 speaks of "better things" (plural), and things that "accompany salvation," not "salvation" itself. The writer of Hebrews is not saying in verse 9, "I am confident that you are saved." Rather, he is saying, "I am confident that you will go on to bear good fruit, which accompanies salvation," just as they already and previously had done (v. 10). For this reason, he reminds his readers that God will be faithful to reward them one day: "for God is not unjust to forget your work and labor of love which you have shown toward His name" (v. 10). Hebrews 6 is about genuine believers going on to maturity in the Christian life, not about believers assuring themselves that they possess eternal life.

If We Sin Willfully (Hebrews 10:26)

> 26 For if we sin willfully after we have received the knowledge of the truth, there no longer remains a sacrifice for sins, 27 but a certain fearful expectation of judgment, and fiery indignation which will devour the adversaries. 28 Anyone who has rejected Moses' law dies without mercy on the testimony of two or three witnesses. 29 Of how much worse punishment, do you suppose, will he be thought worthy who has trampled the Son of God underfoot, counted the blood of the covenant by which he was sanctified a common thing, and insulted the Spirit of grace? 30 For we know Him who said, "Vengeance is Mine, I will repay," says the Lord. And again, "The Lord will judge His people." 31 It is a fearful thing to fall into the hands of the living God.

Next to Hebrews 6:4-6, this passage is perhaps the second most widely-known and cited portion of the epistle. Hebrews 10:26-31 is used both to deny eternal security and to teach the perseverance of the saints. Arminians see in this passage once-genuine Christians, who later abandon their faith and lose their salvation. Calvinists see here an example of mere professing Christians, who eventually prove the inauthentic nature of their professed faith by turning away from Christ and perishing eternally in hell. Neither view is accurate.

The details of the passage and its context show that Hebrews 10:26-31 is addressing genuine Hebrew Christian believers, who had not yet gone back to Judaism but were susceptible to doing so. If they did go back, they would align themselves with the unbelieving nation of Israel—the adversaries of Christ (vv. 27, 29). Since the rebellious nation was facing God's severe discipline that would fall during the Jewish-Roman war of A.D. 66-70, Christians who went back to Judaism, with its feasts and sacrificial system headquartered in Jerusalem, would experience along with the nation maximum divine discipline via physical death. This is similar to other passages in the New Testament depicting sin unto death for the believer, like Acts 5:1-11 and 1 Corinthians 11:30-32, but in more corporate, nationalistic language than those passages. As such, Hebrews 10:26-31 is a warning about the possibility of genuine Jewish believers going apostate and the severe temporal, national judgment of God that would ensue.

There No Longer Remains a Sacrifice for Sins

Verse 26 begins with a conditional statement pertaining to the writer and his readers, as well as the resulting circumstance if that condition were met: "For if we sin willfully after we have received the knowledge of the truth, there no longer remains a sacrifice for sins." This verse is sometimes interpreted by Arminians as saying essentially, "If you as a believer willingly continue to sin, then Christ's sacrifice will no longer cover your sins and you will lose your salvation—at least until you stop sinning continually, and then Christ's sacrifice will apply to you again and you will regain your salvation." This popular interpretation completely disregards the context of verse 26, where the preceding verses in chapter 10 show that Christ's sacrifice was the last sacrifice and that the ongoing sacrifices "of bulls and goats" (v. 4) "can never take away sins" (v. 11). Since Christ's "once for all" sacrifice (v. 10) is the only sacrifice that put away sin "forever" (v. 12), the sacrifices required under the Law are no longer necessary in the plan of God or effective in accomplishing anything for sin. Now that Christ has died for all sin and believers are forgiven on the basis of His work alone, "there is no longer an offering for sin" (v. 18). Virtually the same expression occurs in verse 26: "there no longer remains a sacrifice for sins." Verse 26 continues the same thought as verse 18 by saying that if Hebrew Christians now reject Christ as the last sacrifice by turning back to Judaism with its empty temple-based sacrifices, then there are no sacrifices left to turn to as the basis for daily forgiveness and fellowship with God as a child of God (John 13:10; 1 John 1:3-9). Instead, the disobedient and apostate child of God can expect only God's severe temporal judgment.

This interpretation is supported by other key terms and statements in the context, such as "For" (v. 26), "after we have received the knowledge of the truth" (v. 26), and "spectacle" (v. 33). The Greek conjunction *gar* ("For") connects verse 26 with verse 25. This shows that, as believers, the writer and his readers might deliberately and willfully choose not to assemble themselves together with Christians and instead go to the Temple to participate in its sacrifices. By making a public statement about their rejection of Christ and return to the defunct temple sacrifices, they would practically "trample the Son of God underfoot" and count His blood "a common thing" (v. 29), and put Him "to an open shame" (6:6). This is why the writer reminds his readers that they themselves once "were made a spectacle [*theatrizo-menoi*]" (Heb. 10:33) for Christ. The word "spectacle" comes from the Greek word *theatrizō*, which means "to shame publicly."[30] Now they are not to turn around and put Christ to an open shame. In verse 33, the writer reminds them of their previous sacrifice and investment in serving the Lord Jesus. If they were to go back to Judaism, they would do to Christ what had been done to them. Based on public nature of the sin described in verses 26-29, and the context of chapter 10 dealing with sacrifices, it is safe to conclude that the willful sin of verse 26 is not sin in general but the particular sin of Hebrew Christians returning to the sacrificial system of Judaism.

Identity of the Apostates

In order to interpret this passage correctly, the people described with the third person in verses 26-29 must be accurately identified. Are they unbelievers, who profess, but do not possess, faith in Christ? Or, are they genuine believers? Evidence in the passage points to these people being believers who fall away. First, the believing writer uses the first person "we" in verses 26 and 30 to address his readers. By saying, "If we sin willfully," the writer includes himself and his readers as those who are capable of incurring the judgment described in verses 27-29. Later, the readers are addressed with the second person "you" in verses 32-36, which must describe believers because of the promise of eternal reward given there. Reformed interpreters often point out that the third person ("anyone," v. 28; "he," v. 29) is used in verses 27-29 to describe those who commit apostasy. They conclude that the apostates are separate from the writer and readers—as though the writer is seeking to distinguish between true believers,

---

30. Johannes P. Louw and Eugene Nida, eds. *Greek-English Lexicon of the New Testament Based on Semantic Domains*, Vol. 1 (New York: United Bible Societies, 1988), 311.

who persevere in their faith, and false professors, who never really possessed faith to begin with. However, these verses are not addressing the question of whether a profession is genuine or not. They are describing the possibility of genuine believers ("we," v. 26) sinning willfully by returning to Judaism. The reason for the shift in pronouns from the first person in verse 26 to the third person in verses 27-29 is because the writer does not think that his readers have yet fallen into the category "adversaries." This is why he uses conditional language in verse 26 when addressing the readers: *"if* we sin willfully."

Second, those who turn away from Christ in verse 29 match the description of believers, not unbelievers. In the statement, "the blood of the covenant by which he was sanctified," the word "sanctified" (*hēgiasthē*) is the aorist-tense, indicative-mood form of the verb *hagiazō*, describing a past-tense event. The context of Hebrews 10 shows that only believers in Christ have been sanctified by Christ's blood. Earlier in the chapter, the writer uses "we" and states, "By that will we have been sanctified [*hēgiasmenoi*] through the offering of the body of Jesus Christ once for all" (10:10). Likewise, Hebrews 10:14 says, "For by one offering He has perfected forever those who are being sanctified [*hagiazomenous*]." The description "perfected forever" only applies to genuine believers in Christ, who have been positionally washed, sanctified, and justified (1 Cor. 6:11).

Third, the appeal of the writer to his readers in Hebrews 10:32-29 shows that the readers were true believers facing the realistic alternatives of either sinning willfully by returning to Judaism (10:25-31) or forging ahead in their Christian faith. Verse 32 begins, "But recall the former days in which, after you were illuminated, you endured a great struggle with sufferings." Verses 33-34 further describe how the readers had been reproached, plundered, and publicly put to shame for their faith. They initially paid a high price for following Christ as His disciples and were already deeply invested in Him, with the prospect of an enduring "reward" in heaven (vv. 34-35), so why turn back now through willful sin and apostasy? If, as Calvinism teaches, these genuine believers were incapable of becoming weary in the battle (Gal. 6:9. 2 Thess. 3:13; Heb. 12:3) to the point of leaving their faith in Christ and turning back to Judaism, then why insert the warning to them in verses 26-29 about the willful sin of apostasy that incurs God's severe judgment? What would be the point of that? Obviously, the writer saw the readers as genuine believers like himself, who were capable of apostatizing from the faith.

Fiery Indignation and Worse Punishment

Calvinists and Arminians normally interpret verses 27 and 29 as references to hell when they speak of "judgment, and fiery indignation which will devour the adversaries" (v. 27) and a "worse punishment" (v. 29) than physical death. There is no dispute about the fact that physical death is referred to in verse 28: "Any who has rejected Moses' law dies without mercy on the testimony of two or three witnesses." But verse 29 goes on to speak of a "worse punishment" than the physical death of verse 28. The assumption is that only hell could be worse than physical execution under the Law. There are several reasons why this assumption is incorrect.

First, although the Law commanded the Israelites themselves to carry out the execution of those in willful rebellion and violation of the Law based on two or three witnesses, in some cases, God did the execution Himself with fire. The Law tells of the rebellion of Nadab and Abihu, priests and sons of Aaron, who offered strange fire to God instead of following His will regarding proper worship. As a result they were consumed by fire from God (Lev. 10:2). Later, 250 leaders of Israel followed Korah, Dathan, and Abiram in their insurrection against Moses and Aaron, and all 250 died by fire from the Lord (Num. 16:35; 26:10). In addition, Numbers 11:1 says that some of Israel's rank and file were destroyed by fire for their disobedience: "Now when the people complained, it displeased the Lord; for the Lord heard it, and His anger was aroused. So the fire of the Lord burned among them, and consumed some in the outskirts of the camp." In each of these instances under the Law, the fire came directly from God in His displeasure, resulting in a physical death that was a worse punishment than physical death by a human executioner. But these deaths by divine fire were still physical, not eternal, judgments. What is more, in each of the previous examples, the "fiery indignation" of God's judgment consumed adversaries of the Exodus generation of Israelites, who were true, redeemed believers, as explained previously with Hebrews 3:14.

Furthermore, if the writer of Hebrews were describing hell in verses 27 and 29, rather than serious temporal judgment, then why did he not use a term conveying the eternality of the judgment? Many passages in the New Testament contain the adjective "eternal," "everlasting," or "forever," to clarify that *eternal* judgment is in view.

- "everlasting fire" (Matt. 25:41)
- "everlasting punishment" (Matt. 25:46)
- "eternal condemnation" (Mark 3:29)
- "everlasting destruction" (2 Thess. 1:9)
- "blackness of darkness forever" (2 Peter 2:17)
- "everlasting chains under darkness" (Jude 6)
- "vengeance of eternal fire" (Jude 7)
- "blackness of darkness forever" (Jude 13)
- "their torment ascends forever and ever" (Rev. 14:11)
- "they will be tormented day and night forever and ever" (Rev. 20:10)

The writer of Hebrews freely employs terms expressing eternality or an ongoing state for many subjects in the epistle, as seen in the following list. But conspicuously he never uses such terms as "eternal" or "forever" or "continual" in reference to the judgment coming upon those who do not persevere in their faith.

- "eternal salvation" (5:9)
- "eternal judgment" (6:2)
- "remains a priest continually" (7:3)
- "He continues forever" (7:24)
- "eternal redemption" (9:12)
- "eternal Spirit" (9:14)
- "eternal inheritance" (9:15)
- "which they offer continually year by year" (10:1)
- "one sacrifice for sins forever" (10:12)
- "He has perfected forever" (10:14)
- "everlasting covenant" (13:20)

The writer of Hebrews did not hesitate to use terms expressing eternality or an ongoing state for many different subjects. Therefore, he certainly could have done the same in Hebrews 10:26-31, if he were describing *eternal* judgment. Even when the writer speaks of "eternal judgment" in Hebrews 6:2, this phrase has a dual application to believers and unbelievers. To the unbeliever, "eternal judgment" will mean eternal condemnation; but to the believer, it will mean an imperishable crown. The writer of Hebrews could have described the fiery judgment in chapter 10 as something eternal or continual, but he chose not to, which supports the fact that he was referring to temporal judgment.

Third, even the description of a "worse punishment" (v. 29) than the death penalty of the Law (v. 28) is not a reference to hell. Verse 29 goes on to speak of "the blood of the covenant" by which the apostates were previously sanctified. Why use covenant language here? The "blood" referred to in verse 29 is obviously Christ's blood that ratified the new covenant, as the whole preceding context of 9:12–10:19 makes explicit. But why refer to it here as "the blood of the covenant," when the writer could have just said "the blood of Jesus" as he did earlier in 10:19? The use of "covenant" gives the passage a national, corporate connotation since Hebrews had previously taught that the new covenant was made "with the house of Israel and with the house of Judah" (8:8, 10). The nation of Israel was still God's covenanted people, even after the crucifixion of Christ (Acts 3:25). But Israel was also a nation facing imminent divine judgment, which may be the implication of Hebrews 10:25 since the mention of the approaching "day" leads right into the topic of judgment (vv. 26-31). While the approaching "day" of verse 25 may refer to the day of Christ's coming to resurrect and reward His church, which also fits the context (9:28; 10:37), the flow of the immediate context of 10:25-27 most naturally fits "day" being the day of God's temporal judgment on Christ's adversaries.[31] Dennis Rokser explains how the approaching day of national judgment in verse 25 corresponds with the "worse punishment" of verse 29.

> But this leaves a vital question unanswered, namely, what is the "worse punishment" described in verse 29? It clearly is not eternal Hell since this passage is describing believers who "have been sanctified" (v. 10) and "perfected forever" (v. 14) through the once-for-all sacrifice of Jesus Christ. But

---

31. Arnold G. Fruchtenbaum, *Israelology: The Missing Link in Systematic Theology*, rev. ed. (Tustin, CA: Ariel Ministries, 2001), 971; idem, *The Messianic Jewish Epistles: Hebrews, James, First Peter, Second Peter, Jude*, Ariel's Bible Commentary (Tustin, CA: Ariel Ministries, 2005), 141; Pentecost, "The Apostles' Use of Jesus' Predictions of Judgment on Jerusalem in A.D. 70," 140-41; Kurt Witzig, "Distinguishing God's Punishment and His Discipline," in *Should Christians Fear Outer Darkness?*, Dennis Rokser, Tom Stegall, and Kurt Witzig (Duluth, MN: Grace Gospel Press, 2015), 367.

if they do apostatize and "draw back" because of their present persecution, they could anticipate God's displeasure (v. 38) and serious divine discipline (v. 29). This would involve physical death (v. 28) with the loss of a great present opportunity (v. 39b) and future reward (v. 35) at the Judgment Seat of Christ. But this could involve realities worse than physical death, since to simply die is an easier option than facing certain consequences in this life.

This passage also appears to have national overtones regarding the pending destruction of Jerusalem (A.D. 70). Because of Israel's backsliding, this judgment constituted God's predicted fifth cycle of discipline (Lev. 26; Deut. 28), resulting in massive death and worse (e.g., starvation, mothers eating their children, mass crucifixion, and so forth). Church historians note that there were those believers who took to heart the exhortations of this epistle to the Hebrews and escaped this divine judgment on Jerusalem by specifically heeding Hebrews 13:12-14: "Therefore Jesus also, that He might sanctify the people with His own blood, suffered outside the gate. Therefore let us go forth to Him, outside the camp, bearing His reproach. For here we have no continuing city, but we seek the one to come."[32]

If first-century Hebrew Christians in Israel failed to continue in their faith in Christ and returned to the sacrificial system of Judaism, they would place themselves in the "line of fire" of God's judgment and face the destruction that was soon to envelope the nation during the Jewish-Roman war of A.D. 66-70. When the war began, Jewish freedom fighters enjoyed a few small victories over pockets of Roman troops. But the Romans garnered their forces and soon crushed all such resistance. One attack on Roman troops stationed in the Galilean city of Sephoris "provoked fierce hostilities from the Romans, who spread fire and blood over all of Galilee, killing any who were capable of bearing arms."[33] This "fiery indignation" was by no means localized to towns and villages in Galilee, for the Romans burned their way to Jerusalem and its temple. At the war's conclusion, Josephus records that Israel was viewed as "a land still on fire upon every side."[34]

---

32. Rokser, *Shall Never Perish Forever*, 246.

33. *Josephus: The Essential Works*, translated and edited by Paul L. Maier (Grand Rapids: Kregel, 1988), 302.

34. Josephus, *Jewish Wars* 7.5.5 §145. See also 3.7.1 §§132-34; 4.8.1 §446; and 6.5.1 §275.

Not only was the Roman campaign against the Jewish nation characterized by fiery destruction, but also by unimaginable suffering and death. Historian Philip Schaff recounts the stubborn resistance of the Jews that led the Romans to finally lay siege to Jerusalem.

> In April, A.D. 70, immediately after the Passover, when Jerusalem was filled with strangers, the siege began. The zealots rejected, with sneering defiance, the repeated proposals of Titus. . . . The crucifixion of hundreds of prisoners (as many as five hundred a day) only enraged them the more. Even the famine which began to rage and sweep away thousands daily, and forced a woman to roast her own child, the cries of mothers and babes, the most pitiable scenes of misery around them, could not move the crazy fanatics.[35]

Josephus describes the sheer carnage on the day that Jerusalem's temple was finally burned and razed, mingling blood with fire.

> Yet was the misery itself more terrible than this disorder; for one would have thought that the hill itself, on which the temple stood, was seething hot, as full of fire on every part of it, that the blood was larger in quantity than the fire, and those that were slain more in number than those that slew them; for the ground did nowhere appear visible, for the dead bodies that lay on it; but the soldiers went over heaps of these bodies, as they ran upon such as fled from them.[36]

One scholar concludes from all of Josephus's recorded figures that "the total number of killed, from the beginning to the close of the war, to be 1,356,460, and the total number of prisoners 101,700."[37] Schaff says of those captured and left alive, "Ninety-seven thousand were carried captive and sold into slavery, or sent to the mines, or sacrificed in the gladiatorial shows at Caesarea, Berytus, Antioch, and other cities."[38] The combination of all these miseries associated with the war, coupled with death itself, constitutes "worse punishment" (Heb. 10:29) than the death inflicted for breaking the Law of Moses (v. 28).

---

35. Schaff, *History of the Christian Church*, 1:396-97.
36. Josephus, *Jewish Wars* 6.5.1 §§275-76.
37. Schaff, *History of the Christian Church*, 1:400 n. 2.
38. Schaff, *History of the Christian Church*, 1:400.

For those Hebrew Christians who did not "insult the Spirit of grace" (v. 29) and who continued following Christ by faith, the Lord provided a way of escape from this grave judgment. Schaff explains, "The Christians of Jerusalem, remembering the Lord's admonition, forsook the doomed city in good time and fled to the town of Pella in the Decapolis, beyond the Jordan, in the north of Peraea, where king Herod Agrippa II, before whom Paul once stood, opened to them a safe asylum."[39] According to the book of Acts, this same Agrippa was at least empathetic to the gospel of Christ, though he did not yet believe it. For upon hearing Paul's teaching and testimony, he confessed, "You almost persuade me to become a Christian" (Acts 26:28). Agrippa also found Christ's apostle to be innocent, declaring, "This man is doing nothing deserving of death or chains" (v. 31). Therefore, it is not surprising that God would graciously and providentially make a way of escape from the judgment that befell the Jewish nation by providing a temporary safe haven from the war's desolation in Pella. Eusebius provides the earliest account of the flight of Hebrew Christians, who went "outside the camp" (Heb. 13:13) of Jerusalem to Pella. Between A.D. 290–300, Eusebius wrote:

> The whole body, however, of the church at Jerusalem, having been commanded by a divine revelation, given to men of approved piety there before the war, removed from the city, and dwelt at a certain town beyond the Jordan, called Pella. Here, those that believed in Christ, having removed from Jerusalem, as if holy men had entirely abandoned the royal city itself, and the whole land of Judea; the divine justice, for their crimes against Christ and his apostles, finally overtook them, totally destroying the whole generation of these evildoers from the earth.[40]

Hebrew Christians who rejected Christ as their final sacrifice and returned to Judaism had been forewarned. Christ Himself predicted this approaching day of God's judgment nearly four decades prior; now they had the Epistle of Hebrews as another extension of God's grace. Although God's grace makes full and free provision for pay-

---

39. Schaff, *History of the Christian Church*, 1:402.

40. *The Ecclesiastical History of Eusebius Pamphilus*, trans. Christian Frederick Cruse (reprint, Grand Rapids: Baker, 1989), 86. For a defense of the historical veracity of Eusebius' account, see P. H. R. van Houwelingen, "Fleeing Forward: The Departure of Christians from Jerusalem to Pella," *Westminster Theological Journal* 65 (2003): 181-200.

ment of sin's penalty, it never tolerates sin. It always warns against sin, while beckoning men to come to the fount of grace Himself—Jesus Christ. Following the warning of Hebrews 10:26-31, it is no wonder that the writer of Hebrews goes on to say: "Therefore, since we are receiving a kingdom which cannot be shaken, let us have grace, by which we may serve God acceptably with reverence and godly fear. For our God is a consuming fire" (12:28-29).

Those Who Draw Back to Perdition (Hebrews 10:39)

35 Therefore do not cast away your confidence, which has great reward. 36 For you have need of endurance, so that after you have done the will of God, you may receive the promise: 37 "For yet a little while, and He who is coming will come and will not tarry. 38 Now the just shall live by faith; but if anyone draws back, My soul has no pleasure in him." 39 But we are not of those who draw back to perdition, but of those who believe to the saving of the soul.

These verses are often read as if they say, "You have need of endurance, so that after you have done the will of God, you may receive eternal salvation," thus making perseverance in faith the condition for salvation from hell. But the content and context of the passage show once again that perseverance in the Christian life leads to a reward, while a failure to persevere leads to a loss of reward, and in the case of these Hebrew Christians who faced temptation to return to Judaism, it might also lead to the destruction of God's temporal judgment. Before clarifying the meaning of "perdition" and the "saving of the soul," it is essential to consider the context of verse 39.

The context shows that the passage is about rewards rather than salvation from hell. Following the explicit reference to "great reward" in verse 35, the next two verses begin with the explanatory conjunction *gar* in the Greek text, which is translated "for." These conjunctions express the reason for the readers to persevere. They should endure in their faith because of God's "promise" (v. 35) to give a "great reward" (v. 35), which will be given to them when Christ comes back (v. 37). The coming of Christ is frequently associated with rewards in Scripture since the bestowal of rewards will occur at the judgment seat of Christ following the Rapture and resurrection (Luke 14:14; 1 Cor. 3:13-15; 4:5; Phil. 2:16; 1 Thess. 2:19; 2 Tim. 4:7-8; 1 Peter 5:4; Rev. 3:11; 22:12). Hebrews 10:34 had just stated that the readers' earthly possessions were taken from them because of their faith in Christ, but they had a better and an enduring possession in heaven. This reflects the teaching of Christ Himself, who said concerning rewards, "Do not lay up for yourselves treasures on earth, where moth and rust destroy and where thieves break in and steal; but lay up for yourselves treasures in heaven, where neither moth nor rust destroys and where thieves do not break in and steal" (Matt. 6:19-20). The writer of Hebrews uses this illustration in the next chapter with respect to Moses being rewarded for his perseverance in faith amidst persecution: "By faith Moses, when he became of age, refused to be called the son of Pharaoh's daughter, choosing rather to suffer affliction with the people of God than to enjoy the passing pleasures of sin, esteeming the reproach of Christ greater riches than the treasures in Egypt; for he looked to the reward" (Heb. 11:24-26).

In addition, Hebrews 11:6 speaks of reward for pleasing God by one's faith: "But without faith it is impossible to please Him, for he who comes to God must believe that He is, and that He is a rewarder of those who diligently seek Him." The references in this verse to faith, pleasing God, and reward all point back to the end of chapter 10 where each of these concepts occurs. In 10:38, the expression "no pleasure" (*ouk eudokei*) is used: "but if anyone draws back, My soul has no pleasure in him." The Greek verb for "pleasure" (*eudokeō*) occurs only three times in Hebrews, once in verse 38 and twice earlier in chapter 10, where in each instance it speaks of God having no pleasure in animal sacrifices: "In burnt offerings and sacrifices for sin You had no pleasure [*ouk eudokēsas*]" (10:6) and "Sacrifice and offering, burnt offerings, and offerings for sin You did not desire, nor had pleasure [*oude eudokēsas*] in them" (10:8). These three uses of the expression "no pleasure" in Hebrews 10 confirm once again that the original readers of the epistle were facing temptation to return to the sacrificial system of the Law which was still functioning at the Temple in Jerusalem.

Hebrews 10:35-39 set before the readers two paths. If they would resist the temptation to return to Judaism and endure in their faith in Christ, they would receive a "great reward" from Him (v. 35) at His coming (v. 37), in fulfillment of God's promise (v. 36; cf. Heb. 6:10). The writer of Hebrews was optimistic that the readers would not go back; thus, he affirmed, "we are not of those who draw back to perdition" (v. 39). He stated this previously in the epistle, saying, "we are confident of better things concerning you" (6:9). He reaffirmed this confidence in 10:39. But what if the readers did go back to Judaism? Verse 38 says those who returned would face "perdition."

In the context, "perdition" does not refer to hell but to the physical, temporal destruction that would soon come upon the Christ-rejecting, covenant nation of Israel (vv. 26-29). Kurt Witzig clarifies the meaning of Hebrews 10:37-39.

> In verses 37-38, the writer quotes from Habakkuk 2:3b-4 to encourage the faithful to wait for Him who is coming and to remind them to live by faith. The reference to Habakkuk is significant because of the contextual parallel between the two different groups of readers. The prophet Habakkuk was perplexed over God's allowance of evil in Judah and asked God how long before He comes and physically judges the unfaithful nation. Like Habakkuk, the readers of Hebrews were also wondering how long before God brings the promised physical judgment on the city of Jerusalem for the rampant unfaithfulness of that generation. The writer concludes in verse 39 saying that he and the readers were not of those who draw back to the temple and to the practice of Judaism and thus to perdition (coming physical judgment), but rather they were of those who believe to the saving of the life.[41]

For those who fell away and went back to Judaism, "perdition" would come in the form of physical destruction, which, to the fallen-away believer, would be God's temporal chastening (Heb. 12:5-11) and would also result in a loss of eternal reward. The "saving of the soul" in 10:39 is not a reference to hell. That is, unless we are prepared to say that Jesus threatened Peter with hell! When Jesus told the disciples that He must go to Jerusalem and be killed and rise from the dead (Matt. 16:21), Peter rebuked Him (v. 22). In response, Christ rebuked Peter (v. 23) and taught all the disciples:

> 24 If anyone desires to come after Me, let him deny himself, and take up his cross, and follow Me. 25 For whoever desires to save his life will lose it, but whoever loses his life for My sake will find it. 26 For what profit is it to a man if he gains the whole world, and loses his own soul? Or what will a man give in exchange for his soul? 27 For the Son of Man will

---

41. Kurt Witzig, "Distinguishing God's Punishment and His Discipline," in *Should Christians Fear Outer Darkness?* (Duluth, MN: Grace Gospel Press, 2015), 370.

come in the glory of His Father with His angels, and then He will reward each according to his works.

Jesus Christ taught that the saving of the "soul" refers to the saving of a person's "life" (v. 25), which results in an eternal reward (v. 27). The writer of Hebrews uses "saving" and "soul" in the same sense.[42]

The Author and Finisher of Our Faith (Hebrews 12:2)

1 Therefore we also, since we are surrounded by so great a cloud of witnesses, let us lay aside every weight, and the sin which so easily ensnares us, and let us run with endurance the race that is set before us, 2 looking unto Jesus, the author and finisher of our faith, who for the joy that was set before Him endured the cross, despising the shame, and has sat down at the right hand of the throne of God.

The phrase "the author and finisher of our faith" is often misinterpreted to mean that just as Jesus gave His elect their original, "saving faith," He will sovereignly work to insure that their faith perseveres to the end. Reformed apologist James White explains Hebrews 12:2 this way:

Jesus is the origin and source of faith, the goal of faith, the one who completes and perfects faith. . . . We are kept indeed by the power of faith, but it is not a merely human faith, but a divine faith, a gift from God! Why do some stumble and fall while others persevere? Is it that some are better, stronger, than others? No. The reason lies in the difference between having saving faith and a faith that is not divine in origin or nature. Many are those who make professions not based upon regeneration, and the "faith" that is theirs will not last. . . . There are those who have false, human faith that does not last. But those with true faith produce fruit and remain.[43]

This interpretation of Hebrews 12:1-2 grossly errs by imposing the theology of Calvinism onto the passage instead of drawing the meaning out of the passage in its context. Hebrews 11 presents

---

42. The phrase "saving of the soul" is explained in more detail in the next chapter in connection with its use in 1 Peter 1:9.

43. James R. White, *The Potter's Freedom* (Amityville, NY: Calvary Press, 2000), 293.

examples of faith from the lives of many Old Testament saints. This
was designed to encourage the Hebrew Christian readers to do the
same in their own spiritual race. The great company or cloud of witnesses did not watch the earthly lives of these first-century Hebrew
Christians from some heavenly grandstand in the sky. No, the Old
Testament saints of chapter 11 witnessed *to* the first-century Hebrew
Christians; they were not witnesses or spectators *of* the lives of these
Hebrew Christians. Each of the Old Testament saints recorded in
chapter 11 left a lasting legacy and testimony for future generations
(11:1, 4, 5, 39), including the first-century readers of Hebrews. Jesus
Christ was the greatest and last example of a faithful witness (12:1-2),
to whom these tempted and beleaguered Hebrew Christian readers
were now instructed to look and consider by faith (v. 3; cf. 3:1). Consequently, the expression "author and finisher of our faith" has nothing to do with God causing the gift of "saving faith" to persevere to
the end in each elect person's life.

The word "author" (*archēgon*) refers to Christ being the captain
or leader of our faith in the sense of Him being the highest in rank
among the runners in the race, and the One who leads by His own
example (i.e., the premiere runner). In Acts 3:15, *archēgon* is translated "the *Prince* of life." It is also translated this way in Acts 5:31:
"*Prince* and Savior." This word is also used in Hebrews 2:10: "the
captain of their salvation." Thus, one Greek lexicon defines this word
as "pioneer leader" or "a person who as originator or founder of
a movement continues as the leader"[44] Thus, the word *archēgon* in
Hebrews 12:2 implies Christ's priority or preeminence among believers because of His supreme position and His own perfect example
of unfailing, implicit trust in God the Father over the course of His
earthly life. As the *archēgon* of faith, Jesus Christ is "the exemplar, the
champion of faith."[45]

The word "finisher" (*teleiōtēn*) in Hebrews 12:2 is the same word
that occurs just two verses prior in 11:40, where it says of the many
Old Testaments saints of chapter 11 that "they should not be made
perfect [*teleiōthōsin*] apart from us." In the plan of God, the "cloud" is
not complete until faithful church-age believers add their testimony
to it. This is possible only because church-age saints are positionally
in Jesus Christ, who Himself is part of this "cloud of witnesses" as

---

44. Louw and Nida, *Greek-English Lexicon of the New Testament Based on Semantic Domains*, 466.

45. William L. Lane, Hebrews 9–13, Word Biblical Commentary (Nashville: Thomas Nelson, 1991), 411.

the last and greatest witness. What immediately follows the statement in 11:40 is the chief example of what it means to run the race with patience, namely, Jesus Christ Himself, who faithfully persevered amidst suffering and persecution (12:1-3).

While English Bibles often translate verse 2, "the author and finisher of *our* faith," the Greek text has the definite article before "faith," so that instead of the translation *"our* faith," it would be more appropriate for verse 2 to say *"the* faith." The point of the passage is simply that Jesus Christ is the principal (*archēgon*) and final (*teleiōtēn*) example in a long line of witnesses of those who endured in the collective faith—in God's plan for a life of faith among all His saints—whether they be Old Testament saints who lived by faith or New Testament, church-age saints who must do the same. In this sense, Jesus Christ is literally "the author and finisher of *the faith.*" For the Hebrew Christian readers, this would mean continuing to have faith in Christ rather than denying the *archēgon* and *teleiōtēn* of the faith by returning to Judaism.

In summary, the phrase "author and finisher of the faith" in Hebrews 12:2 is simply teaching that the object of the Christian's faith, Jesus Christ, is the One who went before us as a pioneer leader ("author") and the highest example of all those who finished ("finisher") the race. Hebrews 12:2 is *not* saying that Jesus Christ is the One who sovereignly initiates each person's faith (i.e., as the "author" of their faith) and who deterministically makes believers persevere in their faith to the end of their lives or races (i.e., as the "finisher" of their faith). Hebrews 12:2 *is* saying that the One in whom Christians believe, Jesus Christ, is also the principal ("author") and final ("finisher") example of all those who finished the race before us.[46]

Holiness to See the Lord (Hebrews 12:14)

Hebrews 12:14 says, "Pursue peace with all people, and holiness, without which no one will see the Lord." This is another frequently cited verse from Hebrews used to support the teaching of Lordship Salvation and its concomitant doctrine of the perseverance of the saints. For example, Robert Peterson claims, "perseverance in faith is a condition of final salvation. . . . Believers must also persevere

---

46. Erich Sauer, *In the Arena of Faith: A Call to the Consecrated Life* (Grand Rapids: Eerdmans, 1994), 20-21.

in holiness (v. 14) if they are to be finally saved."[47] Calvinist Michael Horton likewise asserts regarding verse 14, "The New Testament lays before us a vast array of conditions for final salvation. Not only initial repentance and faith, but perseverance in both, demonstrated in love toward God and neighbor, are part of that holiness without which no one shall see the Lord (Heb. 12:14)."[48] Is Hebrews 12:14 really teaching that faith must be accompanied by a holy life, or else one's faith is not genuine and he or she will never get to see the Lord in heaven?

Observe, first of all, what this verse does *not* say: "Pursue peace with all people, and holiness, without which *you* will not see the Lord." Rather, it says, "Pursue peace with all people, and holiness, without which *no one* will see the Lord." The writer of Hebrews is not warning his readers that they must live a holy life to make it to heaven, which would blatantly contradict biblical teaching elsewhere that believers are eternally saved by God's grace, through faith, and apart from our works (Rom. 4:4-8; Eph. 2:8-9; Titus 3:5). Hebrews 12:14 is simply saying that other people will not see the Lord in the believer's life without that believer also manifesting God's attributes of peace and holiness. There is nothing in the context to suggest that the clause "see the Lord" means entering heaven one day. Instead, the context deals with human relationships that are affected by the believer's relationship to the Lord. The passage focuses on the effect of the believer's spiritual life toward other people. The verses before verse 14 deal with believers accepting God's discipline in their lives, so that they "may be partakers of His holiness" (v. 10) and have cultivated in their lives "the peaceable fruit of righteousness" (v. 11). The verse after verse 14 says, "lest any root of bitterness springing up cause trouble, and by this many become defiled" (v. 15). Other people to whom believers witness will "see the Lord" when they see His attributes of holiness, peace, and righteousness manifested.

Rather than setting forth a condition for entrance to heaven, Hebrews 12:14 is simply teaching that the believer's witness and testimony to others will only be effective if he or she displays God's character. It is sheer eisegesis and adding to the gospel of grace to interpret this verse as conditioning eternal life on the believer's personal holiness and sanctification.

---

47. Robert A. Peterson, "The Perseverance of the Saints: A Theological Exegesis of Four Key New Testament Passages," *Presbyterion: Covenant Seminary Review* 17/2 (1991): 102.

48. Michael Horton, *Introducing Covenant Theology* (Grand Rapids: Baker, 2006), 182.

Conclusion

Perhaps more than any other book of Scripture, Calvinists refer to the Epistle of Hebrews in an attempt to prove the doctrine of the perseverance of the saints. This is not surprising in light of the abundance of warning passages in the book dealing with God's judgment, combined with repeated exhortations to hold fast and endure. Yet, what is striking is the absence of any explicit warning to the effect that if the readers do not persevere in their faith they will be *eternally* lost, condemned, or destroyed in hell. The judgment facing the reader throughout Hebrews is consistently temporal, not eternal. Likewise, one cannot find even a single verse explicitly stating that perseverance in faith and holiness is necessary for eternal life, justification, redemption, or anything resembling *eternal* salvation. There are several descriptive statements about being part of Christ's house (3:6) and partaking of Him (3:14), falling away (6:6), land being cursed and burned (6:8), fiery indignation devouring adversaries (10:27), the saving of the soul or life (10:39), and not seeing the Lord (12:14). But where are the specific statements about God requiring perseverance in faith to be eternally saved from hell?

When comparing Calvinism's doctrine of perseverance to the Epistle of Hebrews, one gets the distinct impression that a theological tradition and construct has been imposed upon the text of God's Word. This has very unfortunate consequences. The original recipients of the book, who were true believers, but spiritually stagnant and tempted, now come under suspicion as possibly being unbelievers. The effect is the same for modern-day believing readers who are led to question and doubt whether they themselves, or their Christian peers, have true, "saving faith." Perseverance in faith and holiness is no longer rightfully viewed as a matter of fellowship with God and practical sanctification, but is now seen as proof that one truly possesses eternal, final salvation. This practically devastates personal assurance of salvation. If the requirement for eternal life is persevering and productive faith, but you have not yet come to the end of the race, then how can you presently be sure you will still be faithful when you draw your last breath on earth? And how holy must you be before you can know you are holy enough to be accepted by God into heaven?

To be sure, Hebrews contains strong warnings—perhaps the strongest in the New Testament—to the believer about the importance of enduring faith. But these warning passages pertain to the prospect of believers losing fellowship with God and their eternal reward, and facing temporal judgment or chastening from the Lord, not eternal condemnation in hell. Within the book of Hebrews, believers are not on a quest for personal assurance of eternal salvation. Instead, the book assumes its readers already possess assurance; and they just need to continue in that confidence and hope (3:6, 14; 6:11, 18-19; 10:22-23, 35). The message of Hebrews is equally clear that this assurance is not based on one's performance, but on the promises of God (6:16-18; 13:5-6), and the person (1:3-13; 6:18-19; 7:25) and finished work (1:3; 2:9, 17; 9:12-15, 25-28; 10:1-18; 13:20) of the "great Shepherd of the sheep" (13:20), Jesus Christ.

Chapter 13

Perseverance vs. Preservation in Peter's Epistles

Consistency is one of the chief characteristics of truth. When law enforcement officials investigate crimes, the evidence gathered must be consistent to justify an indictment. When a criminal case goes to trial, in order for an indictment to result in a conviction the testimonies of the prosecution's witnesses must not be contradictory. Similarly, in the realm of science, a hypothesis is confirmed only when the observable facts supporting it are consistent with one another. All truth requires consistency. Yet more than consistency is required for something to be spiritually true. After all, two propositions may agree with one another, but they may both be consistently wrong! As important as consistency is, consistency alone does not guarantee that a spiritual claim is true. The real test of spiritual truth is consistent agreement with the Bible.

Previous chapters have shown that the Lord Jesus, the apostle Paul, and the writer of Hebrews all teach consistently that God alone does the saving work of preserving, keeping, and securing the eternal salvation of sinners who place their faith solely in Christ. This chapter calls forth the apostle Peter as an additional witness and finds his testimony to be completely harmonious with that of Christ, Paul, and Hebrews concerning the fact that God requires perseverance for an eternal reward, not for eternal salvation.

The Testimony of Peter

In the opening chapters of Peter's epistles, he emphasizes perseverance in faith. Peter teaches that the outcome of perseverance in the faith will be a practically sanctified life now and an earned reward hereafter. But when 1 and 2 Peter is read through the lens of the Reformed doctrine of the perseverance of the saints, Peter is misinterpreted to be saying that persevering faith is necessary to escape hell and enter heaven. For example, when Peter instructs his readers to diligently persevere so as to "make [their] calling and election sure" and "never stumble" (2 Peter 1:10), many think Peter is telling his readers to assure themselves that they are one of God's elect by not falling fatally into unbelief and perishing in hell. In the next verse, Peter concludes that if believers are diligent to make their calling and election sure, then "an entrance will be supplied . . . abundantly into the everlasting kingdom of our Lord and Savior Jesus Christ" (v. 11). This verse is also commonly assumed to be requiring perseverance as the necessary proof of initial, saving faith so that a believer can be sure he will enter the kingdom and escape hell. Regarding these verses, popular Reformed author and teacher John MacArthur writes:

> The apostles saw counterfeit faith as a very real danger. Many of the epistles, though addressed to churches, contain warnings that reveal the apostles' concern over church members they suspected were not genuine believers. . . . Peter wrote, "Therefore, brethren, be all the more diligent to make certain about His calling and choosing you; for as long as you practice these things, you will never stumble" (2 Pet. 1:10).[1]

The same Calvinistic assumptions are often brought to the text of 1 Peter 1, where Peter speaks of being "kept by the power of God through faith for salvation ready to be revealed in the last time" (v. 5) and "receiving the end of your faith—the salvation of your souls" (v. 9). Since verses 5 and 9 both refer to "salvation" and "faith," it is assumed that Peter is requiring perseverance in faith in order to be sure of one's salvation from sin's penalty in hell. Peter is assumed to be teaching that the child of God is "kept by the power of God through faith for salvation [from the lake of fire] ready to be revealed in the last time" (v. 5) and that if you are a child of God you will receive "the end of your faith—the salvation of your souls [from eternal condemnation]" (v. 9). Is this really what Peter is teaching in 1 Peter 1? What kind of salvation are verses 5 and 9 referring to?

---

1. John F. MacArthur, Jr., *Faith Works: The Gospel According to the Apostles* (Dallas: Word, 1993), 141.

Faith for Present Trials & Future Glory (1 Peter 1:5, 9)

The meaning of "salvation" in 1 Peter 1:5 and 9 must be determined by Peter's own contextual use of this word and not by theological assumptions brought to these verses. It is essential to begin by considering the spiritual status of the readers of the epistle. Did Peter suspect that some of his readers had a false, spurious faith? Did he think they merely professed faith in Christ but did not possess a "true, working, persevering, saving faith"? Consider what the apostle Peter himself concluded about his readers.

- *They were elect or chosen by God.* "Peter, an apostle of Jesus Christ, to the pilgrims of the Dispersion in Pontus, Galatia, Cappadocia, Asia, and Bithynia, *elect* according to the foreknowledge of God the Father, in sanctification of the Spirit, for obedience and sprinkling of the blood of Jesus Christ: grace to you and peace be multiplied" (1:1-2). "But you are a *chosen* generation, a royal priesthood, a holy nation, *His own special people,* that you may proclaim the praises of Him who called you out of darkness into His marvelous light" (2:9).

- *They had believed the gospel.* "Though now you do not see Him, yet *believing,* you rejoice with joy inexpressible and full of glory" (1:8). *"Who through Him believe in God,* who raised Him from the dead and gave Him glory, so that *your faith* and hope are in God. . . . Now this is the word which by the gospel was preached to you" (1:21, 25). "Therefore it is also contained in the Scripture, 'Behold, I lay in Zion a chief cornerstone, elect, precious, and he who believes on Him will by no means be put to shame.' Therefore, to *you who believe,* He is precious; but to those who are disobedient, 'The stone which the builders rejected has become the chief cornerstone'" (2:6-7). Notice, Peter does not use the pronoun "you" when referring to those who are unbelievers, because he was not directly addressing them. His readers are described only as "you who believe," not "you who are disobedient."

- *They were already regenerated.* "Blessed be the God and Father of our Lord Jesus Christ, who according to His abundant mercy *has begotten us again* to a living hope through the resurrection of Jesus Christ from the dead" (1:3). "Since you have purified your souls in obeying the truth through the Spirit in sincere love of the brethren, love one another fervently with a pure heart, *having been born again,* not of corruptible seed but incorruptible, through the word of God which lives and abides forever" (1:22-23). "Like *newborn babies,* long for the pure milk of the word, so that by it you may *grow* in respect to salvation, if you have tasted the kindness of the Lord" (2:2-3, NASB). The clause "if you have tasted" does not reflect any doubt in Peter's mind that they had already tasted God's kindness. Grammatically, the "if" clause is a first-class conditional statement in Greek, which is the condition of assumed reality. The idea is "if, and you have tasted" (i.e., "since you have tasted").

- *They were redeemed by Christ's work on their behalf.* "Knowing that you were not *redeemed* with corruptible things, like silver or gold, from your aimless conduct received by tradition from your fathers, but *with the precious blood of Christ,* as of a lamb without blemish and without spot" (1:18-19).

- *They had a permanent, heavenly inheritance.* "Blessed be the God and Father of our Lord Jesus Christ, who according to His abundant mercy has begotten us again to a living hope through the resurrection of Jesus Christ from the dead, to *an inheritance incorruptible and undefiled and that does not fade away, reserved in heaven for you"* (1:3-4).

Chosen by God? Regenerated? Redeemed? Having a permanent, heavenly inheritance? Having already believed the gospel? Does this sound like Peter was questioning his readers' salvation? Not at all! If we take Peter's own description of his readers at face value, there is no way we can conclude that their status as truly regenerated people still had to be proven by perseverance to the end of their lives in faith and holiness. But if Peter was not requiring his readers to persevere either to maintain their eternal salvation or to prove the reality of it, then what was he teaching about salvation in 1 Peter 1?

One possible interpretation of 1 Peter 1:5 is that it is promising eternal security. This verse describes children of God as those "who are kept by the power of God through faith for salvation ready to be revealed in the last time." This verse may be describing believers being kept eternally secure from the threat of future condemnation in hell, solely by God's power, once the condition of *initial* faith is met. This interpretation sees the instrumental, human condition ("through faith") as something instantaneously fulfilled, not a continual, ongoing requirement in the life of the believer. In addition, this view holds that the "salvation ready to be revealed in the last time" refers strictly to third-tense salvation by grace when the child of God is delivered from the very presence of sin and receives a new, glorified, resurrected body when Christ appears. This interpretation correctly views verse 5 as a hinge statement between the past, settled, salvation blessings of verses 2-4 (election, regeneration, permanent inheritance) and the present-to-future salvation of verses 6-10.

While this interpretation is doctrinally true and harmonizes well with the Bible's teaching elsewhere on the eternal security of every child of God, it also requires the conclusion that verse 5 refers to momentary, initial faith in contrast to the clear continual, persevering faith of verses 7-9. Both verse 5 and verse 9 refer to salvation through faith, but verse 7 speaks of faith being "tested by fire" and verse 9 says, "receiving the *end* of your faith—the salvation of your souls." Verse 9 does not say "receiving the *beginning* of your faith—the salvation of your souls." This raises a legitimate question—did Peter really intend for the faith of verse 5 to be interpreted as momentary faith, in distinction to the persevering faith of verses 7-9?

There is no evidence in the passage of a transition from one kind of faith in verse 5 to a different kind of faith in verses 7-9. Instead, verses 5 and 7 appear to be linked thematically by the references to Christ's coming. Verse 5 refers to salvation through faith "ready to be *revealed* in the last time" while verse 7 refers to the reward for enduring faith bestowed "at the *revelation* of Jesus Christ." This shows that these verses likely form a conceptual unit that is not addressing first-tense salvation but present and future salvation through ongoing faith. Thus, the salvation of verses 5-10 does not refer to eternal salvation from hell but to *present, practical sanctification, resulting in a greater degree of future glorification and eternal reward.* This present-to-future salvation is supported by several observations.

Present-to-Future Salvation

First, after mentioning "salvation" in 1 Peter 1:5, 9-10, Peter uses the term again in 2:2. The type of salvation Peter had in mind for his readers in chapter 1 is most likely the same type of salvation he mentions at the beginning of chapter 2, where he exhorts them: "So put away all malice and all deceit and hypocrisy and envy and all slander. Like newborn infants, long for the pure spiritual milk, that by it you may grow up into salvation [*eis sōtērian*]" (2:1-2, ESV).[2] In 1 Peter 2:2, the prepositional phrase "into salvation" (*eis sōtērian*) parallels Peter's earlier statement in 1:5 about being "kept by the power of God through faith for salvation [*eis sōtērian*]." The statement in 2:2 that we "may grow up [*auxēthēte*] into salvation [*eis sōtērian*]" does not reflect any doubt in Peter's mind that his readers are elect or regenerate, for he has already declared them to be chosen and born again (1:2-3). Instead, the phrase "may grow up into salvation" means that Peter desired his readers to grow spiritually and be saved from a wasted life of sin. His readers' first-tense salvation from the penalty of sin was already certain and complete; and their third-tense deliverance one day from the very presence of sin was also certain and guaranteed. But what was not certain or guaranteed was whether they would persevere in a walk of faith and practical holiness to be saved from the damaging effects of sin in their lives and receive a glorious, future reward from the Lord.

This sense of "salvation" is confirmed later in 4:1-4, where Peter uses a negated form of the word for "salvation" (*sōtēria*) in a manner similar to its use in 2:2.

> 1 Therefore, since Christ suffered for us in the flesh, arm yourselves also with the same mind, for he who has suffered in the flesh has ceased from sin, 2 that he no longer should live the rest of his time in the flesh for the lusts of men, but for the will of God. 3 For we have spent enough of our past lifetime in doing the will of the Gentiles—when we walked in lewdness, lusts, drunkenness, revelries, drinking parties, and abominable idolatries. 4 In regard to these, they think it strange that you do not run with them in the same flood of dissipation (*asōtia*), speaking evil of you.

---

2. Although the Greek Textus Receptus and Majority Text omit *eis sōtērian*, this phrase is contained in all modern critical editions of the Greek New Testament for good reason. The words *eis sōtērian* are found in virtually all known extant Greek manuscripts from the first millennium of church history, as well as the manuscripts of all three primary language versions (Latin, Coptic, and Syriac). Conversely, manuscripts that omit this phrase come almost entirely from the second millennium, are more recent, and therefore are not as reliable as witnesses to the original text of 1 Peter 2:2.

The word *asōtia* is formed from the Greek letter alpha ("*a*") pre-fixed to the root for "salvation" (*sōt-*), resulting in a word that means the opposite of salvation. Besides 1 Peter 4:4, *asōtia* occurs only two other times in the New Testament, and in each case, it refers to an earthly life that is wasted by sin. Titus 1:6 says that a pastor must be "blameless, the husband of one wife, having faithful children not accused of dissipation [*asōtia*] or insubordination." Likewise, Paul commands the Ephesians: "And do not be drunk with wine, in which is dissipation [*asōtia*]; but be filled with the Spirit" (Eph. 5:18). The word *asōtia* is used in all three of its New Testament occurrences to warn against dissipating or wasting one's life—losing versus saving one's life. For the believer to have a life that is *asōtia* means his life is misspent, squandered, or dissipated like smoke particles that vanish into the air. To be saved in this sense—from a wasted life—not only fits with the reference to "growing up into salvation" in 1 Peter 2:2 but also with "the salvation of your souls" in 1 Peter 1:9.

A second reason "salvation" in 1:5 and 1:9-10 most likely refers to present, practical sanctification resulting in a greater degree of eternal reward and glory is because of the concept of the salvation of the soul. Throughout Peter's letter he refers to the souls of his readers (1:22; 2:11, 25; 3:20; 4:19). In 1:22 and 2:25, Peter says that the "souls" of his readers were already saved in the past (i.e., eternally and judicially); but in two other passages he expresses his concern for the current and future welfare of their Christian lives or "souls." In 2:11, the apostle pleads with his elect readers: "Beloved, I beg you as sojourners and pilgrims, abstain from fleshly lusts which war against the soul." Then he concludes in 4:19: "Therefore let those who suffer according to the will of God commit their souls to Him in doing good, as to a faithful Creator." These references to the "soul" are fitting with earlier conclusions in the previous chapter about the meaning of "the saving of the soul" (Heb. 10:39). (See also James 1:20; 5:20.) The concept of the saving of the soul in Hebrews deals with the deliverance of one's life from destruction by continuing to run the race of the Christian life with perseverance. The child of God will have nothing in eternity to show for the moments he lived for self and sin—those moments when he sought to do his own will and preserve his own life rather than living the Christ-honoring life to which he was called. All such opportunities to serve the Lord will go unrewarded at the judgment seat of Christ and be lost forever!

Peter understood this principle very well. It was deeply personal for him. One particular event in his life left an indelible impression on him. In Matthew 16, after attempting to correct the Lord Jesus about the Father's will for His life, the Lord turned to Peter and said to him, "Get behind Me, Satan! You are an offense to Me, for you are not mindful of the things of God, but the things of men" (Matt. 16:23). This was the only time in Peter's life when the Lord rebuked him so strongly. When Jesus finished correcting Peter, He then used Peter's abject failure as a lesson to teach all of the disciples, saying,

> If anyone desires to come after Me, let him deny himself, and take up his cross, and follow Me. For whoever desires to save his life will lose it, but whoever loses his life for My sake will find it. For what profit is it to a man if he gains the whole world, and loses his own soul? Or what will a man give in exchange for his soul? For the Son of Man will come in the glory of His Father with His angels, and then He will reward each according to his works. (Matt. 16:24-27)

Evangelists often apply these verses toward those who are unregenerate; but in their original context, Christ spoke these words directly to the regenerate disciples as a warning to them to let their lives count eternally for the Lord, for to do so would constitute the saving of their souls or earthly lives. Only a life presently lived in the will of God will result in an eternal reward. A life lived for self-gratification will be a wasted or lost life, as believers often remind one another: "One life will soon be past and only what's done for Christ will last." Peter never forgot this valuable and humbling lesson about the saving of the soul, which explains why he taught it to others in his first epistle, where he emphasizes the "soul" (1:9, 22; 2:11, 25; 3:20; 4:19) and the importance of doing the "will of God" (2:15; 3:17; 4:2, 19), especially being willing to suffer for the Lord (1:6; 2:21; 3:14, 17; 4:1-2, 13, 16, 19; 5:9-10), just as Jesus told Peter He must do to fulfill the Father's will (Matt. 16:21-22; 1 Peter 1:11; 2:4, 21-24; 3:18; 4:1, 13; 5:1).

A third evidence that "salvation" in 1 Peter 1:5-10 refers to a practically "saved" life that is rewarded at future glorification is the fact that the immediate context of these verses deals with future reward, not deliverance from future condemnation or consignment to the lake of fire. After referring in verse 5 to the "salvation ready to be revealed in the last time," Peter goes on to say in verses 6-7, "In this you greatly rejoice, though now for a little while, if need be, you have been grieved by various trials, that the genuineness of your faith, being much more precious than gold that perishes, though it is tested by fire, may be found to praise, honor, and glory at the revelation of Jesus Christ" (1:6-7). Elsewhere the New Testament teaches that the time when Jesus Christ is revealed at His coming is also the time when the saints will be rewarded (1 Cor. 3:13; 4:5; Phil. 2:16; 1 Thess. 2:19; 2 Tim. 4:8; 1 Peter 5:4; Rev. 3:11; 22:12).

Some think that the "praise, honor, and glory" of 1 Peter 1:7 is not a reward from God to the believer but a description of what the believer gives God in that day. While there is no doubt that believers will praise, honor, and glorify the Lord in that day, the mention in verses 6-7 of believers' trials, refinement as gold, and Christ's coming suggests that "praise, honor, and glory" is a reward from God to believers for persevering in faith through their trials. We often think of rewards only in the form of crowns, but the Bible frequently describes the believer's reward that will come from the Lord in the same manner as 1 Peter 1:7—as praise (Matt. 25:21, 23; 1 Cor. 4:5), honor (John 12:26), and glory (Matt. 13:43; Rom. 8:18; 2 Cor. 4:17; 1 Peter 5:4). But if future glory is, at least in part, considered to be a reward, then how do rewards relate to the third tense of salvation called theologically "glorification"?

At third-tense salvation, believers will be resurrected and glorified based solely on God's grace. Peter speaks of this future *grace*, commanding his readers: "Gird up the loins of your mind, be sober, and rest your hope fully upon the grace that is to be brought to you at the revelation of Jesus Christ" (1 Peter 1:13). But a few verses later, Peter also mentions *good works*, which will be rewarded at the judgment seat of Christ. He reminds believers to "conduct the time of your stay here in fear" because God "judges according to each one's work" (1:17). Peter also associates rewards with glory. He refers to the crown given to faithful pastors at Christ's coming as the "crown of glory": "when the Chief Shepherd appears, you will receive the crown of glory that does not fade away" (1 Peter 5:4). In the same epistle, Peter clearly taught two aspects of glorification—a grace aspect and a works aspect—that on the one hand glorification will be based on God's grace, yet on the other hand glorification will also involve an element of reward for the works of worthy believers.

The fact that every believer will be resurrected and saved from the presence of sin is sheer grace. But the extent of additional glory that each believer receives in that day will reflect the extent to which each person sought to glorify the Lord during his or her Christian life on earth. This explains why the Bible teaches that there will be degrees of reward (Ruth 2:12; 2 John 8), and thus degrees of glory, based on the relative faithfulness of each believer's earthly walk with the Lord (Matt. 25:21, 23; Luke 19:17, 19; Rev. 3:4-5). In this sense, glorification or third-tense salvation is related to practical sanctification or second-tense salvation.

Regarding glory, Daniel 12:2-3 describes the believer's glorification at the resurrection in terms of radiance: "And many of those who sleep in the dust of the earth shall awake, some to everlasting life, some to shame and everlasting contempt. Those who are wise shall shine like the brightness of the firmament, and those who turn many to righteousness like the stars forever and ever." Though all believers will shine for the Lord in the sense that we will reflect His glory back to Him, not all will shine equally. Some, perhaps, will be like a 25-watt bulb, while others will be more like a 200-watt floodlight. But together all will contribute to the supreme goal of history, namely, glorifying God (1 Cor. 10:31). Since there will be degrees of reward, and rewards will be used to glorify the Lord (Rev. 4:10), there will be a correlation between each believer's faithfulness on earth and his or her capacity to glorify God in eternity. This connection between the believer's faithfulness and his or her God-given glory is also found in 1 Peter 1:6-7, where believers who faithfully persevere through difficult trials (v. 6) receive "praise, honor, and glory at the revelation of Jesus Christ" (v. 7).

There is a fourth reason "salvation" in 1:5 and 1:9-10 most likely refers to present, practical sanctification that will result in a greater degree of eternal glory and reward. First Peter 1:9 says, "receiving [komizō] the end of your faith—the salvation of your souls." The Greek word for "receiving" (komizō) occurs only 10 times in the New Testament, and over half the time it is used for the receiving of a reward (2 Cor. 5:10; Eph. 6:8; Col. 3:25; Heb. 10:35-36). Peter uses this term twice, with 1 Peter 5:4 being an unmistakable reference to a reward since it speaks of receiving "the crown of glory that does not fade away." These clear New Testament uses of komizō in reward contexts do not necessarily prove that the "salvation" of 1 Peter 1:5, 9-10 is a greater degree of glorification and kingdom entrance as a reward for sanctification. But the usage of komizō in 1 Peter 5:4 and the rest of the New Testament is certainly consistent with this view of "salvation." This broader sense of present-to-future salvation also agrees with Peter's teaching in 2 Peter 1:5-11 on *abundant* kingdom entrance, not merely kingdom entrance, as explained in the next section.

Putting all of these exegetical observations together clarifies Peter's point in 1 Peter 1:5-9. When Peter writes in verse 5, "who are kept by the power of God through faith for salvation ready to be revealed in the last time," he is not saying that perseverance in faith is required for God to save a person from eternal condemnation. Rather, verse 5 is simply saying that God empowers and guards His children, as they walk by faith, from a life wasted by sin that will not result in greater future glory when Christ appears.

The word "kept" in verse 5 is *phroureō*. It occurs only four times in the New Testament (2 Cor. 11:32; Gal. 3:23; Phil. 4:7; 1 Peter 1:5) and is not the word that occurs elsewhere (*tēreō*) for the believer's eternal security and preservation in Christ (John 17:11-12, 15; 1 Thess. 5:23; Jude 1), even by Peter (1 Peter 1:4). In two occurrences, *phroureō* is used literally (2 Cor. 11:32) and figuratively (Gal. 3:23) of someone being guarded in a prison. This term is also used in Philippians 4:7 of God's peace guarding the hearts and minds of believers who pray with thanksgiving. "Be anxious for nothing, but in everything by prayer and supplication, with thanksgiving, let your requests be made known to God; and the peace of God, which surpasses all understanding, will guard [*phroureō*] your hearts and minds through Christ Jesus" (Phil. 4:6-7). Only as the child of God casts his anxieties upon the Lord in faith, and prays with thanksgiving and supplication, will he experience God's continual guarding of his heart and mind with divine peace. In a similar manner in 1 Peter 1:5, Peter explains that the believer is kept or guarded (*phroureō*) "through faith" from a wasted life of sin to a sanctified life that leads to a glorious, future reward. The ongoing exercise of faith is essential in this process, as shown by the context of verses 7-9.

In verse 7, Peter explains that trials are used by God for the purpose of testing the faith of His elect—not to prove that they are truly elect or regenerated but to refine the faith of God's child and ultimately reward him. Verse 7 declares: "that the genuineness [*dokimion*] of your faith, being much more precious than gold that perishes, though it is tested [*dokimazō*] by fire, may be found to praise, honor, and glory at the revelation of Jesus Christ." The words "genuineness" (*dokimion*) and "tested" (*dokimazō*) are related to one another and carry the idea of putting something to the test for the purpose of approval.[3] This word group was used by Paul in 1 Corinthians 3:13

---

3. Walter Bauer, William F. Arndt, and F. Wilbur Gingrich, *A Greek-English Lexicon of the New Testament and Other Early Christian Literature*, 3rd ed., rev. and ed. Frederick W. Danker (Chicago: University of Chicago Press, 2000), 255.

to speak of the believer's works being "tested" (*dokimazō*) at the judgment seat of Christ to see if they are like "gold, silver, and precious stones" (1 Cor. 3:12) so as to reward the believer. Later in 1 Corinthians, Paul speaks of a reward in the form of an "imperishable crown" (9:25), which he could gain by persevering in the race so as not to be disapproved (9:27, *adokimos*). Just as Paul uses the terms and concepts of approval and testing through fire in contexts clearly dealing with rewards, Peter does the same in 1 Peter 1.

All of these exegetical observations lead to one conclusion. Peter is *not* teaching in 1 Peter 1:5-9 that perseverance in faith is necessary to escape the final judgment of eternal separation from God in hell, as both Arminianism and Calvinism have historically understood this passage. Instead, Peter is teaching that endurance in faith will result in a "saved" life that will be richly rewarded by God when Christ appears to establish His eternal kingdom.

Adding Perseverance to Faith (2 Peter 1:5-11)

Second Peter 1 is another pivotal chapter of Scripture dealing with perseverance. On the one hand, this chapter shows that genuine believers in Christ do not necessarily persevere (vv. 5-6, 8-9). On the other hand, this chapter also shows that perseverance is both commanded and possible (v. 10) and leads to an eternal reward (v. 11).

As with 1 Peter, this epistle begins with the writer acknowledging the genuine faith of his readers. Peter writes in verse 1, "Simon Peter, a bondservant and apostle of Jesus Christ, to those who have obtained [*lachousin*] like precious faith with us by the righteousness of our God and Savior Jesus Christ." The participle *lachousin* ("have obtained") comes from the verb *lagchanō* and is in the active voice, meaning that Peter's readers exercised their volitions when they placed their trust in Christ to be born again. In verses 3-4, these believers are told that God's power has made available to them all things that pertain to life and godliness (v. 3), so that they may be partakers of the divine nature, or have fellowship with God, by sharing in His moral attributes rather than the corrupt character of the world (v. 4). Verses 1-4 form the basis for the command of verses 5-7, where believers are exhorted to add seven positive spiritual characteristics to faith.

> 5 But also for this very reason, giving all diligence, add to your faith virtue, to virtue knowledge, 6 to knowledge self-

control, to self-control perseverance, to perseverance godliness, 7 to godliness brotherly kindness, and to brotherly
kindness love.

Verses 5-7 pose a serious problem for the Calvinist doctrine of
the perseverance of the saints since they show that genuine believers do not necessarily persevere but must still *add perseverance* to
their faith. The Calvinist view of faith and perseverance is summed
up by D. A. Carson, who claims, "In other words, genuine faith, by
definition, perseveres; where there is no perseverance, by definition
the faith cannot be genuine."[4] But if genuine, saving faith by definition includes perseverance, then why does Peter command that it
be added to one's faith? Faith should just continue as it is. Calvinists often claim that "true, saving faith" always perseveres in holiness and good works because God sovereignly and deterministically
causes perseverance in the lives of His elect. But in 2 Peter 1:5, the
word "add" (*epichorēgēsate*) is an aorist-tense, active-voice, imperative-mood verb. The active voice and imperative mood show that
those with true faith must still choose to add perseverance to their
faith. In addition, believers must choose to add to their faith the other
six positive traits mentioned in verses 5-7, which do not always, necessarily characterize the lives of every believer.

Being Neither Barren Nor Unfruitful

Verses 8-9 are a contrast to verses 5-7. Verses 8-9 describe a negative spiritual condition that is the opposite of the seven positive traits
spelled out in verses 5-7.

8 For if these things are yours and abound, you will be neither barren nor unfruitful in the knowledge of our Lord Jesus
Christ. 9 For he who lacks these things is shortsighted, even
to blindness, and has forgotten that he was cleansed from his
old sins.

Verses 8-9 prove that it is possible to be a genuine believer and
still be barren and unfruitful. In verse 9, the one who "was cleansed
from his old sins" must be a believer since only believers have had
their sins forgiven. The believer described in verses 8b-9 does not

---

4. D. A. Carson, "Reflections on Christian Assurance," *Westminster Theological
Journal* 54 (Spring 1992): 17.

have the positive traits of verses 5-7. Verse 8 uses a conditional (i.e., "circumstantial") participle in Greek[5] to form a conditional statement: "if these things are yours" (*tauta hymin hyparchonta*). Notice, Peter does not say "these things *are* yours" or "these things *will be* yours." Clearly, the seven positive characteristics of verses 5-7 must be added to the believer's faith because they are not inevitable in every believer's life. This also explains why Peter uses another conditional participle in verse 10,[6] saying, "if you do [*poiountes*] these things you will never stumble." Three times in three verses, Peter uses the expression "these things" (*tauta*) in reference to the seven positive traits of verses 5-7 that are added to faith, and in each case he does not assume that these traits are necessarily true of his readers, who are genuine saints.

- For if these things are yours and abound (v. 8)

- For he who lacks these things is shortsighted (v. 9)

- For if you do these things you will never stumble (v. 10)

According to the Calvinist and Lordship Salvation doctrine of the perseverance of the saints, it is not possible for a genuine believer to be barren and unfruitful and lack the traits of verses 5-7. The believer will supposedly have at least *some* visible fruit in his or her life. Regarding the seven positive spiritual traits that must be added to one's faith, Reformed commentator Thomas Schreiner claims: "it should be noted that progress in all these moral virtues is necessary for one's heavenly inheritance, and hence progress in knowledge is necessary, ultimately, for eternal life."[7] But how can progress in these things be necessary for heaven when verses 8-9 show that it is possible for a genuine believer to lack these things and be barren, unfruitful, and myopic? Peter does not say that "he who lacks these things" lacks regeneration, eternal life, or anything approximating eternal salvation. Nor does he say, "For if you do these things you will never perish eternally." Interpreting these verses through the lens of Calvinism's lifelong test of regeneration and confirmation of one's elect status completely misses Peter's

---

5. A. T. Robertson, *Word Pictures in the New Testament*, Vol. VI (Grand Rapids: Baker, n.d.), 151.

6. Ibid., 153.

7. Thomas R. Schreiner, *1, 2 Peter, Jude* (Nashville: Broadman & Holman, 2003), 299-300.

point that a godly life is *possible* and *commanded* for all believers through God's abundant promises and provisions (vv. 3-4), but it is not *certain* for all believers.

Making Your Call and Election Sure

> 10 Therefore, brethren, be even more diligent to make your call and election sure, for if you do these things you will never stumble; 11 for so an entrance will be supplied to you abundantly into the everlasting kingdom of our Lord and Savior Jesus Christ.

Verses 10-11 have also been greatly misunderstood when the template of Calvinism is pressed upon them. These verses are often distorted to teach that believers must prove they are elect and personally assure themselves they will enter the kingdom by persevering in the traits of verses 5-7 rather than fatally stumbling through apostasy and unbelief. For example, notice how two leading Calvinists, MacArthur and Schreiner, interpret verses 10-11 as a prescription for personal assurance of entering heaven:

> Can Christians rest in the firm and settled confidence that they are redeemed and bound for eternal heaven? Scripture categorically answers yes. Not only does the Bible teach that assurance is possible for Christians in this life, but the apostle Peter also gave this command: "[Be] diligent to make certain about His calling and choosing you" (2 Pet. 1:10).[8]

> Those who live ungodly lives show no evidence that they truly belong to God, that they have genuinely received forgiveness. Hence, Peter exhorted his readers to exercise diligence . . . to confirm their calling and election. . . . Believers who confirm their call and election by living in a godly manner will not "stumble," that is, they will not forsake God, abandon him, and commit apostasy. . . . Peter was not concerned here about rewards but whether people will *enter* the kingdom at all.[9]

---

8. MacArthur, *Faith Works*, 157.

9. Thomas R. Schreiner, *1, 2 Peter, Jude* (Nashville: Broadman & Holman, 2003), 304-06.

Is 2 Peter 1:10-11 really commanding believers to diligently assure themselves that they will enter heaven by adding the positive traits of verses 5-7 to their faith? In the context of verses 10-11, Peter himself expresses no doubts about his readers' eternal salvation; nor is there any evidence that his readers were lacking personal assurance of their own salvation. What is driving the personal-assurance-of-eternal-life interpretation is neither the context nor the actual content of verses 10-11 but a theological system imposed on the text. So, if verses 10-11 are not a prescription for the personal assurance of entering heaven, then what are they teaching? These verses are instructing believers to become firm, steadfast, or established in the godly traits of verses 5-7, to which they were called and chosen by God, with the result that they will not stumble in their Christian lives but will receive an abundant reward at the time when they enter Christ's kingdom. There are several evidences to support this interpretation.

First, the words "call and election" in verse 10 are often wrongly assumed to mean only God's call and election of believers for deliverance from hell to heaven. But the concepts of calling and election are not so limited in their meaning either in Peter's epistles or the rest of Scripture. Peter develops the idea of calling and election more in his first epistle than he does in his second. He says in 1 Peter 1:15, "as He who called you is holy, you also be holy in all your conduct." While this verse does not state specifically what believers are called to, a holy life appears to be associated with calling. Next, 1 Peter 2:9 includes both concepts of calling and choosing: "But you are a chosen generation, a royal priesthood, a holy nation, His own special people, that you may proclaim the praises [*aretas*] of Him who called you out of darkness into His marvelous light." Here Peter states that another purpose for God calling believers is that they may proclaim His praises, or perhaps more literally, His virtues (*aretē* is translated "virtue" in 2 Peter 1:3, 5). In addition, believers are called to suffer for Christ's sake: "For what credit is it if, when you are beaten for your faults, you take it patiently? But when you do good and suffer, if you take it patiently, this is commendable before God. For to this you were called, because Christ also suffered for us, leaving us an example, that you should follow His steps" (2:20-21). Believers are also called to bring blessing to others: "be of one mind, having compassion for one another; love as brothers, be tenderhearted, be courteous; not returning evil for evil or reviling for reviling, but on the contrary blessing, knowing that you were called to this, that you may inherit a blessing" (3:8-9). Not only are believers called to be a blessing to others, but God's purpose is for believers to inherit blessing from Him in the process, which certainly fits with believers receiving a reward at the end of life for their faithfulness.

Furthermore, 2 Peter 1:3 refers to God's calling of believers, saying, "as His divine power has given to us all things that pertain to life and godliness, through the knowledge of Him who called us by glory and virtue." The phrase "by glory and virtue" contains two dative nouns, which could also be translated "to glory and virtue." Believers are not only called *by* God's own glory and virtue but also *to* His glory and virtue. A major emphasis of Peter's teaching on God's calling and election is that believers are called and chosen to reflect the character traits and actions of God the Father and the Lord Jesus Christ. The highest calling in life is to be like the Lord of glory. This higher purpose of calling and election corresponds well with biblical teaching outside of Peter's epistles, where believers are also said to be called and chosen to fruitful discipleship (John 15:15-16), to fellowship with God's Son (1 Cor. 1:9), to peace with one another (1 Cor. 7:15), and to liberty (Gal. 5:13). The concepts of calling and election in Scripture go well beyond simply being called and chosen for deliverance from hell.

As this pertains to one's "call and election" in 2 Peter 1:10, the context of 2 Peter 1 shows that believers have been called by God in their Christian lives to reflect His own glory and virtue (v. 3), and this can be done by adding several godly attributes and traits to their faith (vv. 5-7). If believers will diligently pursue being like God, then they will become well grounded and steadfast in their calling and election and avoid stumbling in their Christian lives (v. 10).

This also leads to the question of what Peter meant in 2 Peter 1:10 by "sure"—"be diligent to make your call and election sure [*bebaian*]." Many assume that the word *bebaian* ("sure") here refers to personal certainty or assurance that one has been effectually called and chosen to eternal salvation from hell. But instead of referring to personal certainty of one's elect status, *bebaios* in its various forms, depending on the context, may also mean "steadfast," "established," or "well grounded" (2 Cor. 1:7, 21; Col. 2:7; Heb. 2:2; 3:14; 13:9). One standard lexicon says this word can mean "firm, steady . . . steadfast, durable" and when used "of persons . . . steadfast, constant . . . more certain to make no change."[10] One theological lexicon concludes, "In

---

10. H. G. Liddell and R. Scott, *A Greek-English Lexicon*, rev. and augmented by H. S. Jones and R. McKenzie, with a Revised Supplement by P. G. W. Glare and A. A. Thompson (New York: Oxford University Press, 1996), 312.

general, *bebaios* maintains its original character in the NT, i.e., that a thing is firm in the sense of being solidly grounded."[11] *Bebaios* and its various forms also has this meaning in several places outside of the New Testament. For example, notice how this term is used throughout the Septuagint (Greek Old Testament) and Apocrypha.

> Aman, who excels in soundness of judgment among us, and has been manifestly well inclined without wavering and with **unshaken** fidelity [*bebaia pistei*], and has obtained the second post in the kingdom . . . (Esther 3:13)

> As for me, You uphold me in my integrity, and **set** [*bebaioō*] me before Your face forever. (Ps. 41:12)

> My soul melts from heaviness; **strengthen** [*bebaioō*] me according to Your word. (Ps. 119:28)

> Love means the keeping of her laws; to observe her laws is the **basis** [*bebaiōsis*] for incorruptibility. (Wisdom 6:18)

> For wisdom, which is the worker of all things, taught me. For in her is a spirit intelligent, holy, unique, manifold, subtle, agile, clear, undefiled, certain, not subject to hurt, loving what is good, quick, kind towards men, **firm** [*bebaion*], sure [*asphales*], tranquil, all-powerful, all-seeing . . . (Wisdom 7:23)

> . . . and taking into consideration their **constancy** [*bebaian*] and good will towards us and towards our ancestors, we have, as we ought, acquitted them of every sort of charge. (III Maccabees 7:7)

The word *bebaios* also has this meaning when used in early Christian writings from the Koine Period shortly after the completion of the New Testament. Notice how *bebaios* and its forms are used in the Apostolic Fathers.

> For has anyone ever visited you [the church at Corinth] who did not approve your most excellent and **steadfast** [*bebaian*] faith? (*1 Clement* 1:2)

---

11. Heinrich Schlier, "*bebaios, bebaioō, bebaiōsis,*" in *Theological Dictionary of the New Testament*, ed. Gerhard Kittel and Gerhard Friedrich, trans. and ed. Geoffrey W. Bromiley, vol. 1 (Grand Rapids: Eerdmans, 1964), 601.

It is disgraceful, dear friends, yes, utterly disgraceful and unworthy of your conduct in Christ, that it should be reported that the **well-established** [*bebaiotatēn*] and ancient church of the Corinthians, because of one or two persons, is rebelling against its presbyters. (*1 Clement* 47:6)

Be diligent, therefore, to be **firmly grounded** [*bebaiōthēnai*] in the precepts of the Lord and the apostles, in order that "in whatever you do, you may prosper." (*Ignatius to the Magnesians* 13:1)

When *bebaios* is interpreted as "steadfast" or "established" in 2 Peter 1:10, it becomes clear that Peter is not telling believers to personally assure themselves or make certain that they are truly saved from hell by persevering in faith and holiness to the end of their lives. Instead, he is simply telling believers that if they will diligently add to their faith the Christ-like traits of verses 5-7, they will become steadfast, established, and well-grounded in the Christ-likeness for which they were called and chosen.

This meaning of *bebaios* harmonizes well with Peter's conclusions to his two epistles. In 1 Peter 5:9-10, he writes, "Resist him [Satan], steadfast [*stereo*] in the faith, knowing that the same sufferings are experienced by your brotherhood in the world. But may the God of all grace, who called us to His eternal glory by Christ Jesus, after you have suffered a while, perfect, establish [*stērizei*], strengthen, and settle you." Likewise, in 2 Peter 3:17-18, Peter concludes, "You therefore, beloved, since you know this beforehand, beware lest you also fall from your own steadfastness [*stērigmou*], being led away with the error of the wicked; but grow in the grace and knowledge of our Lord and Savior Jesus Christ. To Him be the glory both now and forever. Amen." Although the two word groups for *stērizō* and *bebaioō* are not the same, they are semantically parallel, as one theological lexicon concludes, "Yet the two words are interchangeable, as may be seen from a comparison of 2 Th. 2:17 with Hb. 13:9."[12] This interchangeability of terms shows that, just as Paul so frequently exhorts believers to be established in their faith and good works (Rom. 16:25; Col. 2:7; 1 Thess. 3:2, 13; 2 Thess. 2:17; 3:3), Peter does likewise at the beginning and ending of his two epistles. By warning believers about the steadfastness of their Christian lives in 2 Peter 3:17, Peter is returning to the theme of 2 Peter 1:10 about making their calling

---

12. Ibid.

and election steadfast, established, and firmly grounded.[13] As long as believers are diligent to do this, they will not stumble or fall into the error of the wicked but will receive a rich reward from the Lord one day at the beginning of His kingdom.

An Abundant Kingdom Entrance

If believers will faithfully fulfill the conditions stipulated in 2 Peter 1:5-7 and 10, the Lord promises to provide them with an abundant entrance in Christ's kingdom. "For so an entrance will be supplied to you abundantly into the everlasting kingdom of our Lord and Savior Jesus Christ" (2 Peter 1:11). Scripture is clear that only believers in Christ—those who are born again (John 3:3-5)—will enter the coming kingdom (Matt. 5:20; 7:21; 18:3; 19:23-25; 21:31-32; Mark 10:23-27; Rev. 21:27). But not all believers will enter it "abundantly" (*plousiōs*) or richly (2 Peter 1:11). Calvinists often assume that Peter is speaking here merely of *entering* the kingdom, rather than entering it *abundantly*. For example, Schreiner dogmatically asserts, "Peter was not concerned here about rewards but whether people will *enter* the kingdom at all."[14] Schreiner's conclusion completely disregards the use of the word "abundantly" (*plousiōs*) in verse 11. The emphasis of verse 11 is on a rich or abundant entrance into the kingdom, not merely an entrance. Two observations from the verse support this conclusion.

First, the word for "abundantly" (*plousiōs*) is emphasized in the order of the Greek sentence since it comes first in the sentence after the conjunction "for" (*gar*) and adverb "so" (*houtōs*):

> *houtōs gar* **plousiōs** *epichorēgēthēsetai hymin hē eisodos eis tēn aiōnion basileian tou kyriou hēmōn kai sōtēros Iēsou Christou.*

English Bibles sometimes put the adverb "abundantly" towards the middle of the sentence, obscuring Peter's emphasis on an *abundant* kingdom entrance.

> for so an entrance will be supplied to you *abundantly* into the everlasting kingdom of our Lord and Savior, Jesus Christ. (NKJV)

---

13. Robert L. Deffinbaugh, "A Secured Faith that Keeps the Saints from Stumbling (2 Peter 1:8-11)," https://bible.org/seriespage/4-secured-faith-keeps-saints-stumbling-2-peter-18-11 (accessed 31 May 2016).

14. Schreiner, *1, 2 Peter, Jude*, 306.

for in this way the entrance into the eternal kingdom of our Lord and Savior Jesus Christ will be *abundantly* supplied to you. (NASB)

However, if we were to provide an English rendering that corresponds more strictly to the Greek word order, the emphasis of the verse on the faithful believer's rich or abundant entrance would become apparent.

for so *abundantly* it will be supplied to you the entrance into the eternal kingdom of our Lord and Savior, Jesus Christ.

In addition, there is a word association in the Greek text of 2 Peter 1 between verses 5 and 11 that is not readily apparent in English Bibles. This word association underscores Peter's emphasis on a *rich* entrance into the kingdom, not merely an *entrance*. According to 2 Peter 1:5, believers who "add" (*epichorēgēsate*) or supply in their faith the positive character traits listed in verses 5-7 will also be "supplied" (*epichorēgēthēsetai*) abundantly by God an entrance into His eternal kingdom (v. 11). The repetition of the verb *epichorēgeō* connects the command of verse 5 to "add" with the promise of verse 11 about an "abundant" entrance. While faith alone results in entering Christ's kingdom, adding to one's faith the Christ-like qualities of verses 5-7 will result in an entrance coupled with great reward.

There simply is no exegetical evidence to support the view that 2 Peter 1:5-11 is a passage about persevering in faith and godliness to prove that one is saved from hell. Instead, the evidence indicates that it is a passage about genuine believers living a Christ-like life that fulfills the purpose for which God called and chose each believer, resulting in a rich future reward from the Lord.

Conclusion

If you are a professing believer in the Lord Jesus Christ, these passages from Peter's epistles should cause you to reflect and ask yourself, "Have I been basing my expectation of kingdom entrance on my perseverance? On my changed life? Do I think that I *will* never fall into unbelief but others might?" If this is how you think, then your faith has been gravely and presumptuously misplaced in the wrong object—yourself! Now, you must transfer your trust from yourself and your good works to the Lord Jesus Christ alone—the only One who faithfully and sufficiently perseveres in keeping saved all who have been born again.

If you have based your assurance of everlasting life solely upon Christ as the only One who can guarantee you eternal life, then you must also realize that God never meant your faith to be temporary so that you would merely be justified in His sight. He desires so much more for you! He has a life of abundant fellowship and good works planned for you, to which He has called and chosen you. This involves transformation into Christ-likeness that glorifies Him. While this undoubtedly also involves suffering and trials in this life, just as it did for your Savior, God promises that it will be worth it all when we are caught up to be with Christ, to receive our eternal reward, and then to return with Him to the earth to rule and reign with Him in His eternal kingdom. Do you believe this? Will you accept Peter's message and exhortation?

Chapter 14

Perseverance vs. Preservation
in James, John, & Jude

Having heard the testimony of Jesus Christ, the apostles Peter and Paul, and the writer of Hebrews, this chapter calls forth three final witnesses regarding the question of perseverance and preservation—the Lord Jesus' half brothers, James and Jude, and the apostle John. These three witnesses agree with one another like a gospel trio, singing in perfect unison about the fact that eternal salvation depends on the perseverance of the Savior and that the saint's perseverance in faith and holiness results in a reward from the Lord, not the unmerited free gift of eternal life.

The Testimony of James

Understanding perseverance in the Epistle of James begins by recognizing the audience to whom James is writing. The epistle begins in 1:1-4: "James, a bondservant of God and of the Lord Jesus Christ, to the twelve tribes which are scattered abroad: Greetings. My brethren, count it all joy when you fall into various trials, knowing that the testing of your faith produces patience. But let patience have its perfect work, that you may be perfect and complete, lacking nothing." Was James writing to unbelievers who professed faith in Christ but did not actually possess "real, saving faith"? Who did James have in mind by "My brethren" in verse 2? Were these "brethren" merely James's fellow ethnic Jews, consisting of both believers in Christ and unbelievers?

It would be wrong to assume that James wrote in order to distinguish true believers from false believers, for he consistently addresses his readers as believers, who are regenerated. In 1:3, he says, "knowing that the testing of your faith produces patience." James would not have written this to an unbeliever since only one who possesses faith can have his faith tested. A few verses later in 1:5-6, James directly addresses his readers again: "If any of you lacks wisdom, let him ask of God, who gives to all liberally and without reproach, and it will be given to him. But let him ask in faith, with no doubting, for he who doubts is like a wave of the sea driven and tossed by the wind." A person cannot "ask in faith" if he does not already have faith in Christ and is on a praying basis with God as His child. In 1:18, James includes himself with his readers ("us") and declares that they have been brought forth or born from God: "Of His own will He brought us forth [*apokueō*] by the word of truth, that we might be a kind of firstfruits of His creatures." The term *apokueō* literally means "to give birth," which is how it is translated three verses earlier in James 1:15: "Then, when lust has conceived, it gives birth [*apokueō*] to sin." By saying that his readers had been "brought forth" (*apokueō*) in verse 18, James is unmistakably identifying them as regenerate—as believers. The next instance of James directly addressing his readers as believers occurs in 2:1: "My brethren, do not hold the faith of our Lord Jesus Christ, the Lord of glory, with partiality."

From all of these references, it is clear that the readers of this epistle were believers in Christ and already regenerated, but they still needed to walk in faith and fellowship with God so as to endure and mature (1:2-4), do good works toward other people and be justified in their sight (2:14-26), and ultimately be rewarded by God (1:12). Since James describes his readers as believers, who were already born again and justified in God's sight, it is only logical and consistent that he would then speak to them about persevering in their faith for the purposes of spiritual maturity, blessing, and reward (1:3-4, 12; 5:7-8, 10-11), rather than eternal salvation.

James 1:2-4

In the first reference to perseverance in his epistle, James teaches that endurance is necessary for maturity in the Christian life. In 1:2-4, he writes, "2 My brethren, count it all joy when you fall into various trials, 3 knowing that the testing of your faith produces patience [*hypomonē*]. 4 But let patience [*hypomonē*] have its perfect work, that you may be perfect and complete, lacking nothing." The word translated "patience" (*hypomonē*) in verses 3-4 is commonly used in the Greek New Testament for perseverance or endurance. This compound word comes from the preposition *hypo* ("under") and the noun *monē* ("dwelling" or "abiding place"). The noun *hypomonē* is often used for the endurance of believers who abide or remain under trials and adverse circumstances. God knows that human beings are like water in the sense that we naturally take the path of least resistance, and even genuine believers are prone to look for the easy way out of the trials and tests of our faith. We do not naturally prefer to keep ourselves under difficult circumstances. But according to James 1:2-4, the Lord desires us as believers "to abide or remain under" the trials in our lives until they have served His purposes of refining or testing our faith, so that we may grow in sanctification.

The words "perfect" (*teleios*) and "complete" (*holoklēros*) in verse 4 do not support the idea of "sinless perfection." James 1:3-4 is not teaching that a believer in this earthly lifetime can reach a state whereby he or she becomes incapable of ever sinning again. That would be glorification, and glorification for the believer occurs only *after* this lifetime. Instead, "perfect" (*teleios*) and "complete" (*holoklēros*) speak of maturity. Thus, James 1:2-4 simply teaches that trials, tests, and perseverance in faith are necessary for spiritual maturity, not to obtain eternal life or to prove that one is born again or justified before God.

James 1:12

The next reference to perseverance in James occurs in 1:12. This verse teaches that perseverance through trials and temptations results in an eternal reward, not final salvation: "Blessed is the man who endures temptation; for when he has been approved, he will receive the crown of life which the Lord has promised to those who love Him." Since crowns in the Bible always refer to eternal rewards for faithful Christian service and never to eternal salvation (as explained earlier in chapter 6), the crown for endurance here in verse 12 is describing neither the possession of eternal life nor the necessary proof of it, but an earned reward. According to James, perseverance results in Christian maturity and an eternal reward from the Lord. But that's not all, for James 5 also teaches that perseverance brings God's blessings upon believers.

James 5:7-8

The subject of James 5:1-6 is the unjust treatment of poor believers at the hands of the rich, which James says requires patience on the part of believers (vv. 7-8) in light of Christ's return for them (v. 9), when He will richly reward them. This is the context for James's next reference to perseverance in verses 7-8: "Therefore be patient [*makrothymeō*], brethren, until the coming of the Lord. See how the farmer waits for the precious fruit of the earth, waiting patiently [*makrothymeō*] for it until it receives the early and latter rain. You also be patient [*makrothymeō*]. Establish your hearts, for the coming of the Lord is at hand."

The threefold use of the verb *makrothymeō* marks a return to the theme of perseverance found in chapter 1. Like *hypomonē* used in James 1, *makrothymeō* in James 5:7-8 is a compound word for the concept of patience, endurance, or perseverance. This word is formed from the adjective *makro* ("large" or "long") and *thymos* ("anger"). The basic idea behind this word is being long-tempered or having a long fuse. The verb *makrothymeō* and its noun form *makrothymia* are often used of perseverance or longsuffering towards *people*, rather than *hypomonē* or its verb form *hypomenō*, which are often used of enduring adverse *circumstances*. Here in James 5:7-8, believers are exhorted to patiently endure ill treatment at the hands of rich people, while waiting for Christ's return. There is no implication in this passage that believers must persevere because it is required for eternal life. Instead, believers are to persevere in order to be justly compensated by the Lord in terms of reward when He returns.

James 5:10-11

James 5:10-11 is the final passage in this epistle that speaks explicitly of perseverance. "10 My brethren, take the prophets, who spoke in the name of the Lord, as an example of suffering and patience [*makrothymia*]. 11 Indeed we count them blessed who endure [*hypomenō*]. You have heard of the perseverance [*hypomonē*] of Job and seen the end intended by the Lord—that the Lord is very compassionate and merciful." Once again, perseverance has nothing to do with securing or proving one's eternal salvation. By referencing "the prophets" and the example of "Job" (and later "Elijah," v. 17), James uses examples of exceptional, rather than typical, saints. In Job 1:8, God describes His servant Job, saying that "there is none like him on the earth, a blameless and upright man, one who fears God and shuns evil." The perseverance of Job is held up as an example of what all believers should aspire to, not an example of what all believers do already. Thus, James 5:11 says of Job and the prophets, "we count them blessed," not "we count them born again." In verse 11, "the end intended by the Lord" in Job's trial was *not* his deliverance from hell or to confirm whether his initial faith was genuine and thus prove he was truly regenerated. Instead, the passage itself makes very clear that "the end intended by the Lord" was threefold:

- to provide a positive example and encouragement for other believers that endurance is possible with the Lord (v. 10);

- to show that enduring trials and suffering for the Lord is always worthwhile as Job was "blessed" and richly rewarded by God in the end (v. 11a; cf. Job 42:12);

- and to magnify God's character as being very compassionate and merciful (v. 11).

Having examined all four passages in James dealing with the perseverance of the saints, it is conspicuous that none of them speak of perseverance in order to prove the reality of initial, "saving faith." Instead, perseverance is only stated to be necessary for maturity, blessing, and eternal reward from the Lord.

The Testimony of John

The Epistle of 1 John and Book of Revelation contain several verses that are relevant to the doctrines of perseverance and preservation (1 John 2:19; 5:18; Rev. 3:8-10; 13:10; 14:12). In the Epistle of 1 John, there is one verse that is commonly cited by Reformed advocates to prove that perseverance is necessary for eternal life: "They went out from us, but they were not of us; for if they had been of us, they would have continued with us; but they went out that they might be made manifest, that none of them were of us" (1 John 2:19). On the other hand, 1 John 5:18 offers support for the truth that Christ is the One who preserves the child of God: "We know that no one who is born of God sins; but He who was born of God keeps him, and the evil one does not touch him" (NASB). Regarding Revelation 3:10, when this verse is correctly understood according to its context and grammatical patterns of New Testament usage, it is seen to be an unconditional promise of deliverance from the global judgment of the Tribulation, not a requirement for eternal salvation based on perseverance in faith and good works. Likewise, Revelation 13:10 and 14:12 use the expression "the patience [or perseverance] of the saints" to describe the need for saints to persevere in the coming time of tribulation, not as a condition for everlasting life for all saints throughout all ages.

1 John 2:19

Theologian D. A. Carson gives the standard Calvinist interpretation of 1 John 2:19:

> Those who have seceded from the church are described in telling terms: "They went out from us, but they did not really belong to us. For if they had belonged to us, they would have remained with us; but their going showed that none of them belonged to us." In other words, genuine faith, by definition, perseveres; where there is no perseverance, by definition the faith cannot be genuine. . . . In short, genuine faith is tied to perseverance; transitory faith is spurious.[1]

Is 1 John 2:19 really tying perseverance to the reality of saving faith? Are "those who have seceded from the church" necessarily unregenerate? Rather than making continued church affiliation proof that one is born again, or even a condition for entrance to heaven, John is simply describing false, professing Christians, who never really believed the truth about Jesus as the Christ, the Son of God. Those who went out from John and his readers are described in the previous verse as antichrists: "Little children, it is the last hour; and as you have heard that the Antichrist is coming, even now many antichrists have come, by which we know that it is the last hour" (v. 18). The "they" of verse 19 ("They went out from us, but they were not of us") refers back to the "antichrists" in verse 18. The antichrists were those who associated with the early church under the guise of being fellow believers, but in reality they were unbelievers who denied the truth about Jesus as the Christ, the Son of God. Their denial of the truth about Christ eventually manifested itself and they

---

1. D. A. Carson, "Reflections on Christian Assurance," *Westminster Theological Journal* 54 (Spring 1992): 17.

withdrew themselves from John and his readers. In what way did they deny that Jesus is the Christ, the Son of God? John answers this a few verses later:

> 22 Who is a liar but he who denies that Jesus is the Christ? He is antichrist who denies the Father and the Son. 23 Whoever denies the Son does not have the Father either; he who acknowledges the Son has the Father also. 24 Therefore let that abide in you which you heard from the beginning. If what you heard from the beginning abides in you, you also will abide in the Son and in the Father. (2:22-24)

The antichrists had rejected the truth about Christ that John's readers knew from the beginning—that Jesus is the Christ, the Son of God. Consequently, the antichrists had not fulfilled the condition to receive eternal life explicitly stated in John's Gospel: "But these are written that you may believe that Jesus is the Christ, the Son of God, and that believing you may have life in His name" (John 20:31). How did these unbelievers and antichrists mentioned in 1 John 2 deny that Jesus was the Christ, the Son of God? The larger context of John's first two epistles implies that they denied Christ's true humanity.

> 1 Beloved, do not believe every spirit, but test the spirits, whether they are of God; because many false prophets have gone out into the world. 2 By this you know the Spirit of God: Every spirit that confesses that Jesus Christ has come in the flesh is of God, 3 and every spirit that does not confess that Jesus Christ has come in the flesh is not of God. And this is the spirit of the Antichrist, which you have heard was coming, and is now already in the world. (1 John 4:1-3)

> For many deceivers have gone out into the world who do not confess Jesus Christ as coming in the flesh. This is a deceiver and an antichrist. (2 John 7)

John not only declares and defines Jesus to be the Christ, the Son of God by His real humanity but also by the reality of His death and the fact that He guarantees eternal life.

> 5 Who is he who overcomes the world, but he who believes that Jesus is the Son of God? 6 This is He who came by water

and blood—Jesus Christ; not only by water, but by water and blood. (1 John 5:5-6)

33 But when they came to Jesus and saw that He was already dead, they did not break His legs. 34 But one of the soldiers pierced His side with a spear, and immediately blood and water came out. 35 And he who has seen has testified, and his testimony is true; and he knows that he is telling the truth, so that you may believe. (John 19:33-35)

In 1 John 2:19, John was referring to those who professed faith in Christ but held to an early form of Gnosticism, which viewed the material world as inherently evil and thus denied the reality of Christ's incarnation, death on the cross, and bodily resurrection.[2]

9 If we receive the testimony of men, the testimony of God is greater; for the testimony of God is this, that He has testified concerning His Son. 10 The one who believes in the Son of God has the testimony in himself; the one who does not believe God has made Him a liar, because he has not believed in the testimony that God has given concerning His Son. 11 And the testimony is this, that God has given us eternal life, and this life is in His Son. 12 He who has the Son has the life; he who does not have the Son of God does not have the life. 13 These things I have written to you who believe in the name of the Son of God, so that you may know that you have eternal life. (5:9-13, NASB)

Since 1 John 5:9-13 follows on the heels of 1 John 5:6 about the reality of Christ's humanity and death, it is likely that the antichrists also denied that Jesus Christ guarantees eternal life. The fact that Jesus guarantees eternal life also identifies Him as the Christ, the Son of God (John 11:25-27). If someone has never believed that Jesus became a man, died and rose from the dead, and guarantees eternal life to all who believe in Him, then such a person has never been born again.

Had the antichrists ever been born again? There is nothing in the record of 1 John to indicate this. John never says they once believed

---

2. "The Revelation of Peter," in *The Nag Hammadi Scriptures*, ed. Marvin Meyer (San Francisco: HarperCollins, 2007), 495-96; idem, "The Letter of Peter to Philip," 589.

in Christ before they denied Him. They are never said to have been born of God; nor are they ever called children of God, like John's readers. They are never said to possess eternal life, the Holy Spirit, or God's anointing. Instead, when John describes the antichrists in 2:19, notice what he *does* say and what he *does not* say. He says, "They went out from us, but they *were* not of us." He does not say, "They went out from us, but they *are* not of us." John used the imperfect indicative *ēsan* ("they were") rather than the present tense *eisin* ("they are") to show that these antichrists did not merely deny Christ at the time John was writing but they had denied Him in the past, which precipitated their departure. The people John described in 1 John 2:19 appear to be unbelievers who were unregenerate. These antichrists eventually became "manifest" to the whole church by separating from the sound doctrine of the apostles and the churches that followed the apostles' teaching about Christ's person and work.

Having seen what 1 John 2:19 *is* saying, it is appropriate now to consider what it is *not* saying. There are at least three ways that 1 John 2:19 is misinterpreted and misapplied by perseverance of the saints proponents. First, this verse is often misused as a warning to those who currently hold orthodox beliefs about Christ to persevere in orthopraxy—in their good works, practical obedience, and service to Christ. The implication is often drawn from 1 John 2:19 that if a professing orthodox Christian does not continue to live a holy, sanctified life, then that person was never truly saved to begin with and will perish eternally. Sam Storms says regarding the secessionists of verse 19, "If they had in any genuine sense shared the spiritual life of the community of faith, such life would have persevered and produced the fruit of Christlike holiness."[3] But those who are identified as antichrists in 1 John were *not* those who held orthodox views about the person and work of Christ while not persevering or measuring up in practical holiness and sanctified Christian living. There is no evidence that the antichrists were ever doctrinally orthodox.

Second, verse 19 is often misapplied as a warning to those who, despite currently holding orthodox beliefs about Christ's person and work, fail to persevere in this orthodoxy and thereby demonstrate that their faith was not genuine from the beginning. But nowhere in the context of 1 John is there any indication that the antichrists once held the same orthodox views about Christ that John and his readers believed. John says his readers knew from the beginning the truth

---

3. Sam Storms, *Kept for Jesus: What the New Testament Really Teaches about Assurance of Salvation and Eternal Security* (Wheaton, IL: Crossway, 2015), 53.

about Christ (2:24), but John never says anything similar about the antichrists. There is no evidence from 1 John that the antichrists were formerly orthodox in their beliefs about Christ.

According to traditional Calvinist teaching on the perseverance of the saints, if a person commits doctrinal apostasy, then that person never originally believed in Christ. But 1 John 5:13 clearly states that the readers of this epistle were believers ("These things I have written to you who believe"), yet John commands these believers to continue (menō) in the truth they knew and embraced from the beginning: "Therefore let that abide [menetō] in you which you heard from the beginning. If what you heard from the beginning abides [meinē] in you, you also will abide [meneite] in the Son and in the Father" (2:24). The use of menō and the third-class conditional "if" statement shows that John did not assume his believing readers would inevitably continue in their orthodoxy simply because they had genuine faith. Rather, their future continuance was conditional and still uncertain. Believers may or may not continue in sound doctrine. When genuine believers do not abide in Christ, they lose fruitfulness (John 15:4-5) and fellowship with God and one another (1 John 1:3-9), but they do not lose eternal life (John 10:28-29).

Thus, when John uses the verb menō in 1 John 2:19 to say, "if they had been of us, they would have continued [memenēkeisan] with us," he is not teaching that genuine believers will always, necessarily, continue in sound doctrine to the end of their lives, otherwise they prove that they were actually unregenerate antichrists from the beginning. Rather, John is simply saying that if the secessionists had believed the truth about Christ, they would have had no reason to separate from the fellowship of the early church. Although continued unity or perseverance in the faith was the norm, it was not guaranteed or assumed, for verse 24 goes on to show that even John's believing readers had to continue abiding in Christ to remain in fellowship with God and the rest of the early church, which was John's primary reason for writing this epistle (1:1-4).

A third and final way that 1 John 2:19 is misapplied today by Reformed, perseverance theology is by leading believers to think that their faith is proven false by not continuing in church attendance and participation. It is categorically false to conclude that because a person leaves a sound, Bible-believing church, that person never believed the gospel in the first place and therefore must still be eternally condemned. Those who seek to prove from this verse that perseverance in faith is necessary for eternal life actually end up making this verse say too much—that continued involvement in one's local church is a requirement for heaven. If perseverance in faith is necessary for eternal life, and perseverance always manifests itself in continued church involvement, then how can we escape the conclusion that church participation is necessary for eternal life? This would be a blatant form of salvation by works rather than by God's grace.

1 John 5:18

The second verse in John's epistles bearing on the issue of perseverance versus preservation is 1 John 5:18. This verse contains a textual variant so that the translation of verse 18 in some English Bibles supports the truth that Christ preserves His own: "We know that no one who is born of God sins; but He who was born of God keeps him, and the evil one does not touch him" (NASB). Other translations follow a different Greek text and give the impression that each born again person preserves himself: "We know that whoever is born of God does not sin; but he who has been born of God keeps himself, and the wicked one does not touch him" (NKJV). Admittedly, this verse is difficult to interpret, but the evidence favors the view that this verse is teaching that Jesus Christ Himself keeps secure every born again person from the clutches of Satan.

The first main interpretative issue in this verse is the meaning of the statement that "no one who is born of God sins." One common interpretation of this statement is the habitual sin view; that is, that the present tense of *hamartanō* ("does not sin") should be understood as a description of continuous action (i.e., "no one who is born of God continues to sin"). This is the interpretation followed by the New International Version: "We know that anyone born of God does not continue to sin." Naturally, this view is favored by many perseverance proponents, but it faces the problem that the Greek present tense does not necessarily indicate ongoing action, as explained in chapter 4. In addition, Scripture shows elsewhere that genuine believers can continue to sin, even to the point that God must take them home through maximum divine discipline in the form of premature physical death (1 Cor. 3:1-4; 11:28-32). Since Scripture does not contradict itself, the continual sin interpretation must be rejected.

One possible interpretation of the clause "no one who is born of God sins" is that the "one who is born of God" refers to the believer's new nature, so that the verse is really saying that the new nature of the regenerate man does not sin. This view is doctrinally correct and is supported by John's earlier teaching in 1 John 3:9: "Whoever has been born of God does not sin, for His seed remains in him; and he cannot sin, because he has been born of God." In addition, this interpretation harmonizes with the fact that Christians obviously still sin, for John has just stated two verses earlier that a "brother" can still sin (1 John 5:16), just as he stated earlier in the epistle that believers still sin (1:10; 2:2).

The second main interpretative issue to resolve in 1 John 5:18 is the question, who keeps whom? Does the believer keep himself or does Christ keep the believer? Verse 18 contains a textual variant where the Greek Majority Text says that the one who has been born of God keeps "himself" (*heauton*), while the Critical Text says the One who has been born of God keeps "him" (*auton*), in reference to Christ keeping the believer. The textual evidence slightly favors *auton* over *heauton* as the original reading since *auton* has greater geographical diversity among the different text types supporting each reading. The exegetical evidence from John also favors the reading of Christ keeping "him" (*auton*), the one who is born again, from Satan.

First, regarding "himself" (*heauton*) versus "him" (*auton*), John uses *tereō* ("keeps") 25 times in his Gospel and epistles, but not once is *tereō* used with *heauton* as the direct object (i.e., "he keeps himself"). On the other hand, the plural form of *auton* ("they") is used in John 17:11-12 and 15, which are verses that are parallel passages theologically to 1 John 5:18 since they promise eternal security for those who belong to Christ.

Second, although it is unusual in the New Testament to describe Christ as "He who has been born of God," this description of Him is supported by at least one other passage. The verb *gennaō* in the phrase "He who has been born [*ho gennētheis*] of God" is used by the Lord Jesus in John 18:37 to describe His own origin: "You say rightly that I am a king. For this cause I was born [*gegennēmai*]."

Third, *gennaō* is used twice in 1 John 5:18. The first time it is a perfect-tense participle and is used in reference to the new birth of all believers ("We know that no one who is born of God"). In the second clause of the verse ("He who was born of God keeps him"), it is an aorist participle. The switch from the perfect tense to the aorist tense for the second clause seems fitting if the second clause refers to Christ's birth as opposed to the new births of all believers. Elsewhere, when referring to believers as those who had been born, John always uses the perfect-tense participle *gegennēmenos*. John uses *gennaō* 10 times in his first epistle (1 John 2:29; 3:9 [2x]; 4:7; 5:1 [3x], 4, 18 [2x]), and refers to believers as the ones who are born 8 of those 10 times, and always with the perfect tense. Thus, the shift to the aorist tense (*gennētheis*) for the second clause of 1 John 5:18 is unusual if John is still referring in the verse to the believer's new birth.

Fourth, from a theological standpoint, believers do not have adequate power to keep themselves from the prying fingers of Satan; but Christ certainly does. A similar point was underscored earlier by John in the same epistle when he wrote, "You are from God, little children, and have overcome them [the lying spirits of Antichrist]; because greater is He who is in you than he who is in the world" (1 John 4:4, NASB).

Based on these reasons, 1 John 5:18 should be added to the many other verses of Scripture that support the conclusion that believes are kept or preserved by the perseverance of the Savior, not the saints' own perseverance.

Revelation 3:8-10

Revelation 3:8-10 is not often cited in discussions about perseverance versus preservation, but it is another key Johannine passage supporting preservation by God's grace. The context of these verses is Jesus Christ as the Head of the church addressing one of the seven churches of Asia Minor in Revelation 2–3. In this case, He is speaking words of encouragement and promise to the church at Philadelphia:

> 8 I know your works. See, I have set before you an open door, and no one can shut it; for you have a little strength, have kept My word, and have not denied My name. 9 Indeed I will make those of the synagogue of Satan, who say they are Jews and are not, but lie—indeed I will make them come and bow down before your feet, and to know that I have loved you. 10 Because you have kept My command to persevere, I also will keep you from the hour of trial which shall come upon the whole world, to test those who dwell on the earth.

One might get the initial impression from the punctuation and translation of verses 9-10 in the New King James Version above that Christ will keep believers out of the coming Tribulation because they have persevered. Since deliverance from this unprecedented time of God's wrath that will be poured out on the world is part of the church-age believer's salvation (1 Thess. 1:10; 5:9-10), some might be prone to conclude that salvation from God's judgment is predicated on the believer's perseverance in faith and good works. But neither the context nor the grammar of the passage supports this conclusion. Instead, the Lord Jesus is promising believers a reward for their perseverance, coupled with an unmerited, gracious promise to deliver believers from the time of tribulation on the earth. The Philadelphians' reward and preservation are distinct.

The way the end of verse 9 and beginning of verse 10 have been punctuated and divided into verses has led to theological confusion. Reformed interpreters see in these verses support for perseverance as a requirement for spiritual salvation.[4] On the other hand, Partial Rapturists, who reject Reformed theology's doctrine of perseverance, find support for the notion that the Pretribulation Rapture will include only worthy church-age believers who persevered, rather than all believers of the church age based on God's grace.[5]

Traditionally, verses 9-10 have been translated so as to give the impression that the dependent clause at the beginning of verse 10 ("Because you have kept My command to persevere") is connected to the independent clause that follows it in verse 10 ("I also will keep you from the hour of trial which shall come upon the whole world"). However, it is far more likely based on grammatical patterns of usage throughout the New Testament that the dependent clause at beginning of verse 10 ("Because you have kept My command to persevere") completes the thought of verse 9, so that the independent clause of verse 10 ("I also will keep you from the hour of trial which shall come upon the whole world") stands by itself. Accordingly, verses 9-10 should read:

> Indeed I will make those of the synagogue of Satan, who say they are Jews and are not, but lie—indeed I will make them come and bow down before your feet, and to know that I have loved you, because you have kept My command to persevere. 10 I also will keep you from the hour of trial which shall come upon the whole world, to test those who dwell on the earth.

The difference between this rendering of the versification and punctuation versus the traditional rendering can be seen as follows:

---

4. Robert H. Mounce, *The Book of Revelation*, New International Commentary on the New Testament (Grand Rapids: Eerdmans, 1977), 119.

5. D. M. Panton, "An Open Door," *The Dawn* 26 (November 11, 1948), 327.

9. . . . I will make them come and bow down before your feet, and to know that I have loved you. 10 Because you have kept My command to persevere, I also will keep you . . . (Traditional)

9 . . . I will make them come and bow down before your feet, and to know that I have loved you, because you have kept My command to persevere. 10 I also will keep you . . . (Revision)

Is this revised rendering justified? There is no dispute about the fact that verse divisions were not part of the original text of Scripture but were added relatively late in church history.[6] Therefore, they should not be viewed as part of the inspired text. Likewise, English punctuation should not be considered inspired since it is also largely arbitrary and not part of the original text. These facts do not in themselves justify changing the punctuation and versification of Revelation 3:9-10, but they do allow it. Actual support for the revised rendering of these verses comes from patterns of grammatical usage in the Greek New Testament.

Is the dependent clause "Because [*hoti*] you have kept My command to persevere" the start of a new verse and sentence as it traditionally has been translated? Or does this dependent *hoti* clause conclude the thought of verse 9? New Testament usage supports the latter. Commentator David Aune states that it is "unusual" to begin a new sentence with *hoti*. He writes, "The *hoti* clause that begins the sentence is in an unusual position, since in the vast majority of instances dependent clauses follow the main clause."[7] John Niemelä is even more specific, observing that John starts a sentence with *hoti* only 6 percent of the time (11 out of 180 occurrences).[8] Therefore, to insist upon the traditional translation, where the phrase "Because you have kept" begins verse 10 rather than ends verse 9, is to insist upon the rare usage of *hoti* throughout the New Testament and in John's own writings.

Moreover, it is exceedingly rare for the word *kagō* ("I also") to connect a dependent clause ("Because you have kept My com-

---

6. Modern verse divisions were first added in the fourth edition Greek New Testament of Robert Estienne (aka – Stephanus [Latin] or Robert Stevens [English]) in A.D. 1551. Paul D. Wegner, *The Journey from Texts to Translations: The Origin and Development of the Bible* (Grand Rapids: Baker Academic, 1999), 269.

7. David E. Aune, *Revelation 1–5*, Word Biblical Commentary (Dallas: Word, 1997), 231 n. 10.

8. John Niemelä, "For You Have Kept My Word: The Grammar of Revelation 3:10," *Chafer Theological Seminary Journal* 6 (January 2000): 20.

mand to persevere") with an independent clause ("I also [*kagō*] will keep you from the hour of testing"), as it does in the traditional translation of Revelation 3:10. Regarding this point, John Niemelä writes:

> *Kagō* is a compound Greek word (*kai* "and" + *egō* "I"). The normal function of *kai* is to connect equivalent items. For example, it joins: a full sentence to another full sentence, or a dependent clause to another dependent clause. It is extremely uncommon for it to connect a dependent clause to an independent clause. . . . only one passage in the entire New Testament has this usage: 2 Corinthians 11:18. The traditional punctuation of Revelation 3:10a-b would make it only the second passage. This does not give confidence in the traditional punctuation.[9]

The patterns of grammatical usage throughout John's writings and the rest of the New Testament provide better support for the revised rendering of Revelation 3:9-10 than the traditional translation. According to the revised rendering, the dependent clause about perseverance ("because you have kept My command to persevere") should be connected to Christ's promise of a future reward in verse 9. Christ saw the Philadelphians' works and perseverance (v. 8) and consequently promised to reward them (v. 9). This reward will come in the form of future vindication before the unbelieving Jews who had opposed the Philadelphian believers, when every knee will bow to acknowledge Jesus Christ as Lord (Rom. 14:11; Phil. 2:9-11). Thus, verse 9 should read: "Behold, I will make those of the synagogue of Satan, who say they are Jews and are not, but lie—behold, I will make them come and bow down before your feet, and to know that I have loved you, because you have kept My command to persevere." Therefore, what follows in verse 10 is an additional, separate, and distinct promise of deliverance from the Tribulation based on God's grace rather than the Philadelphians' perseverance: "I also will keep you from the hour of trial which shall come upon the whole world, to test those who dwell on the earth."

Since all church-age believers will experience the Rapture promised in Revelation 3:10, and this event is based solely on God's grace rather than believers' works, this verse should be counted as another supporting passage for the truth that believers will be spared God's

---

9. Ibid., 23-24.

judgment because they are preserved by Christ, not because they have persevered in faith and good works.[10]

Revelation 13:10; 14:12

Revelation 13:10 and 14:12 are occasionally cited as proof texts for the view that perseverance to the end of one's life is required for eternal salvation. Reformed, Dortian Calvinism takes the name of its fifth point from these verses where the phrase "perseverance of the saints" is found in some English Bibles.[11] Though some translations of Revelation 13:10 and 14:12 contain the *expression* "the perseverance of the saints," this does not mean these verses contain the Reformed, Calvinist *doctrine* of perseverance. These verses say:

> If anyone is destined for captivity, to captivity he goes; if anyone kills with the sword, with the sword he must be killed. Here is the perseverance and the faith of the saints. (Rev. 13:10, NASB)

> Here is the perseverance of the saints who keep the commandments of God and their faith in Jesus. (Rev. 14:12, NASB)

Although both verses describe saints persevering through tremendous persecution in the future tribulation, it must be observed that neither verse in its context actually prescribes perseverance as a condition for deliverance from hell. Nor do these verses say that every saint today perseveres in faith and keeping Christ's commandments. The correct interpretation of these verses is often affected by one's view of prophecy or eschatology. When Revelation 4–22 is not viewed from a dispensational, premillennial perspective as describing events that are still future and unfulfilled, Revelation 13:10 and 14:12 can be wrongly interpreted as descriptions of church-age believers in the present. However, the events of chapters 13–14 transpire after the rapture of the church in that future, unique, and unprece-

---

10. For support of the Pretribulation Rapture in Revelation 3:10, see Jeffrey L. Townsend, "The Rapture in Revelation 3:10," in *When the Trumpet Sounds*, ed. Thomas Ice and Timothy Demy (Eugene, OR: Harvest House, 1995), 367-79 and Andrew M. Woods, "John and the Rapture: Revelation 2–3," in *Evidence for the Rapture: A Biblical Case for Pretribulationism*, ed. John F. Hart (Chicago: Moody, 2015), 196-212.

11. Curt Daniel, *The History and Theology of Calvinism* (Dallas: Scholarly Reprints, 1993), 415.

dented time of global testing and persecution by the Antichrist (Matt. 24:21-22), during the seven years prior to Christ's return to the earth in judgment.[12] For these reasons, Revelation 13:10 and 14:12 should not be viewed as requirements for eternal life for all saints today, but as encouragements to all believers to persevere, particularly for those living in that unique, future period of the Tribulation.

The Testimony of Jude

The Epistle of Jude is short (only one chapter), but it contains several verses that are some of the most relevant and frequently cited on the topic of preservation versus perseverance. The emphasis of this epistle concerns warning against false teachers and their destructive doctrines and practices, which are a perversion of God's grace. Consequently, it is not surprising to see several verses in this epistle about the need for perseverance, mixed with reminders about believers being kept from eternal judgment by God and His ability to guard believers from stumbling into apostasy. Verse 1 describes believers as those who are preserved or kept by Christ. Verse 5 gives a negative example of genuine believers not continuing in their faith. Verse 21 commands believers to "keep yourselves in the love of God," which is often misunderstood as a requirement for believers to keep themselves saved or prove that they are saved, as if it is the believer's responsibility to make God continue to love him. Finally, verse 24 says that "God is able to keep you from stumbling," which is a promise of what God is *able* to do in the lives of believers, not necessarily what He always *will* do.

Jude 1

The first verse of this epistle contains a description of believers as those who are preserved either in, by, or for Jesus Christ. Three different translation possibilities for this verse are listed below.

Jude, a bondservant of Jesus Christ, and brother of James, to those who are called, sanctified by God the Father, and preserved in Jesus Christ. (NKJV)

---

12. Thomas D. Ice, "The Perseverance of the Saints: Some Biblical, Theological, and Historical Observations," Free Grace Alliance National Conference, Dallas, TX, October 6, 2009.

> Jude, a servant of Jesus Christ and a brother of James, to those who have been called, who are loved by God the Father and kept by Jesus Christ (NIV)

> Jude, a bond-servant of Jesus Christ, and brother of James, to those who are the called, beloved in God the Father, and kept for Jesus Christ (NASB)

Jude 1 gives a threefold description of believers as those who are called, sanctified or beloved, and preserved. The description of believers as those who are called emphasizes God's initiation, grace, and seeking of believers in salvation. Though people must respond in faith to God's drawing of the Holy Spirit (John 16:7-11) and calling through the gospel (2 Thess. 2:14), no one will enter heaven or the eternal kingdom without an invitation from the King (Matt. 22:1-14). Grateful guests who attend royal galas and banquets do not boast in their reception of the invitation to such an event but in the host's graciousness in inviting them in the first place.

The second description of believers in Jude 1 may be either "sanctified in God the Father" (NKJV) or "beloved in God the Father" (NASB, NIV). The difference in translations stems from a textual variant among supporting manuscripts, where "beloved in God the Father" is supported by the earlier Greek manuscripts, translations into other languages (such as Latin and Coptic), and quotations of this verse by professing Christians from the first few centuries of church history. While it is true that believers are "sanctified" in God the Father, the best support stands behind the reading "beloved in God the Father." The fact that believers are viewed as divinely-loved ones is an important truth reiterated later in Jude 21, where believers are told to continually abide in God's love.

Jude 1 also describes believers as "preserved" either "in" (NKJV), "by" (NIV), or "for" (NASB) "Jesus Christ." The reason for this variation among English Bibles is based on the dative case of "Jesus Christ" (*Iēsou Christō*), which permits all three possible translations. Regardless of which translation is correct, all three possibilities support the scriptural truth of the eternal security of the saint. For example, being preserved "*in* Jesus Christ" emphasizes the sphere in which the believer is preserved, that is, in Christ. To be "preserved in Jesus Christ" speaks of the believer's identification with Christ and position in Him. This position or standing before God is unchanging and does not depend on the believer's fluctuating faithfulness.

Being preserved "*by* Jesus Christ" underscores the Savior as the active agent of preservation, rather than the believer himself. The passive voice of the participle for "preserved" (*tetērēmenois*) in verse 1 fits the pattern for datives of agency, which normally follow passive-voice verbs.[13] The passive voice here indicates that believers are not the ones who perform the action of keeping or preserving themselves, rather it is done to them by Jesus Christ. Eternal salvation is the result of the perseverance of the Savior, not the perseverance of the saints.

Verse 1 may also be saying that believers are kept or preserved "*for* Jesus Christ." This reading interprets the dative case as a dative of interest or advantage, where believers are kept for the benefit or interest of Jesus Christ.[14] Does the Lord have an interest in believers? He most certainly does since He gave everything to save and secure them to Himself. Scripture teaches that believers are a gift from God the Father to the Son, that the Son might be glorified by them (John 6:37; 17:6, 9-12; 1 Cor. 6:19-20). In John 6:39, Jesus expresses His interest in believers in terms of keeping them: "This is the will of the Father who sent Me, that of all He has given Me I should lose nothing, but should raise it up at the last day." Commenting on the translation "preserved in Jesus Christ" in the King James Version, C. I. Scofield writes that this "should be 'kept for Jesus Christ.' It carries out the thought of John 17:11, according to which our safety depends, not upon our faithfulness to God, but upon the Father's faithfulness to His Son's trust."[15] No matter whether Jude 1 is saying believers are kept *in, by,* or *for* Christ, all three possibilities point to the eternal security of the saint by the Savior, not the perseverance of the saints as a requirement for eternal salvation.

Jude 5

Jude 5 is sometimes interpreted as a warning to believers not to lapse in their faith lest they end up being lost forever. Verses 3-8 are given below to provide the context for verse 5.

---

13. Daniel B. Wallace, *Greek Grammar Beyond the Basics: An Exegetical Syntax of the New Testament* (Grand Rapids: Zondervan, 1996), 165; Richard A. Young, *Intermediate New Testament Greek: A Linguistic and Exegetical Approach* (Nashville: Broadman & Holman, 1994), 50.

14. Wallace, *Greek Grammar Beyond the Basics*, 142-44.

15. C. I. Scofield, *Scofield Bible Correspondence Course*, Vol. IV (Chicago: Moody Bible Institute, 1960), 940.

3 Beloved, while I was very diligent to write to you concerning our common salvation, I found it necessary to write to you exhorting you to contend earnestly for the faith which was once for all delivered to the saints. 4 For certain men have crept in unnoticed, who long ago were marked out for this condemnation, ungodly men, who turn the grace of our God into lewdness and deny the only Lord God and our Lord Jesus Christ. 5 But I want to remind you, though you once knew this, that the Lord, having saved the people out of the land of Egypt, afterward destroyed those who did not believe. 6 And the angels who did not keep their proper domain, but left their own abode, He has reserved in everlasting chains under darkness for the judgment of the great day; 7 as Sodom and Gomorrah, and the cities around them in a similar manner to these, having given themselves over to sexual immorality and gone after strange flesh, are set forth as an example, suffering the vengeance of eternal fire. 8 Likewise also these dreamers defile the flesh, reject authority, and speak evil of dignitaries.

In verses 5-7, Jude cites three examples of God's judgment for disobedience. Verse 5 describes the example of God's covenanted people Israel, and in particular the Israelites of the Exodus generation. This generation was saved out of Egypt but later destroyed by God in the wilderness because they "did not believe" God could give them victory in the Promised Land, and so they refused to go forward in faith. In verse 6, a second category of intelligent created beings is employed as an example of God's judgment, namely, the fallen angels. Jude's point in citing the example of the demons was obviously not to show that salvation can be lost or that genuine salvation is proven by perseverance in faith and obedience. After all, the demons did not initially possess salvation, even in their pre-fall state of innocence, and thus they could neither lose nor disprove a salvation they never possessed. Verse 7 describes a third example of God's judgment for disobedience—the judgment of the unregenerate and immoral Gentile cities of Sodom and Gomorrah. Jude uses these three diverse examples to remind his readers of the gravity of apostasy and that the Lord will not stand idly by and ignore the false teachers who had crept in among them (vv. 3-4). Just as God judged disobedience in the past, sometimes with severe temporal discipline to the point of physical death (v. 5; cf. 1 Cor. 11:28-32) and sometimes with eternal judgment (vv. 6-7), Jude emphasizes that the unsaved false teachers will also not escape His judgment.

Verse 5 is the only one of the three examples of God's judgment that uses the word "believe" and it is sometimes cited by Arminians as proof that the Bible teaches one can lose eternal salvation by not continuing in faith.[16] On the other hand, Calvinists sometimes use this verse in an attempt to prove that those who are truly elect always heed the warnings of Scripture to persevere.[17] Regarding this, Reformed theologian Thomas Schreiner writes:

> The main point Jude made is clear. No person in the believing community can presume on God's grace, thinking that an initial decision to follow Christ or baptism ensures their future salvation regardless of how they respond to the intruders. Israel's apostasy stands as a warning to all those who think that an initial commitment secures their future destiny without ongoing obedience. Those who are God's people demonstrate the genuineness of their salvation by responding to the warning given. The warnings are one of the means by which God preserves his people until the end. Those who ignore such warnings neglect the very means God has appointed for obtaining eschatological salvation.[18]

Aside from Schreiner's false premise about eternal life being conditioned on works such as making a commitment to Christ, getting water baptized, or ongoing obedience, the question must be asked, to whom was Jude applying the example of Israel's unbelief in verse 5? Was he warning his *believing readers* that they must continue to believe lest they perish in hell? Or, was he using the example of Israel's unbelief to inform his believing readers about the fate of the *false teachers*? In other words, was Jude seeking to apply verse 5 to his readers or to those about whom he was writing? Even some Arminians, who believe salvation can be lost, admit that it is the latter.[19] This conclusion fits with the context of verses 5-7, where in verses

---

16. Guy Duty, *If Ye Continue: A Study of the Conditional Aspects of Salvation* (Minneapolis: Bethany House, 1966), 144-47.

17. Thomas R. Schreiner and Ardel B. Caneday, *The Race Set Before Us: A Biblical Theology of Perseverance & Assurance* (Downers Grove, IL: InterVarsity Press, 2001), 215, 222, 225, 258.

18. Thomas R. Schreiner, *1, 2 Peter, Jude* (Nashville: Broadman & Holman, 2003), 446.

19. I. Howard Marshall, *Kept by the Power of God: A Study of Perseverance and Falling Away* (Minneapolis: Bethany House, 1969), 163.

3-4 Jude describes the false teachers, not the readers. Then, after the three examples of rebellion against God in verses 5-7, Jude refers to the false teachers once again in verse 8, saying to his readers, "Likewise also these dreamers." Jude clearly applied verses 5-7 to the false teachers rather than his readers. This is relevant because the false teachers about whom Jude is writing were unbelievers, while Jude's readers were true believers. Yet according to Calvinism's doctrine of perseverance, it is impossible for genuine believers to duplicate Israel's sin of unbelief which incurs divine judgment to the point of physical death. So what evidence exists that Jude's readers were believers while the false teachers were unbelievers?

Jude 12 says the false teachers were "twice dead," which Jude could never say of one who possessed new life from God. Jude 19 also describes the false teachers as being void of the Spirit. Since every believer in the church age is indwelt by the Holy Spirit (Rom. 8:9), those who do not have the Spirit must be unbelievers who are lost.

Conversely, there is ample evidence within the epistle showing that Jude's readers were genuine believers. In verse 1, they are described as called, beloved in God, and preserved in, by, or for Jesus Christ. In verse 3, Jude refers to the "common salvation" shared by him and his readers. According to verse 20, Jude's readers are described as being able to pray in the Holy Spirit, which means they were indwelt by the Spirit, in contrast to the false teachers in verse 19. Finally, in verse 20, Jude explicitly states that his readers had faith: "building yourselves up on your most holy faith." There is no question that Jude's readers were genuine believers, in contrast to the false teachers.

But if Jude knew that his readers already possessed faith in Christ, and genuine faith always perseveres to the end according to Calvinism, then why would Jude use the example of Israel's unbelief in verse 5 to warn his readers about the possibility that they may also stop believing and supposedly be lost? Apostasy should have been impossible for these genuine believers, according to the Reformed doctrine of perseverance.

The example of the Exodus generation of Israelites shows that it is possible for those who once believed to become unbelieving and incur the temporal judgment of God in the form of severe chastening. Prior to leaving Egypt, the Israelites believed in the Lord and even worshipped Him (Exod. 4:5, 31; 14:31). But after the Exodus, they refused to walk by faith, rebelliously choosing not to believe the Lord at Kadesh Barnea so as to enter Canaan (Num. 14:11; Deut.

1:32; 9:23). Consequently, they were chastened by God to the point of physical death as their carcasses fell in the wilderness over forty years (Num. 14:33). Even Moses did not believe the Lord at one point and was barred from entering the Promised Land (Num. 20:12). The example of the Exodus generation in Jude 5 actually disproves the Calvinist assumption that genuine faith always perseveres to the end of one's life. These examples also show that, although one's justification and eternal life can never be lost, the sin of unbelief still has grave consequences.

Jude 21

In Jude 20-21, believers in Christ are reminded of four responsibilities to combat the effects of the false teachers: "20 But you, beloved, building yourselves up on your most holy faith, praying in the Holy Spirit, 21 keep yourselves in the love of God, looking for the mercy of our Lord Jesus Christ unto eternal life." Verse 21 is often interpreted as the human responsibility for salvation, in contrast to God's responsibility of keeping the believer in verse 1. According to the Calvinist view, Jude is supposedly teaching that God loves and preserves His own, but His own must also persevere in their love for God, otherwise they will prove to be lost and not receive Christ's saving mercy on the last day.[20] But is verse 21 really teaching that God's love toward believers is conditioned on their continual faith and love toward Him? Is Jude really teaching that God's mercy and the possession of eternal life remain uncertain or unproven for believers unless they persevere in faith and love for Christ?

The assumption is often made that if believers do not continue to love God and others, then God will not love them. But this is not what Jude means by the command to "keep yourselves in the love of God." The love of God in verse 21 is God's own love for us, not our love for Him. God's love toward believers is not like He is on a swivel chair, where every time we sin, He turns away from us and stops loving us. God's love toward believers is fixed and it is actually believers who are on the swivel chair! God's love toward believers is constant and unchanging because it is an unmerited, gracious love; but when believers sin and break fellowship with Him, believers are the ones who turn away from God, not vice-versa.[21] Even when

---

20. Schreiner, *1, 2 Peter, Jude*, 483-84.
21. Dennis M. Rokser, *Shall Never Perish Forever* (Duluth, MN: Grace Gospel Press, 2012), 202.

believers turn away from Him, His love does not cease but continues uninterrupted toward them.

Because of God's unceasing love for His own, believers are described throughout the Epistle of Jude as "beloved" or divinely-loved ones (vv. 1, 3, 17, 20). Jude expresses God's disposition toward his readers in verse 2, saying, "Mercy, peace, and love be multiplied to you." God's love toward His own is never in question in Jude—it is assumed. What is not certain is whether believers will continue in their love for the Lord. According to Revelation 2:4, it is possible for believers to leave their first love. This is why Jesus commanded His disciples, saying, "abide in My love" (John 15:9). This speaks of the personal enjoyment and experience of God's love by the believer in Christ as he abides in fellowship with the Lord (John 15:4-5; 1 John 1:3-10). But once a person becomes a believer in Christ and is born again, God's love toward the believer is permanent, unchanging, and unconditional (Rom. 8:38-39; Eph. 3:17-19). This is why David could speak of his own eternal security in terms of God's constant love toward him: "Surely goodness and mercy [*hesed*] shall follow me all the days of my life; and I will dwell in the house of the Lord forever" (Ps. 23:6). The Hebrew word for "mercy" (*hesed*) here speaks of God's loyal love and is sometimes translated "steadfast love" or "unfailing love."[22] Thus, believers keep themselves in the love of God, in essence, when they keep their swivel chairs pointed toward God by abiding in fellowship with Him and occupying themselves with His unchanging love for them (2 Cor. 5:14).[23]

Similarly, when the rest of Jude 21 says believers should be "looking for the mercy of our Lord Jesus Christ unto eternal life," this does not mean Christ's mercy and eternal life are uncertain until the believer successfully perseveres to the end of his earthly life. Eternal life is already possessed by believers from the moment of new birth (John 5:24; 6:47; 1 John 5:11, 13). Because this new life from God is everlasting in duration, it continues from the new birth into eternity. Therefore, the believer can look forward to the full manifestation of that eternal life as his future hope and inheritance (Matt. 19:27-29; Titus 1:2; 3:7), even though it is also his present possession. "Hope" in the Bible does not speak of something questionable or doubtful,

---

22. R. Laird Harris, *"hesed"* in *Theological Wordbook of the Old Testament*, ed. R. Laird Harris, Gleason L. Archer, Jr., and Bruce K. Waltke, 2 vols. (Chicago: Moody, 1980), 2:305, §698a.

23. Edward C. Pentecost, "Jude," in *The Bible Knowledge Commentary, New Testament*, ed. John F. Walvoord and Roy B. Zuck (Wheaton, IL: Victor, 1985), 923.

like the English connotation of the word. Instead, biblical hope is simply faith that is cast forward to something that is still future, yet certain. Biblical hope is certainty about something that is still future, such as Christ's coming (Titus 2:13; 1 John 3:2-3) and the consummation of the believer's salvation at glorification (1 Thess. 5:8). Since eternal life is both a new quality of life and an unending life, believers in their earthly walk of faith are to lay hold on the abundant quality of this life that is available to them in the present (John 10:10; 1 Tim. 6:12, 19).

The same is true with mercy, which God provides for all three tenses of salvation—past, present, and future. Believers have already been saved eternally from hell by God's mercy rather than their works (Eph. 2:4-5; Titus 3:5; 1 Peter 1:3; 2:10). But God's mercy must still be appropriated for fellowship, not eternal salvation, in one's daily walk of dependence on the Lord (Heb. 4:16; Jude 2). Jude 21 speaks of God's future mercy, which believers should look forward to as the consummation of their salvation at the coming of Christ. In verse 21, the participle "looking" (*prosdechomenoi*) is the same word used in Titus 2:13, where it says that the grace of God teaches believers to be "looking [*prosdechomai*] for the blessed hope and glorious appearing of our great God and Savior Jesus Christ." Clearly, the mercy that believers are to look for at Christ's return for the church is something certain, not something merely possible or contingent on the believer's perseverance and faithfulness. Just as the new birth was based solely on God's mercy rather one's merits (Titus 3:5), God knows that His children still sin in their earthly walks, and therefore the future salvation, bodily resurrection, and transformation of sinful believers into Christ's likeness will also be unmerited and based purely on His mercy and grace. That is something to look forward to!

Jude 24

The Epistle of Jude ends with a doxology: "24 Now to Him who is able to keep you from stumbling, and to present you faultless before the presence of His glory with exceeding joy, 25 to God our Savior, who alone is wise, be glory and majesty, dominion and power, both now and forever. Amen." Verse 24 is often assumed as support for the doctrine of the perseverance of the saints, as though it were saying, "Now to Him who *will* keep you from stumbling *fatally into apostasy and unbelief.*" The italicized words emphasize two problems with such an interpretation.

First, this interpretation reads Calvinist theology into the meaning of the word "stumble," without any support from the context. The word "stumble" (*aptaistous*) here is commonly assumed to mean a fatal fall from grace into apostasy, which would ostensibly prove that a person never truly believed or was born again. The root word for "stumble" (*ptaiō*) occurs in only four other verses in the New Testament (Rom. 11:11; James 2:10; 3:2; 2 Peter 1:10). None of these references carries the theologically-freighted meaning assigned to *aptaistous* in Jude 24. In fact, James 2:10 implies, and James 3:2 explicitly states, that all believers stumble in sin to some extent. The last reference in 2 Peter 1:10 says that not stumbling is conditional for the believer based on whether the believer will add the spiritual virtues of 2 Peter 1:5-7 to his faith, as explained in the previous chapter.

Second, the assumed Calvinist interpretation of Jude 24 confuses what God is *able* to do and with what He *will* do. While God provides sufficient wisdom and strength through His Word and Spirit to enable the believer not to stumble into false teaching and apostasy, this verse stops short of guaranteeing that He will necessarily do so in every believer's life. Other passages clearly promise that God will keep every one of His children from perishing in hell and preserve them blameless before Him in heaven (1 Cor. 1:8; 1 Thess. 3:13; 5:23-24), but Jude 24 emphasizes God's ability, not what He has decreed to do. The Lord promises to preserve every one of His saints as a matter of His own will and work, but He does not override the will of His children by making them persevere to the end of their lives. If God is able and willing to change every believer's will so as to make them all persevere to the end, then why doesn't He also prevent all sin over the course of each believer's Christian life? The insistence that God only preserves believers from the particular sin of apostasy is neither logical nor scriptural.

Conclusion

The testimonies of the Lord Jesus' half-brothers, James and Jude, along with the apostle John, agree with one another concerning perseverance and preservation. Positively, they show that God Himself is the active agent who performs the task of preserving every child of God (1 John 5:18; Jude 1; Rev. 3:10). Believers are never said to preserve or keep themselves saved from condemnation. The security of the believer's salvation does not rest on the fulfillment of any conditions following initial faith in the Lord Jesus Christ for eternal life.

Although certain passages are often cited as proof texts for the fifth point of Calvinism on the perseverance of the saints, neither the context nor the actual content of these passages support the claims of Calvinism. First John 2:19 does not describe people who once initially believed in Christ but manifested a false, temporary faith because they did not persevere in that faith. Rather, 1 John 2:19 describes those who were never saved in the first place because they did not believe the truth about Jesus as the Christ from the very beginning. Conversely, the unbelief of Israel's Exodus generation in Jude 5 is not a case where Israel's false, spurious faith and non-elect status manifested itself through a failure to persevere. The Old Testament makes clear that Israel initially believed in the Lord but did not continue in faith following the Exodus. The judgment in the wilderness for unbelief took the form of national, temporal, and physical discipline from God, not eternal condemnation, which is reserved for those who have never believed and been justified. Thus, Jude 5 shows what Calvinism's fifth point does not allow or admit—that genuine, initial faith for justification may not necessarily endure.

There are no passages in the epistles of James and Jude or the writings of John which teach that perseverance in faith is required for eternal life. But there are several that show an ongoing walk of faith is absolutely necessary for daily fellowship with the Lord (Jude 21), spiritual growth (James 1:2-4), and a future, eternal reward from the Lord (James 1:12; 5:7-8, 10-11; Rev. 3:9).

Chapter 15

Must You Persevere to Be an Overcomer?

The year was 1971. A small, upstart tennis shoe company based in Portland, Oregon, needed a marking concept to promote its young brand. The solution was a whole new company name that would embody the spirit of victory and athletic achievement. What better name to choose than the Greek name for victory and the name of the Greek goddess of victory herself—Nike. An appropriate symbol was quickly designed to represent this goddess's wings of victory. By the next year, the Nike swoosh began appearing on the sides of tennis shoes and a world-famous brand was off to the races. Later, a simple marketing slogan was chosen to inspire great achievement—"Just Do It!"

In the Christian world today, many also subscribe to the Nike philosophy when it comes to salvation. They teach that the real overcomers are those who "Just Do It!" If one fails to achieve, they claim this only demonstrates that he is not a real victor or overcomer after all. Such a person is not a Nike Christian since the real overcomers are those who experience ongoing, practical victory over sin, Satan, and the world all the way to the finish line of their Christian lives. But is this Nike philosophy biblical?

Theological traditions that require faith plus good works in order to obtain, maintain, or prove one's eternal salvation invariably view the overcomers in the New Testament as being true believers who are characterized by faithfulness and good works to the end of their lives. For Arminians as well as Calvinists, a real, living, persevering, and saving faith is one which practically overcomes.

Views on the Identity of the Overcomer

The Arminian view asserts that an overcomer is one who believes in Christ for justification and perseveres in faith and holiness to the end of life in order to *maintain* eternal salvation. This is the normal Arminian interpretation.[1] Thus, according to the first view, all true believers practically overcome sin, Satan, and the world in their lives and are considered to be overcomers by their faith and good works. Noted Arminian theologian I. Howard Marshall expresses this view: "The true Christian is the victorious Christian, and he is prom-ised salvation in the world to come. The Christian life is a constant struggle for victory, and in some cases this struggle may include fac-ing martyrdom. If a person fails to be victorious, his faith must be regarded as of doubtful character."[2] Marshall goes on to explain that overcoming requires "faithfulness unto death," "keeping the com-mandments of God," "active endurance of trials," and "performing the works of God."[3] But if overcoming is essential for salvation in the world to come and these things are required to truly "overcome," then salvation must be by works and not by grace alone.

The Calvinist interpretation of the overcomer is no less merito-rious. It also holds that overcomers are true believers whose lives are characterized by a consistent pattern of practical holiness that overcomes sin, Satan, and the world. But this view is distinguished from the Arminian view in that perseverance to the end of one's life does not maintain salvation but *proves* or *demonstrates* the genu-ineness of one's initial faith.[4] Like the Arminian view, the Calvinist

---

1. Daniel D. Corner, *The Believer's Conditional Security: Eternal Security Refuted* (Washington, PA: Evangelical Outreach, 2000), 89; Guy Duty, *If Ye Continue: A Study of the Conditional Aspects of Salvation* (Minneapolis: Bethany House, 1966), 148-52; I. Howard Marshall, *Kept by the Power of God: A Study of Perseverance and Falling Away* (Minneapolis: Bethany House, 1969), 174-75; David Pawson, *Once Saved, Always Saved? A Study in Perseverance and Inheritance* (London: Hodder & Stoughton, 1996), 82-84.

2. I. Howard Marshall, *Kept by the Power of God: A Study of Perseverance and Fall-ing Away* (Minneapolis: Bethany House, 1969), 174. See also Guy Duty, *If Ye Continue: A Study of the Conditional Aspects of Salvation* (Minneapolis: Bethany House, 1966), 148-52.

3. Ibid, Marshall.

4. G. K. Beale, *The Book of Revelation*, New International Greek Testament Com-mentary (Grand Rapids: Eerdmans, 1999), 234-35, 269-72; Matthew R. Edwards, "The Identity of the Overcomer in Revelation 2-3" (Th.M. thesis, Dallas Theological Semi-nary, 2005), 75-79; George E. Ladd, *A Commentary on the Revelation of John* (Grand Rapids: Eerdmans, 1972), 40-41; John F. MacArthur, Jr., *The Gospel According to Jesus*, Revised and Expanded Edition (Grand Rapids: Zondervan, 1994), 229; James E. Rosscup, "The Overcomer of the Apocalypse," *Grace Theological Journal* 3 (Fall 1982):

view also concludes that all true believers are overcomers by virtue of their faith and good works but that perseverance and good works are the necessary result of being elect. Schreiner and Canaday claim that "those who refuse to acknowledge Jesus and fail to overcome will be judged in the lake of fire. From these two overcomer texts (Rev. 2:11; 3:5) it seems fair to conclude that the reward in view in every overcomer text is eternal life itself. Thus, the crown of life in Revelation 2:10 is not a reward above and beyond eternal life; it is eternal life."[5] This interpretation fails to recognize the critical biblical distinction between the free gift of eternal life and rewards for good works explained in chapter 6 and demonstrates once again that Reformed theology's doctrine of salvation is not truly consistent with God's grace.

But if being an overcomer means being a Christian with a continual pattern of spiritual victory over sin, then how continual must your victory be? At what point will you know whether you have overcome enough? Can you really know whether you are an overcomer or not, or must you wait until the end of your life to know your fate? Though the biblical concept of the overcomer is often obscure and uncertain in many Christians' minds, it does not need to be. God wants everyone to know whether they are overcomers or not. This chapter seeks to demonstrate from the Bible that all believers in Christ are overcomers by virtue of their position in the perfect Overcomer, Jesus Christ Himself, and that this classical dispensational interpretation[6] is not only the most consistent with the text of

---

261-86; Thomas R. Schreiner and Ardel B. Caneday, *The Race Set Before Us: A Biblical Theology of Perseverance and Assurance* (Downers Grove, IL: InterVarsity, 2001), 11-12, 83-84; J. B. Smith, *A Revelation of Jesus Christ* (Scottdale, PA: Mennonite Publishing House, 1961), 79; Sam Storms, *Kept for Jesus: What the New Testament Really Teaches about Assurance of Salvation and Eternal Security* (Wheaton, IL: Crossway, 2015), 168-73; Robert L. Thomas, *Revelation 1-7* (Chicago: Moody, 1992), 155, 198, 231-32; and Daniel K. K. Wong, "The Johannine Concept of the Overcomer," (Th.D. dissertation, Dallas Theological Seminary, 1995).

5. Thomas R. Schreiner and Ardel B. Caneday, *The Race Set Before Us: A Biblical Theology of Perseverance and Assurance* (Downers Grove, IL: InterVarsity, 2001), 84.

6. Lewis Sperry Chafer, *Systematic Theology*, 8 vols. (Dallas: Dallas Theological Seminary, 1948; reprint, Grand Rapids: Kregel, 1993), 3:306; Thomas Constable, *Expository Notes on Revelation* (Garland, TX: Sonic Light, 2012), 23-24; W. Robert Cook, *The Theology of John* (Chicago: Moody, 1979), 173; Mal Couch, *A Bible Handbook to Revelation* (Grand Rapids: Kregel, 2001), 164-65; Theodore H. Epp, *Practical Studies in Revelation*, 2 vols. (Lincoln, NE: Back to the Bible, 1970), 1:198-201; Charles L. Feinberg, *A Commentary on Revelation: The Grand Finale* (Winona Lake, IN: BMH, 1985), 43; Samuel L. Hoyt, *The Judgment Seat of Christ*, Revised Edition (Duluth, MN: Grace Gospel Press, 2015), 197-205; Tim LaHaye, *Revelation Unveiled* (Grand Rapids: Zondervan, 1999), 49, 71, 76; J. Vernon McGee, *Thru the Bible with J. Vernon McGee*, 5

Scripture but also with the truth of eternal salvation and Christian living by God's grace.

Overcomers Positionally, Even If Not Practically

In every New Testament reference to the Greek words for victory or overcoming (*nikos, nikē,* or *nikaō*) applied to believers prior to the book of Revelation, all believers are consistently identified as already being overcomers, victors, or victorious (Rom. 8:37; 1 Cor. 15:54-57; 1 John 2:13-14; 4:4; 5:4-5).[7] This status as an overcomer is based on the believer's union with the overcoming One, Jesus Christ, not the believer's own works. The sole human condition for being an overcomer, according to 1 John 5:4-5, is to believe in Jesus Christ: "For whatever is born of God overcomes the world. And this is the victory that has overcome the world—our faith. Who is he who overcomes the world, but he who believes that Jesus is the Son of God?" In reference to this key Johannine passage defining the overcomer as a believer, Ryrie states, "No contingency is attached to the promise in these verses. Every believer, whether new or mature, has victory simply because he is a believer."[8] The only way it is possible for every believer to be an overcomer is if this status depends on one's position in Jesus Christ and His spiritual victory rather than the believer's own performance or practice.

With respect to practically overcoming and the use of *nikos, nikaō,* and their associated forms in the New Testament, it is significant that only God the Father (Rom. 3:4) and the Lord Jesus Christ (Matt. 12:20; Luke 11:22; John 16:33; Rev. 5:5; 17:14) are said to be victors by their own worth or accomplishments. Christ Jesus Himself is the ultimate Overcomer who has already gained the victory by His

---

vols. (Nashville: Thomas Nelson, 1983), 5:904; William R. Newell, *Revelation Chapter-by-Chapter* (reprint, Grand Rapids: Kregel, 1994), 42, 52, 339; Charles C. Ryrie, *Basic Theology* (Wheaton, IL: Victor, 1986), 154; idem, *Revelation* (Chicago: Moody, 1968), 22-23; Erich Sauer, *The Triumph of the Crucified* (Carlisle, UK: Paternoster, 1964), 115-16; Lehman Strauss, *Revelation* (Neptune, NJ: Loizeaux, 1965), 107-10; John F. Walvoord, *The Revelation of Jesus Christ* (Chicago: Moody, 1966), 59, 98-99; and Warren W. Wiersbe, *The Bible Exposition Commentary,* 2 vols. (Wheaton, IL: Victor, 1989), 2:572.

7. Significantly, only the Greek aorist, present, and perfect tenses are used in these epistolary verses to describe the present status of all believers in Christ. The future tense (the only tense in which there is no dispute about time being grammaticalized in the tense form) is never used for *nikaō* to describe being a victor or gaining a victory, as if this was only a potential future status for some believers. In other words, there are no verses that say in essence, "You *will be* an overcomer if you persevere in faith and good works."

8. Ryrie, *Basic Theology,* 154.

perfect character and work. Now in this age of grace, the moment a lost sinner places his or her faith in Christ for eternal salvation, that believer is baptized by the Holy Spirit into spiritual union with Jesus Christ (Rom. 6:3-4; 1 Cor. 12:12-13; Gal. 3:26-28) and has a blessed position in Him by grace (Eph. 1:3). At that same moment of faith and union with Christ, the believer is constituted a spiritual victor or overcomer by his or her position in the One who has already overcome sin, Satan, and the world by His perfect, finished work.

Thus believers do not fight the good fight of faith in order to become overcomers; rather believers fight because they are already victors on the side of the Victor Himself. Believers do not fight the good fight of faith in order to *obtain* the standing of "overcomer"; rather they fight by faith in the present battles of life *from* their standing as spiritual victors in Christ. Lehman Strauss explains this vital relationship between Christ and the believer.

> Presently there is only one perfect Overcomer. He could say, "I also overcame, and am set down with My Father in His throne" (Revelation 3:21). All other overcomers are such by virtue of their position in Him. Jesus said, "Be of good cheer; I have overcome the world" (John 16:33). I am so glad that our Lord Jesus Christ has overcome the world because I know that I never could.
>
> The Apostle John wrote, "For whatsoever is born of God overcometh the world: and this is the victory that overcometh the world, even our faith. Who is he that overcometh the world, but he that believeth that Jesus is the Son of God?" (1 John 5:4-5). The overcomer here is he who has been born again. The [second] verb rendered "overcometh" is in the aorist tense, and this takes us back in point of time to when we first received Christ by faith and were born again, when we passed spiritually out of death into union with Christ. Faith in Christ did not merely make us God's children, but overcomers as well. The day we trusted Christ was a day of victory, the day we overcame the world. "Who is he that overcometh the world, but he that *believeth* that Jesus is the Son of God?" Not merely certain ones among the believers, but all of them. From the very moment of our conversion we were overcomers. "This is the victory that overcometh the world"—even our fighting? No! "Even our faith." Since our blessed Lord overcame the world, must we fight the battle all

over again? How foolish! Rather we trust Him who by His death and resurrection has won the battle for us.[9]

But if being an overcomer is a status or reward only for diligent, deserving believers yet to be determined at Christ's future judgment seat, then how can God already view all believers as overcomers throughout the New Testament? Not only does the Lord already view all believers as overcomers, He even views them as "superovercomers"! According to Romans 8:37, all believers are already considered "superovercomers" or "more than conquerors" (*hypernikōmen*): "Yet in all these things we are more than conquerors through Him who loved us." This status of being a superconqueror or superovercomer is not merited by believers since Romans 8:37 states that we as believers are overcomers "through (*dia*) Him who loved us." We are superovercomers through Christ who loved us, not through our works. The fact that all believers are overcomers positionally, even if not practically, finds support in the subsequent verses, "For I am persuaded that neither death nor life, nor angels nor principalities nor powers, nor things present nor things to come, nor height nor depth, nor any other created thing, shall be able to separate us from the love of God that is in Christ Jesus" (vv. 38-39). The reason why every believer is an overcomer is because they are positionally "in (*en*) Christ Jesus" (v. 39) and eternally secure in Him. According to Romans 8:37-39, all believers are overcomers by (*dia*, v. 37) Christ and in (*en*, v. 39) Him. This speaks of the believer's position in Christ solely because of God's grace rather than their own merit.

But simply because a believer is an overcomer positionally in Christ (Rom. 8:37) does not mean he or she practically overcomes sin. The book of Romans goes on to teach that a believer can still be overcome practically by evil in his or her earthly life: "Do not be overcome (*nikō*) by evil, but overcome (*nika*) evil with good" (Rom. 12:21). It would be pointless to command believers "not be overcome by evil" if every believer automatically and necessarily overcame evil in their practical, daily walk, as the perseverance-of-the-saints view teaches. A comparison of Romans 8:37-39 with Romans 12:21 demonstrates that all believers are overcomers (even superovercomers) in position but not necessarily in practice.

First Corinthians 1:2; 3:1-4; and 15:57 also demonstrate that all believers are overcomers positionally in Christ. In 1 Corinthians 1:2, Paul explains the spiritual position of the Corinthian Christians, "To

---

9. Strauss, *Revelation*, 109-10.

the church of God which is at Corinth, to those who are sanctified in Christ Jesus, called *to be* saints, with all who in every place call on the name of Jesus Christ our Lord, both theirs and ours." These believers were positionally "sanctified in Christ" and literally "called saints." However, in their present spiritual state or walk, they were anything but saintly, for in 1 Corinthians 3:1-4, Paul repeatedly calls them carnal, "And I, brethren, could not speak to you as to spiritual people but as to carnal. . . . for you are still carnal. . . . are you not carnal and walking like mere men? . . . are you not carnal?" Yet despite their evident carnality, the Corinthians were still considered to be spiritual victors, for Paul goes on to write in 1 Corinthians 15:54-57:

> 54 So when this corruptible has put on incorruption, and this mortal has put on immortality, then shall be brought to pass the saying that is written: "Death is swallowed up in victory [*nikos*]." 55 "O Death, where is your sting? O Hades, where is your victory [*nikos*]?" 56 The sting of death is sin, and the strength of sin is the law. 57 But thanks be to God, who gives us the victory [*nikos*] through our Lord Jesus Christ.

The Corinthians were carnal in their present walk with God and even faced the prospect of divine chastening to the point of death for their persistent carnality (1 Cor. 11:28-32). But they were also guaranteed future bodily glorification and victory over sin and death because of Christ's victory over the grave (1 Cor. 15:57). This is attributable only to the grace of God, not the believer's own worthiness, dedication, and good works.

These passages in Romans and 1 Corinthians refute the entire Lordship Salvation, perseverance-of-the-saints position, which teaches that all believers are overcomers both positionally in Christ and practically in daily life. Taken together, these passages Romans and 1 Corinthians demonstrate that "every church saint is an overcomer in standing even if not in practice."[10]

This conclusion is based solely on New Testament evidence rather than Old Testament or extra-biblical usage of the *nikaō/nikos* word group. Though the terms *nikos* and *nikaō* and their associated forms occur many times in the Septuagint of the Old Testament[11]

---

10. Cook, *The Theology of John*, 173.
11. See 2 Samuel 2:26; 1 Chronicles 29:11; Psalm 51:4; Proverbs 6:25; and Habakkuk 3:19.

and Apocrypha,[12] and hundreds of times in extra-biblical writings of the same era (Philo, Josephus, Pseudepigrapha), such occurrences never parallel the New Testament concept of the overcomer as referring to all church-age believers and their exalted position in Jesus Christ. New Testament studies typically explore the Old Testament and extra-biblical backgrounds of a word or concept in order to demonstrate a connection to its New Testament usage. This practice, however, would be ill-advised for the New Testament concept of the believer as an overcomer since it is a unique church-age concept. The church itself, and truth related to it, was a mystery that was unrevealed until the time of the apostles and New Testament prophets (Rom. 16:25-26; Eph. 3:1-10; Col. 1:24-27). Thus, since being an overcomer in Christ is a positional concept and only church-age believers are privileged to have such a spiritual position or standing, then we should not expect to find the positional concept of an overcomer revealed anywhere in the Old Testament or extra-biblical writings—and we don't. The fact that the words *nikos* and *nikaō* (and their associated forms) are used prior to the New Testament Epistles only of one who overcame something practically (in war, athletics, over vice, etc.) rather than positionally fits with the pattern of usage we would expect of an overcomer in the New Testament referring to a church-age believer in Christ, where the believer has a spiritual position in Him solely by God's grace.

"He Who Overcomes" Does Not Mean Ongoing, Practical Victory

A second reason why the "overcomer" is simply a "believer" is that the grammatical form of the phrase "he who overcomes" (*ho nikōn*) functions as a person's title without necessarily describing that person's continual pattern of life. Just as a person may forever be known negatively as a "murderer" for a one-time act of murder or positively as a "benefactor" for a one-time donation, so the New Testament uses "overcomer" to refer to those who place their faith in Christ at a point in time and are born again (1 John 5:1-5).

However, many interpreters still wrongly assume that the present tense, substantival participle *ho nikōn* indicates a pattern of life in which the believer experiences continual, practical victory over sin,

---

12. See 1 Ezra 3:9; 4:5, 59; Wisdom 4:2; 1 Maccabees 3:19; 2 Maccabees 3:5; 10:28, 38; 13:15; 15:8, 21; 3 Maccabees 1:4; and 4 Maccabees 1:11; 3:17; 6:33; 9:30; 17:12.

Satan, and the world.[13] James Rosscup is one who holds this view of the overcomer.

> [1 John 5:5] goes on to utilize present tenses, quite plausibly customary or iterative presents, to denote the general overall pattern of overcoming for the Christian who believes in an ongoing sense (v 1, *pisteuō*, present tense) that Jesus is the Son of God. Later, in Revelation 2–3, "he who overcomes" is virtually the same as "he who believes." As Robertson says: "... *nikaō* [is] a common Johannine verb. ... Faith is dominant in Paul, victory in John, faith is victory (1 John 5:4)." John also uses the present tense of *nikaō* in Revelation 2–3, suggesting that continuing victory is characteristic of the saved just as continuing faith is (1 John 5:1).[14]

As explained previously in chapter 4, the Greek present tense is often misinterpreted as indicating a verb or participle's *Aktionsart* or kind of action, namely, that it is continual. However, the ten examples given in chapter 4 of the present tense, substantival participle dispel this myth of Greek grammar. The grammatical construction *ho nikōn* ("he who overcomes") is identical to the construction for "he who believes" or "whoever believes" (*ho pisteuōn*) and such constructions do not inherently denote an ongoing pattern of belief or practical victory.

Furthermore, the only place in the entire New Testament where the overcomer is explicitly defined is 1 John 5, and there the issue of whether one is an overcomer (i.e., true believer) is determined by the object or content of faith, not the duration of faith: "Whoever believes that [*ho pisteuōn hoti*] Jesus is the Christ is born of God. . . . For whatever is born of God overcomes the world. And this is the victory that has overcome the world—our faith" (5:1, 4); "Who is he who overcomes the world, but he who believes that [*ho pisteuōn hoti*] Jesus is the Son of God?" (5:5). The expression "whoever believes" or "he who believes" (*ho pisteuōn*) combined with "that" (*hoti*) indicates the content of what is believed, namely, that Jesus is the Christ, the Son of God. According to John 20:31, when a person believes "that

---

13. Beale, *The Book of Revelation*, 234-35, 250-51, 266-67; Donald W. Burdick, *The Letters of John the Apostle: An In-Depth Commentary* (Chicago: Moody, 1985), 347; D. Edmond Hiebert, *The Epistles of John: An Expositional Commentary* (Greenville, SC: Bob Jones University Press, 1991), 223-30; Mounce, *The Book of Revelation*, 90; Thomas, *Revelation 1-7*, 155, 198.

14. Rosscup, "The Overcomer of the Apocalypse," 264.

Jesus is the Christ, the Son of God," that person receives eternal life. But notice what 1 John 5 does not say. It does not say "Who is he who overcomes the world, but he who believes *and perseveres in that belief to the end."* Neither 1 John 5, nor any other passage of Scripture defines the overcomer according to the duration or fruitfulness of belief. Instead, being an overcomer is defined by believing the right biblical content concerning Jesus Christ.

There is no evidence, whether grammatical, lexical, or contextual, proving that the phrase "he who overcomes" (*ho nikōn*) in Revelation 2–3 refers to continual, practical victory over sin as a Christian. In contrast, the Bible teaches that the moment a person fulfills the one condition for being an overcomer, namely, believing in Jesus Christ (1 John 5:4-5), that person is viewed by God as being positionally in Christ (Rom. 8:37; 1 Cor. 1:2; 15:57), the victorious One, even if that believer does not thereafter walk in practical victory over sin (Rom. 12:21; 1 Cor. 3:1-4).

Overcomer Promises and Crowns Are Distinct

A third reason for an overcomer simply being a believer in Christ is that the promises to the overcomers in Revelation 2–3 are distinct from the rewards that are offered to the seven churches. There are two passages (Rev. 2:10; 3:11) where Christ offers "crowns" to the churches as a reward for service. But this is distinct from the promises to all believers/overcomers in the following verses (2:11; 3:12):

> 10 Do not fear any of those things which you are about to suffer. Indeed, the devil is about to throw some of you into prison, that you may be tested, and you will have tribulation ten days. Be faithful until death, and I will give you the crown of life. 11 He who has an ear, let him hear what the Spirit says to the churches. He who overcomes shall not be hurt by the second death. (Rev. 2:10-11)

> 11 Behold, I am coming quickly! Hold fast what you have, that no one may take your crown. 12 He who overcomes, I will make him a pillar in the temple of My God, and he shall go out no more. I will write on him the name of My God and the name of the city of My God, the New Jerusalem, which comes down out of heaven from My God. And I will write on him My new name. (Rev. 3:11-12)

Notice that in 2:10 and 3:11, the two references to a "crown" come *before* the overcomer statements of 2:11 and 3:12. Conspicuously, "crowns" are never mentioned *within* any of the seven overcomer statements of chapters 2–3. This indicates that Christ never promises a crown "to him who overcomes" because not all overcomers receive crowns—only deserving overcomers/believers do. Therefore, in keeping with the biblical distinction between salvation and rewards, the two crown passages (Rev. 2:10; 3:11) should be interpreted as references to rewards and the following two overcomer statements (2:11; 3:12) as promises of future salvation blessings for all believers, which are designed to give believers incentive to persevere in the present conflict because of guaranteed future victory.

This conclusion harmonizes well with the content of the promises to the "overcomer" in Revelation 2–3, which are clearly salvation promises rather than offers to earn rewards: "To him who overcomes I will give to eat from the tree of life" (2:7); "He who overcomes shall not be hurt by the second death" (2:11); and "He who overcomes . . . I will not blot out his name from the Book of Life" (3:5).

Good Works Are Additional to Being an Overcomer

A fourth reason "overcomer" in Revelation 2–3 is simply describing a believer is because the language and syntax of overcomer verses do not support the conclusion that doing good works is inherent to being an overcomer. A few key overcomer references, such as Revelation 2:26, 3:4-5, and 12:11, are often cited as proof texts to support the idea that all overcomers are persevering, obedient believers. Revelation 2:26 is perhaps cited more often than any other verse to support this claim.

Revelation 2:26

In this verse, Christ says to the church in Thyatira, "And he who overcomes [*ho nikōn*], and [*kai*] keeps [*ho tērōn*] My works until the end, to him I will give power over the nations." There is nothing contextually or grammatically, including the presence of the conjunction *kai* ("and"), that requires "he who overcomes" (*ho nikōn*) and "[he who] keeps" (*ho tērōn*) to be synonymous or inseparable concepts. What this passage *is* teaching is that a person must first be an overcomer/believer (one who possesses eternal life), and second, he must persevere in good works (to receive a reward). This appears to correspond well with the promises in the passage. To the one who is an overcomer/believer, he will receive the promise of reigning with Christ (v. 27). In addition, if he fulfills a second condition, namely, perseverance in good works, he will receive the reward of the morning star (v. 28).[15]

Robert Thomas offers an explanation of Revelation 2:26 based on Greek syntax that tries to equate "he who overcomes" (*ho nikōn*) with "[he who] keeps (*ho tērōn*) My works to the end."

> The occurrence of the article with each participle has the effect of making the two participles equal. Its repetition with the second serves to emphasize the two conditions of success: "The victor is he who keeps Christ's works; he who keeps Christ's works is the victor" (Swete, *Apocalypse*, p. 46; Charles, *Revelation*, 1:74). The nominative case of the participles affords another example of the nominative absolute (cf. 3:12, 21), the person so designated being picked up by a dative *autō* in the next clause (Robertson, *Word Pictures*, 6:311). More normal constructions are those found in 2:7, 17 and 6:4; 21:6 (Charles, *Revelation*, 1:74). The nominative absolute is common in John's other writings (cf. John 6:39; 7:38; 1 John 2:24, 27) (Lee, "Revelation," 4:529).[16]

---

15. Scripture teaches that all believers, regardless of their walk, will reign with Christ in some capacity by virtue of being positionally in Christ and being His corporate bride (1 Cor. 3:1-4, 21-23; 4:8; 6:2-3; Rev. 3:21; 19:7-9). But the promise of Revelation 2:28, "and I will give him the morning star," although somewhat enigmatic and subject to various interpretations, seems to promise something additional to salvation. Since Revelation 22:16 explicitly states that the morning star is none other than Jesus Christ Himself, it seems best to follow this same interpretation in 2:28. Other passages confirm this interpretation (Num. 24:17; Mal. 4:2; 2 Peter 1:19). But this raises an important question. If every believer already has Christ (1 John 5:12a), yet in Revelation 2:28 Christ promises that He "will give" (in the future) persevering overcomers/believers the morning star (i.e., Himself), in what sense will He give Himself to believers if they already have Him? He promises in Revelation 2:26-28 that He will give Himself as the bright morning star in a special way, as a reward, to persevering, deserving believers. (This is similar to the twofold promise of Revelation 3:4-5 explained below.) To the believer who seeks to glorify Christ through an abiding walk of personal intimacy with his Savior and perseverance in faith and good works, Christ will reward that believer with a special reflection of His own glory—with an increased capacity to glorify the Lord (Dan. 12:3; 1 Cor. 15:41-42; 2 Cor. 3:18; 4:16-18)—a capacity that reflects the degree to which that believer sought to glorify the Lord in his earthly life. In this sense, although the believer already has Christ (1 John 5:12a), Christ also promises Himself to the abiding, obedient believer as a reward (Rev. 2:28).

16. Thomas, *Revelation 1-7*, 232.

Thomas's explanation of the overcomer in this passage requires a rather technical response. First, the nominative absolute construction has no bearing on the issue of perseverance. The nominative case of the two participles (*ho nikōn* – "he who overcomes"; *ho tērōn* – "[he who] keeps") being picked up by the dative case of *autō* serves only to identify "he who overcomes" and "he who keeps" as the same individual. But this does not equate the *actions* of overcoming and persevering; nor does it lead to the conclusion that all overcomers keep Christ's works to the end or that one must keep His works to the end in order to be an overcomer. Rather, it shows only that there are two separate requirements for one person to receive the promise of authority over the nations (vv. 26-27) and the morning star (v. 28)—first, being an overcomer, and second, keeping Christ's works to the end. In other words, this passage is requiring that the believer/overcomer, who will receive the salvation blessing of reigning with Christ (vv. 26-27), must also persevere in good works in order to receive the reward of the morning star (v. 28).[17]

Second, Thomas also claims that the use of the article (*ho*) before each participle, with the two articular participles being separated by *kai*, has the effect of making the two participles equal. But the syntax simply does not sustain such a conclusion. The only sense in which the two participles may be considered "equal" is that they refer to the *same person* performing the activity described in the two participles. The grammatical structure does not equate the two *actions* of the participles—overcoming and keeping.

A computer search of the New Testament for this exact syntactical structure reveals that there are only three parallel examples to the construction found in Revelation 2:26.[18] The three parallels to Revelation 2:26 are all found in the Gospel of Mark (6:31; 11:9, 15). These three verses demonstrate that it is invalid to equate, or inseparably

---

17. Some may reasonably wonder, if the phrase in 2:26 "and keeps My works until the end" is an additional requirement to "him who overcomes" rather than a further explanation of what it means to be an overcomer, then why is verse 26 the *only* overcomer statement in Revelation 2–3 that has this additional requirement of "he who overcomes *and* . . ."? The answer appears to be as simple as observing the unique context. A few verses earlier Christ had just given the Thyatirans a promise that is not stated anywhere else to the seven churches, namely, to "give to each one according to his works" (2:23). It appears that in verse 26 Christ is simply being consistent with the preceding promise of verse 23 to give a reward according to one's works that is additional to being an overcomer.

18. This search looked for all known examples of *kai* separating two articular participles that mirror each other with the same tense, case, gender, and number (and that are not the participles of equative verbs, such as *eimi*, as in Revelation 1:8; 4:8; 11:17; 16:5).

connect, the actions of the two articular participles on either side of the conjunction *kai*.

Mark 6:31 states, "And He said to them, 'Come aside by yourselves to a deserted place and rest a while.' For there were many coming and going (*hoi erchomenoi kai hoi hypagontes*),[19] and they did not even have time to eat." In Mark 6:31, the activities of "coming" and "going" are not the same. "Going" is not epexegetical to "coming." Nor are the two participial phrases parenthetical, as if the verse were saying, "There were many coming (that is, there were many going)." Although the two activities expressed by the participles ("coming," "going") are not equal or epexegetical, the *people* who came and went may have been the same individuals, just like Revelation 2:26 where the one who receives the promised reward is the individual who both overcomes (believes) and keeps Christ's works.

Mark 11:9 provides a second syntactical parallel to Revelation 2:26.

Then those who went before and those who followed (*hoi proagontes kai hoi akolouthountes*) cried out, saying: "Hosanna! 'Blessed *is He who comes in the name of the* LORD!'"

In Mark 11:9, those who went before and those who followed after Christ as He entered Jerusalem may not have been the same people or one homogeneous group (as in Rev. 2:26), but this example shows nevertheless that having the same construction of two articular participles separated by *kai* does not make the actions of the participles synonymous or equivalent since going "before" Christ and "following" after Him clearly do not have the same meaning. In the same way, the activities of overcoming and keeping/persevering in Revelation 2:26 do not mean the same thing.

Mark 11:15 provides the final New Testament parallel to the construction in Revelation 2:26. Consistent with Mark 6:31 and 11:9, this verse also does not equate the activities of the two participles separated by *kai*. This verse says, "So they came to Jerusalem. Then Jesus went into the temple and began to drive out those who bought and sold (*tous pōlountas kai tous agorazontas*) in the temple, and overturned the tables of the money changers and the seats of those who sold doves." Again, while those "selling" and those "buying" in the temple may not be referring to the same individuals, the activities

---

19. Note that the difference in voice between *erchomenoi* and *hypagontes* is irrelevant and does not disqualify Mark 6:31 as a parallel example to Revelation 2:26 since *erchomai* is deponent and does not have an active voice form.

of those individuals cannot be equated since buying and selling are opposite of one another. The passage cannot logically be making the second participial phrase parenthetical or epexegetical to the first, as if the passage were saying, "Jesus . . . began to drive out those who were buying (that is, those who were selling...)." Such an interpretation becomes nonsensical.

There are only three constructions in the entire New Testament that are syntactically parallel to Revelation 2:26. These three examples demonstrate that an article preceding each participle of the same tense, case, gender, and number, separated by *kai*, does not make equal or epexegetical the two entities described by the participles or the two activities of the participles. This means that *there are no examples in the New Testament to support the conclusion that the two acts of overcoming and keeping/persevering are equivalent to one another or that overcoming is parenthetically modified and defined by keeping Christ's works to the end.* Rather, the three parallel examples from Mark's Gospel demonstrate just the opposite, namely, that the two participles separated by *kai* are distinct from one another. The second articular participle does not necessarily follow the first, just like the one who keeps Christ's works to the end does not necessarily follow being an overcomer.

Revelation 3:4-5

Revelation 3:4-5 is a second passage often cited to support the interpretation that being an overcomer means being a faithful, obedient believer who perseveres in holiness and good works. In this passage, Christ says, "You have a few names even in Sardis who have not defiled their garments; and they shall walk with Me in white, for they are worthy. He who overcomes shall be clothed in white garments, and I will not blot out his name from the Book of Life; but I will confess his name before My Father and before His angels." The promises of Christ in Revelation 3:4-5 are similar to those in Revelation 2:26-28. In Revelation 2:26, the description of the recipient is twofold—"he who overcomes *and* keeps My works to the end." Similarly in Revelation 3:4-5, all overcomers will "wear" white garments (v. 5), but only those who "walk" in a "worthy" manner will receive the privilege of being able to "walk with" Christ in white (v. 4), which is a reward of greater privilege and intimacy with Christ.

It was previously noted that Revelation 2–3 contains a pattern of Christ promising a reward to faithful believers in a particular church (2:10, 23, 25; 3:11) followed later by a promise of salvation blessings to the overcomers within that church (2:11, 26-28; 3:12). Revelation 3:4-5 follows this same pattern of a reward promised to faithful believers (v. 4) followed by a promise of salvation blessings to all believers (v. 5). In these verses, Christ states that the faithful believers in Sardis "shall walk with Me in white, for they are worthy" (v. 4) and that the overcomer "shall be clothed in white" (v. 5). Wearing white will be a blessing possessed by all the saved (v. 5); whereas walking with Christ in white garments (v. 4) will be an added blessing or reward conditioned on one's walk of fellowship with the Lord now. This principle is found throughout Scripture (Gen. 3:8; 5:22, 24; 6:9; Lev. 26:11-12; Deut. 23:14; 2 Chron. 17:3-4; 2 Cor. 6:16; Eph. 4:1; Rev. 2:1). Even though all believers will be in a state of purity and fellowship with God after the resurrection by virtue of being in sinless, glorified bodies, walking with Christ in white in the coming Kingdom will be a reward for a walk of purity and intimacy with the Lord now.

Imagine being at a royal ball hosted by a wealthy foreign monarch where hundreds of well-dressed guests are assembled inside the royal palace and you are among them. It is an honor just to be present on such a grand occasion. But imagine the honor you would have if, during the ball, the king invited you to leave the palace for a while and go for a walk with him on the palace grounds. What a privilege that would be! This is the privilege that awaits the overcomers in white (Rev. 3:5) who are also found "worthy" to walk with Christ (Rev. 3:4).

Therefore, Revelation 3:4-5 is simply teaching that all who are overcomers (believers) will wear white (v. 5), but those who are believers (overcomers) *and* who walk worthily shall not only wear white but also receive the reward of *walking* with Christ in white (v. 4). This pictures a greater degree of intimacy with the Lord. The Greek text does not support the idea that overcoming in verse 5 is defined or explained by walking worthily in verse 4.

Revelation 12:11

Revelation 12:11 is also used sometimes to support the idea that all overcomers are faithful, working, persevering believers. This verse describes overcomers who are martyred by the Antichrist in the Tribulation, saying, "And they overcame him by [*dia*] the blood of the Lamb and by [*dia*] the word of their testimony, and they did not love their lives to the death." Many interpreters wrongly assume that this verse is teaching that being an overcomer requires more than faith in Christ's blood, requiring at least two other things—testifying for Christ and enduring persecution or martyrdom.

In order to correctly interpret this verse, it should be carefully observed once again what this verse *is* saying and what it is *not* saying. First, it is not saying that there are three activities by which a person is an overcomer: believing in Christ's substitutionary death, witnessing for Christ, and being a martyr. Instead, it is teaching that being an overcomer is based on two things: Christ's "blood" (substitutionary death) and "the word" of their testimony (the Word of God or the gospel). The word "testimony" (*martyria*) is a noun, not a verb (*martyreō*). The passage does not say that they overcame the Antichrist because they testified, but by the word "of their testimony," i.e., by the content of what they testify, namely, the word (singular) of God or the gospel, which they had believed and was the power of God unto salvation for them (Rom. 1:16; 10:16-17; James 1:18; 1 Peter 1:23-25). Once Christ's blood and the Word of God are stated in the verse as the basis for regeneration or being an overcomer, the verse concludes by telling the reader what these overcomers will do in the Tribulation—they will be willing to die for Christ—"and they did not love their lives to the death."

Regarding the basis for being an overcomer in Revelation 12:11, the preposition *dia* is used twice with the nouns "blood" and "word" in the accusative case: "And they overcame him by (*dia*) the blood of the Lamb and by (*dia*) the word of their testimony." When *dia* is used with the accusative case, it expresses cause and should normally be translated or interpreted "because of." When *dia* is used with nouns in the genitive case, it means "through" or "by." Therefore, since *dia* occurs here twice with the accusative case, Revelation 12:11 is more accurately saying, "And they overcame him *because of* the blood of the Lamb and *because of* the word of their testimony." This shows more clearly that these Tribulation believers are overcomers "because of" two things—the blood of Christ and the Word of God. Neither of these refer to activities done by the overcomers, but rather to the contents of their faith. Observe again what Revelation 12:11 does *not* say. It does not say what many people assume it says, that is, that these Tribulation saints are overcomers "*because* they did not love their lives to the death." The preposition *dia* with the accusative case occurs twice in the first clause of the sentence but not a third time in the final clause dealing with martyrdom—"and they did not love their lives to the death." The language and syntax of this verse show that being an overcomer is not defined by being a martyr for the Lord (which is additional to being an overcomer) but because of Christ's blood and God's Word rather than a believer's sacrifice for Christ and evangelism for Him.

Overcomer Statements Are Promises,
Not Commands or Warnings

A fifth reason all believers are overcomers in Christ, the overcoming One, is because the Lord gives only positive promises, rather than commands or warnings, to the overcomer in Revelation 2–3. Many people assume that when Christ says "to him who overcomes" or "he who overcomes," He is issuing a command that the believer must still obey ("to him who *will* overcome") as proof of their status as a believer or overcomer. According to this view, the phrases "to him who overcomes" and "he who overcomes" set forth an ongoing condition that must be fulfilled between the believer and the Lord until the time of the believer's death. For the believer to truly be an overcomer, he must persevere to the end of his life in faith and good works. If he does not persevere, he either forfeits his status as an overcomer (Arminianism) or proves he was never truly an overcomer or believer in the first place (Calvinism).

As was explained earlier in this chapter and in great detail in chapter 3, the grammatical constructions for "he who overcomes" and "to him who overcomes" in Revelation 2–3 function like titles that describe those who share a common activity, namely, overcoming (i.e., believing, 1 John 5:4-5). But whether the description is "to him who overcomes [*tō nikōnti*]" (2:7, 17) or "he who overcomes [*ho nikōn*]" (2:11, 26; 3:5, 12, 21), both expressions are virtual titles that describe those who share the common act of overcoming but say nothing about the duration and nature of that act, whether it is instantaneous or ongoing, or whether it was accomplished in the past, is being accomplished in the present, or will be accomplished in the future. Thus, the grammatical construction of Christ's seven promises to "him who overcomes, I will . . ." are ideally suited to function as standing promises to all who have either already overcome by believing or who may yet believe in Christ before they die. It is the same as Christ's promise that all things are possible "to him who believes" (Mark 9:23) or "he who believes in Me has everlasting life" (John 6:47).

In addition, both types of overcomer expressions in Revelation 2–3 ("to him who overcomes [*tō nikōnti*], I will . . ." and "he who overcomes [*ho nikōn*], I will . . .") are always followed by a promise of spiritual blessing. There is never a negative consequence presented to any of the seven churches for *not* overcoming that is similar to the positive promise statements. For example, nowhere does Christ say, "To him who does *not* overcome, I will..." followed by a negative consequence. This means that *the seven overcomer statements should not be viewed negatively as warnings or threats that the believer must overcome or else lose his or her salvation or prove to be unbelievers in the end.* Instead, these seven statements should be viewed as positive promises whereby Christ encourages His church to endure in view of guaranteed future blessings and spiritual victory for those who are born again.[20] Such hope can have a strengthening (Acts 14:22; Rom. 8:25; 2 Cor. 4:16-18), purifying effect (1 John 3:3) in the present conflict.

Others read into the seven overcomer statements a general tone of warning based on the fact that in the verses preceding each overcomer statement, Christ rebukes the churches for their various transgressions. Five out of the seven churches are critiqued by the Lord with respect to their sins, with repentance required in each instance (Rev. 2:4-5, 14-16, 20-24 [implied]; 3:1-3, 15-19). Some cite this fact as evidence that being an overcomer means that all overcomers/believers are obedient and persevering in their Christian lives. However, if believers were overcomers by practically overcoming and repenting of the sins identified by Christ to each church, as some assume, then this presents a glaring problem with the churches of Smyrna and Philadelphia. These churches are never confronted with any sins to repent from! How then will they become "true" overcomers if the overcomer statements to them in 2:11 and 3:12 are supposedly warnings? A better solution is to recognize from the structure of Christ's addresses to the churches that the correction for each church always comes before the closing encouragement of the overcomer statement. Observe carefully the following order and pattern of Christ's address to the Ephesian church, which reflects the same order and pattern of His address to all seven churches in Revelation 2–3.

---

20. Constable, *Notes on Revelation*, 23.

- **the church** – "To the angel of the church . . ." (2:1a)

- **the city** – "of Ephesus write . . ." (2:1b)

- **the Critic** – "These things says He who holds the seven stars in His right hand, who walks in the midst of the seven golden lampstands." (2:1c)

- **the commendations** – "I know your works, your labor, your patience, and that you cannot bear those who are evil. And you have tested those who say they are apostles and are not, and have found them liars; and you have persevered and have patience, and have labored for My name's sake and have not become weary" (2:2-3). "But this you have, that you hate the deeds of the Nicolaitans, which I also hate" (2:6).

- **the criticism** – "Nevertheless I have this against you, that you have left your first love." (2:4)

- **the correction** – "Remember therefore from where you have fallen; repent and do the first works, or else I will come to you quickly and remove your lampstand from its place—unless you repent." (2:5)

- **the closing encouragement** – "He who has an ear, let him hear what the Spirit says to the churches. To him who overcomes I will give to eat from the tree of life, which is in the midst of the Paradise of God." (2:7)

In the middle of these addresses, Christ critiques each church for its faults (except the Smyrnans and Philadelphians). He then immediately follows each critique with a negative warning or consequence for not repenting (2:5, 16, 22; 3:3, 16, 19). Some churches, like those in Ephesus and Sardis, even have another commendation (2:6; 3:4) between the correction (2:5; 3:3) and the closing encouragement to the overcomer (2:7; 3:5). But conspicuously and significantly, the critique and the warning in each case are always concluded *before* the closing encouragement of the overcomer statements at the end of Christ's address to each church. This shows that the general tone of rebuke and warning always occurs in the *middle* of each address to the churches, not at the *end*, where Christ always gives a *positive* promise to the overcomer/believer.

Seven Addresses Are Epistles, Ending with Grace

A final reason why all believers are overcomers is because Christ's addresses to the seven churches of Asia Minor are like distinct, miniature epistles, and the positive ending to each "epistle" is consistent with the pattern found in other New Testament epistles. In many of Paul's epistles he gives severe pastoral correction, but without exception he ends on a note of grace, saying essentially in one form or another, "the grace of the Lord Jesus be with you all" (Rom. 16:20; 1 Cor. 16:23; 2 Cor. 13:14; Gal. 6:18; Eph. 6:24; Phil. 4:23; Col. 4:18; 1 Thess. 5:28; 2 Thess. 3:18; 1 Tim. 6:21; 2 Tim. 4:22; Titus 3:15; Philem. 25). This is also how the book of Revelation ends, "The grace of our Lord Jesus be with you all. Amen" (Rev. 22:21).

In a book, such as Revelation, that is all about spiritual victory and Christ's triumph over every evil, it is only fitting for the addresses to the seven churches to end on a positive note of victory through God's grace. This is also more consistent with the general approach to the Christian life found in the New Testament epistles, where God appeals to believers to live a holy life of practical sanctification in light of their positional sanctification in Christ. Position should always affect practice. Christ says in effect to each of the seven churches, "Since you are already overcomers by your position in Me, the Overcoming One, and you are guaranteed ultimate spiritual victory (glorification) on that basis, won't you fight the good fight of faith now in the arena of this earthly life?" Therefore the overcomer statements in Revelation 2–3 should be viewed as gracious, promissory incentives to live faithfully for the Lord in light of these guaranteed salvation blessings awaiting every believer in Christ.

Conclusion

The biblical evidence overwhelmingly supports the conclusion that all church-age believers are overcomers based on their position in Christ and identification with Him. This spiritual standing or position is not based on the believer's imperfect walk but on the grace of God and the perfection of the Savior—the Overcoming One, Jesus Christ. Laying hold of this conclusion can have a liberating effect for the child of God as he comes to realize that he cannot gain any more spiritual victory over sin, Satan, and this evil world system than Jesus Christ has already gained for him by His own perfect, finished work. Believers are simply called now to stand by faith upon the Savior's merits, perfection, and victory (Gal. 2:20; 3:3-5; 5:1). Has He not already conquered the world, the flesh, and the Devil? Is His work for believers not the provision for practical victory now in each of these theaters of conflict (Gal. 6:14; Rom. 6:6; Heb. 2:14)? Believers are never told to fight in order to gain or seize new ground from the enemy, but rather to fight the good fight of faith from the spiritual high ground of their standing in Christ and identity in Him as overcomers (1 John 2:13-14; 4:4, 17-18; 5:1, 4-5). Having the assurance that the Victor has already won the war (John 16:33) and that believers are already on the winning side (Rom. 8:37-39; 1 Cor. 15:54-57) should give each believer great boldness rather than complacency to endure life's toughest battles.

The sure promises in Revelation 2–3 awaiting the overcomer provide powerful incentives to persevere through adversity in this world as believers reckon that the sufferings of this present time are not worthy to be compared to the glory guaranteed each one in Christ (Rom. 8:18). Christians today are at a crossroads. We can either accept a merit-based approach to the doctrine of the overcomer or a grace-based view. We can either accept a false theology of "grace" that threatens us with hell for failure to sufficiently and consistently overcome, or we can accept by faith the testimony of God's Word regarding our real identity as overcomers in Christ by grace. The former will lead to greater fear, failure, and despair, while the latter will surely lead to greater assurance, joy, encouragement, and practical victory.

Chapter 16

Why Should Every Believer Persevere?

Must faith endure for salvation to be sure? I trust by now you are convinced from Scripture that the answer is an emphatic "No!" God's Word is clear and consistent in its testimony that all who have trusted in Christ for salvation will be kept secure forever, not because of their imperfect obedience but because God's saving grace is always undeserved, Christ's work on the sinner's behalf stands perfect and complete, and God is faithful to fulfill His promise to keep and preserve each one of His children despite their unfaithfulness to Him.

But as reassuring as these biblical truths are, this book would not be complete or biblically balanced without an exhortation to persevere in the faith if you are a child of God. While the Bible is clear that not all children of God *will* necessarily persevere, it is equally clear that every child of God *should* persevere. Even though perseverance is not required to be saved from hell to heaven, there are many reasons why you should persevere in the faith if you have been born eternally into God's family.

The Love and Grace of God

First, God's infinite love and amazing grace toward you are reason enough to persevere in the faith. The apostle Paul knew this love, and it drove him to live for Christ and not for himself: "For the love of Christ compels us, because we judge thus: that if One died for all, then all died; and He died for all, that those who live should live no longer for themselves, but for Him who died for them and rose again" (2 Cor. 5:14-15). When Paul wrote that "the love of Christ compels us," he did not mean that *our* love for Christ motivates us to serve the Lord; rather, it is *Christ's* incomparable love for us that should motivate us. Which is greater: our love for God or His love for us? "In this is love, not that we loved God, but that He loved us and sent His Son to be the propitiation for our sins" (1 John 4:10).

The love that God has for His own is truly unfathomable and life-transforming. For this reason Paul prayed that the Ephesian Christians would be rooted and grounded in God's love for them, that they may be "able to comprehend with all the saints what is the width and length and depth and height—to know the love of Christ which passes knowledge; that you may be filled with all the fullness of God" (Eph. 3:18-19). God's love for the believer in Christ is without limit—infinite, just like God Himself.

Do you realize what this means practically? If you are God's child, He cannot love you any more or any less than He already does! God does not love us on the basis of our spiritual performance (Rom. 5:8) but for His Son's sake since we are in His Son, where He has "made us accepted in the Beloved" (Eph. 1:6)! Since He loves us for His Son's sake and not on the basis of our abilities or achievements, nothing can separate us from His love (Rom. 8:38-39). This kind of love and acceptance provides a powerful incentive to love and serve Him eternally in return. The dreadful prospect of not enduring to the end and missing final salvation should never be our motive in serving Him. On the other hand, His unchanging, unconditional love and the guarantee of eternal life provide a powerful motivation to continue serving Him.

While some consider fear of hell a valid stimulus to serve the Lord, serving Him on that basis is inconsistent with His unconditional love and grace, and it is an affront to the finished work of His Son. The apostle John writes, "Love has been perfected among us in this: that we may have boldness in the day of judgment; because as He is, so are we in this world. There is no fear in love; but perfect love casts out fear, because fear involves torment. But he who fears has not been made perfect in love. We love Him because He first loved us" (1 John 4:17-19). In essence, the Christian life ought to be one big "thank you" note of gratitude to God for His undeserved favor and kindness procured by Christ's perfect work on our behalf. With grace comes not only thanksgiving but encouragement to press on, and by doing so, to receive an even greater, glorious future reward.

15 For all things are for your sakes, that grace, having spread through the many, may cause thanksgiving to abound to the glory of God. 16 Therefore we do not lose heart. Even though our outward man is perishing, yet the inward man is being renewed day by day. 17 For our light affliction, which is but for a moment, is working for us a far more exceeding and eternal weight of glory, 18 while we do not look at the things which are seen, but at the things which are not seen. For the things which are seen are temporary, but the things which are not seen are eternal. (2 Cor. 4:15-18)

Provision for the Race

A second reason every believer should persevere in the race of the Christian life is because God has provided us with everything necessary to successfully run the race and cross the finish line according to the riches of His grace (Eph. 1:3; 3:8, 16). The apostle Peter tells us that "His divine power has given to us all things that pertain to life and godliness, through the knowledge of Him who called us by glory and virtue, by which have been given to us exceedingly great and precious promises, that through these you may be partakers of the divine nature, having escaped the corruption that is in the world through lust" (2 Peter 1:3-4).

When God sends out His soldiers to the spiritual battlefield, they are fully equipped with every means necessary to achieve victory over every foe. The believer has a position in Christ in which he has already died to the sin nature (Rom. 6:4-6), so that "we should walk in newness of life" (Rom. 6:4). This walk is possible because Christ's resurrection power is constantly available to us as we go through life (2 Cor. 1:8-10; 4:7-14; 12:9-10; Phil. 3:10). Every believer now has the third person of the Triune Godhead permanently indwelling him as the internal dynamo to empower him to accomplish God's will (Zech. 4:6; Rom. 8:1-4; Gal. 5:16; Eph. 5:18). The believer also has the Word of God as his spiritual sword (Eph. 6:17), which is quick and powerful (Heb. 4:12). If all this were not enough, the believer is also already on the winning team simply by virtue of his spiritual standing or position in Christ as a victor in the spiritual war of the ages—a war whose ultimate outcome of victory is already certain (John 16:33; Rom. 8:37; 1 John 4:4; 5:1, 4).

Fullness of Joy

A third reason you should persevere to the end of your Christian life in faith and holiness is because this is the only life that offers true joy and fulfillment. The carnal Christian surrenders this great blessing for a mere mirage dangled in front of him by his flesh, the world, and the Devil. While a believer cannot lose his eternal salvation by sinning, he can lose the joy of it, as David wrote in repentance after committing adultery, "Restore to me the joy of Your salvation" (Ps. 51:12). It is possible "to enjoy the passing pleasures of sin" (Heb. 11:25); but that is all it is—a "passing" thrill. Sin never produces real, lasting happiness. It only deceives, robs, and destroys. It always promises more than it delivers, costs more than we are willing to pay, and keeps us longer than we want to stay. While there is some degree of momentary pleasure in sin; invariably it results in death (James 1:15-16) or separation from fellowship with God (1 Tim. 5:6) and a hard life—"the way of transgressors is hard" (Prov. 13:15, KJV).

In contrast, Jesus Christ came not only to provide salvation but an abundant life of rich fellowship with Him. The Good Shepherd Himself declared, "I am the door. If anyone enters by Me, he will be saved, and will go in and out and find pasture. The thief does not come except to steal, and to kill, and to destroy. I have come that they may have life, and that they may have it more abundantly" (John 10:9-10). When believers walk by the power of the Holy Spirit (Gal. 5:16) in fellowship with God (1 John 1:7), this results in the Spirit's fruit of joy in their lives (Gal. 5:22)—and not merely joy but fullness of joy (Ps. 16:11; John 15:11; 16:24). While the Christian life is certainly no "Easy Street" since it involves trials, opposition, and at times suffering for Christ, you can still experience tremendous joy as a believer amidst tribulation (1 Thess. 1:6; James 1:2), "for the joy of the Lord is your strength" (Neh. 8:10). Do you have this joy? This joy can be yours as you abide in fellowship with Jesus Christ (1 John 1:3-4).

Christ-like Character

A fourth reason every believer should persevere in the faith is because spiritual growth and conformity to the character of Christ depends on it. According to the unfailing plan of God laid out in Romans 8:28-30, God's revealed will is that all believers be "conformed to the image of His Son" (Rom. 8:29). Ultimately, this will occur for all believers at glorification, but before that time arrives the

Lord wants to transform our characters to be like His as part of the process of spiritual growth and sanctification, which will be richly rewarded in glory.

The vital relationship between perseverance and character can be seen in Romans 5:3-4, which says, "knowing that tribulation produces perseverance; and perseverance, character; and character, hope." The Lord loves us too much to see us remain in our sinful state, so He desires to conform us to the likeness of His Son. This passion is reflected in the apostle Paul's statement to the Galatian Christians, "My little children, for whom I labor in birth again until Christ is formed in you" (Gal. 4:19). This forming process requires trials and our perseverance (James 5:10-11). The Lord knows that without trials or tribulations in life, our faith would not be tested, and we would not grow or persevere; and without perseverance our characters would not be transformed. James understood this well when he wrote, "knowing that the testing of your faith produces patience. But let patience have its perfect work, that you may be perfect and complete, lacking nothing" (James 1:3-4).

While God supplies the trials, His Word, and His Spirit in order to accomplish our growth and inner transformation, the believer's responsibility is to behold Christ by faith in the Word of God (Rom. 12:2) and let the Spirit of God do His internal, transforming work to the glory of God. This uniform process intended by God for every member of Christ's body is summarized by Paul in 2 Corinthians 3:18: "But we all, with unveiled face, beholding as in a mirror the glory of the Lord, are being transformed into the same image from glory to glory, just as by the Spirit of the Lord." The Lord desires this transformation for all believers. The question is, do we? Are you willing to yield yourself to the sanctifying process of the Holy Spirit in transforming you into the character of your Savior?

Testimony to Others

A fifth reason every believer should persevere in the faith is for the sake of his or her testimony to others. By giving up in the race, we lose our testimony to the lost and fail to fulfill our God-appointed role and privilege of being ambassadors for Christ (2 Cor. 5:20). The apostle Paul knew well the direct correlation between his own perseverance and his witness to others. Paul wrote, "Therefore I endure [*hypomenō*] all things for the sake of the elect, that they also may obtain the salvation which is in Christ Jesus with eternal glory" (2

Tim. 2:10). The reason Paul endured was not to attain his final salvation but for the eternal salvation of others through Christ! Elsewhere he testified, "We give no offense in anything, that our ministry may not be blamed. But in all things we commend ourselves as ministers of God: in much patience [*hypomōnē*], in tribulations, in needs, in distresses" (2 Cor. 6:3-4). The words translated "endure" and "patience" are simply the verb and noun forms of the same word. These passages show that quitting the race not only adversely affects us but also those to whom we should minister and witness.

Eternal Reward

A sixth reason believers should persevere is because God has promised a glorious, eternal reward in heaven for their perseverance. Paul knew his martyr's death was fast approaching when he penned his own epitaph in his last epistle: "I have fought the good fight, I have finished the race, I have kept the faith. Finally, there is laid up for me the crown of righteousness, which the Lord, the righteous Judge, will give to me on that Day, and not to me only but also to all who have loved His appearing" (2 Tim. 4:7-8). Throughout the New Testament, there is a close correlation between perseverance and rewards (Phil. 3:11-15; Heb. 6:10-12; 10:35-39; 11:6, 35; James 1:12; Rev. 2:10, 26b; 3:8-10a). James 1:12 contains one of the most explicit connections of these two themes, stating, "Blessed is a man who perseveres under trial; for once he has been approved, he will receive the crown of life which the Lord has promised to those who love Him" (NASB). Crowns in the Bible do not speak of the free gift of eternal life but of an earned reward. Our magnanimous God delights to bestow both.

Though the believer's perseverance or failure to persevere cannot change his already perfect salvation by God's grace, the prospect of receiving a greater degree of reward definitely provides a tremendous incentive to lead a Christ-honoring life. Throughout history believers have faced intense persecution and pressure to compromise; but the promise of a potentially greater reward has encouraged them to persevere in faithfulness. This is likely the meaning of Hebrews 11:35, which recalls how believers of the past "were tortured, not accepting deliverance, that they might obtain a better resurrection." Since believers will be "repaid" for their faithfulness to Christ at the resurrection of the righteous (Luke 14:14), believers can make that payday "better" by persevering in faithfulness to God's will. It will be worth it all when we see Christ!

The Glory of God

Finally, though your faith need not endure for your eternal salvation to be sure, you should still persevere for the highest purpose of glorifying God (2 Cor. 4:15-16). I have saved this reason to persevere for last since it is the greatest of all motivations. Reformed theology is right on the mark by concluding that the chief end of man is to glorify God and enjoy Him forever. We were created and born anew for the express purpose of glorifying our God in all that we do (1 Chron. 16:28-29; Ps. 96:7-8; Rev. 4:11), as 1 Corinthians 10:31 commands, "Therefore, whether you eat or drink, or whatever you do, do all to the glory of God." If even eating and drinking may glorify God, certainly our perseverance in the faith should as well. May the doctrine of salvation that we believe and the life of sanctification and perseverance that we live give honor and glory to God!

Scripture Index

OTHER BOOKS & BOOKLETS
BY
GRACE GOSPEL PRESS

available through
amazon.com & barnesandnoble.com

10 Principles to Ponder When the Unexpected Happens by Shawn Laughlin

Bad News for Good People and Good News for Bad People: "You Must Be Born Again!" *(John 3:1-21)* by Dennis M. Rokser

The Coming Kingdom: What Is the Kingdom and How Is Kingdom Now Theology Changing the Focus of the Church? by Andrew M. Woods

David: A Man after the Heart of God by Theodore H. Epp

Disciplined by Grace by J. F. Strombeck

Don't Ask Jesus into Your Heart: A Biblical Answer to the Question: "What Must I Do to Be Saved?" by Dennis M. Rokser

Faith & Works: A Clarification of James 2:14-26 by Dennis M. Rokser

Freely by His Grace: Classical Grace Theology edited by J. B. Hixson, Rick Whitmire, and Roy B. Zuck

The Epistle to the Galatians by C. I. Scofield

Getting the Gospel Wrong: The Evangelical Crisis No One Is Talking About by J. B. Hixson

The Gospel of the Christ: A Biblical Response to the Crossless Gospel Regarding the Contents of Saving Faith by Thomas L. Stegall

The Gospel of Grace and Truth: A Theology of Grace from the Gospel of John by Michael D. Halsey

Grace: The Glorious Theme by Lewis Sperry Chafer

Holding Fast to Grace by Roy L. Aldrich

I'm Saved! Now What? by Dennis M. Rokser

I'm Saved But Struggling With Sin! Is Victory Available? Romans 6-8 Examined by Dennis M. Rokser

Interpreting 1 John by Dennis M. Rokser

Job: A Man Tried as Gold by Theodore H. Epp

The Judgment Seat of Christ: A Biblical and Theological Study by Samuel L. Hoyt

The King of the Kingdom of Heaven: A Commentary of Matthew by Thomas O. Figart

Let's Preach the Gospel: Do You Recognize the Importance of Preaching the Gospel to Both the Unsaved and the Saved? by Dennis M. Rokser

LifeQuakes: God's Rescue Plan in Hard Times by Leah Weber Heling

Moses: 2 Volumes in 1 by Theodore H. Epp

The Need of the Hour: A Call to the Preaching of the Supremacy and Sufficiency of Jesus Christ, Verse-by-Verse, from a Grace Perspective by Dennis M. Rokser

Never Alone: From Abandoned to Adopted in Christ by Becky Jakubek

Planting & Establishing Local Churches by the Book by Dennis M. Rokser

The Powerful Influence of the Christian Woman by Donna Radtke

Promises of God for the Child of God by Dennis M. Rokser

Repentance: The Most Misunderstood Word in the Bible by G. Michael Cocoris

Salvation in Three Time Zones: Do You Understand the Three Tenses of Salvation? by Dennis M. Rokser

Seven Key Questions about Water Baptism by Dennis M. Rokser

Shall Never Perish Forever: Is Salvation Forever or Can It Be Lost? by Dennis M. Rokser

Should Christians Fear Outer Darkness? by Dennis M. Rokser

The Strombeck Collection: The Collected Works of J. F. Strombeck by J. F. Strombeck

A Tale of Two Thieves by Shawn Laughlin

Trophies of God's Grace: Personal Testimonies of God's Gift of Salvation

Truthspeak: The True Meaning of Five Key Christian Words Distorted through Religious Newspeak by Michael D. Halsey

What Cancer Cannot Do by Debbie Fetter

Where Faith Sees Christ by C. I. Scofield

For other helpful resources from a biblically-based, Christ-honoring, and grace-oriented perspective, please visit us at:

www.gracegospelpress.com